A MURDER IN WELLESLEY

# a MURDER in WELLESLEY

THE INSIDE STORY OF AN IVY-LEAGUE DOCTOR'S

DOUBLE LIFE, HIS SLAIN WIFE, AND THE TRIAL THAT

GRIPPED THE NATION     *Tom Farmer & Marty Foley*

*Northeastern University Press   Boston*

Northeastern University Press
An imprint of University Press of
New England
www.upne.com
© 2012 Thomas J. Farmer
and Martin T. Foley
All rights reserved
Manufactured in the United States of
America
Designed by Mindy Basinger Hill
Typeset in 10.5/15 pt. Minion Pro

University Press of New England
is a member of the Green Press Initiative.
The paper used in this
book meets their minimum
requirement for recycled paper.

For permission to reproduce
any of the material in this book,
contact Permissions, University Press
of New England, One Court Street,
Suite 250, Lebanon NH 03766; or visit
www.upne.com

Library of Congress Cataloging-in-
Publication Data

Farmer, Tom (Thomas J.)
A murder in Wellesley: the inside story
of an Ivy-League doctor's double life, his
slain wife, and the trial that gripped
the nation / Tom Farmer and Marty Foley.
    p.    cm.
Includes bibliographical references and index.
ISBN 978-1-55553-791-3 (cloth: alk. paper) —
ISBN 978-1-55553-797-5 (ebook: alk. paper)
1. Greineder, Mabel, d. 1999. 2. Greineder,
Dirk. 3. Murder—Massachusetts—
Wellesley—Case studies. 4. Murder—
Investigation—Massachusetts—
Wellesley—Case studies. 5. Trials
(Murder)–Massachusetts—Norfolk County.
I. Foley, Marty (Martin T.). II. Title.
HV6534.W45F37 2012
364.152'3092—dc23       2012006730

5   4   3   2   1

FOR MAY GREINEDER

AND ALL VICTIMS

OF DOMESTIC VIOLENCE

# contents

A MURDER IN WELLESLEY

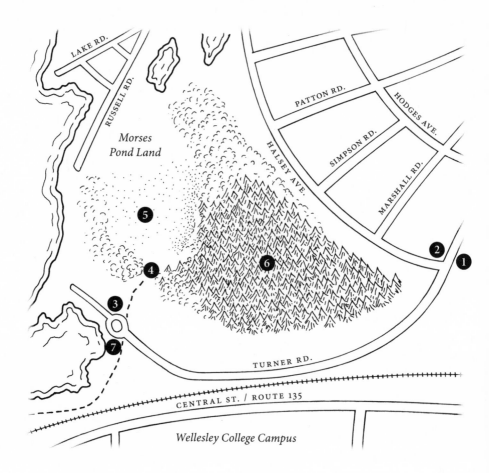

1 Dirk's van parked

2 Storm drain: left glove found

3 Traffic circle

4 May Greineder crime scene

5 Sand pit

6 Pine tree forest

7 Knife, hammer, right glove found
   in beach access road storm drain

# 1

NESTLED IN THE MIDDLE OF NEW ENGLAND is the affluent community of Wellesley, Massachusetts, a prosperous town of twenty-six thousand residents where the quality of life embodies the best of what the six-state region has to offer. Located just thirteen miles west of Boston, it is home for many of the state's captains of industry and its professional elite.

Dirk and Mabel "May" Greineder embodied all the desirable qualities of a typical Wellesley family. Highly respected medical professionals — he a renowned allergist and asthma researcher and she a nurse — they had raised three accomplished children, Kirsten, Britt, and Colin, who like their father had all graduated from Yale University, with Kirsten and Colin embarking on medical careers of their own. Now empty-nesters, Dirk and May were basking in the recent news that Kirsten had become engaged.

Even though the clocks had been turned back an hour for Daylight Savings Time, and despite having been up late the previous night, the couple rose before sunrise the Sunday morning of October 31, 1999, as was their usual practice. Eating breakfast in their modest split-level home at 56 Cleveland Road, Dirk and May were looking forward to getting out of the house on what was emerging as a glorious fall day. Weekend mornings at the Greineder home were reserved for walks with their German shepherds, Wolf and Zephyr, at nearby Morses Pond, although in recent months their male dog's aggressive behavior had prevented them from bringing him to the expansive public recreation area. Only the smaller female, Zephyr, was now allowed to romp through the pond's wooded trails and swim at its beach.

With bright sun and unusually warm weather stretching into the seventies, the only thing marring the perfect Indian summer day were wind gusts of thirty-two miles an hour from the southwest. Still, for the last day of October, no one was complaining. Loading Zephyr into their silver Chrysler Town and Country minivan just before 8:30 A.M., Dr. Greineder backed out of his driveway and headed up Cleveland Road for the two-minute ride to Morses Pond.

In the summer, residents are allowed to drive down a winding access road and park in a sandy parking lot where a spacious beach beckons a thousand feet away. Surrounded by woods and a large open sandpit, the pond was used year-round by joggers and walkers, many like the Greineders finding the serene surroundings perfect for exercising their dogs.

After Labor Day, the town locked the steel barrier at the top of the access road, so after making a U-turn at the end of Turner Road just in front of the padlocked gate, Dr. Greineder backed the van into his regular off-season parking spot. After letting out Zephyr, Dirk and May slipped around the gate and strolled a short distance down the access road before veering right onto a trail in the woods the locals called the "pine tree forest."

Across town at the Wellesley Police Department, dispatcher Shannon Parillo was almost an hour into her daylong shift, thankful she would be leaving at 4 P.M. before the annual Halloween nuisance calls started after sunset. The phones had been quiet that morning with many residents taking advantage of the extra hour to sleep or ease into their Sunday morning routines.

When a police line rang at 8:56 A.M., Parillo was not prepared for the hysterical, blubbering caller on the other end. After offering a friendly, "Wellesley Police. This call is recorded," Parillo was greeted with rapid-fire, nasally pitched pleas for help from a male caller.

"Help. I'm at the pond. I need some, someone attacked my wife, trying to get . . ." the breathless caller sputtered as Parillo struggled to understand him.

"Sir, where are you?"

"I'm at, at the pond, at Morses Pond. Walking . . ."

"At Morses Pond?" Parillo asked, still confused by the man.

"Walking the dog, someone attacked. I left her 'cause she hurt her back."

"Okay, you just need to relax because I can't understand what you're saying," Parillo said soothingly.

"Please, please, please send a car."

"Okay, you're at Morses Pond?"

"Pond, yeah," the caller panted.

"Whereabouts at the Pond? Whereabouts at the pond," Parillo shot back, trying to stop the caller's rambling.

"I'm, I'm outside my, my car's outside the gate."

"Okay. Hold on one second, okay," Parillo instructed, now knowing where to send Patrolman Paul Fitzpatrick, whose patrol sector that morning included Morses Pond.

"Wellesley Control to fourteen zero five," Parillo radioed to Fitzpatrick.

"Oh my God," the caller gasped, interrupting Parillo's dispatch.

"What, what happened," she asked.

"I, I, I, we were walking the dog," the caller answered.

"Fourteen zero five," Fitzpatrick responded, Parillo now trying to maintain separate conversations.

"She hurt her back," the caller said, his voice still hurried and high-pitched.

"Is she injured?"

"I think she's dead," the caller replied excitedly. "I'm not sure. I'm a doctor. I went back. I . . ."

"Can you start over to Morses Pond," Parillo radioed Fitzpatrick, the caller stating simultaneously, "She looks terrible."

" . . . For an unknown medical at this time," Parillo continued, now sending Fitzpatrick to the pond along with Wellesley firefighters and an ambulance.

"The dog heard something. She went back," the caller continued.

Now able to focus on the caller, Parillo continued her effort to calm him. "Okay. Just relax. Is this your, is this your, is this your daughter?" Parillo said, trying to interrupt the man.

"My, my wife," the caller gasped.

"You're right at the entrance to Morses Pond?" Parillo inquired, now slowing the caller's breathless delivery.

"I'm right at the entrance where, where it's blocked. And, and you got to have someone unlock the gate so the cars can get in," the caller replied, growing frantic again.

"Okay, what's your name?" Parillo asked.

"Dirk, Dirk, Greineder. G-R-E-I-N-E-D-E-R," he responded, out of breath as he spelled his last name.

"Okay. Listen. Listen to me," Parillo ordered sternly.

"Yeah," the caller obeyed.

"You need to relax," Parillo ordered, finally gaining control of the conversation. "I have people on the way. But I can't understand you. So you need to just relax."

"All right. Yeah, I just ran over here," the caller replied apologetically.

"Okay. What's your name?" Parillo asked.

"Dirk."

"Dirk?" Parillo repeated.

"Yeah."

"And this is your wife?"

"Yeah, yes, yes."

"And you were walking your dog and what happened?"

"She, she twisted her back. She's got a bad back," the caller stressed.

"She twisted her back?" Parillo asked.

"I left her," the husband responded.

"Okay, is she conscious and breathing?"

"I, I don't think so. I don't think so," Dr. Greineder stammered, Parillo now realizing the injury was worse than a twisted back.

"I went back for her," the husband continued, while Parillo radioed Fitzpatrick with the update that the caller "doesn't think she's conscious."

Now almost in complete control and speaking more slowly and clearly, Dr. Greineder kept talking while Parillo conversed with Fitzpatrick.

"The dog . . . someone attacked her," he said. "It's definitely an attack," he added with emphasis.

"Okay. Just hold, are you with her right now?" Parillo asked.

"No, no, I'm way out. I had to go out to call you."

"How old is she?"

"Oh God, please send someone. I don't know."

"They're on their way. How old is she?" Parillo demanded.

"Fifty-eight. We live; we lived in Wellesley for twenty-five years, thirty years. I don't even know," he added excitedly.

With more information, Parillo tried to update Fitzpatrick while the husband continued to speak.

"Hold on one second, okay sir?" she said. "Wellesley Control to fourteen zero five."

"Zero five," Fitzpatrick replied.

"I found her and I'm . . ." Dr. Greineder interrupted.

"Be advised, that's a fifty-eight-year . . ."

"I tried to see if there was anything to do," he added, oblivious to Parillo's conversation with Fitzpatrick.

" . . . Old woman . . ."

"There's nothing I can do," he went on.

"Fell possibly," Parillo continued over the caller's talking. "Twisted her back. Unknown if she's conscious and breathing at this time."

"Sir?" she asked, turning her attention back to Dr. Greineder. "Are you on a payphone?"

"No, I'm on, I'm on my cell phone in the car."

"Okay. Can you take your cell phone and go to her."

"No, it's in the car. I don't have my portable," said the doctor now more composed and conversational.

"Just send someone," he pleaded. "I, someone inside with her, there was someone else walking his dog, and I, he went in there. There's a runner here," Dr. Greineder stuttered.

"Do you see the ambulance?" Parillo asked. "We have them on the way."

"No. I don't see anything yet. Do they have a key to this gate? Because they can't get in unless they have the key. DPW has the key, I think that they're always in there."

"Sir?" Parillo interrupted, again halting his rambling.

"Yeah," he responded.

"What I'm gonna do is, I'm gonna hang up the phone with you. I want you to keep an eye out for the ambulance and the police officer," Parillo instructed.

"All right. All right."

"When you see them, get them," she added.

"I'm waiting. I'm waiting. I'm waiting," the doctor stammered.

"Go back to your wife. See if she's okay," Parillo ordered before hanging up.

# 2

TROOPER MARTY FOLEY'S PAGER began shrieking at 9:20 A.M. The Massachusetts State Police detective had been up early Halloween morning for a meeting at the Office of the Chief Medical Examiner in Boston, where his pager was now telling him to call his department's General Headquarters. A state trooper for seventeen years, Foley was a homicide detective in the office of Norfolk County District Attorney William R. Keating.

Being on call that weekend, Foley had to respond to any unattended or suspicious deaths in the affluent county aligned southwest of Boston. The day before, he had been paged to two unattended deaths, but neither involved foul play. Now he was at the ME's office to ensure the necessary toxicology screens were done on them. Afterward he would head to the DA's office in Dedham to write both case reports.

The silver-haired former University of Massachusetts–Boston linebacker had wanted to clear some time for his two teenage sons and a blissful afternoon of watching NFL football, but when he saw the familiar number for his GHQ on the pager he had a sinking feeling. As he pushed the numbers on his cell phone, something told him he wouldn't be watching any football with his sons that day.

The dispatcher at State Police headquarters confirmed it. Foley's football-playing boys, Tim and Dan, would be watching the games without him. He was needed in the town of Wellesley, the dispatcher told him; the local police were requesting he respond to Morses Pond. Foley jotted down some directions, and with an entrance to the Massachusetts Turnpike right down the street from the ME's office, he was quickly rolling west toward Wellesley.

A seasoned trooper, Foley had investigated white-collar crime for eight years while assigned to the Massachusetts Attorney General, but he had been in Norfolk County for less than a year and had never worked with the Wellesley Police Department. So he was a bit unsure of what to expect as he checked his directions and zipped through the sparse Sunday morning traffic.

Wellesley Detective Jill McDermott had reported for duty at 8 A.M. McDermott was the only detective on duty, but she expected a typically easy Sunday shift. Scheduled to work just a half day, she was thinking about a Halloween party she had been invited to after work as she lazily thumbed through the *Boston Globe*.

The daughter of Lieutenant William McDermott, of the Brookline Police Department, McDermott had found herself following her dad's career path almost by accident. Never aspiring to be a cop, she was a sophomore at Pine Manor College studying biology in 1994 when her father paid the $35 registration fee for her to take the Massachusetts Civil Service exam.

When McDermott walked into Brookline High School the morning of the exam, she found the bedlam of hundreds of anxious police hopefuls, including her older brother Billy. McDermott "flew in, took the test and never thought about it again." Eighteen months later, she was preparing to graduate with her biology degree and contemplating a career as a physical therapist when postcards arrived from the Brookline and Wellesley police departments offering jobs pending additional testing. McDermott talked it over with her father and decided on a career change. She sailed through the added qualifying requirements before choosing Wellesley. As a rookie uniformed officer, McDermott was assigned to the four-to-midnight shift, but less than two years later, at the age of twenty-five, she made detective.

With her radio on to monitor the patrol units on the street, McDermott had flipped through the bulky Sunday paper in rare seclusion. She hadn't thought much of Shannon Parillo's dispatch to Morses Pond until she heard an update that a woman might not be breathing. If photographs had to be taken or other specialized services provided, it would be McDermott's responsibility. She shuffled the newspaper aside and started to gather her belongings, wondering how a twisted back could result in someone not breathing. Her thoughts were interrupted by a call from Parillo. "You should head over to Morses Pond," the dispatcher advised. "Sergeant Nahass wants to see you there."

Two hundred miles south, Belinda Markel had also been up early that morning. A New Yorker since birth, Belinda had left her apartment in an exclusive high rise in midtown Manhattan with her two youngest children, nine-year-old William and twelve-year-old Amy. They were bound for a swim meet outside the city in Newburgh. Belinda's oldest daughter, fifteen-year-old Alexis, was swimming in another meet in Flushing and would return home hours before her mother and siblings.

A Halloween party was planned for that evening. Although the party would be an orgy of candy consumption and horseplay that would probably trash her place, Belinda didn't care. She genuinely enjoyed the company of her children's companions. And she was in a great mood that morning, bouncing to her feet for yet another strong race by one of her children and proudly contemplated how well they were swimming. Chatting with the woman seated next to her, Belinda was very interested to learn that she was a well-known bridal author and magazine editor.

The mention of weddings jolted Belinda's memory, however. With a touch of guilt, she realized she had forgotten to telephone her aunt May the day before. When Belinda had spoken to May the previous Friday morning, the hour-long conversation had centered on the recent news that Kirsten had become engaged to a man from Denmark. Belinda's twenty-eight-year-old cousin had met M. Aleks Engel while studying medicine at Harvard, and they were now living near Ann Arbor, where Kirsten was a second-year resident at University Hospital, University of Michigan.

Belinda and her aunt were extremely close, more like a mother and daughter than aunt and niece. May was in her late teens when Belinda was born in 1958 and was with her nearly every day during her early childhood growing up in Queens. Even after May went to Ohio to study nursing at Case Western Reserve, Belinda would still frequently see her during visits with her grandmother. May loved to spoil her niece with surprise trips to the zoo and other outings. She would never get married, she joked, because they went out so often that everyone thought Belinda was her daughter.

Even after May and Dirk married in 1968 and later moved to Wellesley, Belinda continued her regular visits, now with her own children in tow. With their shared experiences of motherhood, over the years, Belinda's relationship with her aunt grew even stronger. In fact, Belinda's kids were almost like May's grandchildren, and she often kidded her aunt that she was a "grandmother-in-training."

In their conversation on Friday, despite her typically upbeat demeanor tinged with joy over Kirsten's marriage announcement, May was somewhat stressed. Her aunt was in the middle of an expensive home renovation that was producing headaches on a daily basis. She also talked about a paper she was trying to finish for one of her classes to become a nurse practitioner. On top of it all, it had not helped that she had stumbled on a small step in her kitchen, injuring her chronically bad back. May had suffered sometimes debilitating back pain for most of her adult life, and it wasn't uncommon to see her strapped in a black flexible brace like those used by workers at building supply and department stores. Belinda had offered to drive up to Wellesley to help May look for a place to have Kirsten's wedding reception, promising to call back Saturday.

But she had completely forgotten to make that call in the bustle of a busy Saturday. Belinda's uncharacteristic forgetfulness would not be repeated today. She silently vowed to call May before the Halloween party. Anyway, she couldn't wait to tell her how well William and Amy had swum. May would also be thrilled that the bridal author had offered to mail May two of her books and was willing to talk to her about Kirsten's wedding. As her thoughts happily returned to the action in the pool, Belinda still couldn't soothe the unexplained urgency to call May she felt welling inside her.

With the light Sunday morning traffic, Trooper Marty Foley had made great time to Wellesley. He swung onto Turner Road and approached what looked to be a vehicle barrier that had been opened, and now Foley could see a uniformed Wellesley officer standing outside a marked cruiser.

Foley stopped to identify himself, noting that the patrolman was recording the names and times of everyone he allowed to pass through the two rectangular steel barriers to an access road. Tracking the comings and goings of everyone at an investigation should always be one of the initial steps taken by the first responders, so Foley was glad to comply. He still didn't know what to expect from the Wellesley Police Department, but it had made a good first impression. "Just go down the road as far as you can go and that's where it is," the officer said, logging Foley in at 9:53 A.M. Foley thanked him, nudged past the officer's cruiser, and proceeded down the sloping asphalt access road that twisted and curved in a left-handed arc.

He didn't hurry. Foley liked to take everything in. Rushing only resulted in mistakes. Coasting slowly, he was immediately struck by the enveloping canopy over the road created by the thick groupings of trees on both sides. It was like passing through a wooded tunnel despite the deciduous trees having already dropped a good portion of their leaves by this date, leaving a blanket on the ground for the coming winter. But enough foliage remained on the branches that Foley could not see much beyond the trees on either side of him. Just yards past the gate, his attention was drawn to what looked like a wide dirt trail extending from both sides of the road. It looked perfect for jogging or mountain biking.

Foley would soon learn that it was an aqueduct linking the Quabbin Reservoir in western Massachusetts to Boston and was, in fact, frequently used for the recreation he envisioned. The detective rolled on, still consumed by the forest around him. The access road was a standard hot-topped street, and although not overly wide, it had two yellow lines running down its center. It certainly wound on for a while.

Foley noticed that the right side of the road had a sidewalk for a short distance, until it dropped and disappeared into the woods. The place was remote enough, he thought. Finally he picked up a boost of gravitational speed on what seemed to be the final downward straightaway, and glancing to his right, he saw a large, sand-covered parking lot.

Emerging from the peaceful, forested access road, Foley was struck by the sudden contrast of the bustling activity behind a paved traffic circle directly ahead. There were at least four marked Wellesley cruisers and almost that many unmarked cars parked in the cul-de-sac. A Wellesley fire engine towered over the police vehicles, and Foley noted the presence of an ambulance as well, but its white-shirted paramedics appeared to be milling with firefighters and a few other men in the jumble of activity, which mostly centered on a crescent-shaped patch of grass behind the traffic circle.

Foley parked almost directly facing the cul-de-sac. To his right, he observed a tall man with a small dog, an Asian man, and a third man dressed in running clothes. To the left stood a patrol officer and a cruiser. Straight ahead, a woman in her mid-twenties was talking to a man in a yellow jacket. Slightly to the right of the man's bright yellow-and-white windbreaker, a marked cruiser was parked on the grass at an angle facing into a trail in the woods.

Foley reached for a notebook and got out of his car, still trying to digest the unfamiliar landscape around him, feeling the warming sun and a strong wind from the southwest. But before he could walk to the traffic circle, a nicely dressed man approached him with a uniformed Wellesley police sergeant. Lt. Wayne Cunningham and Sgt. Peter Nahass introduced themselves and explained that a woman was lying dead down the trail where the cruiser was parked. "The husband is over there, he's wearing the yellow coat," Nahass told Foley, swinging his arm toward the man to emphasize the identification. "Can I see the body?" Foley asked, wanting to look at the deceased woman before meeting her husband.

At the graveled head of the trail, Foley saw an officer who had been stationed there to prevent anyone from walking on it. Foley was happy to see that the first-arriving Wellesley officers had secured the trail and now an accounting of all the footwear that had landed on it had commenced. "Is there a way to view the body without walking on the path?" Foley asked his escorts. Cunningham and Nahass directed him to the left of the trail toward an area covered with low trees and scrub. Stooping to avoid low-hanging limbs and probing pine branches, Foley followed his guides on a weaving course through the grove to a spot about thirty yards behind the body.

He repositioned himself to get a closer look. She was lying on her back in the underbrush with only her legs extending into the trail. A ghastly neck wound was easily visible from this distance of about forty feet. The woman's blue-and-white sweat pants had been pulled down exposing her red panties, and her dark sweatshirt was pushed up showing her black bra. Something that looked like a blue glove was lying near her feet, and there was a clear plastic bag resting on the trail. In the middle of the path a large puddle of blood darkened the soil, and there appeared to be a drag mark coming from it.

No one said a word, but their minds were filled with images of another elderly murder victim in Norfolk County, whose grisly and sexually depraved slaying ten months earlier was eerily similar to the disturbing scene now before them. And it had only been a little over a month since Foley had been sent to the nearby town of Westwood, where, mysteriously, an eighty-two-year-old man had been horribly murdered while fishing at a public pond.

As he soberly studied the woman's neck wound and inspected the terrain around the woman's savaged body, it was disturbingly clear to Foley that the county's homicide detectives had another gruesome murder on their hands. He couldn't help but wonder if some deranged person was stalking the elderly.

The crunch of approaching footsteps from behind took Foley's thoughts away from the grim sight. It was the attractive young woman he had seen with the victim's husband. Wayne Cunningham introduced Foley to Detective Jill McDermott.

"I spoke briefly to the husband," she told Foley and gave him a brief synopsis of her conversation with the man as the four investigators made their return trip to the traffic circle. "He said they came to the park for their morning walk and his wife twisted her back," McDermott recounted. "They had separated for a few minutes so he could take the dog down to the pond, and when he came back he found her like this."

"I'd like to go talk to him now," Foley said.

Sizing up the husband as he neared him, Foley guessed he was in his fifties, but his trim, athletic physique made him appear more youthful. He was a handsome man of average height; his brown hair had probably been lighter when he was younger. Standing with a uniformed officer on the grassy patch behind the traffic circle, the husband seemed slightly agitated, but composed, as McDermott introduced Foley to Dr. Dirk Greineder. "I'm very sorry about your wife," the trooper said. "I know this is difficult, but I need to ask you a few questions. Okay?"

Now face-to-face, Foley could see Dr. Greineder's yellow windbreaker was some kind of swim team jacket with wide, white vertical stripes on the chest. The front of it was mostly coated with blood, as were the insides of both sleeves. Foley noted the bloodstains stopped at the doctor's wrists, where the cuffs were rolled, but in sharp contrast, the husband's hands were conspicuously clean.

Looking closer, Foley noted the doctor was wearing a black shirt and pants, which magnified the brightness of his white Reebok sneakers, also stained with blood. The man's nose was unusually runny, but he was not crying, and Foley noted a bloodstain on the left lens of his eyeglasses.

"My wife and I came here for a walk with our dog," Dr. Greineder began. "I parked our car by the gate and we went for a walk like we do every weekend." Foley patiently listened, both he and McDermott trying to jot down everything the husband said. After years of conducting interviews in white-collar crime investigations, Foley's style was to let his subjects talk as much as they wanted. He was in no hurry to ask questions if information was free flowing, and Dr. Greineder was talkative. Foley got answers to his initial questions and more. The husband was rambling, almost stream of consciousness, as he wove from one topic to another.

"What did you do last night?" Foley asked when the doctor finally paused. "We were home working on a slide presentation for her class. She's studying to be a nurse practitioner," Dr. Greineder replied. "She went to bed about eleven, but I stayed up until twelve-thirty and got up at six. I usually only sleep six hours a night," he added. Foley found the doctor's extraneous detail somewhat odd.

"What did you do when you got up?" Foley asked. "I made breakfast," Dr. Greineder replied. "I cut up some fruit and we had muffins. She got up around seven and we cleaned the house after breakfast. The house was a mess because we were spending a lot of time on her slide presentation. We're also remodeling, and that's made a mess, too."

"Do you and your wife sleep in the same bedroom?" Foley said, shifting the interview toward some personal questions he had to ask. "Yes, we do. It's just been remodeled, and we offered it to my daughter but she didn't want it. I couldn't understand that," the doctor complained. Foley was surprised at the man's irritation with his daughter when his wife was lying dead four hundred feet away.

"Did you have sex with your wife this morning?" Foley asked. It was important to know because it looked like the doctor's wife might have been sexually assaulted. If the autopsy turned up semen or other biological evidence, he would need to know if it was from the husband or the killer. "No, we didn't," Dr. Greineder said quietly.

"Did you have sex last night?" Foley continued. "No," the husband repeated. "Yesterday?" Foley pressed. "No," the man answered. "How about in the last week?" Foley concluded. "We haven't been sexually active for a few years," the husband offered softly. "She has a bad back, and our relationship has moved beyond that."

"What did you do after cleaning the house?" Foley asked, taking Dr. Greineder back to the morning's events. "We decided to take one of the dogs for a walk. We do that almost every weekend," the husband explained. He went on, saying that after parking their van outside the locked gate, they had strolled along the access road, where his wife had briefly debated whether to walk the aqueduct. They opted for the paved bike path through the pine tree forest instead, which Foley had seen from the access road, and then they had turned onto a leaf-carpeted trail leading to the ridge above the sandpit.

When Dr. Greineder's droning account turned disconnected and rambling again, Foley had to interrupt him a second time. "What time did you get to the pond?" the detective asked, the simple query seeming to confuse the husband, who considered the question but didn't answer. "Do you have a clock in the van?" Foley persisted. "I was in the van at eight-thirty. The clock read nine-thirty, but I hadn't changed the clock," Dr. Greineder answered before digressing into a confusing and unnecessary dissertation on Daylight Savings Time and Eastern Standard Time. "I got to the pond at eight-thirty," he finally concluded after Foley let him babble.

Resuming his story in the pine tree forest, Dr. Greineder said he and his wife were throwing a ball to their dog but the shepherd wasn't interested in retrieving it that morning. "The ground was wet, and she was doing a lot of sniffing. There were a lot of great scents for her," he said. Foley again found the statement strange, considering that this man's wife had just been horribly killed.

Coming down the forty-foot slope from the ridge above the sandpit, "She stumbled and had a twinge in her back," the doctor said. "She told me to go on with the dog and take her for a swim and she would meet me at the rock," he added, pointing to a large flat rock near the sandy parking lot that his wife would frequently lie on when her back flared up. "She wasn't hurt too bad," the husband continued. "She was moving slowly. She usually wears a back brace but she must have forgotten it in the van."

To Foley, the story seemed a bit illogical. *The dog has already been for a walk. Your wife is hurt, what are you going to do, leave your wife there?* he thought.

After leaving his wife in the sandpit, Dr. Greineder said he and Zephyr set out for the pond's beach, gesturing to the area several hundred yards past the traffic circle over a footbridge. "When we got to the fence near the beach, the dog started acting funny and ran back toward my wife. We were only gone for ten minutes," the husband said emphatically.

After following the dog up the dirt path leading from the right side of the traffic circle, Dr. Greineder said, he spotted his wife lying supine on the shady trail but wasn't immediately concerned because it seemed like a "reasonable place" for her to soothe her aching back.

It didn't seem reasonable at all to Foley. The top part of her body was lying in overgrown underbrush, and he couldn't imagine anyone wanting to rest there. Maybe the guy's in shock or in denial about what he saw, the detective considered, trying to give the husband the benefit of the doubt.

Zephyr was licking his wife's face, the doctor continued, leading him to think the two were playing. When he got closer, he observed a wound on her forehead. "Did you touch your wife?" Foley asked. "The first time I touched her, I checked her carotid artery on the right side. That was closest to me," he told the detective, demonstrating with his right index and middle fingers pressed together on his neck. "She still felt warm but I couldn't get a pulse."

"Did you touch her anywhere else?" Foley said. "I tried to pick her up," the husband answered. "I couldn't pick her up. She was like dead weight. She weighs a hundred and twenty pounds. I used to be able to lift two hundred and fifty pounds. Now, I couldn't lift her. She was like a dead weight," he repeated.

"Did you have a leash on the dog?" Foley asked, himself the owner of a

German shepherd. "I put Zephy on the leash after I found May," the doctor answered. "The leash was either around her middle or it may have been on the ground next to her. I grabbed the leash and put it on the dog to get the dog off of her. I knew I needed to get help. I didn't see any DPW workers around. I saw a runner on the path," he pointed, forcing Foley to glance up from his notebook toward a paved, single-lane maintenance road roped off with yellow tape on the opposite side of the cul-de-sac.

"I couldn't find anybody on the path. I saw the man with the little dog coming down the road," the husband said. Foley assumed he meant the man he had seen earlier, who was now being interviewed by a Wellesley detective. "I asked him if he had a cell phone and he said no," Dr. Greineder continued. "I told him my wife was hurt, then I grabbed my dog and ran as fast as I could. I was upset because I'm so out of shape and I couldn't run any faster. I thought I was going to throw up."

The husband said he then saw a runner on the paved bike path in the pine tree forest and yelled down to him from the elevated access road. This would be the jogger Foley had seen earlier standing with the man who owned the small dog. He didn't have a cell phone either, so the doctor ran the rest of the way up the long access road to call for help from his van. As he started to run back to his wife, a Wellesley police officer pulled up next to him on the access road. Jumping into the back of his cruiser, the husband directed him to the dirt path off the traffic circle where his wife lay. He returned to his wife's side, Dr. Greineder told Foley, and it was then that he discovered her fatal wound, when he checked the carotid artery on the left side of her neck "where I do a better job."

Foley didn't know what kind of doctor Greineder was, but his description of trying to diagnose his obviously dead wife again struck Foley as bizarre. It didn't make sense that a physician could miss such a gaping wound until the second time he had returned to his wife. "I tried to pull her pants up, they were pulled down around her hips" the doctor continued. "I tried to listen to her heart. I pulled her shirt up and listened with my ear, and I didn't hear anything."

"Did you wash your hands?" Foley asked. "No, I haven't been out of your sight. The police have been with me the whole time," Dr. Greineder replied. "Did you go near the water and wash your hands?" Foley asked again, trying to reconcile why the doctor's hands were so clean when he just said he touched his wife's bloody wound. "No, I didn't wash my hands," Dr. Greineder stressed. "Can I use your cell phone? I need to call my daughter Britt. She lives in Brookline."

During the course of the interview, the doctor had told Foley and McDermott several times that he wanted to call his daughter and that he had to care for his dog in the van and another "vicious" pet named "Wolfie" at home. Both investigators had found the husband's concern for his dogs, seemingly over his wife, more than a little odd.

Foley was getting annoyed. He had left his cell phone back in his cruiser and didn't want to be bothered with phone calls while he was trying to get critical information about what happened to the woman along with a sense of whether her attacker might still be in the area, but the husband kept pestering him about tending to the dogs and calling his daughter. The dog in the van was protected by the shade. The other dog at the doctor's house had been alone for less than two hours. And in any case, it was inappropriate for the slain woman's loved ones to be notified by cell phone several hundred feet from where she lay savagely killed. He assured Dr. Greineder he would be able to make his calls, but they needed to get through his account of what happened first.

Foley couldn't imagine how he would react if his wife had been found like May Greineder, but at the very least, he'd be more distraught than Dr. Greineder. The husband's nose had been continually runny, but he had not cried once during the interview. The trooper was keeping an open mind, but the doctor was acting strangely.

If Dr. Greineder had tried to aid his wife, it made sense his clothing and glasses would be bloodstained, but Foley was somewhat troubled about his clean hands and the pattern of tiny blood drops on his sneakers. The stains on the Reeboks looked more like spatter from inflicting a wound, and the clean hands were not consistent with the lifesaving effort the doctor had described.

Foley had his back to the traffic circle during the interview but could hear the continuous arrival of Wellesley and State Police vehicles, and he could read on the doctor's face that he was taking in the burgeoning police response.

State Police Lt. Joseph Brooks, the commander of the Norfolk detective unit, must have heard Dr. Greineder complaining about his dogs. He politely interrupted Foley's questioning and introduced himself to the husband, suggesting that Foley bring Dr. Greineder to the Wellesley Police Station, where he could make phone calls and whatever arrangements he needed.

It sounded like a good idea to Foley. The doctor was covered with his wife's blood and possibly trace evidence left by her killer. Foley needed to take the man's clothes but didn't want to take him to his house where the evidence might be contaminated. It would be best to have the daughter he had mentioned bring some clothing to her father at the police station. "Why don't we go to the police station and you can make your calls there," Foley offered.

The doctor agreed. "I'm not going to tell Britt what happened. I'll have her come to the police station, and I'll tell her there."

Foley and McDermott walked the doctor to the trooper's cruiser and McDermott settled in the back seat so the husband could ride in front. He again expressed concern for his dogs as soon as Foley turned over the ignition. Passing through the gate at the top of the access road, Foley slowed to show the doctor that his van was safely parked in the shade and the shepherd inside would be fine for the time being.

"We'll take care of the dogs," he reassured him, then asked another question to change the subject and keep his witness talking. "Is your estate in order?" the detective inquired.

"We just signed some papers yesterday," Dr. Greineder responded forlornly, "but there are some problems with the life insurance. It doesn't matter now," he sighed. Before Foley could ask anything else, the doctor suddenly groaned. "I have to tell her family. They live in Queens," he said, his voice filled with dread. "Do you have any guns or knives in the house?" Foley asked, snapping Dr. Greineder from his troubled thoughts. "No, we don't have anything like that," he answered, somewhat surprised. "I know you are just doing your job," he added after a pause. "I always hire professionals to help me and you are doing a good job."

McDermott was letting Foley do the talking. His question about the doctor's estate was a good one, another she had not thought to ask. Foley was clearly a more experienced investigator, but she had not felt intimidated by the older detective. In fact, it seemed Foley was treating her as an equal, including her in the important first dealings with May Greineder's husband.

Before joining the Wellesley department, McDermott had interned at the Norfolk DA's office and knew many of the State Police detectives assigned there. Waiting for someone to respond that morning, she had mentally gone through the list, hoping it would not be this one or that one. Her experience level had grown significantly, but some of the veteran State Police detectives she knew would probably send her for coffee or assign her to a menial role in this, her first murder case.

During the five-minute ride to the police station, Foley observed that Dr. Greineder, who had remained emotionally calm, "lost it a little bit." In the second-floor detective office, Foley sat down with the doctor to explain the need for his clothing and sneakers, suggesting his daughter Britt could bring a change of clothing.

"She's not going to be able to do that," the doctor protested excitedly. "We just changed the locks and the alarm codes and she's not going to be able to get in. A friend of mine, Terry, he's a lawyer and I think I should call him."

Foley decided not to push the issue. He was going to get the clothes even if he had to obtain a search warrant. Feeling it was time to back off a little, he let the doctor make his calls. While McDermott showed Dr. Greineder to a telephone in the small meeting room within the detective office, Foley walked down the hallway to a larger conference room where he began to confront some of the multiplying details in the blossoming investigation.

As she sat behind a computer across from the windowed meeting room, it looked to McDermott like Dr. Greineder made two telephone calls. One of them was to his daughter Britt. McDermott overheard the father telling his middle child that "something bad" had happened to her mother, ordering her to come to the police station right away. The detective was still alone in the office when Dr. Greineder walked out of the meeting room. He told her the first call had been to his lawyer.

"He said not to talk to you anymore," the doctor said, almost apologetically. "I have told you everything. I'm not trying to hide anything. I've given you everything I know," he added with concern. "You say you want my clothes, and it suddenly scares me. This isn't real. This is a movie. I don't know what happened and I was right there."

McDermott didn't respond. *He's lawyered up*, she thought. *I can't talk to him.*

Proceeding cautiously and not wanting to make a mistake by conversing with the doctor against the counsel of his attorney, McDermott sat silently, slightly overwhelmed by the responsibly that her superiors had placed upon her. When Lt. Wayne Cunningham arrived to take charge at the crime scene, McDermott was slightly stunned when he told her she was going to be the department's primary detective for the homicide investigation. Cunningham and his younger brother Terry, who was Wellesley's police chief, had decided to put the promising young officer on the case despite her relative inexperience. Wayne Cunningham had pulled McDermott aside for some soft words of encouragement. "We know this is your first big homicide," he said, "but go with your instincts. We'll support you, but you'll do fine."

The rest of the investigation team was soon assembled. Trooper Julia Mosely arrived at the pond just before 10:30. A state cop for nearly twenty years, Mosely had been assigned to the Crime Scene Services Section based at the State Police crime lab in suburban Sudbury for the previous year and a half, specializing in fingerprints, photography, and evidence recovery. Like Foley, she would be the unit's case officer for the Wellesley investigation, making her responsible for categorizing most of the collected evidence.

Lt. Ken Martin, who worked out of the ME's office in Boston, had been called to Morses Pond to supervise along with Sgt. Deborah Rebeiro, who would videotape and help photograph the scene as well as oversee the analysis of footwear impressions on the murder trail.

A chemist was also needed, but so far headquarters was having a hard time finding Gwen Pino, a highly regarded civilian who was a manager at the crime lab. The sheer size of the area presented its own problems, but the weather looked like it was going to cooperate. There would be no rain to compromise the physical evidence spread around the woman's body.

Foley had also requested the State Police dive team, since the pond was an obvious place the killer could have dumped evidence.

Finally, Trooper Ken Rudolph and his German shepherd, Arek, trained to follow a human scent, were ordered to Wellesley, on a mission to track a sadistic murderer.

# 3

ATTORNEY TERRY SEGAL anxiously identified himself to the Wellesley desk officer a short time before noon, still not believing what Dirk Greineder had just told him. More of a family friend than a legal advocate, Segal had rushed to his friend's aid knowing he must have been devastated over what had happened to May. Terry and Harriet Segal had lived next door to Dirk and May Greineder for many years on Cleveland Road before moving to a more exclusive section of town. The families had remained friendly but had grown a bit distant after the Segals moved. Dirk's call that morning had left Segal speechless.

"What is the status of the investigation?" the lawyer asked State Police Lt. Bob Friend.

"We're in the process of an investigation and all the information we can get would be helpful," Friend answered.

"My client will be happy to cooperate in all aspects of the police investigation. He wants to do everything humanly possible to find out who did this to his wife," the lawyer stressed.

"There's some things on his clothing that could be evidence and we'd like to take his clothes. We could get a search warrant if we have to," Friend said politely.

"That won't be necessary," Segal insisted. "Dr. Greineder wants to cooperate, and he'll give his clothes. Is he under arrest?"

"No, he's not under arrest."

"Do you intend to arrest him?"

"No."

"Is he a suspect?" Segal persisted.

"We don't have any suspects at the moment. It's too preliminary to have a suspect," Friend said.

"Is he free to leave?"

"I have no problem with him leaving, but we'd like his clothes. There could be evidence on them, and I'd rather he leave us his clothes. I'd be happy to see if there is some clothing here in the police station he could wear," the lieutenant offered, explaining the police needed Dr. Greineder to sign a consent form for the clothing and agree to be photographed.

"He is willing to sign a consent form and give you his clothes and be photographed, but he needs something to change into," Segal said. "He does not believe his daughter can get in the house, so we need some clothes provided to him."

Shuffling into the detective office from behind the glass facade of the small meeting room, a worried Dr. Greineder found himself alone again with Jill McDermott. "I'm thinking all these crazy things," he suddenly announced. "Like this morning, May gave me a backrub, so you'll find my skin under her fingernails." McDermott struggled to remain expressionless. The comment, like the one he had made moments before about being scared, had come out of nowhere.

"Did you give your wife a backrub?" she finally asked.

"No," he replied.

McDermott tried to calm her rising panic. *Shit, I asked him a question*, she thought, at the same time reasoning it was the doctor who had initiated the dialogue against the advice of his attorney. McDermott told herself to relax. *He talked to me first and there is a reason he is telling me this*, she considered.

Meanwhile, Wellesley Sgt. Mike Price was in the lobby of the large, modern brick police station with State Police Sgt. Gerry Mattaliano when an obviously upset young woman hurried through the door. Britt Greineder was frantic to know what had happened to her mother. "I'm sorry. Your mother is dead," Mattaliano bluntly told the crying woman. "She died suspiciously while walking with your father at Morses Pond. Are there other family members?" he asked.

"My older sister Kirsten is a doctor in Michigan, and my brother Colin is going to medical school at Yale," she sobbed.

The officers asked if Britt lived locally and what she did for work. "I graduated from Yale and went to Harvard Medical Pre-School for a while. I'm a manager for an athletic club in Boston," she said through tears.

They asked what her parents did.

"My dad's a doctor; he specializes in allergy and asthmatic patients," she replied. "My mom is retired from Harvard Vanguard Medical. She worked in internal medicine, and she was in the masters program at Massachusetts General Hospital to be a nurse practitioner. She goes to class on Monday and Tuesday every week, but my dad wasn't too excited about her taking that program," she added. Mattaliano picked up on the mention of discontent. "Could you tell us about your parent's relationship together?" he asked.

"My parents were very much in love," Britt said defensively, sensing Mattaliano's suspicion. "They're each other's best friend, they do everything together," she stressed. "Have they had any problems lately," Mattaliano pushed.

"They haven't had any unusual problems or arguments, and I know they are faithful to each other," Britt implored. "I had some problems with my parents several years ago, but we are a very close family and have been for years."

Mattaliano asked Britt about the problem with her parents, but she was reluctant to go into it. "I had fallen out with them about a year and a half ago when I dropped out of the Harvard medical program. My mom and I didn't speak for four months, but we made up," she finally told the detectives. "Is that enough for now? Is my father okay? I want to see him."

Britt's growing anxiety prompted Mattaliano to end the interview.

Jill McDermott was still mulling Dr. Greineder's comments about the backrub when a young blonde woman stormed sobbing into the detective office followed by Terry Segal. "What the hell is going on?" the doctor's daughter tearfully yelled. "What happened? Is she really dead? Did someone kill her?" she bellowed. Dr. Greineder didn't respond as his daughter embraced him. "What happened between you and mom today? Did something happen?" Britt wailed.

"No, we were walking and she hurt her back and I went down to the water with Zephy and Zephy heard something and she found her," Dr. Greineder answered, his excitement level rising in response to his daughter's frantic demeanor.

"She's hurt her back before. She usually lies down and she's fine," Britt said as her father guided her to an empty office in an effort to calm her privately.

McDermott walked over to her desk and wrote down the "strange and bizarre" things Dr. Greineder had said to her. She had been wondering what he might say next, when his daughter's emotional arrival had ended their conversation. Returning a few moments later, she found Britt was still upset.

"Why do these fucked-up things always happen to our family," she yelled at her father. "Why do these psychotic, unexplained things happen to our family?"

McDermott waited silently for Dr. Greineder's response. "They are going to think it's me," he coldly told his daughter. "I've seen it on TV."

Drawn back to the detective office by the commotion of Britt's arrival, Marty Foley learned that Dr. Greineder had agreed to provide his clothing and sign a consent form. But now the detective wanted something else as well. It had occurred to him that he should take a look inside the doctor's house and van. The only way he could make an inspection without a search warrant was with the owner's permission. His request was met with silence from the doctor and his attorney.

"I'd hate to have a pool of blood on your kitchen floor and not know about it," Foley said.

The stark comment seemed to jolt the doctor and his lawyer. After a brief consultation with his friend, Segal said the police could see his home and minivan, agreeing to Foley's suggestion that the doctor's permission be included on the consent form.

The information continued to flow into the police station, and the fragmented reports slowly began to illuminate what had happened at Morses Pond before Foley arrived there. As Paul Fitzpatrick, the first officer sent, had approached the gate, he had seen Wellesley Engine 1 in his rearview mirror carrying firefighters Ken Demerchant, William DeLorie, and Ronald Wilson. While looking for the key to unlock the gate, Fitzpatrick told Foley, a jogger named Richard Magnan had approached him before he could even get out of his cruiser. Fitzpatrick had asked if a woman had been injured. "A man told me his wife was attacked," the runner had answered, "and he's running toward the pond. He should just be over that hill," Magnan had gestured toward the sloping access road. "He has blood on him."

The mention of blood had injected Fitzpatrick with an urgency the original dispatch had not warranted.

The officer first saw the man in the yellow windbreaker moving at a brisk walk. He brought his cruiser to a sharp stop even with him and lowered the passenger-side window.

"My wife's been attacked," the man yelled through the window.

"Get in the back and show me."

The man jumped in and Fitzpatrick pressed the accelerator.

"Where are we going?" he asked over his shoulder.

"Down the circle. Down at the beach," the man responded.

Fitzpatrick's passenger pointed out a dirt path and he pulled his cruiser up on the grass toward it. Dr. Greineder frantically tried to open the rear door but couldn't. The back doors, designed to prevent prisoners from escaping, had to be opened from the outside. Fitzpatrick opened it, and Dr. Greineder sprinted down the dirt trail without him before he could say a word. The officer, with twenty-eight years on the job and nearing retirement, struggled to keep up on the uneven terrain.

Now a good fifty feet behind the husband, Fitzpatrick came up a rise in the path, and saw him drop to his knees at his wife's feet, adjusting her clothing at the waist. Moving to within five feet of the woman, Fitzpatrick was stunned to find her lying on her back with a huge, gaping wound to the left side of her neck, her skin color ashen. She appeared to be dead.

Sensing the firefighters coming up the path, Fitzpatrick tapped the husband on the shoulder and told him to move. The three men halted almost instantaneously. Expecting a back injury, they too were jolted to see the woman lifeless on the ground. Observing the woman's ominous skin color, DeLorie directed Demerchant to check for a pulse. Holding one of her wrists, Demerchant felt nothing. Now standing over the woman's head, he went to check her neck for a pulse, pushing her sweatshirt away. Demerchant and DeLorie immediately saw the ghastly slice.

Definitely not wanting to put his hand there, Demerchant gingerly touched the other side. Again, the burly firefighter felt nothing, helplessly looking up at DeLorie, who hovered near the woman's feet. Not willing to forgo every effort to save the patient, especially with her husband there, DeLorie lifted his radio and called the ambulance. "How close are you? The woman's not breathing," he advised. "We're coming up behind you," was the reply.

With the much more serious diagnosis radioed by DeLorie, paramedics Jason Harris and Glenn Davis increased their speed as their ambulance neared the pond. They immediately headed down the path at a run. When Harris crested the rise in the middle of the trail, he saw a man with a yellow jacket standing with three firefighters and a police officer farther down the path. Passing the man with the jacket, the stocky Harris was nearing the patient when a large amount of blood lying in the dirt slowed his run. Now anxious to check his surroundings, the paramedic stopped abruptly, looking at the woman from a distance of eight feet.

The neck wound was clearly fatal, the woman's skin color underlining the obvious. Harris closed to within three feet and knelt down next to the woman to examine her grievous injury. The jagged cut was two inches wide and stretched from the bottom of her left ear to the middle of her neck under her chin. There would be no attempt to resuscitate her. Harris didn't touch her. He stood surveying the scene, noticing what looked to be drag marks near the puddle of blood. There was nothing they could do for the woman now. Aware that she had fallen prey to a vicious crime, Harris led his partner around the murder scene and they retreated back down the path to their ambulance.

Ken Demerchant quietly told Bill DeLorie the woman had other wounds on her head. Looking around, he saw a square piece of plastic on the ground that looked like it had blood on it and a blue fleece glove lying nearby that matched one the woman was wearing on her left hand.

Dr. Greineder dropped to his knees again, obviously upset but not crying. DeLorie noticed he was sweating and his hair was mussed. "My wife. My wife, who could do this to my wife?" he cried.

DeLorie waited a moment for the husband to compose himself, asking if he had lost sight of her.

Dr. Greineder responded he had. "She has a bad back," he added, the information unsolicited. "She was throwing the ball to the dog and twisted her back," he continued, demonstrating what looked like an underhand softball pitch. "She told me to go ahead and take the dog to the pond. When we came back we found her."

Now surveying the trail for the first time after stepping back for the firefighters, Fitzpatrick also spotted the puddle of blood and the drag mark that ended at the woman's left foot. The officer also saw what looked like a plastic Ziploc bag spotted with blood in the pathway and a tennis ball lying nearby. Keying the mike on his radio, Fitzpatrick asked Sgt. Nahass, the street supervisor, to come to the pond. "We have a crime scene here," he told his sergeant. Concentrating on preserving evidence, Fitzpatrick asked Dr. Greineder and firefighters to move away from the body. They looped around the bloody spot in the path, slowly starting back down the trail.

When Nahass hustled up the path minutes later, he quietly surveyed the chilling scene until Fitzpatrick broke the silence. "The husband's here."

"Where is he?" Nahass responded anxiously.

"He's out there somewhere," Fitzpatrick said, pointing down the trail toward the traffic circle.

"Go stay with him," was all Nahass said, thinking about the list of people he had to notify. A Wellesley cop for nearly twenty-five years, Nahass had been around long enough to know the murder would spread an epidemic of fear throughout the prosperous community, where a housebreak was considered a major crime. His superiors would be furious if they were not informed promptly. Carefully trying to retrace his steps down the trail, all Nahass could think about was the sensational murders of two other elderly residents that had recently dominated the news. He couldn't imagine what the coverage would be like once the word got out that a third person had been slain, particularly in an upscale community like Wellesley, where there hadn't been a murder in three decades.

Approaching the husband on the grass behind the traffic circle, Paul Fitzpatrick slowed for a moment to look him over. He could see dried, rust-colored blood staining the yellow nylon of his jacket, what looked like a blood smear on a lens of his glasses, and small, reddish-brown spots on his white Reebok sneakers.

"What happened?" the officer asked.

"My wife and I were walking with the dog in the sandpit and she said she stepped on a pebble or something. She said, 'Oh my God, I twisted my back again.' She's done that before," Dr. Greineder explained. "When I got back to where we had left her, she was lying down and the dog was on top of her, licking her. I knelt down and felt that she was warm and I checked her carotid pulse. It was hard to feel so I ran back to my van to use the cell phone."

Shuffling through his notes one last time, Fitzpatrick would forget to tell Marty Foley until weeks later about two questions the husband had asked him earlier at the pond.

"Is she dead?" Dr. Greineder had inquired, ending an awkward period of silence during the interview. The unexpected query had made the officer pause. Fitzpatrick had confirmed that she was, and then, after several more uncomfortable moments, the doctor had asked, "Am I going to be arrested?" The second question had caught Fitzpatrick even more unprepared. "I don't know; it's not up to me," he had finally said. "There's sergeants and lieutenants here, and that would be their call."

Dr. Greineder's insistence that no one could get into his home set off an almost comedic search for clothing throughout the police station. Cops were rummaging through their lockers looking for street clothes the doctor could change into, but the effort was futile. The doctor and his attorney were getting antsy. Segal again asked Lt. Friend if his client was free to leave. "He's free to leave but we are doing our level best to find him some clothes," Friend responded tersely.

Busy in the conference room, Marty Foley was distressed to hear Dr. Greineder was thinking of leaving despite his earlier agreement to give up his clothing. Legally, the police could not detain him at the police station. But Foley was determined that the doctor was not walking out of there with those clothes on his back.

Meanwhile, State Police Sgt. Kevin Shea had finally managed to reach the Norfolk DA's chief trial counsel, Rick Grundy, who was visiting his mother in Delaware with his wife and infant daughter. He immediately agreed to cut short his visit and return to Massachusetts. "Don't let him leave with those clothes," Grundy had told Shea.

Grundy, a skilled, unrelenting prosecutor, was in charge of the Norfolk homicide unit. He had inherited the two previous killings of elderly residents in the county and was alarmed that another older person had been butchered in a public park, all within ten months. Grundy spent much of the eight-hour drive home with his cell phone pressed to his ear.

Finally, Terry Segal's wife, Harriet, arrived with some of her husband's clothes for Dr. Greineder to change into. He had now been at the police station for more than two hours. Foley explained that Julia Mosely was going to photograph him removing each article of clothing.

"That's no problem. I posed nude for the art students when I was at Yale," the doctor retorted.

*Okay, whatever*, Foley thought, finding another of the doctor's statements peculiar.

Standing before a white wall, Dr. Greineder began taking off his clothes, starting with the yellow windbreaker, while Mosely took pictures.

When the doctor had stripped to his underwear, Foley noticed a fresh, red scratch on his chest and three more on his neck. "How did you get those?" the trooper asked.

"I was wrestling with the dog," the doctor replied.

As Dr. Greineder began changing into his lawyer's much larger clothes, Foley was again drawn to his hands. Several of his fingernails were dirty while the others appeared untrimmed. Foley thought it was odd a doctor would have dirt caked under his nails. If the husband did have something to do with his wife's murder, the dirt under his nails might be important.

"Would you mind cutting your fingernails for us?" Foley asked. The doctor and his attorney reacted indifferently to the request, agreeing to amend the consent form to include the clippings. Someone produced nail clippers allowing Dr. Greineder to snip his fingernails into an envelope held by Foley.

Perhaps sensing he would finally be able to leave, Dr. Greineder's demeanor had improved during the photography and recovery of his clothing. One picture captured a near-smirk on his face, and he had briefly joked with the officers. Foley, hoping to get as much as he could from the man before he walked away, tried for something else. "I'd also like to have your glasses," Foley told the doctor. Since the lens was stained with blood, the trooper figured it had touched the victim.

"You can't have my glasses. I need them to drive," Dr. Greineder said, losing his friendly demeanor.

Foley would regret it later, but he reluctantly let it go. He wanted the glasses but didn't want to jeopardize what the doctor had already agreed to. Bob Friend also appealed to Segal for the glasses, explaining they were stained with blood, but the lawyer was adamant that Dr. Greineder needed them to drive. The supervising lieutenants had also wanted to ask the doctor to submit to an ortho-toluidine test, which could indicate the presence of blood on his hands, but GHQ had yet to track down chemist Gwen Pino.

There was no sense in broaching the subject without a chemist available, Foley thought, and with all the blood on Dr. Greineder's clothes the test would not be necessary. He was going to have the doctor's nail clippings tested anyway and wanted to keep the investigation moving with a look inside the doctor's home and van.

Dr. Greineder was visibly anxious to leave. Despite his strange behavior, Foley had not drawn any conclusions, having no inclination to arrest him. Who is to say how a grieving husband should act, Foley considered. He knew what the statistics said about husbands killing wives, but the other two unsolved cases hovered in his mind.

Satisfied with the signed consent form granting him the clothing, fingernails, and a look into his house and van, Foley told the doctor and Segal he would follow them to Dr. Greineder's home on Cleveland Road.

At about the same time, Sgt. Deborah Rebeiro was getting a general overview of the crime scene, particularly where May Greineder lay. Rebeiro surveyed the various items near the body before studying the large bloody puddle and drag mark in the trail. Earlier, Julia Mosely had discovered a white kitchen-size plastic trash bag folded and tucked under a downed branch, and Rebeiro listed it among the items to be collected. Unfortunately, it would be several months before anyone would tell Foley about the kitchen bag.

Rebeiro could see a large number of footprints and impressions in the dirt near the body. Wellesley police officers had already taken photographs of the shoe bottoms worn by the first responders who had tried to save the woman as well as a pair of sneakers worn by Bill Kear, the man with the small dog who had walked down the trail in an effort to help after his encounter with the woman's husband.

Ten years of collecting footprints had given Rebeiro experience documenting impressions from soil and snow, floors and carpeting, even a window. An impression can be left either three-dimensionally or in the form of a stain from something coating the bottom of the shoe, like blood. Once the impression is recovered, it can be compared to a thousand different brands of footwear, each brand having hundreds, sometimes thousands of common manufacturing characteristics. A manufacturing identifier was always the first thing Rebeiro looked for in trying to match a footprint, but many times, the print was just a general size and shape, devoid of the manufacturer's characteristics. Prints can also be matched through identifiers like cuts or gouges that are particular to that one shoe.

Rebeiro found that the beginning of the dirt trail was hard and topped with gravel. Impressions there were difficult to see with the ground not soft enough to capture a three-dimensional print. Closer to the body, the path was covered by a thick layer of pine needles that again masked the prints of anyone who had walked there. In the small clearing in the wooded section where May Greineder lay, Rebeiro was encouraged to see a number of prints in the trail where the drag mark from the victim's left foot had softened the hard-packed soil.

Most of the impressions were likely left by the first responders who had futilely tried to save the already dead woman. Any prints left unidentified would be painstakingly documented with photographs and then collected using casts made of dental stone. With a hundred-foot tape measure laid along the path, extending about twenty-five feet past May Greineder, each impression would be marked and then logged with its location along the tape. Rebeiro would then lay a ruler next to each print and take close-up photographs. Back in the laboratory, she would be able to make life-size, one-to-one enlargements that could be compared against any suspected piece of footwear.

In addition to the photography, Rebeiro would collect an impression in a dental stone cast made from a mixture that looked like pancake batter. For each cast, Rebeiro combined water and two pounds of dental stone in a Ziploc bag, stirring with a spoon or spatula to the desired consistency. The mixture was then poured on the impression, smoothed across it, and left to harden for thirty minutes. The dental stone captured an accurate three-dimensional image of the print that, through various techniques, Rebeiro could match to a particular shoe.

Completing her initial survey, Rebeiro had nearly forty prints she considered identifiable. She and her assistants then got to work. On their hands and knees they began photographing and trying to identify every one.

Lt. Ken Martin had driven through the access road gate about an hour after Rebeiro. During his twenty years on the job, Martin had been to hundreds of crime scenes, first as a homicide detective, then as a crime scene supervisor. He would assist in May Greineder's autopsy by carefully disrobing her for a close inspection of each garment and then scanning her body and clothing for any trace evidence.

Martin stepped carefully toward the body and halted to take in the crime scene. An expert on blood pattern interpretation, he was particularly interested in the puddle of blood drying in the middle of the pathway.

From the yawning wound in her neck, Martin concluded that the woman had been killed in the path then dragged to where she now lay in the scrub. Standing over the body, Martin could see tiny droplets of blood on the ground next to the woman and on her face and abdomen, where it looked like her pants had been cut. The blood drops told the forensic expert that whoever killed May Greineder had inflicted more blows after dragging her off the trail. He would be able to make a better examination once she was autopsied, but Martin also detected what looked like impact spatter on May's pants and jacket.

Inspecting May's left leg where her pants had been pushed up above her knee, Martin noted a single drop of impact spatter on the side of her knee near the calf. There was also a bloodstain that looked like it had dripped on the leg while she was lying on her back. The rumpled pant leg was further proof that May had been dragged. His suspicion would be confirmed later when May was put in a body bag for the trip to the ME's office. Her pants and red underwear had been forced down to the midpoint of her buttocks, and leaves were bunched up under her back. Like the others who had seen the savaged body, Martin couldn't help but think of the other two unsolved murders in Norfolk County.

General Headquarters had finally located chemist Gwen Pino at her cousin's baby shower in the western Massachusetts city of Chicopee. Her family had a running joke every time Pino visited. "Who's dead?" they would ask. "Really, I'm just here to visit," Pino would joke back. Since she was a backup to the on-call chemist, Pino had not expected to be sent to a crime scene in Wellesley seventy-five miles away. *Oh shit*, she thought as she saw the familiar number for GHQ on her pager. The on-call chemist was going to be tied up for hours at another murder, leaving Pino with the unhappy realization that she had to go to Wellesley. Driving east, she called Deb Rebeiro to go over what they had.

Employed by the State Police crime lab for fifteen years, Pino was an assistant manager of the evidence and case resolution units. Despite her supervisory duties, she still worked at crime scenes, where the procedure was always the same. The forensic investigators had to work as a team, and before anything was done, they huddled to discuss what was known about the case and what steps they would take to proceed. Talking to Rebeiro while driving, Pino reminded her to keep the detectives away from the body until she got there. She wanted to make sure that evidence was not inadvertently destroyed. She and Rebeiro set up a plan that Rebeiro then relayed to the investigators.

Rebeiro was waiting for Pino at Dr. Greineder's van on Turner Road. She had been warned about the doctor's dog inside, but the black and tan German shepherd seemed friendly enough, wagging her tail as Rebeiro peered at the animal through the window. Within a few minutes, a crying young woman with striking blonde hair drove up and identified herself as Dr. Greineder's daughter Britt.

Rebeiro expressed sympathy about her mother's death and asked her for the keys to the van, which the distraught daughter reluctantly surrendered. The German shepherd happily bounced out when she opened the door, slightly buoying the daughter's spirits. Rebeiro took several pictures of the dog, ignoring the daughter's annoyance when she was asked to leave the animal's leash and collar before taking Zephyr home.

Giving the inside of the van a quick survey after Britt's departure, Rebeiro observed a small red backpack with black straps on the front passenger seat. After taking more pictures, she backed away to wait for Pino, who finally arrived moments later from her long drive across Massachusetts. Rebeiro described the husband for the chemist. With the exception of his hands, he had been covered with his wife's blood. Accordingly, Rebeiro continued, the lieutenants wanted Pino to test for blood inside the Chrysler van.

Spotting a reddish stain on the frame of the front passenger seat, Pino took a piece of dry white filter paper and ran the strip across the stain before adding a drop of ortho-toluidine to detect oxidizing reagents associated with blood. Putting a drop of sodium borate to the filter paper caused no change in color. If there had been oxidizing material indicating the presence of blood or heme in the stain, the filter paper would have turned blue.

The test is extremely sensitive, so even with a positive reaction the ortho-toluidine test would not have been conclusive for the presence of blood. The chemical can also test positive for oxidizers in some fruits and vegetables, and partly for that reason, Pino would have recommended against testing Dr. Greineder's hands had she been available when he was at the police station. Even if he had not touched his wife's wound, Pino believed testing the husband's hands would have undoubtedly returned a positive result because his clothing was covered with blood. If he had any cuts on his hands or had handled certain fruits or vegetables, the result would also be positive.

The detectives' observations of Dr. Greineder's clean hands and the photographs taken at the police station would prove far more valuable than the missed ortho-toluidine test. To actually confirm a substance is blood, it has to be swabbed with distilled water and brought back to the lab for a more elaborate test. The preliminary ortho-toluidine tests on the driver's seat and the handset of the cellular phone Dr. Greineder had mounted on the console were both negative for blood. As Marty Foley would later reason, if the husband had blood on his hands, it surely would have shown up on the phone he used to call for help.

Finished with the van, Pino was taken to the crime scene before May

Greineder's body was removed to the medical examiner's office. As she took notes on the items in the path and compiled a list of the woman's clothing, Pino noted that the victim's blue-and-white striped pants appeared to be ripped or cut down the front seam and her right arm was raised. Pino took a lock of hair resting on the woman's upper left arm, then collected the right-hand blue glove, a tennis ball, and the bloodstained Ziploc bag on the trail.

Although hardened from processing hundreds of crime scenes like this, looking at May Greineder, Pino couldn't help but feel sadness. "When a bad guy kills a bad guy it doesn't affect me," she said later. "I knew about the other murders [of elderly residents in the county] and you had them in the back of your head. When you see that kind of viciousness, somebody is very angry with you and it's personal." She added, "You don't think about who did it. I think about what kind of evidence am I going to find to link my victim to my suspect."

Taken to Paul Fitzpatrick's cruiser to test for blood in the back seat where Dr. Greineder had sat, Pino repeated the procedure done at the doctor's van. This time, Pino watched as the filter paper she touched to the cruiser seat turned blue, an indication Dr. Greineder had left blood there. Testing the door handle the frantic husband had desperately tried to open, Pino noted the color of the filter paper remained unchanged. It was, as Foley would observe, another obstacle to the husband's contention that he had touched his wife's gaping neck wound.

# 4

TROOPER MARTY FOLEY FOLLOWED TERRY SEGAL down Cleveland Road. The lawyer turned left into Dr. Greineder's driveway, and Foley parked his cruiser in the street in front of the white, split-level home with the number 56 displayed over the front door. To the left of the black door was a large bay window, and to the right an attached two-car garage. A wooden fence lined the rear yard. The house was in a pleasant neighborhood, but for Wellesley, it was rather middle class, Foley thought.

Foley had driven over with Jill McDermott, Julia Mosely, and Trooper Diane Lilly. They gathered on the front porch behind Dr. Greineder and Segal while the doctor unlocked the door. They could hear a dog barking inside, and Dr. Greineder announced that he would have to put Wolfie out back in his pen so they could walk through the house. He stepped into the foyer and disappeared down a set of stairs to what looked like a finished basement, emerging seconds later holding a German shepherd by the collar. The doctor took the animal to the main level of the house and led the dog out a door in the kitchen to its pen in the rear yard.

Waiting in the kitchen for the doctor to come back, Foley spotted a Star Tec cell phone on a counter. When Dr. Greineder returned, he brought Segal and the officers through the kitchen to the left, rear corner of the house where they entered an office. Going back toward the middle of the main floor, they took a step down into a small eating area next to the office, returned to the kitchen, and walked into a separate, more formal dining room with a sliding glass door leading to a rear deck. Dr. Greineder had told Foley his house was a mess, but it looked clean and free of clutter to the trooper.

Following Dr. Greineder into the living room, they then came to a set of stairs leading to the second floor. Foley climbed the stairs and peered into a bathroom that was being remodeled. While there was nothing ostentatious about the furnishings in the Greineders' home — with the exception of a number of nice artworks — Foley thought the bathroom was quite lavish. The fixtures looked very pricey, as did the ornate glass on the shower door.

The three other rooms on the top floor were bedrooms, all furnished with computers. The detectives did not open closets or look in drawers, as the doctor had only consented to a walkthrough of his home, not a thorough search, which would take court approval. Foley wasn't looking for anything in particular, anyway. He just wanted a visual survey made of the doctor's home and van.

Dr. Greineder was cordial, seemingly more relaxed now that he was home, yet showing no emotion over the murder of his wife only six hours before. The strangely composed host led his visitors back downstairs to the main level, around the corner and down the foyer stairs to the basement. The group turned toward a nicely furnished family room with a wall displaying family photographs, including a picture of a man in a World War II German military uniform.

The doctor then led his guests through the family room to a tidy bedroom in the left, rear of the basement that Foley recognized as the master bedroom. The king-sized electric bed was stripped. "Where are the sheets?" Foley asked. "They're in the laundry, but I didn't start the washing machine yet. Do you want to see them?" Dr. Greineder offered. "Sure," Foley responded. The doctor led him to a nearby laundry area. After pulling the sheets and mattress cover from the washing machine, Dr. Greineder lifted the bedding for Foley to inspect.

Nothing looked amiss, and the detective turned to an adjacent work area where Dr. Greineder had a wooden bench and hanging pegboard. The area was meticulously kept, with everything having a place. The tools had been carefully hung and organized on the pegboard, Foley noticed. Dr. Greineder led everyone back to the kitchen on the main floor, where Foley made another attempt to collect the doctor's glasses. "He needs them to drive," Segal interjected, again rebuffing the detective.

"How about if we take a picture of them, then," Foley countered, looking toward Julia Mosely holding her camera.

Dr. Greineder briefly consulted with Segal, agreeing to let Mosely photograph the eyewear still bearing blood on the left lens. Needing a solid background for the pictures, the glasses were placed on a desk in Colin Greineder's bedroom, where flashes from Mosely's camera blinked off the white ceiling.

During the picture taking, Foley remembered the clear bag from the crime scene. "Did you or your wife bring plastic bags today?" he asked the doctor.

"I don't know anything about plastic bags," Dr. Greineder answered.

Finished with the tour, the doctor showed the four police officers to the door, where Foley thanked Dr. Greineder and his attorney before leaving. It was now about 3 P.M., and Foley drove the half mile back to Morses Pond conscious that nightfall was rapidly approaching.

In Manhattan, Belinda Markel worked through a mental checklist of everything she needed to do for the Halloween party. When she was almost home from the swim meet in Newburgh, her cell phone rang with a call from her oldest daughter, Alexis. Arriving home first from her meet in Flushing, Alexis had found a concerning message on the answering machine left by a distressed Britt Greineder urging Belinda to call "right away."

Belinda didn't recognize the number Britt left as she wrote it down while trying to navigate her large Expedition through Manhattan traffic. "She sounded kind of odd," Alexis told her mother before hanging up. Of Belinda's three cousins, Britt was easily the most unpredictable and dramatic. High-strung and emotional, she was always dealing with some minor crisis.

Belinda dialed the unfamiliar number as she drove down Fifth Avenue. But it was her Uncle Dirk who answered. "Oh, hi, Dirk, I'm calling Britt back," said Belinda.

"She called, but I need to talk to you," he replied ominously. "Where are you?"

Belinda sensed a troubled urgency in his voice. "I'm in my car," she replied haltingly.

"Can you pull over, or do you want to call me when you get home?" The tone in his voice indicated he had something bad to tell her.

Belinda intuitively knew something was seriously wrong and didn't want to wait to find out what it was. She was still trying to find a place to stop when her uncle delivered the worst possible news.

"There's been a terrible accident," he said.

Belinda went numb with fear.

"And May's dead."

The words pierced Belinda to the core, sending waves of grief and shock through her. Struggling to keep both her composure and the big suv under control, Belinda's thoughts swirled about while her uncle went on excitedly about the dogs, something about going to the pond, May being attacked.

"Oh my God, what are you talking about?" Belinda finally gasped. Young Amy and William sitting behind her immediately sensed the distress in her voice. "I'll call you when I get home," Belinda said, unsure she could continue the conversation without causing an accident.

"I'm frightened for you, Belinda," her uncle said before hanging up.

Reeling from what her uncle had just told her, Belinda somehow managed to keep the Expedition on course. From her uncle's confusing account, she deduced her aunt had been killed in her home while the dogs weren't there. *Where were the dogs?* she wondered. *Why weren't they home, and what could have happened to her?*

"What's wrong, Mom?" Amy's apprehensive question from the back seat corralled her mother's runaway thoughts.

"We'll talk about it when we get home," Belinda said. Her response met with rare silence from the two precocious children, who sat rigid and alert, underlining their expectation that something terrible had happened.

Belinda continued her agonizing drive, somehow managing to make it home. Coming through the door of their twenty-first-floor apartment, Belinda caught the expression of fear on Alexis's face, showing that she too suspected devastating news. "There is something really bad," Belinda said quietly, "but I need you guys to wait here for just a few minutes." Feeling herself losing control again, Belinda was not about to have it happen in front of her kids. A few moments alone would help her pull herself together. She hugged and kissed her kids and slipped out the door. "I'll be right back," she promised.

Belinda took the elevator to the lobby and went outside. Forgetting to call her uncle back in her anguish, she instead called her husband's law office. "Greg, May is dead. I need you to come home," she blurted. Speaking the inconceivable words for the first time wrenched May's death into reality.

Greg Markel had barely said hello when his wife rocked him with the dreadful news. "What are you talking about?" he responded in alarm, hoping he had misunderstood but knowing he had not from the trauma in her voice.

"Dirk said something about her being attacked and that she's dead. That's all I know. You have to come home," she insisted.

Normally unflappable, Belinda checked her paralyzing shock with the reality the nightmarish development had to be dealt with. *Holy shit*, she thought, *I have three kids sitting upstairs and I have a whole bunch of kids coming to my house in two hours.*

After ending the call with her husband, Belinda put herself on "automatic pilot," calling the other families who were invited to the Halloween party. She was honest about the reason for the sudden cancellation, and the bewildered parents offered hasty condolences. Then it was time to face her children with the awful reality that May, their "Auntie May," whom they loved, was dead.

Greg Markel soon arrived to help his wife try to console their grief-tormented children, but the shaken parents had few remedies. The suddenness of May's death was frightening enough, but the concept of murder was doubly disconcerting, particularly for the kids. She held them for a long time, letting them cry. As she tried to organize her thoughts, one thing became abundantly clear; she had to go to Wellesley.

At Morses Pond, Trooper Ken Rudolph was interested to learn that Marty Foley had returned. Earlier, Rudolph had followed his K-9, Arek, in an expansive search of the vast recreation area, but nothing seemed out of the ordinary. Later, Arek had hit on an apparent human scent on the narrow, paved beach maintenance road leading from the traffic circle. The dog had pointed its nose at the corner of a granite backsplash in the asphalt curbing, and Rudolph had reached down and felt a draft, realizing that Arek had stopped at a storm drain. The trooper hadn't disturb the matted leaves there but returned to the traffic circle, where the hectic police activity was being coordinated. Rudolph had told Lt. Bob Friend about Arek's behavior. "Let Foley know when he gets back," the lieutenant had ordered.

Absorbed with what he needed to do back at the crime scene, Foley didn't immediately notice the trooper in the black jump suit approaching him. "Hi, Ken Rudolph," he said, extending his hand. "Lt. Friend told me to tell you about a hit my dog had on the trail over there," Rudolph said, pointing out the narrow maintenance road where Dr. Greineder had told Foley he went looking for a jogger.

When the heavy drain was lifted off a short time later, Trooper Scott Jennings got on his knees and peered into the dim catch basin, where he was drawn to a bright blue object on the bottom. He couldn't identify it in the fading daylight. Squinting into the darkened recess, Foley recognized what it was immediately. The brilliant blue was the signature color of an Estwing hammer, a high-quality tool familiar to Foley from his experience as a carpenter. The detective quickly noticed something else near the hammer, lying under what looked like a brown piece of cloth. Looking harder, Foley could see it was the brass handle of a knife under a brown work glove. The sinister implication of the discovery was grimly apparent to the four cops huddled over the catch basin.

After Deb Rebeiro carefully photographed the hammer, knife, and glove on the leafy bottom of the catch basin, Bob Friend, the skinniest cop there, dropped into the drain and gingerly handed up its contents on brown paper.

Foley studied each item as it was lifted to the pavement, now convinced they had found the murder weapons. The hammer, fashioned like a small sledgehammer, was a two-pound model, and it was clearly spotted with blood. The knife, also streaked with blood, appeared new like the hammer. Its folding blade was closed, and Foley studied its silver "Old Timer" logo on the handle. When extended, the blade measured about four inches. Foley could now see that the brown glove was for the right hand, and its top and cuff were made from a knitted brown material. The palm, thumb, and all around the index and baby fingers were covered with black textured rubber dots to improve grip.

Little was said as the murder weapons were lifted from the storm drain. The Wellesley and State Police detectives were well aware of what Bill Kear—the man with the small dog—had told them. Walking down the middle of the access road, Kear had seen Dr. Greineder emerge from the dirt path where his wife lay, cross behind the traffic circle with his German shepherd, and briefly vanish down the small paved road to the beach where the weapons and glove were hidden. Only after returning to the access road did Dr. Greineder turn toward help and ask Kear for a phone. It was now painfully clear that the oddly grieving husband was the obvious suspect in his wife's murder.

For Wayne Cunningham, it was almost like concrete hardening around the husband. He marveled at their good fortune in finding the weapons and glove as well as identifying witnesses who could put Dr. Greineder at incriminating places at specific times. Subdued by the savagery and cold-bloodedness of the doctor's apparent act, another unspoken sentiment swirled around the cops. The investigators didn't know why Dr. Greineder had done it, but it seemed clear that he had planned his wife's murder to look like the highly publicized recent unsolved slayings in the area. A sense of resolve that the doctor was going to be held accountable steeled the detectives.

Gwen Pino had not watched the recovery of the weapons and glove but had felt a mounting excitement as word spread across the crime scene that they had been found. Brought to look at the items, Pino observed a brown stain on the face of the hammer and small reddish-brown smears on the front and back of its bright blue handle. When the knife was opened, Pino noted red stains on both sides of the blade. Filter paper she ran across both weapons rapidly turned blue when drops of sodium borate landed. She carefully put the weapons and glove in three separate brown bags for more detailed testing later.


Belinda Markel called her parents' vacation home in East Hampton, not knowing if her mother was aware her younger sister was dead.

But Murray Stark greeted his daughter with a distressed, "Oh, my God," and the hysterical wailing of Belinda's mother, Ilse, in the background provided the answer.

Britt had called her Aunt Ilse with the shattering news, and Murray Stark had been futilely trying to calm his inconsolable wife ever since. Putting his wife on the phone, Murray hoped she would listen to her daughter.

"It's a mean trick. It's just a mean trick," Ilse Stark screamed into the phone. "Britt's just doing this. It's a mean trick. It can't be true," she repeated over and over.

"Mom, it's true and you need to come home," Belinda said evenly, trying to bring her mother back to her usually controlled and refined demeanor. "You need to calm down, and we need to go up there."

Belinda spoke to her father again, and Murray reported he was doing his best to get Ilse in the car to drive her home. Hanging up, Belinda dialed the Greineder house, where her uncle answered. "I need my family together," he implored, telling his niece that Kirsten and Aleks were flying in from Michigan, and friends were driving Colin home from Yale.

"I'm trying to get organized to get up there," Belinda said. She prodded Dr. Greineder for more information about what had happened to May but still did not get beyond his foggy explanation that someone had attacked her. "My mother's on her way home, and I want to be here when she gets home," Belinda told her uncle. "The kids are putting some stuff together. I'll call you back in a little while."

The phone was ringing again; this time it was Belinda's cousin Britt. "Is Greg going to help us find a lawyer," Britt asked excitedly.

"What are you talking about?" Belinda responded, puzzled by the question.

"We need the help. We need a lawyer. This is going to be a mess," Britt shot back, her excitement rising with every sentence.

"Why don't you calm down and we'll talk about this when I get there," Belinda suggested, still not knowing what her cousin was talking about.

Standing above the catch basin, Marty Foley had come to an obvious conclusion. A closer inspection was needed of Dr. Greineder's home and van, and this time he was going to get search warrants to do it. With the implements of May Greineder's murder safely stowed in evidence bags, Foley surveyed the remainder of the narrow road beyond the storm drain to its end at the pond's beach. It didn't seem logical. *If your wife is hurt and you want to make a phone call you would want to make a beeline up the access road*, Foley thought.

The doctor must have known the maintenance road was a dead end, since he had told police he and his wife walked the recreation area all the time. Foley wanted to meet Bill Kear before he went back to the police station to prepare the search warrants. It was clear Kear was going to be an important witness, and Foley wanted to make his own personal evaluation of what the man with the small dog had seen. Studying the route Kear had described Dr. Greineder and Zephyr taking that morning, Foley realized it was the opposite of where a frantic husband desperate for help should have gone.

Coming out of the dirt path where his lifeless wife lay, Dr. Greineder had turned right toward the back of the traffic circle, hugging the tree line bordering the cul-de-sac, instead of turning left into the traffic circle so he could run directly up the access road. Based on Kear's description, the doctor had moved toward a small retaining pond about forty steps away when he suddenly veered slightly left, heading straight for the maintenance road where the glove and weapons were found.

It seemed to Foley that Dr. Greineder might have used the shadows in the cul-de-sac for cover, intending to hurl the weapons into the retaining pond until he saw Kear and his dog on the access road. Why *didn't he just leave the weapons with the body?* the detective wondered. *Why risk it? Was dumping the stuff in the pond part of the plan?*

There was no way to know, but Foley had already decided Kear would be brought back to Morses Pond at some point to show the trooper precisely where he was when he observed Dr. Greineder. Foley would also have Kear describe the doctor's exact movements from the time he appeared from the dirt path to when he approached the apprehensive Kear and asked for a phone. ·

Satisfied that the crime scene specialists were deep into their evidence recovery on the dirt trail, where lights were being set up for work into the night, Foley and Kevin Shea left for the police station, with a side trip to Bill Kear's house. The sunlight gone early with the fresh implementation of Daylight Savings Time, the luminous beams of extended spotlights beyond the guarded gate to Morses Pond announced that the media had finally caught up to the story.

Passing through the open barrier before turning left on Halsey Avenue, Foley avoided the row of TV trucks and a mob of reporters and photographers hopefully looking past the police sentry down the darkened access road for anything that could reveal the Halloween evil that had befallen May Greineder. Foley was surprised it had taken this long for the media to show up but was happy with the daylong reprieve from the unwanted distraction. It must have been because of the plane crash he had heard about before being sent to Wellesley, he figured, not really caring what the reason was.

Assignment editors at Boston's two newspapers and six television stations were greeted early that Halloween morning with the news that EgyptAir Flight 990 thirty minutes after leaving Kennedy International had inexplicably plunged more than 17,000 feet in just forty seconds. The plummeting plane, nosed straight down, pitched back and suddenly climbed 9,000 feet, where unforgiving gravitational forces tore it apart. The scattered wreckage sprinkled the Atlantic sixty miles south of Nantucket, leaving no survivors.

The shocking murder in tranquil Wellesley had thus gone uncharacteristically undetected until late in the day when word that an older woman had been slain in a public park filtered into the newsrooms. The killing was frighteningly similar to the murder ten months earlier of Irene Kennedy in the Norfolk County town of Walpole.

Kennedy had been in terrific shape for seventy-five. She and her husband of fifty years had driven a short distance from their home in Foxborough to neighboring Walpole. They walked almost every morning there through the hilly meadows and wooded paths of the eighty-nine-acre William Francis Park, more commonly known to the locals as "Bird Park."

Thomas Kennedy, her seventy-seven-year-old husband, could only walk about half the circuit his more active wife enjoyed in the secluded park, which featured a duck pond and a delightful waterfall. Tom Kennedy usually accompanied his wife to a certain spot and then doubled back to the parking lot while she finished her longer stroll. The mother of four grown daughters and grandmother of six did not return from her walk on December 1, 1998. Concerned, the elderly husband went searching. He found his wife shortly before 9 A.M. crumpled in the woods about five feet from a gravel path near Scout Road.

Kennedy's head was bloody and she was lifeless. Her clothes had been torn open, and it looked like someone had bitten her breasts. Investigators would find other signs of sexual assault and mutilation. Police confiscated Tom Kennedy's shoes and clothing, angering his already devastated family, but the elderly man was quickly and publicly ruled out as a suspect.

The autopsy concluded Irene Kennedy had been bludgeoned and fanatically stabbed twenty-nine times, mostly about the head. State and Walpole police quickly focused their attention on Edmund F. Burke, the brother of one of the victim's sons-in-law, who lived in a ramshackle dwelling near Bird Park with his eighty-eight-year-old mother and thirty-two cats.

When Burke was arrested nine days after Kennedy's murder, he vehemently denied he was a twisted killer. After spending several weeks in the county jail, DNA testing exonerated him, and the charges were dropped.

A little over a month before May Greineder's murder, Marty Foley had been sent to Buckmaster Pond in the town of Westwood, where a fisherman had found eighty-two-year-old Richard J. Reyenger unconscious and bleeding at 7:40 A.M. The first responding officers didn't immediately suspect foul play, thinking Reyenger might have had a fishing accident, possibly snagging a hook on his face. The resulting rescue effort covered the flat earthen bank of the pond with the overlapping footprints of cops, firefighters, and paramedics, obliterating any evidence left by Reyenger's attacker.

Still alive when taken to a Boston hospital, the spry retired woodworker passed away despite intensive efforts to save him. An autopsy showed Reyenger had suffered one massive blow to the head with a razor-sharp instrument, probably a sword or an ax, which had penetrated six inches into his skull. The State and Westwood detectives could find no hint as to why someone would want to kill the gentle churchgoer, who had made regular dawn fishing trips to the pond since 1960.

With the early reports from Morses Pond eerily similar to the demise of Irene Kennedy, speculation in the Boston newsrooms centered on the possibility that a serial killer was stalking elderly Norfolk County residents in towns that began with the letter W.

The media had now swarmed onto Cleveland Road with the release of May Greineder's identity. With the renewed aura of a serial killer on the loose, the reporters were anxious to talk to the slain woman's family, but they were met at the door by her neighbor, Dr. Jerome Gans, who had a prepared statement from the Greineders. "The Greineder family and the neighbors are in shock and deeply grieving the senseless murder of May Greineder," Gans read on the front lawn. "The family is doing everything they can to help police catch the murderer."

## 5

SITTING AT BILL KEAR'S DINING ROOM TABLE a short drive from Morses Pond, Marty Foley and Kevin Shea were even more convinced that the stuffy forty-seven-year-old computer trouble-shooter was going to be a damning witness against Dr. Greineder. A resident of Wellesley for nine years, Kear and his Australian silky terrier spent hours together at the pond, Kear walking the dog there nearly every weekend. After leaving his house on nearby MacArthur Road shortly before 8:30 that morning, Kear had set out on his regular circuit ambling down the middle of Turner Road to the pond at his customarily unhurried pace.

At the locked vehicle gate, Kear had noticed the Greineders' silver 1997 Chrysler Town and Country van parked just outside the barrier. After stopping to unleash his dog, he had continued his lazy walk down the middle of the access road almost to the end, where the sight of a familiar man and his much larger dog brought him to an abrupt halt.

Kear didn't know the man by name, only learning it was Dirk Greineder after stumbling upon a slaughter. The man wearing the bright yellow windbreaker and a small, bright red backpack was usually with his pleasant wife, Kear told the two State Police detectives. The sudden appearance of Dr. Greineder and one of his dogs from a wooded trail behind the traffic circle had caused Kear to immediately scoop up his dog, simultaneously fumbling to secure his leash to the collar on the tiny animal.

Kear didn't like the couple's dogs at all; especially the larger one, which was vicious and had once tried to maul Kear's terrier, before the Greineders intervened. The terrier now safely in his arms, Kear warily watched Dr. Greineder and his leashed German shepherd bear right behind the traffic circle and cross behind a large planter in the middle of the roundabout. The man was walking briskly, Kear said, his leash taut from the dog leading him, when Dr. Greineder quickly turned right then disappeared down the paved beach maintenance road. Within twenty or thirty seconds, Kear said, his anxiety returned when he spotted the leashed German shepherd reemerge from the small dead-end road and head straight for him, the expressionless look on her owner's face not hinting why. Standing even with the sandy parking lot near the traffic circle, Kear was almost exclusively watching the dog as Dr. Greineder neared.

"My wife has been attacked. Do you have a cell phone? Can you go make a call for me," the doctor had blurted, leaving Kear so stunned he momentarily forgot about the German shepherd.

"No. I don't have a phone," Kear replied apprehensively, now seeing Dr. Greineder was upset. "Where was your wife attacked?"

The husband lifted his arm and pointed, Kear's gaze shifting toward the hulking water treatment plant at the pond then lowering to the dirt path he had seen the man first emerge from. Still trying to absorb what was happening, Kear didn't respond when Dr. Greineder told him he had a phone in his car and would go make a call for help. Kear could only stare as Dr. Greineder hastened up the access road, still clutching his dog's leash with his right hand.

Shocked by what he had been told but fearful of the unexplained nature of the attack, Kear decided after contemplating his "moral obligation" that he should go see if he could help the woman. Timidly starting down the dirt path bordered by woods and a chain-link fence blocking access to the water plant, Kear jerked to a stop when he saw two legs jutting from the underbrush. Wondering if the assailant still lingered, Kear retreated back down the path, fearing he too might be attacked.

As Foley had learned from the Wellesley detectives, after separating from Kear, Dr. Greineder had come across jogger Richard Magnan as he ran up the access road to his van. Magnan, a regular runner at the pond, was starting to feel warmed up as he approached the gate to Morses Pond. He saw a man driving away, then observed another vehicle, a silver minivan, parked near the gate. Magnan jogged by the vehicle barrier, then hopped onto the sidewalk that gradually extended into the paved bike path in the pine tree forest. Preoccupied with his run, he saw someone out of the corner of his left eye on the access road above him but didn't understand what the man had yelled to him. Stopping, Magnan yelled back, "What?" He could now see through the trees the man elevated over him was wearing a yellow jacket and holding a leashed German shepherd. "My wife's been attacked. Do you have a cell phone?" Dr. Greineder hollered.

"No," Magnan replied less forcefully, taken aback by the man's report. As Dr. Greineder pressed on up the road, Magnan recognized him as a regular walker at the pond. *His wife was attacked? How was she attacked?* he thought, standing dumbfounded on the bike path. Magnan pondered whether he should continue running in the direction where the doctor had just been, his mind consumed by the unexpected exchange. Feeling afraid, he stood idle a minute longer to think about what to do. Finally, he shrugged and started running again. Maybe there was something he could do down there, he thought.

Exiting the path into the sandy parking lot near the traffic circle, Magnan spotted a man with a small dog he had also seen at the pond before. Eyeing each other, the man Magnan would soon come to know as "Bill," motioned him over.

"Someone has been attacked. Can you make a call to the police department," Bill Kear asked.

"I don't have a phone," Magnan responded.

"Did you see anyone?" Kear asked, still spooked by what he had seen on the dirt path.

"Yes, a man asked me if I had a cell phone," Magnan said.

"His wife is lying on the trail over there," Kear informed the runner.

The two men briefly discussed what might have happened to her, wishfully concluding she might have suffered a heart attack. "Do you know CPR?" Kear asked. "No," answered Magnan. "I don't either," said Kear. "I'll run back for help," Magnan offered, turning to make a sustained sprint back up the access road.

Reaching the locked gate, Magnan could see Dr. Greineder in his yellow windbreaker standing outside the driver's door of his van having an animated conversation on a cell phone, the cord extending into the vehicle frequently stretching taut with his gyrations. Dr. Greineder was distraught, and from snippets Magnan heard of his excited conversation he deduced that he was making a 911 call. "Just send someone," Dr. Greineder said urgently into the phone. "I . . . someone inside with her, there was someone else walking his dog, and I, he went in there," Magnan heard him say confusingly. "There's a runner here," Dr. Greineder added, looking up at Magnan.

The bewildered jogger stood about twelve feet from the van, waiting for Dr. Greineder to finish. Studying him, Magnan saw what looked like streaks and spots of blood on his jacket and sleeves. Maybe a dog had bitten his wife, Magnan considered. Ending his call and placing the phone back into the van, Dr. Greineder slammed the driver's door and approached the quizzical runner.

"Why don't you go back and see how she is," Dr. Greineder asked, his skin flushed.

"She's your wife, why don't you go," Magnan answered, caught off guard by the odd request. "I'll wait here for the ambulance. I know where she is," Magnan offered instead.

"But I'm afraid they won't know where to find me," the doctor protested.

"I can tell them exactly where she is. Don't worry," Magnan reassured.

Seeming disappointed, Dr. Greineder agreed, saying "Don't let anyone go in the van; the dog is in there," and he motioned to the German shepherd in the back. Dr. Greineder turned reluctantly toward the gate, and Magnan watched him head back down the access road, more at a jog than a sprint, he judged.

After interviewing Kear, Foley and Shea returned to the police station and made a list of evidence to search for that could link Dr. Greineder to his wife's murder. The discovery of the weapons and glove was the kind of major break that had been missing from the other two unsolved cases. The knife and hammer looked relatively new. Leaves covered the bottom of the drain but none were on top of the hammer, knife, and glove, indicating they had been recently dropped there. The only way the bulbous head of the hammer could enter the basin was through the carved opening on the granite back splash behind the cast iron grate. Foley wondered if Dr. Greineder had known the hammer would fit or had just been lucky in a rushed bid to hide the murder weapons. The brown work glove also explained Dr. Greineder's clean hands, Foley and Shea considered, and all efforts would be made to find its left-handed mate.

Finally having a chance to compare her notes with Foley, Jill McDermott told the trooper that there were inconsistencies in what Dr. Greineder had told her when she first spoke to him and when she stood with Foley during his interview. The young detective said she found the husband odd from the beginning, when he was pointed out to her at the traffic circle. She was surprised to see him lying prone on the pavement, his elbows forming a bipod on which he rested his chin on two balled fists. McDermott thought he looked upset, but he hardly seemed distraught.

After conferring with McDermott, Foley concluded that Dr. Greineder's account of how his wife hurt her back had changed at least four times. He had explained to firefighter Bill DeLorie and then McDermott that May Greineder had wrenched her back while tossing a ball to the dog. But he told Paul Fitzpatrick she had stepped on a rock. He then switched his story to McDermott saying his wife had twisted her back in the sandpit, not the pine tree forest, as he had first reported. When Foley interviewed him, Dr. Greineder said his wife had stumbled coming down the slope into the sandpit.

Just as troubling was his reasoning for going down the paved beach road where the weapons and glove were found instead of heading straight up the access road for help. Dr. Greineder didn't make mention of the side trip until he saw Bill Kear talking with police, later telling Kear when they were standing away from the investigators that he had seen a "shadow" on it, prompting the doctor to go down the road in search of help. But by the time he first spoke to McDermott, the shadow account had changed to the doctor looking for a jogger. When Foley and McDermott queried him, Dr. Greineder said he had definitely seen a runner but could not catch up to him.

While the varying stories certainly darkened the cloud of suspicion, Foley knew he needed harder evidence to expose a highly regarded physician and family man as a cold-blooded killer. Taking a phone call from Lt. Ken Martin, the trooper was informed that the initial forensic investigation also pointed toward Dr. Greineder as his wife's killer. After May Greineder's body had been taken to the medical examiner's office, Martin and Dr. Faryl Sandler had made a more thorough inspection looking for trace evidence, carefully removing and photographing each item of clothing. Martin made a significant observation when he checked the back of the woman's head, scrutinizing a circular wound an inch and a half in diameter.

The circumference matched the twin striking faces of the Estwing hammer. Listening to Martin's description of the injury, Foley visualized May Greineder's terrible final moments. Dr. Greineder had probably surprised his wife with a hammer blow to the back of her head, knocking her to the ground, and he then slashed her neck open with the knife. Her life drained into the trail's dirt. Then he dragged her into the brush where he stabbed her about the head and chest before slicing her pants to make it look like she had been sexually assaulted.

The doctor's white Reebok sneakers with the small bloody dots — mixed with some other type of tiny red stains — painted a grisly picture for Martin, an expert in bloodstain pattern analysis. The blood was impact spatter, meaning Dr. Greineder was within "inches or feet" of his wife during what Martin called "the bloodshed incident."

Spatter resulting from blood in flight is categorized in three velocities — low, medium, and high — with the size of the blood droplets telling a trained expert how fast the blood traveled. Low-velocity spatter moves at less than five feet per second; the blood typically dripped from a wound or a bloody instrument.

Medium spatter travels at more than twenty-five feet per second after blood is propelled by force, in May Greineder's case, being struck by a hammer and stabbed with a knife. Medium-velocity spatter leaves bloodstains between one and three millimeters in diameter depending on the force of the blow. A large number of small stains would indicate to Martin that the bloodshed incident involved a higher degree of energy or force.

High-velocity spatter is classified as anything traveling over 100 feet per second, the staining usually resulting from a gunshot wound. The bullet, traveling at more than 1,500-feet-per-second, turns blood into a mist that leaves droplets measuring a millimeter or smaller. Using physics and mathematical formulas, Martin could determine the velocity of the spatter as well as the direction it traveled.

With basic trigonometry, Martin could also calculate the angle of impact. If spatter is observed on a suspect, Martin could estimate how close the person was to a victim based on the size of the bloodstains. The smaller some of the spatter, the closer the suspect was to the victim. In Dr. Greineder's case, his sneakers, and later the yellow windbreaker, would tell an incriminating tale. Both shoes had more than ten bloodstains, all appearing to be medium-velocity spatter. The husband had to have been right next to his wife when she was killed, Martin told Foley.

The doctor's bloodstained eyeglasses were the first item Foley and Shea listed for the court's permission to seize. In addition to looking for the left-hand glove, the detectives also would want store or credit card receipts, containers or packaging or catalogs for an Old Timer folding knife and an Estwing hammer, as well as any "bloody clothing or instruments."

Shea was helping Foley organize the lengthy itemized affidavit for the search warrant applications that required approval by a judge or clerk magistrate. Starting the first of what would end in six pages from his laptop, Shea typed, *"I, Martin T. Foley, am a Massachusetts State Police Officer and have been a police officer for 17 years. I am presently assigned to the Norfolk County District Attorney's Office as a criminal investigator and have been so for the last 14 years."*

Despite reviewing the affidavit several times before signing it with Dedham District Court Assistant Clerk Phil McCue, it would be several days before Foley noticed the typo that declared he had been at the DA's office for fourteen years instead of saying he had been an investigator that length of time. A seemingly harmless mistake that no one had caught, the ambiguity would result in a huge headache for Foley later.

The affidavit and search warrant applications were completed a little before 11 P.M. Meanwhile, at Morses Pond, the State Police forensic investigators were packing up for the night with plans to be back there early the next day. Laboring in the hot sun all afternoon, then working under floodlights into the night, they had recovered the items near the body, collected blood samples and potential trace evidence, and prepared May Greineder for autopsy the next morning.

While working on identifying footprints with Julia Mosely, Trooper Robert Dateo had glanced into a small open area choked with downed trees and green overgrown vegetation directly across from the body. Something shiny had drawn the trooper's attention. Taking a closer look, he had uncovered an aluminum foil cake pan measuring nine inches long by five inches wide and three inches deep partially covered with branches and pine needles. Inside the pan was a pair of white latex surgical gloves.

It appeared the foil loaf pan and gloves had been recently secreted in the scrub, and their discovery resulted in varied speculation about their intended purpose. Could Dr. Greineder have been wearing surgical gloves under the brown work gloves? Foley wondered. The search of the doctor's home and van would also include a hunt for matching latex gloves.

The forensic investigators had also completed their painstaking analysis of footprints on the earthen trail. Of the thirty-seven impressions Deb Rebeiro marked along the path, thirty-one were matched to the photos Wellesley police had taken of the first responders' footwear. The other six appeared to mirror the bottom of Dr. Greineder's white Reebok sneakers, which Rebeiro had examined and photographed before Ken Martin took them. The Reeboks had distinctive parallel lines that ran horizontally across the toe area and the ball of the foot. Rebeiro also noted a pyramid-shaped indentation into the heel of the shoe.

Adding two dog prints to the six not identified, Rebeiro collected eight impressions with photographs and dental stone casts she numbered F1 through F8. Prints F1 through F4 were all within two feet of each other heading away from the body. The first three impressions showed distinct characteristics of consecutive steps made by the woman's husband, while the fourth print lacked identifiable features.

F5 and F6 were the dog prints. F7 was an impression probably left by May Greineder's killer at the top of the drag mark, partially overlapping the elongated bloodstain in the middle of the trail where she had been killed. F7 was going to be a problem for Dr. Greineder, because it matched his left sneaker.

On the edge of the bloody puddle, Rebeiro had also photographed and casted overlapping heel prints that matched Dr. Greineder's right Reebok. Rebeiro would later conclude the overlap could have only resulted from a moving foot. With Dr. Greineder's Reeboks, Rebeiro would later make comparison impressions by putting powder on the bottom of the sneakers and lifting it off with a sticky clear adhesive backing to make transparent overlays.

The transparencies were then put on a copy machine to make black transparent overlays that Rebeiro applied directly to the white stone casts to examine for similarities. Five of the six footprints she recovered, including the damning F7, would match Dr. Greineder's Reeboks beyond any doubt. The sixth could not be excluded from the doctor or the Reebok sneakers worn by his wife.

F7 and the overlapping right heel prints were going to haunt Dr. Greineder. He had not told anyone he had been on that part of the path, and his sneaker impressions there created another inconsistency on a growing list contradicting what he had told investigators. Dr. Greineder said he had gone directly into the brush and tried to rouse his injured wife, but his bloody, apparently rear-facing footprints near the drag mark and the bloodstained sleeves of his windbreaker were telling the detectives something entirely different. To them, it looked like the husband had picked up his dead wife under the arms from behind then dragged her savaged body off the path.

# 6

MARTY FOLEY KNOCKED on Dr. Greineder's front door at exactly 1:03 A.M. The doctor was up and opened the door right away, the two German shepherds barking downstairs. "Marty, what's going on?" the visibly concerned doctor asked. "We have a search warrant to search your house. Can you put your dogs out back?" Foley replied evenly. Dr. Greineder rushed down the stairs and came back with the agitated shepherds. Stepping inside the doorway, Foley let the doctor pass with the dogs and then followed him into the kitchen, where he kept his suspect in sight until he returned from the dogs' pen outside.

"Marty, what's this all about, you already looked in the house," Dr. Greineder said, his voice tinged with protest and somewhat whiney. The daylong relationship between the detective and doctor had been amicable, even to the extent the two referred to each other by their first names.

"Is there anyone here with you," Foley asked, ignoring the doctor's question.

"The kids are sleeping upstairs. I gave them sleeping pills," the doctor replied.

With Jill McDermott now at his side and the other investigators lining the stairs from the foyer, Foley showed Dr. Greineder the search warrant, telling him what they would be looking for before reading the doctor his Miranda rights. After the near fiasco trying to recover the man's clothes earlier at the police station, Foley wanted to be cautious.

Moving to the living room, Dr. Greineder, casually dressed in a warm-up suit, sat in an easy chair while Foley took a seat across from him on a couch, the knees of the two men touching. Although Dr. Greineder had a lawyer, the detective sensed he wanted to talk. "What's this all about?" Dr. Greineder asked. "You were already here earlier," he complained.

"We found a hammer and a knife and a glove that were used to kill your wife," Foley softly told him, none of the other officers able to hear the muted conversation. "We're here looking for the left-hand glove and receipts and packaging and the other things on the search warrant, and we'd like your help finding them." Thinking of the man's children having to be drugged to force sleep over their grief, Foley looked into Dr. Greineder's eyes and appealed to him as a father. "You could make it easier on your family if you told me what happened today," the detective said compassionately.

Foley's quiet voice had made Dr. Greineder lean closer as the trooper watched for a reaction, hoping his quarry would "cleanse himself" with a confession, as others had done when Foley employed this interview strategy.

Without breaking eye contact, Dr. Greineder slowly sat back in the chair. Foley heard rustling from the Greineder children upstairs. Behind the man's quizzical eyes, Foley could sense he was considering an admission to the horror he had set forth that day. The detective was anxious for a response before his children intruded. *He's thinking this might be the right thing to do,* an optimistic Foley thought, still searching Dr. Greineder's eyes. *He's going to tell me what happened.* Foley was convinced his suspect was going to confess — until the moment was stolen by the wrathful shouts of his incensed oldest daughter.

"What are you doing here?" Dr. Kirsten Greineder railed. "You have no right to be in our house!" The daughter's furious entrance from upstairs abruptly ended the cordial conversation between Foley and her father, smashing the detective's belief that he was going to admit what he had done.

"It would probably be best if I didn't talk to you anymore," he calmly told Foley, leaning back in his chair while the other officers spilled into the home with the onset of Kirsten's ranting.

The shouting had brought Kirsten's fiancé, Aleks, and her sister Britt and brother Colin downstairs, threatening to turn the situation more volatile. But the Greineders agreed to go across the street to Jerry and Nancy Gans's house.

The detectives fanned out, searching for evidence connecting Dr. Greineder to the bloody weapons and glove found in the storm drain. They searched for checkbooks and credit card receipts or anything that would show payment for the murderous items.

Rummaging through Dr. Greineder's office, Foley and Bob Friend seized American Express and Master Card statements listing purchases from Home Depot and Service Merchandise, two stores that might sell the items found at Morses Pond. Trooper Steven McDonald picked up the Star Tec cell phone from the kitchen counter Foley had seen earlier and turned it on. Dialing his own cell phone, McDonald retrieved the phone's number from his phone's caller identification and wrote it down.

Outside, Jill McDermott, Police Chief Terry Cunningham, and Detective Bill Vargas of the Wellesley Police were about to search the Greineders' other vehicle, a beige Toyota Avalon parked in the driveway, when McDermott inadvertently set off its alarm. The racket brought a hostile Nancy Gans, an attorney, who grabbed the keys from McDermott, angrily telling her that she could not search the car. McDermott wrestled the keys back and informed her that their search warrant did in fact allow them access to the vehicle.

McDermott took the driver's side while Vargas rummaged on the passenger side, and Cunningham stood over McDermott shining his flashlight into the sedan. Picking up a small white towel from the floor next to the driver's seat, McDermott could see it was made of a rough, knobby-type material, and noticed some stains that looked liked coffee or dirt. Holding it up to examine it with her flashlight, McDermott didn't see anything else on the towel and set it back in the car without thinking about it again.

Across the street at the Ganses' home, Dr. Greineder was upset that the police had labeled him the suspect in his wife's murder, and his children and neighbors were appalled that he would even be considered. But the doctor was expressing fears that his DNA had been innocently transferred to whoever killed his wife, setting off a discussion between the medically trained Kirsten and Colin about whether the police could have obtained DNA results in just sixteen hours.

"Dad, did they take your blood," Colin asked.

"No," his concerned father responded quickly.

"Without blood or hair, they don't know what your DNA is," the son assured him.

Kirsten and Colin concluded there was no way the police could have genetically linked their father to the murder this quickly. The siblings, still trying to recover from the devastating news that their mother had been horribly murdered, were now growing angrier about the police insinuation that their father was responsible.

The police search lasted about two hours, but nothing obviously linking Dr. Greineder to his wife's murder was found in the house or the beige Avalon. Searching through Britt's room, McDermott had sadly read the beginning of a tribute the daughter was penning about her mother. They left with the doctor's eyeglasses, now cleaned of the bloody swipe they had seen earlier; American Express and Master Card statements; a small bag of latex gloves; and a bag of shredded paper. A search later in the morning of Dr. Greineder's Town and Country van, now impounded at the police station, resulted in the seizure of twenty-one items, most of them mundane. Police collected the small red nylon backpack Dr. Greineder was wearing when Bill Kear first saw him and the three balls, two leashes, and pair of yellow Playtex kitchen gloves inside. May Greineder's black back brace was also recovered from the vehicle.

Getting home for a couple of hours of sleep as sunrise approached, Foley had found his wife awake. He had spoken to her several times from Morses Pond, and Cheryl Foley had watched the late-night television coverage of the murder. She had been married to a police officer long enough to know when to ask questions and when to let it go. This morning, she couldn't resist as her exhausted husband pulled himself into bed. "The husband did it, didn't he?" she asked assertively.

"I think so," he said, his heavy fatigue quickly fading to sleep.

At Morses Pond, State Police Sgt. Walter Carlson could tell from the way dawn was breaking that it was going to be another spectacular fall day. Carlson had been up all night, frequently checking the floodlit path where May Greineder had been killed. Taking yet another survey of the tree-enveloped trail, Carlson saw something yellow in the morning sun, almost as if a beam of light had illuminated the item against the dark background of the scrub where the foil loaf pan and surgical gloves had been found the day before.

Stooping to check the bright object that was mostly hidden under a fallen tree and concealed by pine needles, Carlson found a five-ounce plastic container of Ronsonol lighter fluid bearing a price tag. The fuel was commonly used for wick or Zippo-type cigarette lighters — less popular since the advent of disposable butane lighters — but the bright yellow packaging boasted another use. "ALSO EXCELLENT FOR REMOVING LABELS, TAR, GREASE & OIL STAINS," the container trumpeted under the brand name. The lighter fluid looked new, not like something that had been left outside for an extended period. Carlson was careful not disturb it.

Marty Foley was already up, preparing to leave for Morses Pond. Foley had slept for less than two hours before waking and seeing his boys off to school. The police had made major strides toward solving May Greineder's gruesome killing, but there was much that still had to be done. Only a small part of the crime scene had been searched, with the remainder of the pond's vast terrain still to be scoured.

Meanwhile, Belinda Markel was about to pull out of the first rest stop on the Massachusetts Turnpike when her cell phone rang. She had talked back and forth with the Greineders during the first three hours of her drive to Wellesley, her uncle calling or answering the phone each time. It had been a "terrible night," her uncle reported. "Terrible things" had happened. But despite his rambling, Dr. Greineder had again been short on details.

Belinda had also traded calls with her parents, who left the city more than an hour behind her. They were trying to keep each other updated, but the answers to their many questions remained elusive. The latest call was from Belinda's husband, Greg, who had found some interesting, yet unnerving information about May's murder from *Boston Herald* and *Boston Globe* stories posted on the Internet. "I have to tell you this before you get there," he told his wife. "She was at the park and someone cut her throat."

*Jesus*, Belinda thought, trying not to convey the revulsion to her children seated behind her. Belinda merged onto the Mass Pike heading east toward Wellesley. Her thoughts were consumed with horrifying images of May's killing.

Walter Carlson showed Foley the lighter fluid as soon as the detective got to Morses Pond. Since they were found near the mysterious loaf pan and surgical gloves, Foley wondered how the lighter fluid was connected to the murder. Was Dr. Greineder going to burn evidence? Was he going to use the fluid for its secondary purpose of removing stains — possibly blood or DNA? The detective didn't know. And like many facets of the terrible crime, it would be a constant source of puzzlement for the methodical investigator.

When Belinda Markel and her children finally reached the Greineder home, her disheveled uncle opened the door to greet them. Filing inside, the Markels traded emotional hugs and greetings with the Greineders. Finding her uncle with tears in his eyes, the only time she would see him cry in the coming days, Dr. Greineder gave Belinda an enveloping hug. "Now my whole family is here," he said. "Now we can be together."

Everyone now settled, Dr Greineder told Belinda, "I have to talk to you," bringing her into his office where he sat down in front of his computer. The police had gone through the house earlier that morning, he soberly reported.

"We had intercourse yesterday morning, and there's nothing wrong with that because we're married," he abruptly announced.

The unsolicited comment caught Belinda totally unprepared. *Why are you telling me this?* she thought, far more concerned about hearing what had happened to May. Belinda couldn't imagine why her uncle was making a point to reveal this intimate information "out of the blue in the first two minutes of the conversation."

"May gave me a backrub yesterday, and we went for a walk. My skin might be under her fingernails," Dr. Greineder continued, his thoughts beginning to scatter but not unexpectedly to Belinda, who was used to her uncle's habitual rambling. Going back to what happened at the pond, Dr. Greineder said his wife "had been hit on the side of the head with a hammer" and "her throat had been cut." Referring to the police as "these people," Dr. Greineder told Belinda the detectives had come looking for receipts for a hammer, knife, and glove.

"They came into the house and threw us out and went through all of our things," he complained. "I'm frightened, they are looking at me," he said.

"It's okay," Belinda reassured him. "I'm here now and I'll help you." Belinda was aware that Terry Segal and Nancy Gans were giving her uncle legal advice.

"I'm frightened," he repeated. "I need you to help me and I need Greg to help me. Terry wants to represent me, but I don't know if that's the right thing," Dr. Greineder said.

"I don't know why you need to be represented," Belinda replied, the notion her uncle could be responsible for the murder unthinkable to her. "Some of this must be standard procedure," she reasoned.

"No, no," her uncle disagreed. "I've seen this. I've seen this," he stressed. The more her uncle talked about how he had "seen it" and that the police "knew what they were doing," Belinda noticed more of an edge in his voice as he continued to plead for her help.

"Of course," Belinda reassured.

"I feel so much better now that you are here," he sighed.

At the Office of the Chief Medical Examiner in Boston, Dr. Stanton Kessler was about to prove Dr. Greineder a liar about being intimate with his wife the day before. With May's disrobed body lying on a gurney, Kessler found two vertical, well-healed surgical scars from the earlobe of each ear to the scalp. The benign scars were indicative of a facelift or similar plastic surgery procedure. The evidence turning more gruesome, Kessler announced for the tape recorder and the assembled investigators his observation of blood spatter on both of the woman's hands but no defensive wounds. The ME also marked blood spatter on the lower chest and abdomen.

On her lower extremities, Kessler measured seven bruises and contusions, some appearing fresh with the remainder looking a week to ten days old. On the right side, he recorded two contusions on the woman's lower right leg and two on the right thigh. There were two contusions on her left thigh and one on her lower leg, the size of the marks ranging from the circumferences of a quarter to a half-dollar.

Kessler also studied "a quarter-inch irregularly shaped red contusion" above the left side of May's upper lip and another one on the left chin. On her back were the telltale signs that she had been dragged from the middle of the path at Morses Pond. Kessler measured and photographed two vertical abrasions just below and to the right of where the base of the spine aligns with the buttocks.

"There is skin sloughing [piling] present at the most inferior portions of the abrasion, consistent with drag marks," Kessler noted. From the amount of sloughing, Kessler theorized that the woman had been dragged by the shoulders from behind. The examination showed no indication May had been sexually assaulted or recently had sex, contrary to what her husband had just told Belinda Markel.

Kessler observed obvious wounds of trauma to the woman's head, neck, and chest. Her hair now shorn for a thorough examination of the head injuries, Kessler counted ten wounds on the body, labeling them A through J. Wounds A and B were penetrating stab wounds to the chest. The ME found a small amount of blood in the left chest, about three ounces, indicating May was dead when the wounds were inflicted.

Wound C was an irregular laceration on the back of the head measuring two inches by a half inch. There was an irregular cut in the galea, the tough membrane covering the skull, but the skullcap was intact, X-rays showing no fractures. The wound was caused by something striking the back of the head at an angle, pushing up the skin and tearing it. The blow had caused a lot of damage on the scalp but very little underneath.

Kessler concluded the injury came from a heavy metal object; likely the two-pound hammer police had recovered near the crime scene. Although a bloody, painful wound that would have required suturing, the blow would not have rendered the woman unconscious or dead, Kessler concluded, citing no underlying contusion to the brain.

Wound D was actually two injuries, a one-and-a-quarter-inch stab wound to the left side of the head and a blunt blow to the area. The stab wound penetrated a quarter inch leaving a cut in the galea that was "very superficial." The second injury was more severe. The blow, likely delivered from a gloved fist or a padded object, left a two-and-a half-inch fracture across the left orbital plate extending up into the frontal bone, evidenced by a purple contusion about the upper left eyelid. The impact didn't tear the skin, but Kessler found an area of hemorrhaging within the left temporal muscle.

Wounds E, F, G, H, and I, were more superficial stab wounds to the head that did not penetrate the skull. None of the wounds designated A through I, even the two stab wounds to the chest, would have been fatal had May Greineder received prompt hospital treatment. However, nothing but prevention could have allowed her to survive Wound J.

Kessler described it as a "large, gaping cut-throat-type complex stab wound involving the entire left side of the neck." It measured five inches long and two-and-a-half-inches wide in what Kessler called a "rapidly fatal wound." The thrust of the knife had sliced straight in, stretching five inches to the spine's C5 vertebrae while severing the jugular veins and main draining veins of the brain and face.

It cut some of the muscles that hold the neck and back together, also slicing a portion of the thyroid cartilage deep in the neck above the Adam's apple. The knife's penetration left a nick in the C5 vertebrae with deep damage to the thyroid cartilage about an inch apart, leading Kessler to believe there had been two powerful knife thrusts into the neck. It was possible, he considered, that she was moving during the attack.

The conclusions were chilling. The petite woman had been the victim of a ferocious assault that had resulted in multiple stab wounds to the head, neck, and chest, a skull fracture from being punched or hit with a padded object, and multiple contusions to her lower extremities. "Based upon police investigation and autopsy findings, it is the opinion of the undersigned that the deceased died as a result of multiple incised wounds and blunt head trauma. The manner of death is homicide," Kessler wrote.

Unofficially, the absence of defensive wounds had also left Kessler with the conclusion that May Greineder "had been taken by surprise." She had not reacted to her attacker, Kessler theorized, because she knew her assailant, didn't expect to be set upon, or was just unable to respond.

At the Wellesley Police Station, the collection of evidence against Dr. Greineder was proceeding when Jill McDermott received an astonishing telephone call shortly before noon. Terence McNally, a thirty-nine-year-old resident of Lake Road near the ridge above the Morses Pond sandpit, had telephoned the police as soon as he read about the murder in the newspaper.

After waking on Halloween morning, McNally had lounged in bed for another twenty-five minutes enjoying the extra time Daylight Savings had brought. McNally left his house with his dog, Theo, on a leash, walked up Russell Road, and turned onto a path leading into woods. Marveling at the unseasonably balmy weather, McNally and Theo sauntered the length of the secluded fifty-yard trail that emptied into a clearing high above the yawning sandpit at Morses Pond.

Picking up a stick to toss to Theo, McNally suddenly heard a strange sound that seemed to come from a distant part of the sandpit. The scream was high-pitched, almost not humanlike. Still playing with his dog, McNally told McDermott the scream lasted less than ten seconds, coming in a series of "very quick, short yells, from a distance." The yelling did not make much of an impression, McNally attributing it to kids playing he told the detective. A few minutes later, he left with Theo to go home.

Reading the account of May Greineder's slaying, McNally was horrified to realize he had probably heard her being killed. Anxious to pass along the information but more concerned about being considered a suspect, McNally quickly dialed the police. He told McDermott he had not seen anyone during his morning walk.

While Marty Foley was not convinced the scream came from May, he instantly recognized the significance of McNally's information. If the scream was from her, it significantly narrowed the time frame between when she was killed and the 8:56 A.M. call her husband made to police. "He wouldn't have had time to do all the things he said he did," Foley concluded after reviewing everything Dr. Greineder had told him.

McNally had been in the clearing above the sandpit some seventy-five yards from the wooded trail where the woman was killed, and like Bill Kear and Rick Magnan, who had approached from a different direction, McNally did not see anyone else.

Foley now had three independent witnesses who had not seen a stranger fleeing the area, putting more into doubt Dr. Greineder's claims that he had seen a "shadow" and a "runner" in explaining why he went down the paved beach road where the weapons were found.

When Belinda Markel's parents arrived at the Greineder home, Ilse Stark told her brother-in-law they needed to talk. "Dirk, what happened?" Ilse began.

Calmly, and now somewhat concisely, Dr. Greineder told his rapt audience how he had separated from May after she hurt her back to take Zephy to the pond, only to return to find her injured.

"I was shaking. I was shaking so much I couldn't even tell if she had a pulse," he had told his daughter Kirsten earlier. "I couldn't even do it. I couldn't even get her pulse. I knew she felt a little warm. I tried to pick her up so I could do something and then I ran back to get help because I knew I couldn't do it. I needed help."

Unable to assist his wife, Dr. Greineder said he jumped up, ran back down the path and saw a jogger. He started to chase the runner before spotting a man with a small dog, whom he asked for help. Ilse thought it was odd that Dirk did not have a cell phone with him. Every time she saw him he had one clipped to his belt.

Kirsten had asked him before why he didn't have his cell phone. "I was charging it," he replied.

Ilse asked her brother-in-law how May had been killed. She winced when he said she had been "hit on the back of the head" and "her throat was cut." May's pants had also been pulled down, he said, an added detail he had not told Belinda, who sat silent on the floor, preferring to let her mother continue, even though she had a "million questions" of her own.

"Was she sexually assaulted?" Ilse asked, trying to reconcile why her sister would be the target of such evil.

"No, absolutely not," Dr. Greineder said firmly, leaving Belinda wondering how he could be so sure. Her uncle had been in remarkable control of the conversation other than looking drawn from no sleep.

"Was she robbed?" Ilse asked, thinking of the diamond earrings her sister adored. "I don't know," her brother-in-law responded. "I don't know if she had them on or if they were taken."

Believing Dr. Greineder had told them all he knew, Belinda and her cousins turned to making the arrangements for May's memorial service, and the solemn conference broke up.

When he arrived a short time later, the Rev. Marc Sherrod from the Newton Presbyterian Church where May had worshipped was unaware that her husband was being methodically stalked by the authorities as he made his way around the Greineder kitchen offering his condolences.

Belinda had spoken briefly with Rev. Sherrod about what they wanted for May's service but had left the final planning to May's children.

Her uncle, who was clearly angry and on edge, "was not focused on any kind of arrangements," and was more concerned about himself, Belinda noticed. Dr. Greineder called in to his Boston medical office and was told it had been searched by the police. Throughout the day, especially after receiving word of the office search, he became increasingly obsessed with finding a lawyer. Because of his pestering, Belinda called her husband twice, asking his help in finding her uncle counsel. "Greg has to find someone," Dr. Greineder insisted.

"There's a chance Dirk did this," Greg Markel told his wife. "Are you sure you want me to help?"

Belinda was incensed that her husband could even consider her uncle capable of killing May, sparking a brief argument. "Please, you have to do this. This man needs help," she said. Despite their disagreement, Greg was willing to do whatever his wife wanted.

Later, Belinda found her uncle in Britt's room on the floor with Zephyr. "Dirk, why don't you lie on the bed and get some rest," she suggested.

"No, I'm better on the floor," he answered, indicating he didn't want to stop cuddling with the dog. Rubbing her uncle's shoulders, Belinda persisted with her advice that he try to sleep.

"I'm worried about my pants," he said. "They asked me a lot of questions about my pants. They're really old pants and they have holes in the pockets. I may have had a pair of work gloves like that at one point and I'm worried fibers from them may have been left on my pants," he said, referring to the brown glove found by police.

"Don't be ridiculous," Belinda said. "May was a clean fanatic. May must have washed those pants a million times by now. Don't worry," she reassured.

"No, no, it could be a problem," Dr. Greineder argued. "I don't have gloves like that in the house anymore, but I could have before."

Her uncle kept on about the pants until he launched into another confusing concern about nosebleeds he and May had before going to Morses Pond. They got them at the same time as they were about to leave the house, her uncle explained, and as a result, he and May had shared the same tissue.

May was prone to frequent nosebleeds, but her husband's getting one at the same time was not only strange but also seemed irrelevant to May's death, until Dr. Greineder excitedly expressed his fear that his blood or mucous could have been innocently transferred to May's killer from their shared tissue. May had taken the tissue with her to the pond, and if she still had it in her hand when she was attacked, she could have transferred his blood or saliva to the killer, Dr. Greineder explained, growing more animated as the strange story progressed.

The niece again calmed her uncle, finally convincing him to take a nap. Drifting off on the floor with the dog, Dr. Greineder slept for a half-hour before returning to the kitchen where he again assumed command of the effort to find him a lawyer.

A half mile away at Morses Pond, another methodical search was taking place that for the moment had produced a lot of sweat but not much else. The detectives were convinced the second glove used in the killing had to be there somewhere, and a group of eight officers had been conducting a series of line searches all day at the sprawling recreation area. Turning over rocks and logs, looking in trees and beating the bushes on the unusually warm November day, the police had searched both sides of the narrow beach road where the weapons and glove were found as well as both sides of the winding access road. It was closing in on 4 P.M. and getting dark. Standing at the gate at the top of the long access road, Chief Terry Cunningham was conscious of the line of TV cameras set up on Turner Road, their operators diligently taping their every move. The police had shown up unexpectedly, and the cameramen had scrambled to their tripods, grateful for the chance to video something after being blocked from the pond for two days.

The search had included several storm drains on the way up the access road, each devoid of evidence. With nothing to show from a hard day's work, Cunningham shifted his frustrated gaze across the street where Halsey Avenue intersected Turner Road, settling on the catch basins on each side of the street that had been in police sight for thirty-six hours. "What the hell," he said, "we've looked in all the other ones. We might as well look in these last two."

Cunningham told two of the sergeants, Peter Nahass and Jack Pilecki, to check out the drains before ending the line search. While Pilecki took the catch basin closest to the gate, Nahass got on his knees, peering into the drain across the street. Seeing Nahass stiffen then turn with his eyes wide and face full of expression, Cunningham quietly growled, "don't anybody say anything." Nahass had obviously found something, but Cunningham did not want to alert the media set up twenty-five yards away with powerful zoom lenses.

"What did you see Peter?" Cunningham nonchalantly asked, not fully prepared for the answer. "The fucking glove," Nahass fired back, still trying to contain his excitement. Cunningham ordered some uniformed officers to move the media back, the reporters and photographers now buzzing that something significant was breaking over the storm drain.

Moments later, the telephone rang in Cunningham's office, where Marty Foley was going over the case with prosecutor Rick Grundy. Apprised of the situation, Foley headed straight to the pond, where the cameras were dutifully recording the heightening activity around the drain and a news helicopter was hovering overhead. Foley peered into the catch basin, where he saw a brown glove floating on the flooded bottom. *There it is*, he thought.

More State Police detectives were arriving as nearly a dozen cops encircled the drain and the final light of day expired. None of them were able to get over how close the glove was to where Dr. Greineder had parked his van and made his blubbering call to police. To Terry Cunningham it was "like a door slamming." Whatever doubt he might have had about Dr. Greineder's guilt, the discovery of the glove thirty-five feet from his van erased it.

In a repetition of the recovery process from the day before, the soggy glove was lifted from the drain then placed on an evidence bag where the huddled detectives collectively noticed a red tinge in the water spreading across the brown paper.

As it had for Cunningham, the recovery of the glove just steps from where Dr. Greineder had parked his van removed any lingering thoughts Foley had of May Greineder's attacker being a random deranged killer. Foley had eyewitnesses who could put Dr. Greineder in the three places the killer had been — the path where his wife was killed and the storm drains where the weapons and gloves were found. But why did the left-hand glove wind up in the drain near Dr. Greineder's van? Foley wondered. He might have been startled by the presence of Bill Kear and simply forgot to take it off, Foley considered. Getting back to the van and realizing he was still wearing the glove, the doctor probably strolled over to the drain and dropped it in.

A short drive away at 56 Cleveland Road, the daylong discussion about who should represent Dr. Greineder had come down to several finalists who would be interviewed the following day. One of them was Alan Dershowitz, the brash Harvard Law School professor who had been part of O. J. Simpson's legal "dream team." Dershowitz was also synonymous with other celebrity clients, such as Rhode Island socialite Claus von Bülow; boxer Mike Tyson; disgraced evangelist Jim Bakker; junk bond king Michael Milken; and the "Queen of Mean," hotel magnate Leona Helmsley. Dershowitz had agreed to meet with Dr. Greineder, who was on the faculty of Harvard's prestigious Medical School.

Another candidate was J. W. Carney Jr., a well-known Boston lawyer with a reputation for being confrontational and a fierce willingness to defend any defendant, no matter how notorious the charges. A third attorney who would be interviewed was Martin F. Murphy, a former state and federal prosecutor who had recently gone into private practice. Several people had recommended Murphy, who as it turned out, had worked with Rick Grundy prosecuting criminal cases in Middlesex County.

BELINDA MARKEL WAS UP before the sun on Tuesday morning, the unfamiliarity of her hotel bed only compounding her insomnia induced by incessant questions racing inside her head. Her distress would only increase a few hours later when she returned to her uncle's house. He was waiting with a shocking request.

"Belinda, I want you to go to the medical examiner's office to identify May."

Before the stunned Belinda could muster an answer, her cousin Kirsten interrupted. "I might want to go too."

"Absolutely not," her father said forcefully. "You may absolutely not go. I want Belinda to go." Watching the exchange, Murray Stark could not contain his amazement. "She's an adult. If she wants to go, she should go," he told his brother-in-law. "It's her mother."

"Absolutely not," Dr. Greineder repeated, becoming more visibly upset, his stance absolute. "I want Belinda to go."

Trying to keep the peace, Belinda intervened, and only sparked a heated argument with her father. "It's his family; let him do what he wants. Mind your own goddamn business. Stay out of it."

The rebuff only stoked Murray's fury. "There's no reason you should go," he screamed at his daughter. "She's a grown woman. If she wants to go, she can."

The ugly row continued, Belinda's kids hearing every word and Kirsten's fiancé sitting uncomfortably at the dining room table. Adding to the din of Belinda and Murray's shouting match, Dr. Greineder kept yelling, "Belinda has to go!"

"Why does she have to do it?" Murray yelled back at Dr. Greineder. Murray was now alternating between screaming at his daughter and at his brother-in-law.

Belinda finally stormed out of the house in a rage, casting a comically sardonic wave at a lone reporter parked across the street. Ilse Stark, Kirsten, and Aleks spilled out of the house after her, Ilse running down the street after her daughter. Kirsten and her fiancé shuffled off in the other direction to talk.

Everyone now composed, Belinda went back to the house, agreeing to identify May's body. "Fine, I'll go," she said, ending the fight with her father after some residual grumbling. Thinking the issue was resolved, Belinda held her breath when her mother suddenly announced, "I want to see my sister."

"You can't," Dr. Greineder said. "You can't go. I want Belinda to go," he repeated.

Greg Markel, who had called in the middle of the dispute, listened, expecting another explosion. He also was confused about why his wife was going to identify May. "Why are you going?" he asked. "I don't want you to go. Why doesn't Dirk go?"

Belinda was unable to respond. Her uncle had not given a reason why he had picked her. Getting off the phone with her husband, Belinda watched her mother take Dr. Greineder aside. "I'm going to do whatever the hell I want to do," Ilse said hotly. She had never spoken harshly to her brother-in-law since meeting him more than thirty years before. "You can't tell me what to do. I'm the only one who has the same blood that courses through her veins and that gives me the right."

Murray Stark, who had been suspicious of Dr. Greineder's behavior since he had learned of May's death two days before, gave Dr. Greineder no room to respond. "She's going to do whatever the hell she wants to do," he echoed, leaving his brother-in-law uncharacteristically speechless. The Starks then defiantly asked Kirsten if she wanted to go to the medical examiner's office with them. She declined, telling her aunt and uncle she didn't want to go against her father's wishes.

With this thorny issue resolved, Dr. Greineder abruptly shifted his attention back to the lawyer interviews scheduled that day, now totally focused on getting ready for them. He was going to drive to Boston to meet Terry Segal and Greg Markel downtown while Belinda and her parents went to the medical examiner's office. Kirsten and Aleks had an appointment at the Eaton & Mackay Funeral Home in Newton to make the arrangements for May's cremation. Belinda's kids would stay in Wellesley with Colin and Britt.

Pulling Belinda aside in the kitchen before he got into the shower, Dr. Greineder again complained the police were after him "because they had no one else to look at." He was concerned, he said with a lowered voice, about photographs that had been taken of him at the police station. "I have a scratch on my chest and I don't know where I got it." He didn't show Belinda the abrasion but pulled up the sleeve on his left arm, displaying several dime-sized black-and-blue marks on his biceps that he didn't know the source of either. He pointed out two red marks on his neck and said emphatically that they were from shaving, launching into a long explanation of how it sometimes happened when he shaved.

While Belinda called the medical examiner's office for directions, she noticed Dr. Greineder was still visibly agitated that Ilse was going. But he knew enough not to object again. His sister-in-law had already made very clear that she was not the type to be told what to do. Belinda also noticed a complete change in her uncle's demeanor now that he had showered and was dressed in a suit and tie. He was focused and businesslike, almost as if he were heading off for a normal workday. Colin and Britt were concerned about his ability to drive, but their father waved them away as he grabbed his briefcase and car keys.

"I'm fine," he said, more concerned about a call from Greg Markel reporting that his flight to Boston would be ninety minutes late. "What am I supposed to do?" Dr. Greineder asked his niece helplessly.

"Start the interview," Belinda replied, sarcastically thinking, *What else are you going to do?*

Dr. Greineder had been looking forward to a meeting with Alan Dershowitz until his daughter Britt heard the celebrity lawyer's name. Causing another scene, Britt lashed out at her father about his willingness to talk to an attorney her mother had apparently despised. "He's a piece of shit," she railed. "You know how Mom thought about him. How could you go to somebody like that?"

Dr. Greineder did not want to reject the opportunity to bring in a high-powered attorney like the tenacious Dershowitz, strenuously arguing that he should at least meet with him. "If you need this kind of counsel," he argued, "you don't have to like him. You pay him to help you." Britt would not bend, and before her father left the house she forced him to reluctantly remove Dershowitz from consideration.

On the way to the Office of the Chief Medical Examiner, Belinda Markel and her parents did not know what to expect. Belinda drove in silence, not wanting to add to the tension or rekindle the argument with her father. There was some "mumbling" between her parents during the ride to Boston. Her mother was still complaining about her brother-in-law's attempt to prevent her from going to the coroner's office, while her father grumbled about his blocking "his own children from seeing their mother."

Ilse couldn't get over how Dr. Greineder kept referring to May as "the body" instead of calling her by name. It must be force of habit, she could only conclude, since he was a doctor. They also wondered why Dr. Greineder had insisted that Belinda make the identification. She offered no opinion as she steered her Expedition, because she was wondering the same thing.

Belinda and her parents walked tentatively into the modern, two-story brick building nestled in Boston's South End medical area. They were greeted inside the ME's office by an attendant who made the terrifying process a bit easier with his kindness and compassion. As with most people in this position, they had never done anything like this before, and the attendant sat down with Belinda to explain the process. He would take them to a viewing room where they would identify May through a glass window. He would draw the curtains, he said. Belinda would sign the official papers after the identification was made.

Wracked with grief, apprehension, and uncertainty, Belinda and her parents went into the viewing room, instinctively huddling together for mutual support. The attendant asked if they were ready, then opened the curtains.

May was lying with her right side facing the window. She was completely draped, with her head wrapped and only her face and the right side of her neck exposed to her devastated relatives. Belinda had expected May to appear different, but she wasn't prepared for the sight before her. With the exception of some bruises and wounds on her face, her aunt looked unchanged, almost as if she had closed her eyes and gone to sleep.

Belinda and her parents stood rigidly silent for a minute, almost paralyzed, as they studied the heartbreaking scene before them. Finally their shock was slowly replaced with hushed questions about May's injuries. Why was her face so bruised when she had been found lying on her back? they wondered.

"Somebody must have hit her," Belinda said, starting a brief discussion with her parents about whether bruising occurs after you die.

Why was she cut? they wanted to know. Shielded from the gaping wound on the left side of her neck, Belinda deduced that a blow to the head had killed her aunt.

"Look, her ears aren't ripped," Ilse said. "It wasn't robbery," she surmised, unaware her sister had not been wearing her diamond earrings when she was killed.

Belinda was deeply troubled by the bruising on May's face. *Someone hit her and hurt her,* she thought, more convinced of her uncle's assessment that a blow to the head had killed her. *How did this happen?* she sadly wondered.

Their bewilderment was interrupted by the kindly attendant who entered the viewing room, asking if that was May Greineder. Belinda told him it was. He asked if they needed more time. "I think we're done," she said, the trauma of seeing May dead now surmounted by the disconcerting questions as to why.

Signing the paperwork, the attendant told Belinda the autopsy had been completed, allowing for the body's release for whatever arrangements they had made. The words barely registered through Belinda's confusion and grief. They walked outside, reeling from what they had just seen.

Returning to Cleveland Road, Belinda and her parents learned that Kirsten and Aleks had completed the arrangements for May's memorial service. It would be held the next day, but without her body, based on Dr. Greineder's contention that it would not be released in time from the medical examiner. Even though Belinda had documentation from the ME's office authorizing the release, no one in their numbing grief had thought to question her uncle's position that May's body would be unavailable. They all agreed to gather for a private ceremony when the remains were released, after the public service.

It wasn't long before another controversy ensued after Britt took a call from the Wellesley Police Department that left her near apoplectic. "They want the dogs," she wailed, unable to coherently relay the rest of what she had been told through her rising fury.

When the authorities called again, Belinda took the phone to find out what was going on. The police had a search warrant to take samples from the dogs, they informed her, asking if they could send the animal control officer over to get them. Belinda told them she needed to check with Dr. Greineder first. Britt was now hysterical, throwing a full-fledged tantrum. "They want to harass my father! They want to kill our dogs!" she screamed. "What are they going to do with them?"

Britt's meltdown infected Belinda's kids, who began asking if the police were going to hurt the dogs. Belinda called her husband, who, with Terry

Segal, was on a second lawyer interview with Dr. Greineder. "We have a problem here with the dogs," she said. "They have a search warrant and it seems to me that we have to give them the dogs."

"You do," Greg Markel agreed. "What's the big deal? Give them the goddamn dogs. They're just dogs."

Dr. Greineder did not feel that way, however. "Those bastards," he spat. "My poor kids. My poor dogs. What are they going to do with them?"

State Police Detectives Dermot Moriarty and Gerry Mattaliano had obtained the search warrant after a dog hair had been collected from inside the cuff on the left-hand brown work glove found in the storm drain near Dr. Greineder's van. The investigators wanted a veterinarian to remove blood and hair samples from the doctor's dogs for analysis, but the Greineders, especially Britt, did not want to turn the animals over.

After a long discussion of what to do, the detectives agreed to let Britt and Colin and neighbor Nancy Gans transport the dogs to the vet in Belinda's SUV. The detectives followed the van, and the required samples were collected without further incident. Belinda stayed behind to soothe her children, who were convinced from Britt's histrionics that the police were going to be "shaving and cutting chunks out of them."

When Dr. Greineder got home ninety minutes later with Segal and Greg Markel, the uproar about the search warrant had subsided, but it was clearly a concern for the doctor. Belinda and Murray Stark happened to be near the landing leading from the front door when her uncle entered talking nonstop about a squeegee ball the dogs played with that he and May had handled, saying he was afraid his DNA could have been transferred to May's killer from Zephyr's saliva. Dr. Greineder did not take off his jacket or even greet anyone upon entering the house, lost in his passionate rant about the dog and the ball.

Murray caught his brother-in-law's eye and interrupted him before Dr. Greineder could reach the top of the stairs. "When they find the gloves," Murray said coolly, his growing mistrust of his brother-in-law spilling over, "the killer's fucked."

Dr. Greineder was left momentarily speechless, literally coming to a halt as he looked quizzically at Murray, this self-made businessman who had learned a thing or two in his hardscrabble upbringing.

If wounded by this apparent challenge to his credibility, Dr. Greineder did not show it. Undaunted, he swung back into his spiel about the squeegee ball, repeating a high-five demonstration of how May could have innocently passed genetic material from her husband to her killer while trying to defend herself.

His audience now spread about the main floor, Dr. Greineder began taking questions about the lawyer interviews, but he was still focused on trying to deflect the implications of the latest police search. Sitting on the hassock in the living room, he began another retelling of the strange simultaneous nosebleed he had with May, elaborating with more details than he had told Belinda previously. They were using up the tissue they were sharing as they were walking down to the garage, he said. Dr. Greineder then grabbed a towel out of his car that both he and his wife used to stem the mutual bleeding. Using a high-five motion again as part of his animated demonstration, Dr. Greineder said he was afraid May could have transferred his blood to the killer. He then began talking about leaning toward hiring Marty Murphy to represent him, announcing he was going to take the night to mull it over before making a final decision in the morning.

Much as her husband had done, Ilse Stark stopped his diatribe with a statement that left him outwardly guarded. "May wasn't robbed," she said.

"What?" Dr. Greineder asked, clearly distracted from his focus on the attorney.

"May wasn't robbed," Ilse repeated. "Anybody that would have killed her so savagely would have no compunction of ripping her earrings out of her ears. Was she wearing her jewelry, Dirk?" she asked, repeating her question from the day before.

"I don't know," he replied again.

"Why did May have bruising around her mouth?" Belinda now asked, still troubled by what she had seen at the medical examiner's office.

"I don't know," he said again.

"Do you think she lived for a long time through this?" Belinda asked hesitantly. "Do you think she was aware of what was happening?"

"No, I don't think she lived very long," Dr. Greineder said softly.

Belinda was unsure if he really knew or gave that opinion just to ease her distress. Now nearly 9 P.M., Belinda and her family got ready to leave for the night. She packed the kids in the car and they headed for their hotel, the Crowne Plaza in neighboring Natick.

Settling at a table in the nearly empty lounge, Belinda and her parents asked Greg about the lawyer interviews.

Greg said he could not go into specifics about what had been said in deference to Dirk's client-attorney privilege, but he revealed that he had been impressed by how composed he had been. Controlled and reasonably consistent in telling his story to two prospective defense attorneys, Dr. Greineder had been very detail oriented. But his wife and in-laws were troubled that Dr. Greineder had freely given to the defense attorneys facts that he had not told them or had explained only in lesser detail.

May's pants had been slit and pulled down while her shirt had been pulled up, Dr. Greineder had informed the lawyers, answering, "I just don't know" when he was queried about the possibility that his wife had been raped. This description was almost contrary to what Dr. Greineder had told Belinda and her parents the day before.

He had also described more wounds for the lawyers than he had for his wife's distraught relatives. There was a blow to the head, he repeated in the interviews, but May had also suffered multiple stab wounds, and her throat was cut, he disclosed. Greg was not revealing all that Dirk had said, but his wife and her parents had heard enough to realize he "knew a whole lot more than we knew about," Belinda recalled.

"I think he did it," Murray Stark said, thinking still of Dr. Greineder's reaction to his comment about the gloves. He exchanged a knowing glance with Greg. Ilse was undecided about her brother-in-law's guilt or innocence. Belinda was definitely still "a holdout" on the unthinkable idea that her uncle had done it, although a small seed of doubt had been planted.

Greg and Murray were intuitive enough not to push the issue or flaunt their suspicions. They knew their wives would have to come to a conclusion on their own. But the mother and daughter were deeply "troubled" thinking about "the inconsistencies and some of the bizarre things" Dirk had started to say, Belinda later recalled. "In a twenty-four-hour period, it became a runaway train. We were being bombarded with all these stories."

The family was slowly getting the message that Dr. Greineder might be connected to some bad things, but Belinda didn't want to believe her uncle was capable of killing May.

# 8

DEEP INTO HER FIRST REAL SLEEP since the murder three days before, Belinda Markel was jolted awake on Wednesday, November 3, by the shrill ring of the telephone. Her husband had quietly risen for a workout at the hotel gym, happy that his grief-consumed wife was finally getting some rest, but her uncle had apparently forgotten she planned to sleep late that morning. It was 6 A.M.

"Belinda, I was going through some of May's things and I found her dilator," Dr. Greineder gushed excitedly as soon as he heard her semiconscious hello. "It came to me that we had to do a second autopsy," he said urgently. "I need to talk to Marty Murphy. We have to figure out who's going to do this. I have to get on top of this because this is something we have to do."

Belinda had no idea what he was talking about but figured a dilator might be something to expand the vagina to make sex more comfortable for her aunt. Belinda knew from conversations with May that she and her uncle "did not have the best sex life," partly because of physical discomfort May experienced. May had tried several remedies, including making time to be more romantic with her husband by planning intimate dinners at home or going on dates to the ballet, theater, or movies. The effort had worked for them until May's mother got sick the year before. After May's mother passed in late 1998, she had tried to rekindle her intimacy with Dirk but their infrequent dates had trailed off. It got to the point where May usually skipped the obligatory business dinners or parties that Dirk had to attend.

"Is there something wrong, Dirk?" Belinda sleepily asked, still confused about why he had woken her or why the discovery of May's dilator would necessitate a second autopsy.

"No, no, this is very important, this explains everything," Dr. Greineder said, continuing what would become a daylong dialogue with his niece about the need for the second autopsy and who should perform it.

Her uncle's breathless argument "still made no sense whatsoever," but Belinda accepted it on good faith. When she told her husband and parents about the second autopsy they "were kind of surprised but no one interfered," she recalled.

May's memorial service had been planned with the expectation that her remains would not be available, a situation that remained unquestioned even though Belinda had signed the release at the medical examiner's office. She too assumed May's body would not be available for the service, but with the troubling conversation of the night before with her husband and parents still fresh, Belinda got out of bed sensing the second autopsy was another disconcerting development.

Dr. Greineder decided early Wednesday morning to hire attorney Marty Murphy and promptly wrote a retainer check, sealing it in a stamped envelope. With the issue of who was going to represent him resolved, Dr. Greineder concentrated on May's second autopsy. He had already called several colleagues asking their opinion about whom to consult, while attorney Murphy had also suggested someone. Belinda quickly realized that Dirk had not told his children about the second autopsy when her cousins began asking questions after overhearing snippets of a conversation in the kitchen.

The Greineder children seemed unsettled over the plan to have their mother autopsied again. The discussion over why it was necessary went back and forth, but Dr. Greineder was firm. "We absolutely have to do this," he kept saying. The police were out to get him, he hammered home again, and expounded on the idea that the state medical examiner couldn't be trusted either. He needed to hire a private pathologist to use his newly discovered evidence to help prove his innocence, he argued.

Due at the church an hour before the 2 P.M. service and running late, Belinda Markel and family packed into her Expedition. The Greineders and Kirsten's fiancé got into Dr. Greineder's Avalon and Aleks's rental car for the trip to Newton.

The small convoy parked in the lot at the ornate Newton Presbyterian Church, built in 1730. The two families solemnly filed in, the sanctity of the stone church bringing their thoughts solely to May and the heartbreaking reason they were there. After gathering in a small chapel for a preservice prayer, with nearly nine hundred mourners attending in the spacious sanctuary, May's relatives were directed by Rev. Sherrod out to their front-row pew. Joined by Terry and Harriet Segal and Nancy and Jerry Gans, Dr. Greineder led his family, followed by the Markels and Starks.

"I am numb, as you are numbed by this senseless violence," Rev. Sherrod told the hushed mourners, recalling how May joined the church in 1994, mostly attending the early service on Sunday. Warm, caring, and deeply dedicated to her children, she had called Sherrod earlier that month, he said, "bubbling with excitement wanting to know if I would officiate at the wedding of her oldest daughter."

After a musical reflection featuring "In the Garden," May's close friend Carol Ottesen climbed the stagelike altar to deliver the eulogy. There had been a lot of debate among May's children about who would make the keynote tribute, but her husband of thirty-one years had not been a consideration. Dr. Greineder had ignored the preparation of his wife's funeral, and his giving the eulogy "wasn't even discussed," Belinda said. Belinda had been asked to "contribute" to the eulogy, but her cousins decided Ottesen, whom May met when she and Dirk were living in Maryland in the early 1970s, would memorialize May with stories about their friendship, which had stretched nearly three decades.

The decision turned out to be a good one. Obviously disturbed but elegantly composed, Ottesen told the hushed congregation she had talked to May on the phone only two weeks before, finding her fulfilled and happy with her children as well as her marriage to Dirk. "She was looking forward to the marriage of her daughter Kirsten," Ottesen said. "I take such pleasure in the fact she felt so happy these last weeks."

Ottesen drew laughs from the downcast mourners with her recollection that May "could charm any child or dog" and was someone who was so compulsively neat she once cleaned the top of her stove with a toothpick.

May had gone back to work at Harvard Vanguard Medical Associates, Ottesen said, so Kirsten would not have to pay off tuition after graduating from Harvard Medical School. "When Kirsten asked what she wanted in return, May told her that she just wanted her to be happy and that would be payment enough," Ottesen reflected, bringing tears to the eyes of the Greineder children in the front row.

Wondering how her family could go on without her, Ottesen described May through the words of the man who had shared her life for more than thirty years. "The thread woven through May was her tremendous sense of responsibility to everyone. She needed to know that she made a difference to some person or some animal," Dr. Greineder had told his wife's best friend.

Ottesen unsteadily kept her composure as she completed her tribute, finally walking down the stairs from the pulpit in tears to the waiting arms of Dr. Greineder and his weeping children. Surrounding Ottesen with their traditional group hug, the Greineders tearfully consoled her before returning to their seats.

May's hour-long memorial service drew toward a conclusion with the reading of the Lord's Prayer and the singing of "Amazing Grace." After the Benediction, Dr. Greineder gathered his crying children in another collective hug and led them, still clinging together, up the altar stairs to a side exit. Belinda had not realized how many people had come to pay their respects until May's relatives formed a receiving line in the vestry while church volunteers set up a table with food and refreshments.

Belinda was amazed that most of the mourners stayed to pass through the receiving line, the process taking nearly three draining hours. Standing next to her uncle, Belinda found him surprisingly fresh and animated while the rest of the family looked physically and emotionally spent. Belinda was watching her uncle closely, listening to his conversations to figure out who people were from what her uncle was saying. She knew some of the people who had come to say good-bye to May but had never met most of them. Her uncle was unusually jovial, even frivolous, Belinda thought, almost as if the receiving line was for the wedding of one of his children rather than the funeral for his murdered wife.

When Yale swim coach Frank Keefe passed through, Dr. Greineder was almost boisterous as they reminisced about Keefe's tutelage of the Greineder children. "Here they are," Dr. Greineder boomed, proudly gesturing toward his children. "Look at her now," he said of Kirsten. "She's getting married. Can you believe it?" Belinda didn't expect her uncle to be morose, but his almost upbeat demeanor "seemed a little much, and it went on forever."

When May's young hairdresser offered her condolences, Dr. Greineder asked about her belly button, which she had just gotten pierced. He had extended conversations with some of the contractors who were working on his home, asking them questions about the progress of their respective jobs. When one of his nurses approached, Dr. Greineder went over things that needed to be done at work and asked her how it was going there. He "got all worked up," Belinda noticed, when the office search warrants were mentioned. The final mourner completed the receiving line shortly before 6 P.M.

Ilse Stark reflected on how much May had given her husband and family. She and Dirk had been unusually close, more so than any married couple she knew. They did nearly everything together and made no decisions without the other's approval. Something as simple as buying a wastebasket required both of their participation. Whatever arrangements were made for the family or the house, no matter how major or minor, it was something May had to do with Dirk. Everything was done in tandem.

Ilse had never seen a family so bonded. They had regular meetings to discuss household issues and air grievances, much like business executives running a corporation. Despite the children's input, Dirk usually steered the direction of the meetings to his desired conclusion, giving the kids a false sense that they actually participated in the decision making.

But during May's weekly visits to New York to help care for her dying mother, Ilse had noticed some subtle changes in her sister's marriage. Dirk's work responsibilities had increased, including traveling all over the country for medical seminars, leaving him uncharacteristically less available. He used to take his family to spend a week at Ilse and Murray's vacation home every summer, but Dirk had been absent the past four years.

He had not come to New York with May, even when it was evident her mother was about to die. For that reason, Ilse had found it odd that Dirk and May seemed to be struggling financially. Ilse had frequently given her sister money to help out with things, and their mother traditionally sent May about $3,000 every year even though she wasn't a wealthy woman.

May "had asked very little for herself," although Ilse had paid for a facelift for May. Ilse's financial assistance was usually in the form of airfare so May's kids could come home for a visit or for a television or a car for one of her nieces or nephew. Both Ilse and Belinda had helped May pay her Amtrak or air shuttle costs to New York when her mother was sick.

Belinda had also given May $500 to defray her travel expenses, surprised when her aunt said "it would help." With her husband's medical salary, Belinda couldn't understand why $500 would mean so much or why the traveling had created a financial hardship to the point where Dirk got irritated when May flew to New York instead of taking the less expensive train. "I guess it just sort of shocked me at that point that five hundred dollars would have made that big a difference," Belinda recalled.

Her first recollection of May and Dirk together came from her childhood visits to Cleveland, where the couple had met at Case Western Reserve. Her uncle was primarily a researcher early in his career, forging Belinda's early impression of him as a scientist. Even though May's kids were grown and out of the house, their mother was "still very involved in their lives." Still, she seemed "somewhat lonely," Belinda had observed. Dirk had taken a new position at Brigham and Women's Hospital in Boston, subsequently working longer hours and traveling more than he ever had. He and May were spending more time away from each other "and I think she really felt that," Belinda said.

In the year before her death, May had started to dress more nicely, whereas she used to prefer walking around in jeans and a sweatshirt. She had started to coordinate her clothing, had begun exercising, and had lost some weight. Then she had the facelift and began to travel on her own, "which she had never done before with Dirk." The trips to New York and one to see Carole Ottesen in Maryland were "a change for her." Over the years, Dirk had been able to limit May's time with her relatives, occupying her with her immediate family's needs.

In the past, May would arrive in New York for whirlwind, "obligatory" visits, showing up for twelve hours and then disappearing until the next time. Belinda would drive her grandmother to Wellesley so she could see

May, but she did not enjoy staying at her son-in-law's house. Often they stayed the night, then Belinda drove her grandmother home the next day.

Dr. Greineder had been even less supportive while his wife was in New York taking care of her mother. May did not talk to her husband unless he telephoned, the conversation invariably turning to Dirk complaining about money. He expected Belinda to give May an advance on her anticipated $50,000 inheritance from her mother's estate to put toward travel costs. Dirk and May had certainly paid their share of college and medical school tuition — nearly $400,000 between 1989 and 1999 — but their self-described financial woes perplexed Belinda.

Her aunt "was not the best money manager in the world," but Belinda knew Dirk took care of the couple's finances. As the weeks passed, he grew increasingly upset about the travel costs to New York. The complaining "irritated the hell out of me," Belinda said. "I was angry at May for letting him do that because she wasn't paying for anything while she was here, but she said, 'He's really mad and we have these bills to pay and I'm here.' I wrote her a check and said, 'Take the goddamn money. I don't want to hear it.'"

After her mother's death, May would frequently call her niece to ask about the progress of probating her estate; Belinda suspected Dirk was putting pressure on May to collect her share of the inheritance. "It was constant," Belinda remembered. "She would ask, 'Do you think the lawyer's ready? Have you sold the house? When are you going to close?'" May said she needed the money "because they had been doing this work in the house and she had already spent that money," Belinda said.

The renovations at 56 Cleveland Road had started in the kitchen with the purchase of a new stove then snowballed to replacing the other appliances along with the installation of granite floors and counters. Redoing the upstairs bathroom had caused May the most grief. It was gutted and then enlarged, but the tile, fixtures, and a custom glass door for the shower May had selected put her way over budget. She had estimated her $50,000 inheritance would cover the entire renovation project, but work in the master bathroom had skyrocketed to $40,000 on its own.

May had been uncharacteristically left alone by Dirk to make most of the renovation decisions, with the exception of the couple's laborious search for a formal dining room set. After shopping for dozens of hours over a period of months, they spent more than $15,000 for a table, chairs, and a buffet at Roche Bobois. The dining room set May had longed for since the beginning of her marriage was delivered a week after she died.

Even the joy of her daughter's engagement was tempered with financial worry. "When Kirsten got engaged May was thrilled, but when she started figuring out how much things cost, she said she didn't know how she was going to do it," Belinda said. "I told her I would give her some money to help her." May would usually return from New York on Fridays to find a batch of household chores waiting. Her husband routinely called toward the end of the week, Belinda said, "to remind her the laundry needs to be done and this needs to be done and he was bugging her about a Christmas party he had to have at the house for work," Belinda said.

When May told her husband, "Look, I really can't do this and have this party, can't you find someone else?" Dr. Greineder "got pretty irritated," Belinda recalled. He had hosted a Christmas party for his coworkers the year before, but May had "done everything herself. He didn't seem to miss her as a companion. It was an inconvenience that she was away," Belinda remembered. Dr. Greineder grumpily decided to have the holiday party at another doctor's country club.

Belinda had also been aggravated with her cousin Colin, who would arrive home from Yale expecting May to do his laundry after she had spent the week taking care of his dying grandmother. "At that point my kids were doing laundry for me, and they were a whole lot younger," said an exasperated Belinda. She began noticing "that something was missing," from Dirk and May's relationship. They had shown plenty of affection toward each other early in their marriage, but their life together "was routine and became kind of a coexistence," Belinda observed. They still called each other by their pet names, "Mom" and "Dirky," but Dr. Greineder was not the type to walk into a room after coming home from work and give his wife a hug and a kiss.

Belinda found May to be "brilliant, smarter than Dirk." But her aunt "would get annoyed" when Dirk and Colin "would get into a deep conversation about computers or something and kind of put her down because she wasn't as informed. That was one of her big complaints," explained

Belinda. "She got tired of them treating her like she didn't know anything and [saying], 'Look, you don't understand what we're talking about.'"

Belinda felt Colin took advantage of his mother, demanding too much from her. "He expected things to be cooked for him, and he always had a Jekyll-and-Hyde personality," she said. "He had a terrible temper, and they would get into terrible arguments. He could be nasty and mean. He loved his mother but didn't seem to respect her."

May could be hard to live with as well. She was tough and very demanding, and her newfound independence "created a lot of tension in that household," Belinda said. May used to look at her niece with wonder when Belinda would take her kids to Florida on a whim or travel without her busy husband, "but she was learning how to do that."

May had been somewhat of a free spirit before she married Dirk, and in the year before her death she had started "escaping that control. She picked up and went to see Carol Ottesen in Maryland for a few days. She would never have done that" in years past, Belinda said. "She had the facelift, and I thought he was going to have a nervous breakdown, and he didn't even pay for it. It had been May's idea, and he was not terribly helpful in that."

The Greineder children had noticed their father's increasing time away from home. They had also noticed the tension between their parents and had planned to have a family meeting when they were all home for Thanksgiving to discuss it. Instead, they had been hastily summoned home on Halloween for the unimaginable.

After the service, Belinda, beyond exhausted, loaded her family into the Expedition for the drive back to Wellesley — where one of the more bizarre moments of the week occurred. Taking a pan of lasagna out of the oven, Belinda was visibly startled to see her uncle hovering near her with a large kitchen knife. "Oh my God, I thought you were going to stab me," she blurted in reaction to Dr. Greineder's inquisitive stare. Her uncle silent, Belinda glanced at her mother and two of her kids standing behind Dirk. Ilse Stark also didn't speak, but the disbelieving look she gave her daughter did not need words. "I tried to make a joke of it," Belinda said later, "but I don't know why I said it."

Cleaning up in the kitchen, Belinda began rinsing one of the numerous foil pans the Greineders' friends and neighbors had brought food in. She was surprised when her uncle told her "to throw that damn thing away." Dirk and May were the "king and queen of recycling," recalled Belinda, who was quite familiar with their stringent sorting system. Following her uncle's instruction, she tossed the foil pans in the trash.

Later, her uncle pulled her aside. "Before you leave, I want to talk to you," he said, leading her into his office down the hall from the kitchen. "You really need to give me some time tomorrow," he said. "We have to discuss my fund-raising and what we're going to do about all this. I don't know what kind of evidence they might have, and you need to help me," he said with obvious concern.

"Dirk, of course I'm going to help you but right now, I'm really tired and getting sick, and I just want to get my mother and the kids back to the hotel."

"Let me put you on some antibiotics," her uncle offered.

Belinda declined. All she wanted was some sleep.

# 9

FOR THE SECOND STRAIGHT DAY, Belinda Markel's sleep was shortened by a predawn telephone call from her uncle. Where Wednesday's preoccupation had been about finding a pathologist to conduct a second autopsy on May — a search that would continue — Thursday's urgency was setting up a "defense fund." Trying to wake up in her hotel room and make sense of why he was calling her so early again, Belinda listened to another rehash of Dr. Greineder's concern that evidence might be innocently connected to him.

His latest worry centered on the mysterious towel he and May had supposedly shared to stem their nosebleeds and the question of whether the police had seen it during the search of his Avalon. "I don't know what to do with it," he whined. "What if they saw it? If I throw it away, they might come back and look for it," he feared.

"Where's it been all this time?" Belinda groggily asked, finally starting to privately question the strangeness of his dilemma.

"It's been in the car but I don't know if the police saw it," he repeated.

"Why don't you give it to Marty Murphy," Belinda suggested.

Dr. Greineder seized on the idea. "I'm going to give it to Marty," he ebulliently agreed, and then began giving Belinda a step-by-step account about the nosebleeds. "I'm going to send it to Marty Murphy," he reiterated, "because it's the right thing to do."

Belinda agreed, but she would never see the towel in his possession.

When Belinda and her mother arrived at Dr. Greineder's house, he had a special task ready for them. "The bastards still have my van," he complained. "I need you to take the trash to the dump. I don't want the kids to go because I don't want them to attract any attention. I don't want it to look like they are throwing the garbage out."

Her uncle's reasoning seemed warped, but Belinda had no problem helping him out with something as easy as driving some rubbish to the dump. "That's fine," she said, wondering what difference it really made who went but hesitant to say it with the bitter argument over who should go to the medical examiner's office still raw in her memory.

Going to the Wellesley dump turned out to be quite an experience for two residents of Manhattan. As they pulled in with Belinda's big Expedition loaded with trash bags, Ilse Stark was captivated by the activity going on there. It turned out the dump, shared by Wellesley and neighboring Needham, was a prime spot for trash picking. Legend has it one wealthy resident who couldn't be bothered trying to sell his boat trailer and an engine had simply left them at the dump for whoever wanted to claim them. People brought their old TVs, stereos, and furniture, which were quickly taken, sometimes before the former owners could even get them out of their vehicles.

Ilse's fascination abruptly ended when her daughter told her she needed help lugging the Greineders' trash out of the truck. The garbage was sorted for the various refuse and recycling containers. Belinda asked a man what the procedure was. "I've never done this before," she said with a laugh. "You have to help me out." Ilse added, "We're from New York." The two city dwellers laughed about their adventure while they completed several other errands for Dirk before returning to Cleveland Road. It would be several weeks before Belinda became haunted by speculations about what she might have unwittingly helped her uncle get rid of.

Back at his house, Doctor Greineder renewed his urgency about funding his defense effort. Taking Belinda into Colin's room, he again went over all his evidentiary fears and "wanted me to hear everything . . . three times," Belinda said. His biggest concern involved DNA, and how it could be transferred, sparking yet another retelling of how he and May had shared the bloody tissue and towel. Coming out of the fog of her grief, Belinda found herself beginning to question more of what her uncle was telling her.

The concept of sharing a tissue was repulsive, and with tissues all over the Greineder home, Belinda had to wonder why May and Dirk needed to share one. Besides, May was known to carry small travel packages of tissues. In fact, unknown to Belinda, two small packets of Kleenex had been found by investigators in a front pocket of her jacket, along with a crumpled tissue that tests concluded was devoid of blood. *I wouldn't even share a tissue with one of my kids*, Belinda thought, sitting patiently on a bed while her uncle outlined the reasons he needed her help.

"They're coming after me. I have a lawyer but I need money. I don't have much money," he whined.

"Maybe you can mortgage your house," Belinda suggested, surprised, as she had been during May's visits to New York, at her uncle's claim that he was financially strapped.

"That's funny," he responded without humor. "I was going to ask you the same thing. Do you have a big mortgage on your apartment?"

"No," Belinda replied, *and it's going to stay that way*, she thought.

"Everyone is going to rally together for a defense fund, but I know they are coming after me," Dr. Greineder repeated. Nancy Gans was going to start the fund, and his neighbors and medical colleagues were going to invest, but the bottom line was he was going to need, he said, "at least a half-million dollars to start. Belinda, give me your pledge that you will help me with whatever you can."

He then told her what he wanted if the police arrested him. "You need to get up here as fast as possible to get me out on bail and take care of the kids," he ordered.

"I'll do what I can," Belinda replied unconvincingly.

"No, you have to promise me. You have to come up," he replied forcefully, his voice rising.

Belinda didn't know if it was because she was tired and sick, but she was, as she said later, "starting to get a little pissed off." *I have three little kids and he has three big kids who should be able to take care of themselves,* she thought. "Dirk, I'll do the best I can," she reiterated, her uncle backing off a bit.

Sitting on the bed facing each other, Belinda recalled, she "didn't know why," but she "got this horrible chill" up and down her back. Deciding she was just tired and stressed, Belinda and her uncle "sort of bantered back and forth" about the evidence he was convinced the police were gathering against him. "They have the weapons and they are going to do everything they can to arrest me," he said, turning the conversation back to his need for money.

"Dirk, the defense fund sounds good, and I'll do whatever I can to help you, but I'm not going to mortgage my apartment," Belinda finally revealed. "Did you ask Marty Murphy what this is going to cost?"

"At least a half million dollars," he repeated.

Belinda, needing a break, went out and sent her mother in to talk to Dirk. But if he thought he was going to tell his sister-in-law what he wanted, he was mistaken.

"Well, you know, Ilse," he began as they descended the stairs to the living room. "No, Dirk, let me tell you something," Ilse interrupted. "I'll try to help, but you should try to help yourself. The defense fund sounds good, but you should put your finances in order and see what you have."

"May has two hundred thousand dollars in life insurance, and that will help, but do you think they will pay me?" he asked. "I sent Marty Murphy a check, but I hope I have enough money to transfer to cover it. I've got a paycheck coming from Harvard but I don't know if it will be enough."

Listening to the conversation, it sounded to Belinda like her uncle was not going to make ends meet for the rest of the month. "If it's a question of keeping a roof over your head, we're going to do whatever it takes," Belinda told him.

Dr. Greineder vented his frustration by slighting the investigators.

"They're such bastards," he said. "They're only coming after me because they didn't go after anyone else. They have to come up with somebody to solve the crime. There's been other murders in the area, but they are trying to blame me."

Listening to his tirade, Ilse thought her brother-in-law to be "exceedingly agitated and nervous." With still no idea when May's remains would be available for the family funeral, Belinda and her mother decided it was time to return to New York.

Across town on Linden Street, Marty Foley walked through the door of F. Diehl and Sons Hardware about ten minutes before the store's 5 P.M. closing, commencing what would be an almost obsessive search for the distinctive brown work gloves worn by May Greineder's killer. He was looking for ones where the rubber textured dimples went around the baby finger, thumb, and index finger, picking up a pair that seemed identical to those recovered from the Morses Pond storm drains. The label advertised them as "Men's Work Gloves, Mini-Dot for Sure Grip, Distributed by Durable Products, a division of Norman Librett Inc., New Rochelle, N.Y."

Diehl's sold about six different types of brown work gloves, and Foley bought a pair of each. Some of the other investigators had already seen the mini-dot gloves at Diehl's, which was located a street over from the police station, but, Foley said, "I wanted to see them for myself. I wanted to have them in my possession. I wanted to be able to have them on my desk so I could get a feel for what they were."

Paying for the gloves, Foley did not tell the clerk he was a police officer. "Diehl's will tell you they never sold so many pairs of brown work gloves, and most of them were bought by us," the detective laughed. Foley also noticed that Diehl's sold the Estwing two-pound drilling hammer. Over the coming months Foley would check two dozen stores for the mini-dot gloves distributed by Norman Librett. He shopped in department stores, pharmacies, supermarkets, general stores, convenience stores, hardware stores, and gasoline station mini-marts.

"Wherever I might be, if there was a store that might sell gloves, I would look at the gloves," he said. He looked in and around Wellesley and outside the area, keeping a handwritten chart of the store, its location, and whether it sold gloves. If the store did sell gloves, Foley noted what kind and whether they sold the same mini-dot gloves used in May's murder. No matter where he looked, the only place that sold the high-quality brown work gloves was Diehl's Hardware, where Dr. Greineder's financial records proved he was a frequent customer. Foley also maintained a chart of area stores that sold the two-pound hammer. Other than Diehl's, only Harvey's Hardware in neighboring Needham carried the unpopular item.

Wellesley Sgt. Mike Price and Trooper Scott Jennings had also started a search to see who sold the nine-by-five-inch E-Z Foil loaf pan and the five-ounce Ronsonol lighter fluid. Carrying Polaroid photographs of the two items recovered near May's body, the detectives found the loaf pans during a visit to the Roche Bros. supermarket in Wellesley, also located on Linden Street near Diehl's. The loaf pans came in pairs, secured with a clear plastic wrapper bearing an E-Z Foil label affixed to the bottom of the top pan in the package.

In another aisle, the detectives found the lighter fluid, quickly determining that it appeared to have the same price tag and code numbers as the container found at Morses Pond. Price and Jennings had already checked half a dozen stores for the items, but Roche Bros. was the only one that sold both the pans and lighter fluid. Carrying the items to the front of the supermarket, the detectives asked for the store manager before being directed to his basement office, where Dan Lanzillo easily recognized the items in the photographs.

"That's my product. They both have the same numbers," he said of the price tags on the lighter fluid. Price asked if the store was able to track when it sold the items. Lanzillo wasn't sure and dialed Joseph "Jeff" Dineen, who managed the information system and computerized cash registers for the chain of thirteen stores.

Talking to Dineen, the detectives were disappointed to learn the register system in the Wellesley store was unable to match particular products to customers unless it was done the day of the sale or possibly the next morning.

Price was unconvinced. Believing the computer system had to be able to store that information, he urged Dineen to investigate further and check with the software manufacturer. Despite Dineen's willingness to help, the customer purchase information would never materialize. The best Dineen would be able to do was tell the investigators how often the Greineders shopped at Roche Bros. by tracking the use of their Advantage Club membership for cashing checks.

Looking back over the eighteen months before May's killing, the investigators realized the couple were "very religious shoppers, on a weekly basis," said Foley. In the weeks leading up to the murder, the Greineders had shopped at Roche Bros. five times.

Although Dineen could not tell the detectives what specific items the Greineders bought, the Roche Bros. computer system could determine the weekly sales of the loaf pans and lighter fluid, which were brought into the store by an outside vendor. Between July and November 1, 1999, sixty-two pairs of loaf pans and eight containers of the five-ounce lighter fluid were sold at the Wellesley store. During the week of October 10–16, two weeks before May's murder, two containers of lighter fluid and seven packages of loaf pans were sold. Lanzillo told the detectives that this seven-day period in October was the only one dating back to July in which the pans and lighter fluid were both sold in the same week.

Other pairings of Wellesley and State Police detectives had fanned out in search of the Estwing two-pound hammer, the Shrade Old Timer knife, and the distinctive brown work gloves.

Reading the *Boston Globe* on Friday, November 5, Marty Foley and Rick Grundy were very interested to learn that Marty Murphy would be defending Dr. Greineder. The press was still clamoring over the case, finally confirming that the Greineder home had been searched sixteen hours after May was found dead at Morses Pond. Murphy would not acknowledge the search, instead releasing a statement thanking the community for its sympathy.

Grundy and Murphy had worked together in Middlesex County, where Murphy was the first assistant under DA Tom Reilly. The two men liked and respected each other, and although the stakes in the Greineder case were astronomical, the colleagues-turned-adversaries would never lose sight of their friendship or professionalism. Like Grundy, Murphy came from a modest background, growing up in the Massachusetts city of Haverhill, a town of former shoe manufacturing mills on the Merrimack River bordering New Hampshire.

The son of a state trooper, Murphy excelled at academics, graduating from Princeton University summa cum laude in 1980. From there he went to Harvard Law School, graduating cum laude in 1983. Murphy was an assistant U.S. attorney in Boston from 1987 to 1991 before becoming Reilly's first assistant in 1992. As the top prosecutor in the largest county in Massachusetts, he had tried — and won — a number of notable cases.

In 1997, Murphy left Reilly's office for a lucrative private practice at the prestigious Boston firm of Bingham Dana & Gould where Grundy had worked at the beginning of his career. The Greineder murder would be Murphy's first major criminal defense case.

Foley also knew Murphy, finding him likable and talented. Their fathers had served together on the State Police, and Foley worked with Murphy's brother Matt, who was also a state trooper. Foley and Murphy had golfed together several times and had spent one Friday afternoon interviewing a judge for an investigation. While Foley's friendship with Murphy was more casual, Grundy knew him very well. Foley realized there was a certain advantage in that: "If nothing else, Rick knew the enemy and knew exactly what Murphy would be looking for and how he would be doing this case. Rick's thought was Murphy's going to do his homework. He's going to do a good job, and we're going to have to make sure we do."

Grundy had no illusions that prosecuting Dr. Greineder was going to be easy. He was all too familiar with Murphy's meticulous trial preparation, and his client was a prominent member of the community whom a jury might be reluctant to find guilty of murder. They were in for a battle. "If we screw up, we're going to lose this case," Grundy had warned. But Foley sensed that Grundy was more comfortable facing off against Murphy than some of Boston's other top defense attorneys whose courtroom theatrics were more unpredictable.

Back in New York City, Belinda Markel was still getting frequent updates from her uncle about the police investigation aimed at him. Dr. Greineder had told his niece that the second autopsy on May would likely be done soon. As she tried to catch up on some chores and paperwork at home,

Belinda took a constant stream of calls from her uncle reporting what the police were up to and what Marty Murphy was doing to counter them.

Dr. Greineder was planning to honor his out-of-state lecturing commitments but was annoyed when he received a call saying he had been replaced for an upcoming trip. "They said they didn't think I would be up to it, but I need to get back to things," he complained.

"I guess they are just being considerate," Belinda told her uncle, trying to soothe his irritation.

Dr. Greineder was more agitated to learn that Marty Foley had spoken to Greg Markel about interviewing Belinda. His wife was willing to cooperate, Greg told the detective. Deep down, Belinda privately "didn't know what side" she was on. But it wouldn't hurt to talk to the police, she thought, and besides, the most important thing was for May's killer to be brought to justice. Belinda could not understand why her uncle and his children were refusing to cooperate with the police, her opinion sparking "a long, heated discussion" between them. "Don't you want them to find out who killed May?" an exasperated Belinda had finally asked.

No matter how much Belinda tried to convince her uncle and cousins to support the investigation they would not budge, calling the police "bastards" who were out to get him. Belinda herself had moments of hostility toward Foley and his colleagues for suspecting her uncle. "I wanted to go knock on their door and say, 'What the hell are you doing? Have you found this person who killed May?'" she recalled.

Her uncle and cousins were unconditionally united, Dirk's children readily agreeing to his directive that they avoid all media coverage of the case, which he felt was slanted against him. He had convinced his children that the investigators were unfairly targeting him for the murder of their mother.

For Belinda, the Greineders' contempt for the police was another unsettling development. "There were times during that week that I started to get uncomfortable," she said. "Greg's description of Dirk at the attorneys' and the Wednesday and Thursday conversations I had with him" about getting an attorney and doing a second autopsy "were in the back of my mind. I thought, 'Something doesn't make sense.' But I was not at a point to say Dirk did this."

Unfortunately for Dr. Greineder, Marty Foley and Rick Grundy were.

Meeting at the State Police crime lab in Sudbury, they sat down with manager Gwen Pino to start sorting through all the evidence that had been gathered. The biggest issue facing the two investigators was how to go about testing the weapons and gloves for DNA to assure them that they were connected to May's murder and, more critical, prove her husband was responsible.

The knife and hammer found in the storm drain had tested positive for human blood; the next step was to confirm that it came from May. Pino told Foley and Grundy she didn't think she could capture the suspect's DNA from the weapons because human cells were unlikely to adhere to the smooth surfaces on the knife and hammer, but she would try.

Pino had taken swabs from the blade and handle of the knife as well as the head and handle of the hammer, hoping to connect the suspect with the victim. Even if only May's DNA was profiled, the investigators could be sure they had the actual murder weapons. The gloves would be a little more complicated. If they were tested in their entirety, the process would destroy them, and Grundy would not be able to display them at trial. Pino had taken cuttings from areas that tested positive for human blood as well as places where the wearer might have left skin cells or other biological matter that could yield DNA.

Going through her notes, Pino said she had seen a clear liquid on one of the gloves that she swore looked like semen until it tested negative. Foley immediately thought of Dr. Greineder's runny nose the day of the murder, telling Pino he had probably wiped the fluid onto the glove. "You mean, snot?" said Pino, the slang description drawing smiles from the two serious investigators. There wasn't a high chance of skin cells being found in the nasal discharge, but the cutting with the clear liquid would be tested anyway.

A total of eight cuttings would be taken from the brown right-hand glove found with the hammer and knife. Pino made seven cuttings from the left-hand glove recovered from the storm drain on Turner Road, where Dr. Greineder had parked his van. Three animal hairs had been found inside the left glove and would be sent to the Celera AgGen laboratory in Davis, California, where commercial animal DNA testing had been pioneered just a few years before.

Foley and Grundy had hoped to link the hairs to Dr. Greineder's dog

Zephyr, even though animal DNA had not been accepted as evidence by the Massachusetts courts. As with humans, scientists can extract animal DNA through two methods. The more identifying technique, short tandem repeats, or STR typing, requires nuclear DNA, the sample having to contain a sufficient quantity of intact cells.

In humans and animals, those cells are more commonly found in blood, saliva, semen, and hairs in which the roots or bulbs are intact. If a profile is developed from nuclear DNA, it is virtually unique because it is inherited from each parent. Even if a partial profile is obtained, it can be powerful evidence that the DNA likely came from a single human or animal. In cases where the sample does not contain suitable cellular material or in testing hairs without roots, the scientists would perform less identifying mitochondrial typing.

Mitochondrial DNA can be profiled from samples in which STR testing fails or wasn't feasible because the sample was too small or degraded. Mitochondrial DNA is present in hundreds of thousands of copies in each cell, whereas nuclear DNA is singular to a cell. Where nuclear DNA maps the person or animal's complete genetic makeup, mitochondrial DNA is inherited only from the mother. Animals that are related through maternal DNA would have the same sequence variants, or haplotype.

But mitochondrial DNA is not unique to the person or animal that carries it. Since it is passed maternally, siblings or even maternal cousins can share the same profile. A mitochondrial DNA match simply means the person or animal cannot be excluded as the source of the sample once the DNA sequence is determined.

The first criminal case that saw the introduction of animal DNA evidence was in Canada in 1996 when prosecutors used cat hairs on a bloody jacket to link a Prince Edward Island man to the killing of his estranged wife. At the time of the Greineder murder, only two juries in the United States had heard evidence of animal DNA in a homicide case.

Gwen Pino did not think Celera could recoup nuclear DNA from the dog hairs found in the brown work glove, but she believed there was a good chance the hairs would yield mitochondrial DNA that would not exclude Dr. Greineder's female German shepherd as being the source. Grundy and Foley's hopes of setting a legal precedent in Massachusetts would be dashed, however, when the California lab refused to stand by its results showing that one of the hairs taken from the work glove matched the genetic profile of Dr. Greineder's male dog, Wolf.

When testing for DNA, scientists include a known genetic standard, or "ladder," that they expect to see in the results. The presence of the known standard tells the scientist that the testing was done properly. In the Greineder case, Celera AgGen used the profile for Wolf's breed of German shepherd as the ladder and the result from the test sample was an exact match to the known standard. The male dog's hair in the glove would be just as incriminating for Dr. Greineder as one from the female, Zephyr, who had been at the pond the day of the murder, but the California lab would not say the test hair was a match with Wolf.

"It matched him," said a frustrated Pino, but the scientists would not testify about their results. "They would have had to defend their result, and once they realized the result was the same as their ladder they were opening themselves up to be harshly questioned on the stand," explained Pino. "They were not going to have any part of that, so they called it inconclusive."

Beth Fisher, who had worked in the trace analysis unit at the State Police crime lab for eight years, determined that swabs collected from May Greineder did not contain seminal fluid. Her vaginal, perianal and oral swabs tested positive for blood, as did swabs taken from her abdomen and left shin. Nothing of any evidentiary significance was found from fingernail scrapings taken from May Greineder's right hand. On her left hand, which had been found gloved, Fisher noted the screening test for blood had been positive on three fingernails.

Pino had collected fibers from inside one of the brown work gloves for Fisher to compare with material recovered from Dr. Greineder's fingernail clippings. She had also commenced a detailed forensic examination of Dr. Greineder's clothing and glasses. Pino catalogued the yellow-and-white windbreaker, a red-and-black jersey, a pair of dark socks, black jeans with a belt, and his white Reebok sneakers. She had also been given the red backpack the doctor was seen wearing containing three rubber balls, three dog leashes, and latex kitchen gloves.

Before turning the jacket over to Lt. Ken Martin for bloodstain analysis, Pino documented stains on the right and left sleeves, the right shoulder area, and the front and inner lapel that all tested positive for human blood. On Dr. Greineder's dark jeans, Pino found bloodstains on the knees and cuffs at the bottom of the pants. On the red-and-black long-sleeved jersey, Pino noted a bloodstain that was small and "smearlike" on the right chest and also found a small bloodstain on the white piping that ran across the chest a few inches under the neck.

Two one-millimeter stains on the right front and top of the red nylon backpack tested positive for blood, but no traces of blood were found inside the backpack. Foley had theorized that Dr. Greineder might have hidden the hammer, knife, and gloves inside the backpack that Bill Kear had seen, but the absence of blood there made it unlikely.

When Foley finally seized Dr. Greineder's glasses during the search of his home, the bloodstain the trooper had seen and ordered photographed had been cleaned. Removing the lenses, Pino tested the eyeglass parts for blood, getting a positive result where the right side of the left lens fit into the frame.

Pino also conducted tests on Dr. Greineder's sneakers, finding multiple bloodstains on the toe and tongue of the right shoe as well as along the top and outside portion of the left shoe. Other spatter-type stains were negative for blood, turning out to be red deck stain. Pino took cuttings from both sneakers for DNA testing.

Turning to May's clothing, Pino told Foley and Grundy that her jacket was saturated with blood in the collar area and upper chest, with blood smears across the chest and along both arms. Some animal hairs were removed from the jacket, and in the pockets Pino found two travel packs of Kleenex, a used tissue, a Claritin pill, a quarter, and a toothpick. The used tissue and two travel packages tested negative for blood, a result Grundy would seize upon later in the case after learning about the doctor's bloodstained towel.

May's blue-and-white-striped pants with an elastic waist and side zipper had been cut from the waist to the crotch and stained with blood. Pino found two crumpled tissues in the pants pockets that also tested negative for blood. The woman's Victoria's Secret black bra had a one-and-a-half-inch cut in the left cup an inch from its bottom edge. Her red Victoria's Secret panties bore a four-inch cut from the waistband to the crotch with a large amount of sand in the crotch area. Both undergarments tested positive for blood.

Pino had taken particular notice of the slain woman's underwear. Here was a woman in her mid- to late fifties, and she's got Victoria's Secret underwear on, Pino thought. "As a woman what that tells me is she was trying to be something for her husband. She was trying to do something. She just seemed like a nice woman and it made me mad that he had done this to her."

As a scientist, Pino could not pick sides between the prosecution and defense. She had a responsibility to properly test the evidence, knowing if an unidentified DNA profile turned up, it would be probative for both sides. Many times, Pino would have bad news for the investigators. "Would I do anything to help get a conviction? No," she stressed. "I'll tell them what I have."

Pino was unable to observe any stains on the blue fleece right-hand glove found on the dirt path, despite it testing positive for blood. Cuttings would be taken from both of May's gloves for DNA testing. Pino found it likely Dr. Greineder's DNA would be on the gloves, hardly unexpected between a husband and wife, but she wanted to make sure no other profiles existed there.

As expected, the red smear on the plastic Ziploc gallon bag found at the crime scene was blood. Examining the bag, Pino noticed that it contained two other bags, another gallon Ziploc and a pleated half-gallon storage bag. She did not remove the two bags but took a swabbing from the bloodstain for DNA testing. Pino then sent the three bags to Trooper Julia Mosely to be tested for impressions and fingerprints.

Foley and Grundy were interested to learn that the leash taken from Zephyr had blood on the handle and along the edges of its flat webbing. The blood along the edges was twelve inches from the handle and about four inches from where the leash attached to the dog's collar.

To get blood along the edges of the leash, Foley envisioned it would have had to pass through a bloody hand or in Dr. Greineder's case a blood-soaked glove. The doctor said the leash had been wrapped around his wife after the dog had run back to her but Foley would have expected blood to be on the flat part of the leash, not along the sides. The blood on the handle seemed even more damning. Dr. Greineder's hands had been conspicuously clean, yet Bill Kear clearly remembered him holding Zephyr's leash as the dog led him across the back of the Morses Pond traffic circle.

Bloodstains were going to be a definite problem for Dr. Greineder. Ken

Martin had already determined that the blood on his sneakers was impact spatter, putting the husband within "inches or feet" of his wife when she was killed. But before drawing a final conclusion, Martin always looked at the evidence in total to see how it fit with the crime scene. Examining Dr. Greineder's windbreaker, Martin noted bloodstains on both sleeves and the right shoulder that appeared to be transfer stains made by something bloody coming in contact with the material.

He observed impact spatter on the front of the jacket; the left side having in excess of ten small bloodstains while the right side bore about six. A bloody hair swipe on the right sleeve was also telling when matched with the transfer patterns. Martin deduced that after killing his wife at close proximity, Dr. Greineder scooped her under the arms from behind and then dragged her off the trail.

The husband's dark jeans were more difficult to analyze because of their color but knowing the small stains on the cuffs had tested positive for blood, Martin believed they too were impact spatter. Looking at the weapons, Martin could see a pattern of several "dots or dimples" on the rubber handle of the hammer in two places. Checking the Shrade Old Timer knife, Martin found another dot pattern on the handle two inches from where the blade folded open. The tiny blood marks were almost uniform, like they had been left by the same source.

Whereas blood evidence abounded in the Greineder case, the oddly stashed items found near May's body did not yield a single fingerprint, bolstering the investigators' belief that Dr. Greineder was wearing the brown gloves with possibly surgical gloves underneath when he killed his wife. After slicing open the three Ziploc bags and the white kitchen bag found stuffed under the tree branch along the dirt path, Julia Mosely placed the bags under an overturned fish tank then fumed them with a heated chemical similar to Super Glue. She then treated the bags with a dye that would reveal fingerprints, but none were observed.

Repeating the process with the hammer, knife, and container of lighter fluid, Mosely again found no fingerprints or "ridge detail." Turning to the foil loaf pan and latex surgical gloves that were found in it, she determined that the rubber gloves also were devoid of any prints, but on the loaf pan, on the bottom edge, a tiny area of ridge detail — or a partial fingerprint — appeared. However, the print was far from having the minimum eight characteristics the State Police mandated to make identification.

To Foley and Grundy, it was obvious the items had been wiped free of fingerprints then brought to the pond by someone wearing gloves. If they could connect the gloves to Dr. Greineder through DNA, it would make it that much harder for the plotting husband to get away with murder.

Wrapping up their meeting, Pino and the two investigators talked about where the evidence should be sent for DNA testing. Grundy suggested the Bode Technology Group in Springfield, Virginia, which he had used with success while a prosecutor in Middlesex County. The turnaround time from the Virginia lab, the largest forensic DNA company in the country, had been relatively quick, and the scientists were willing to provide a statistical breakdown of how the DNA profile compared to the rest of the world's population.

Pino told Grundy and Foley that Cellmark Diagnostics, the Maryland laboratory often mentioned during the O. J. Simpson trial, was working with the State Police lab on its accreditation and had a testing procedure that was more extensive. The drawback was that the testing took longer and Cellmark normally did not make a statistical report of the results.

"That was something we needed and we talked about that," Foley recalled of the statistical breakdown. Since Cellmark was already working with the lab, Pino was confident its scientists would provide the statistical analysis as well. "We wanted to know what we had," said Foley. "We talked about it, and a decision was made to go with Cellmark."

As the afternoon faded to November's early darkness, Foley left the Sudbury crime lab with his cruiser pointed west toward home. He and Jill McDermott planned to be at Morses Pond before sunrise on Saturday morning, but Foley would take an important break from the Greineder case that Friday night. His oldest boy, Tim, only a sophomore, was starting for the Marlborough High School football team under the lights at home against Doherty Memorial High School from Worcester.

Foley had barely seen his family for the past six days and relished the anticipation of spending the evening with them. "I missed them all week long, and I would have hated to have missed the game," he recalled. Foley had been up every morning by 5:30 but his wife, Cheryl, knew enough not to ask "what was going on or how's it going? She understood," said Foley.

Watching his boys play sports, Foley liked to stand off alone away from the boisterous, fiercely partisan parents rooting for the Marlborough Panthers. He wasn't a yell-and-scream kind of fan but instead enjoyed savoring his pride in his sons at play in solitude or with his wife. While watching the action from field level, Foley was approached by a woman he had known for several years, who was a civilian employee of the State Police.

"Dr. Greineder is my allergist, and he is a brilliant man," she told her coworker. "I hope Marty's not thinking he could have done this," the woman added, looking at his wife. Foley politely responded without answering her question. The woman was not the first and would not be the last to approach Foley or the other investigators with a comment like this. Most extolled Dirk Greineder's skill as a physician or parent and found it preposterous that he had fallen under suspicion.

Foley had planned to escape the rigors of the high-profile case for just a few hours, but it was not meant to be. "No matter where I went it was going to be there," he said. "It also showed how affected the community was. We came across a lot of people who knew Dirk or went to Dirk as a patient. He was brilliant in his field, and you can't take that away from him."

Murdering your wife, however, was an entirely different endeavor, and Foley wanted to expose Dr. Greineder's dark side. Tim Foley and the Marlborough Panthers easily handled Doherty Memorial 34–12 that Friday night, on the way to a respectable 6–5 season. His father found it refreshing to spend some time with his family, even though he couldn't remove himself from the image of May Greineder lying hideously murdered off a tranquil pathway.

# 10

MARTY FOLEY AND JILL MCDERMOTT had almost immediate success Saturday morning as they asked residents arriving at Morses Pond if they had used the recreation area the week before. Wellesley resident Duncan Andrews, an affable middle-aged man walking his dog about 8:15 A.M., told the detectives he had arrived at the pond about the same time the previous Sunday, returning home by nine o'clock. He and his wife were familiar with the Greineders and had heard about the sensational slaying. "I was here last Sunday and walked my dog and left, but I didn't see anything. I parked my car right over there," Andrews said, pointing to the intersection of Turner Road and Halsey Avenue, across the street from where Dr. Greineder had parked his van.

Andrews and his wife, Patricia, knew the Greineders from having walked their dog at Morses Pond for the previous five years, but the relationship only extended to friendly greetings. They were careful to keep their dog, Allie, away from the Greineders' more aggressive German shepherds.

Gliding down Turner Road on Halloween morning, Andrews had seen a silver minivan parked to the left of the gate in the spot he frequently used. Easing toward the curb on the right, he had parked his car across the intersection from the van. Feeling rushed because he had to get home to prepare for a function on the North Shore later, Andrews began his regular walk, which would take him in a loop around the recreation area, but he had noticed nothing amiss.

Shortly after meeting Andrews, Foley spotted his key eyewitness, Bill Kear, ambling up to the Turner Road gate, stopping to pick up his small terrier. Foley watched as Kear unhooked the tiny dog from its leash, putting the animal back down for the walk down the access road. Foley had planned to re-interview Kear at some point, but not then. They exchanged "good mornings," and then, looking at the second hand of his watch, the detective discretely timed the man's leisurely pace from the gate to a signpost about two hundred feet down the access road "to get an idea of how fast he walked."

Foley did the same thing with Duncan Andrews the following day when he showed up at the pond with his wife for a walk. Although it wasn't planned, the detectives asked the couple if they could accompany them on their morning circuit with Allie. Joining Duncan in front with the dog while Patricia trailed behind with McDermott, Foley noted it was 8:29 A.M. as they started into the woods of the pine tree forest.

Andrews told Foley he liked to meditate as he made his way in a long circle around the area, a revelation not particularly pleasing to the trooper, who wanted to know everything Andrews had seen or heard during the minutes surrounding May Greineder's killing. "We wanted to jog his memory and wanted to time how long it took him to do his walk," said Foley. "I thought if I could be with him and experience his walk, his exact route of travel, I might be able to solidify where Dirk was and where Dirk wasn't and the walk did that."

Andrews led the small procession through the pine tree forest to the elevated clearing that rimmed the sandpit where Terry McNally had played fetch with Theo. With the pond to their right, they started down a sloping trail in the woods that eventually emptied to a grassy area next to the pond, bordered by a chain-link fence that blocked access to the water treatment plant.

Foley followed Andrews through a large hole in the fence that permitted them to enter the grassy area where the pond's "old beach" was once located before the new one was built in 1976. Foley was struck by how much closer the area was to the crime scene than the newer beach a thousand feet distant. With his wife nearly debilitated with back pain, why didn't Dr. Greineder take his dog here for exercise and a swim rather than go nearly a quarter-mile farther? Foley wondered. Gazing over the old beach, the veteran investigator thought Dr. Greineder's claim that he was headed for the new beach when his wife was killed seemed even more implausible.

From the old beach, Andrews made his way toward the traffic circle, following a trail near the dirt path where May was killed that emptied into the sandy parking lot. The foursome strolled across the lot and reentered the bottom of the pine tree forest, starting their ascent away from the traffic circle on the paved bike path through the woods that ran parallel to the access road.

Reaching the point where the paved path was at its lowest elevation and greatest distance from the access road, Andrews suddenly stopped and turned to Foley. "I remember seeing someone up there last Sunday," he told the detective, motioning toward the access road high above them about eighty feet away.

Because of the differing elevation, Andrews had only seen the "tall guy" from the knees to the torso, he told the trooper, but the man was definitely walking down the access road toward the traffic circle. Because

Allie had a penchant for chasing joggers, Andrews had been stirred from his meditation and reached down to snap the leash on his roaming dog's collar. Continuing to his car, Andrews had again surveyed the silver van parked across the street.

Trying to swing a U-turn back up Turner Road, Andrews was irked by his vehicle's limited turning radius, having to stop and back up so he could clear the minivan. Finally started home, Andrews remembered seeing a runner wearing shorts and a T-shirt jogging toward him as he picked up speed on Turner Road. It was getting close to nine o'clock, Andrews told Foley, because he had felt rushed and was behind schedule for his trip to the North Shore.

Based on the time Andrews had started his walk on Halloween morning and considering it had taken him about twenty-five minutes to complete it a week later with Foley, the "tall guy" Andrews had seen had to be Bill Kear. It couldn't have been Rick Magnan because Magnan had jogged down the same bike path Andrews had used to leave the area. Magnan had not encountered Dr. Greineder until after the doctor had spoken to Kear near the traffic circle and then made the long trip back up the access road to his van. Andrews had arrived home about the time Dr. Greineder made his 8:56 A.M. call to the Wellesley police, so the runner Andrews had seen while leaving the pond had to be Magnan.

Mentally figuring the timeline, Foley was now sure that Andrews had been circling Morses Pond when May was killed. He had clearly recalled seeing Dr. Greineder's van parked near the Turner Road gate when he arrived that morning because that was where Andrews usually parked. He was equally certain the van was still there when he left because it blocked his car from making an easy U-turn up Turner Road.

Even though Andrews had not seen or heard Dr. Greineder at the pond, he hadn't seen anyone else who could have killed May either. Foley was pleased with the results of spending the weekend at Morses Pond.

"What I'm seeing in my mind is we're surrounding this place," he said. "We have Terry McNally on the hill above the sandpit. We have Bill Kear coming down the middle of the access road. We have Duncan Andrews circling the crime scene and coming back up, and they are all in there at the same time and no one sees anyone else. And Duncan had walked by the area leading to the beach where Dirk said he had been." Any doubt Foley still had that a mystery killer had attacked May had now evaporated.

Finishing at the pond, Foley turned onto Weston Road, quite possibly passing Belinda Markel and her family on their way to the Greineder home. Receiving a call from her uncle the day before, she had learned that the second autopsy on May had been completed, so the family funeral would take place on Monday. The Markels went by the Greineder house and got updated on what was going on.

While Belinda and her family readied for May's service on Monday morning, State Police Sgt. Dermot Moriarty strolled into the lobby of the Hilton at Dedham Place carrying a copy of one of Dr. Greineder's American Express statements, interested in a charge he had made at the hotel on the previous June 2. A prototypical state trooper, standing well above six feet, the pleasant Moriarty spoke to a general manager before being directed to Nan Shifflett, the hotel's manager of human resources.

In scouring financial and phone records obtained through a subpoena, investigators saw that Dr. Greineder used his cell phone to call 781–614–3040 on June 3, the day after the Dedham Hilton charge, as well as the day before and the day after his wife's murder.

Marty Foley had recognized the 614 prefix from another investigation as one used by the Pagenet paging company, wondering if Dr. Greineder had met someone at the Dedham Hilton off busy Route 128 a few miles from his Wellesley home. Clicking away at her computer keys, Shifflett told Moriarty that a "Girk" Greineder had stayed at the hotel on June 2, checking out the same day. Looking at a list of business conferences held at the hotel that day, Moriarty found nothing remotely related to asthma or allergy, Dr. Greineder's field of expertise.

The detectives, probing for a reason why Dr. Greineder would so heartlessly kill his wife, now had an indication that there may be someone else in his life, since he had apparently not gone to the hotel on business. Hardly elated, but encouraged, Foley realized they only had more work to do.

About the same time that Moriarty left the Dedham Hilton that morning, Belinda Markel and her family were headed for another ordeal perpetrated by her uncle. Walking into the chapel at Newton Cemetery for May's family service, the Markels and Starks entered a small anteroom already occupied by the Greineders, Segals, and Ganses. After exchanging solemn greetings, Belinda walked around the corner to the chapel, her children just ahead of her. Just inside, they all stopped short, seeing May lying in some kind of casket fully exposed.

At May's public memorial service five days before, Belinda had specifically asked her uncle if May's casket was going to be open at the family funeral. "I have three kids," she told him. "I want them to be prepared for what they are going to see."

"No. No. No," her uncle had stuttered in response. "Don't worry about it," he had assured. While May had looked almost peacefully asleep when Belinda identified her at the medical examiner's office a week before, that was far from the case now. But Belinda gently ushered her kids into the chapel.

Belinda could barely contain her rage. Her fury fell squarely on Dr. Greineder. "You should have told me," she hissed. "I told my kids it wasn't going to be open because you told me it wasn't going to be open."

"I wanted it to be open," interrupted her cousin Britt. "We need it to be open so everyone can see. Everybody needs to see my mother's face. I want everybody to look at my mother's face," she repeated demonstratively. With the tense discussion escalating at the back of the chapel, Dr. Greineder suddenly burst into tears, and almost at the same moment, Britt also began to cry. The father and daughter embraced and walked out of the chapel still holding each other. Her anger now mixed with total confusion, Belinda glanced at her other cousins, seeing that Kirsten and Colin were also furious with their sister.

While it was not unusual for them to be annoyed with their more volatile and unpredictable sibling, they were clearly exasperated by Britt's histrionics in front of their dead mother. Whatever was going on between Dirk and Britt didn't directly involve May, Belinda sensed. Her uncle had been remarkably composed for a week in dealing with May's killing, but now he had unexpectedly gone to pieces over something concerning Britt.

"He cried with Britt, but it was very bizarre," Belinda recalled. "It was clearly between the two of them, and I could tell from the reaction of my cousins that it was clearly something else other than grief over May." Having composed themselves, Dr. Greineder and Britt returned to the chapel several minutes later, where Britt continued to assert how "beautiful and radiant" her mother looked despite the obvious.

With the situation already fraught with tension and hostility, Ilse Stark now returned to Belinda's side after paying her final respects to her adored younger sister. She was seething. "They put my sister in a cardboard box," Ilse quietly told her daughter, her voice laced with outrage. "How could they put her in a goddamn cardboard box?" she spat. Ilse had also been astonished and further enraged to find May dressed in an outfit she had borrowed from Ilse during May's last visit to New York.

The distressing events were now openly affecting her children, and Belinda took Alexis, Amy, and William to say a prayer at May's side. She too was taken aback by the construction of her aunt's casket. "It was true. May was in a cardboard box," Belinda softly recalled with sadness. "It was cardboard covered with felt. I had never seen a casket like that and as recently as the previous January I had bought one for my grandmother." Even though Belinda's family members were cremated, as May would be, they were still afforded the dignity of a traditional casket, never considering something flimsy such as the one her aunt was resting in.

Belinda gently moved her disconsolate children away from May's side while Kirsten and Aleks replaced them to pay their respects. Her cousin Colin, Belinda noticed, had not ventured near his slain mother's body, and would not be able to, despite the hurt of his loss. May's husband, the man police were pursuing as her killer, also declined to kneel at her side to say good-bye. Still mulling her uncle's bizarre concerns and actions since May's murder, Belinda had taken to "watching him very carefully at that point because there was so much going on." Aside from his tearful breakdown with Britt, Dr. Greineder had mostly controlled his demeanor, almost as if he had moved on from his wife's horrific slaying.

The Rev. Marc Sherrod, who had presided over nearly a thousand crestfallen mourners at May's first memorial service, had also noticed the husband's unwillingness to have a final moment with his wife of three decades. Sherrod found himself thinking unholy thoughts. "I began to feel a bit uneasy myself, wondering why he didn't go forward to view the body as did his children and the small group of close friends there for the service," the minister admitted.

With the mournful trips to May's paperboard casket completed, Rev. Sherrod gathered the edgy group of relatives and friends together for an abbreviated funeral in the nondescript cemetery chapel. "We had a little service and that was it," said Belinda, the memory of that morning still bitter. "They didn't make arrangements to take the casket out. We just left. We got up and walked out. I don't even know if it took fifteen minutes."

Belinda assumed the family would go to lunch somewhere, since they had done that after funerals for her grandparents, but the small convoy returned to the Greineder home where it was apparent nothing had been planned. She silently watched with irritation as her uncle and cousins changed, then rummaged through the refrigerator, the conversation dominated by Kirsten's wedding plans, with an occasional mention of May. "Everybody seemed to have their own agenda," Belinda said. "We went back to the house for a while, but none of us really knew what to do."

Dr. Greineder used the opportunity to corner his niece yet again about how the police were trying to screw him, resuming his constant refrain about how much he needed her help. Steaming through yet another disjointed diatribe, her uncle was particularly angry that the police had taken his glasses. "He was really pissed about the glasses," said Belinda. "He wanted his glasses. He needed his glasses. It was very strange."

After the trauma Belinda and her family had been put through that morning, she was unsympathetic to her uncle's complaints. He had tried to rehash some of his odd stories about nosebleeds and fibers on his pants, but Belinda had heard enough. "I decided I was going to go home," she said. "I was with my parents and said, 'Let's get out of here.'"

There had been a growing undercurrent of animosity between the Greineders and the Markels and Starks, the tension further amplified by the funeral. Belinda's upset was accompanied by confusion. She seemed to be the last one to know about most of the Greineder family's questionable decisions, yet her uncle constantly bombarded her with his fears about the police investigation along with his need for an attorney and money.

Belinda didn't understand how her cousins were so allied with their father when it seemed that issues were never openly discussed. She knew her uncle and cousins had clustered for family meetings since May's murder, but she had seen only a few instances while she was in Wellesley. Months later, her children would provide her with a more revealing understanding of what was going on inside 56 Cleveland Road when Belinda was not there.

"They'd have these family meetings, and a lot of it occurred after I left the house," she said. "Dirk would ask my kids to leave and go downstairs into the family room and take his kids and have a family meeting in one of the bedrooms and close the door." Even though Belinda was far from fully grasping the situation, the growing divide between the Greineders and May's relatives was palpable. "You could feel a little bit of strain, and by the time the actual funeral came around you could feel some sort of division," she recalled. "There was anger from my family in there, and I think a lot of that anger may have come from the way Dirk and his kids were handling this."

# 11

RETURNING HOME TO MANHATTAN after May's funeral on Monday, November 8, Belinda Markel felt something was seriously wrong. The week following May's murder had been a long blur of one devastating shock after another, but back home, she was able to step back and reflect on the bizarre happenings in Wellesley.

Far from convinced that Dirk had killed May, Belinda found herself beginning to doubt her uncle nonetheless. "After the funeral, that's when I started to allow some of those thoughts to go through," she said. "This dominated our lives and our conversations as we started to calm down and back away from it. This was an emotional assault, never mind the loss. Going through the tension of being up there in Wellesley and being in the house and out of the house, there were things that we were learning that didn't sit right. So you sit there and start to review all this, and it took a while for everything to become clear."

Dr. Greineder's insistence that a second autopsy be performed "really bothered" Belinda. Even more disturbing was the Greineder family's pact not to cooperate with the police. Her cousins had been subpoenaed to appear that week before the Norfolk County Grand Jury and Belinda "couldn't believe it" when she found out that her uncle and his attorney, Marty Murphy, were going to send a lawyer with May's children. She was even more surprised to learn that Murphy wanted her cousins "prepped" before they testified.

"I said to Dirk, 'I can't imagine why you would need to do that,' but he said, 'Well, they're not used to doing things like this like you are and they would just be more comfortable.'" Her uncle was overly worried about what his daughter Britt might say before the grand jury, which was already hearing testimony from the first emergency responders who went to Morses Pond on Halloween morning. Belinda said that her uncle told her Britt "was a nervous wreck and he had given her medication. She had taken Xanax in the past, and they were trying to get her back on it," Belinda said.

Anytime Belinda questioned Dr. Greineder about his actions, he always turned it around and railed about how he was the one who was being persecuted by the police. "It was always, 'Those sons of bitches,' and 'They're coming after me' and 'they screwed up my van,'" said Belinda. "He didn't want to leave the house and he was upset his colleagues had cancelled one of his lecturing trips."

She got the same response from her cousins. "They were really angry that they were being put through this," Belinda said. "They were very guarded in what they were going to say to the grand jury, which at that time didn't make any sense to me."

With each passing day and more telephone conversations with her uncle and cousins, Belinda slowly began to doubt her uncle's innocence. "I knew something wasn't right," she said. "Something didn't make sense, but I wasn't at the point to say, 'Wow, Dirk did this.'"

Belinda gradually realized he was only telling her what he wanted her to know. She had her husband, Greg, call Marty Foley and then prosecutor Rick Grundy to find out how things were going. "I was looking to see if they were proceeding on this," she said. "I felt like Dirk was only keeping me updated on what he wanted me to know."

Foley and Grundy spoke to Greg Markel only in general terms about their investigation, careful not to tell the attorney that his wife's uncle was the only suspect. Belinda found herself on the Internet every day checking the Boston newspapers for any news of the investigation. "I was trying to find out what was going on," she said. "Somebody had murdered my aunt, and I wanted to make sure somebody was looking for that somebody. I'm not from the area. I didn't have any reason to have faith in the Wellesley Police Department or the State Police or whatever. I didn't know who was involved and who was doing what."

In keeping in daily contact with the Greineders, Belinda had a more caring motive. "I was keeping in touch because I was concerned about their well-being," she said. "I was putting myself out there as a sounding board for Dirk, and I was trying to be helpful. I still had personal affection for him."

Although Belinda Markel had no way to know it then, there was an intensive effort underway to expose her uncle as the man who had killed her aunt. Nearly two dozen talented, highly trained, and dedicated investigators were still working nearly around the clock to conclusively link Dr. Greineder to his hideous crime. Foley's days during the second week of the investigation were filled with trips to the crime lab and "gearing up for the grand jury," but there was another important issue facing the prosecution team. They had reached the conclusion that a second, far broader search had to be made of Dr. Greineder's home.

With the hammer used in May's killing firmly in evidence, Foley wanted to see if he could match it to tool mark impressions at 56 Cleveland Road, particularly to landscaping railroad ties a contractor working at the home had talked about. Also, Dermot Moriarty's visit to the Dedham Hilton indicated Dr. Greineder might be having an extramarital affair, of which another search might provide further evidence.

Most importantly, Foley wanted to seize his computers. The detectives had been told by some of the contractors working at the home that Dr. Greineder did his banking online. Foley was still hoping to connect his suspect to the weapons and strange items found at the crime scene.

Before applying for the second search warrant, Foley had to add three pages of new information to his original affidavit. Noticing the typo that indicated he had been assigned to the Norfolk DA for fourteen years, Foley corrected the paragraph to read, "I am presently assigned to the Norfolk County District Attorney's Office as a criminal investigator. I have been an investigator for the State Police for the last 14 years." But the damage of the original affidavit had already been done and would be used later by the doctor in an attempt to discredit Foley and have the search warrants invalidated.

As he had the night of May Greineder's murder, Assistant Dedham District Court Clerk Phil McCue carefully read through Foley's application for a second search warrant, finally signing the paperwork late on the afternoon of Friday, November 12, 1999.

Gathering again at the Wellesley Police Station, the State and Wellesley detectives discussed their respective assignments then clambered into unmarked cruisers for the short ride to Cleveland Road. This time, their search would yield a much more incriminating collection of evidence after Foley knocked on the doctor's front door just before 6 P.M.

With the familiar response of frantic barking from the two German shepherds, Dr. Greineder pulled opened the door, staring expressionless at the dozen police officers standing on his porch. "Marty, what's going on?" he asked, pushing open the storm door. "We have another search warrant, and we're going to be doing an extensive search of the house," Foley replied evenly. "I'd ask that no one touch anything while we are here."

Dr. Greineder, now almost conditioned to securing his dogs for a search of his residence, turned toward their continued barking, but Foley stopped him. Slightly amused by his suspect's practiced response, Foley did not want the shepherds put in their pen in the rear yard as they had been during the two previous police visits to the home. "Dirk, can you put them in the garage?" the detective asked politely. "We have some work we have to do outside." Dr. Greineder complied, but Foley could tell he was aggravated, especially when the dogs increased the fervor of their barking, frantically scratching at the garage doors.

Foley turned to follow Chief Terry Cunningham and State Police Lt. Richard Lauria out the kitchen door to check for tool marks in the back-yard, then saw an increasingly angry Kirsten Greineder pursue Cunningham outside. When the detectives had first entered the house she had been almost pleasant but quickly changed her demeanor when she realized the police posse was there to search the house again.

"How dare you!" she screeched at Cunningham and his brother Wayne, who had followed the group outside. "You have no right to be here again."

Going over the events of the first search warrant, Foley had realized the November 1 examination of Dr. Greineder's home had not been as thorough as it could have been. Hampered by the early morning execution of the warrant while fatigued and hungry from having worked nonstop for sixteen hours, the police had overlooked several things.

They had only made a cursory search outside the house, and Foley was determined this time to scour the entire property. Prosecutor Rick Grundy, who was rushing home from Delaware in the hours after May's murder, was there for the second search but sat alone in his car while the officers secured the dwelling.

Kirsten calmed down some but continued to mock the police for targeting her father and harassing their family. Watching the police size up the elaborate doghouse in the back yard, Kirsten loudly boasted to Terry Cunningham how her father had built the custom structure with its surrounding chain-link fence.

Foley watched as the irate woman demonstrated how her father had put hinges on the doghouse roof so it could be lifted for easy cleaning. "It opens right here," she said smugly, swinging the top open with Cunningham's help to proudly show how talented her father was.

Foley saw the police chief's eyes grow wide before narrowing to meet Foley's gaze with a look that told the detective that Cunningham had seen something. Casually moving to the corner of the doghouse where Cunningham was standing, Foley looked in with a rush of excitement. Resting there on a frame made of two-by-fours was a pair of brown work gloves that looked identical to the ones found at Morses Pond. Foley and Cunningham didn't speak or react to the find until Dermot Moriarty was able to shoo Kirsten back into the house.

Illuminating the gloves with their flashlights, the two detectives realized Dr. Greineder's daughter had unwittingly led them to a major discovery. Cunningham did not move from the side of the doghouse until the gloves were photographed and recovered. Dr. Greineder had obviously tucked them up under the hinged roof so they would be handy whenever he cleaned the doghouse, but their uncovering would be a long-standing topic of debate among the investigators.

"I say if Kirsten doesn't open that doghouse roof, we don't find the gloves," said Foley, who was in agreement with the Cunningham brothers. "Rick Grundy says we would have found them, but how would you have known that it opened?" The investigators surely would have looked inside the large wooden structure but it is doubtful they would have reached back up under the doghouse entrance to feel across the top of the frame. "Kirsten was trying to tell us how smart her father was, and she led us right to the gloves," said Foley. "It was a huge break for us."

The police had been at the home for less than twenty minutes, already collecting a damning piece of evidence, but there was much more work to be done. Turning to the railroad ties, Foley was disappointed that Lt. Lauria, an expert on tool impressions, had not found any marks.

Terry and Wayne Cunningham fought back grins when a "whiney" Dr. Greineder told them his private office could not be searched because it contained his medical research, arguing his patients' privacy would be violated. To Wayne Cunningham, the "sniveling" Dr. Greineder seemed to be more than just inconvenienced. It was almost as if he thought the police could not come back after the November 1 search. "I think he thought once he got past the first search warrant that we weren't going to take another run at him," the Wellesley detective recalled.

The brothers assured Dr. Greineder that patient privacy would be respected but their warrant allowed them to search anywhere on the property. Terry Cunningham, having enough of the doctor's objections, suggested it would probably be best if he left with his children until the search was over. In a repeat of the November 1 search, the Greineders eventually went across the street to the Ganses' house, where Dr. Greineder tried to reach Marty Murphy.

While the November 1 search had gone almost undetected, word of the Friday night return by the police pinballed around the Boston newsrooms. The investigators inside the house soon realized that the media had gathered outside, but no one ventured to make a comment.

Marty Foley went to the basement laundry room to look over Dr.

Greineder's work area again. Seeing that many of the things hanging neatly around the workbench bore price tags from Diehl's hardware, Foley had everything photographed. He collected a receipt on the workbench from the store dated September 3, 1999, for a $6.76 cash purchase of six small packages of nails. Putting the small slip of paper into an evidence bag, Foley had no idea what impact the store receipt would have months later.

All the computers and accessories in the house were collected and set aside to be taken to the police station. Opening Dr. Greineder's monthly planner in his office, Foley narrowed on the square for June 2, bearing a handwritten notation reading "Hilton." Foley instantly recognized the date as being the day Dr. Greineder's American Express card had rented a room at the Dedham Hilton, and now here it was in his own date book.

Silently considering the implications of the Hilton reference, the detective was more convinced that whatever happened in that hotel room might tell him why May was killed. Foley slipped the monthly planner into an evidence bag, wondering if Dr. Greineder could offer an innocent reason for being at the hotel that day or had boldly noted an extramarital tryst. It wouldn't be long before he found out.

In the Greineder kitchen anything containing plastic food bags was removed from the pantry and confiscated. Foley had still not been informed about the discovery of the white plastic kitchen bag tucked under the fallen tree branch at the crime scene, so no effort was made to try to connect it to Dr. Greineder's house. An oversight that still angers Foley today, it was an error the investigators would never be able to correct. "I didn't think to have those types of bags seized from the house," Foley said with frustration. "Sure enough, they were there. It was one of those things. We screwed up."

It turned out that some of the detectives who searched the home remembered seeing the white trash bags, Trooper Bobby Chan even managing to photograph some of them. But the failure to seize the trash bags would block an opportunity to test later for a conclusive link between the bag from Morses Pond and the ones in the Greineder home. Fortunately, the same mistake had not been made with the clear plastic food storage bags.

Satisfied that the house had been thoroughly searched inside and out, the detectives were ready to finish with the two-door garage. They started with the beige Toyota Avalon parked in the right-hand bay, where they immediately spotted what looked like blood on the front passenger seat. Backing away from the vehicle, Foley got on his cell phone, making a call to headquarters to have the on-call chemist dispatched to Wellesley.

The Avalon had been searched on November 1, but no one had seen a crescent-shaped stain on the front edge of the leather seat. To Foley, it looked like the blood had dripped there, probably from someone having a nosebleed, with the blood falling between the person's legs. The investigators now stayed clear of the car until chemist Richard Iwanicki arrived. Iwanicki did a presumptive test for blood, which was positive, making it almost certain the seat was stained with blood. A close examination of the car led to the discovery of several small blood droplets on the console between the two front seats and a small bloodstain on an umbrella on the back seat.

Foley wanted the front passenger seat completely removed, as he had done with the filler pipe and gas tank on the doctor's Plymouth van for a stain that ended up not being blood. In trying to access the stain from the doctor's van so it could be tested, Foley had ordered a mechanic using an acetylene torch to cut the pipe away from the gas tank. Dr. Greineder was nearly apoplectic, and later ranted to Belinda Markel about how the police had wrecked his van, forcing him to pay hundreds of dollars to fix it. Perhaps with that in mind, Rick Grundy, in what Wayne Cunningham would later comically describe as a "weak moment," decided that swabbing the stain instead of removing the seat in the Avalon would be sufficient.

Jill McDermott had been wracking her brain wondering if she had missed the bloodstain on the Avalon seat during the November 1 search. The mystery would linger when it was later determined the blood had been left by two contributors with May Greineder being the majority donor. Now pushing 11 P.M. with the unexpected delay of having to wait for the chemist, the detectives turned their efforts to checking the rest of the garage where McDermott began emptying the contents of a rubbish barrel standing between the two parking spots.

As she reached the bottom, her heart began racing when she saw a label for an E-Z Foil loaf pan along with the clear plastic wrapping used to seal two pans together. Her exhilaration spread to the other detectives now huddled over the trash barrel, but just as quickly, their euphoria crashed when McDermott pulled out a Roche Bros. receipt dated November 8, 1999, that showed a $3.39 purchase for foil pans. Purchased eight days after the murder, there was no way to connect the packaging to the loaf pan found at Morses Pond. "I was like, 'Oh my God, a Roche Bros. receipt,'" recalled McDermott. "When I saw the date and realized it was November eight, I felt pretty small."

Foley tried to channel his disappointment by thinking through the discovery. For one thing, no sign of the small metal pans listed on the receipt had been found in the house, and at the very least it showed the Greineders had a history of using them. "It is what it is, but those pans were not in the house," he said. "What are we proving here? We're proving that at least they use these pans. They're buying them. They are not in the house and the receipt is dated eight days after the murder."

With the passing of the eleven o'clock news, most of the media had retreated from the street in front of the house, but the search of the garage was still going as the clock approached midnight.

"Have we done everything?" Foley asked hopefully, aware that the garage had been previously searched on November 1. "The only thing left is the boxes," said Wayne Cunningham, pointing to the back of the garage where cardboard boxes of varying sizes were piled chest-high across the wall. The detectives briefly debated whether the large pile was worth a second look but decided it had to be examined again.

Cunningham began taking the boxes down one by one, checking their contents. Grabbing one marked "Misc. hdw (braces and hinges)," he couldn't believe his eyes when he lifted up the cardboard flaps that formed its top and saw a bright blue box of Trojan condoms. "Hey, what's this," he announced excitedly as he placed the box on the hood of the Avalon. Rummaging through the cardboard container, Cunningham pulled out two prescription bottles, even more surprised when he read the labels. The first was from CVS Pharmacy dated April 30, 1998, for ten 50 mg doses of Viagra. The second prescription was filled on June 2, 1999, for twelve 100 mg doses of Viagra. Both containers of the erection-enhancing drugs had been prescribed by "Dr. Greineder for Dirk Greineder."

"He's prescribing Viagra to himself," Cunningham chortled, the significance of the items already apparent to the others gathered around him. "It looks like the millennium love kit," Cunningham joked, his glee infecting the other weary investigators, prompting other one-liners and guffaws.

Foley's fatigue was erased with a rush of adrenaline as he laughed with the others. June 2 was the same day Dr. Greineder had rented a room at the Dedham Hilton with a corresponding notation in his monthly planner. The doctor had told the trooper the day of the murder that he had not had sex with his wife for several years, but with condoms and self-prescribed Viagra hidden in his garage, it was clear Dr. Greineder was having sex with someone.

Opening the prescription bottles, Cunningham found only three pills in the one dated April 30, 1998, while the other container from June 2 held eight and a half tablets. The twelve-pack of Trojans was open, missing one condom. Setting the condoms and prescription bottles aside, the detectives delved further into the box, the joking commencing in earnest with the removal of the rest of the contents.

Cunningham pulled out a plastic bag marked "Eaton Apothecary," containing two AA batteries, six sterile cotton-tip applicators, and a knotted nylon rope that drew a string of bawdy comments. The Wellesley lieutenant lifted out a piece of Velcro, then a marble, then a small circular brush with a wire handle. "What was he doing with that?" said one investigator eyeing the sharp metal bristles encircling the top of the wire. "Never mind that. What was he doing with the marble?" laughed another detective.

Reaching into the bottom, Cunningham removed the remaining contents of the box; a tube of toothpaste and toothbrush, several screws, and a Diehl's hardware sticker marked $1.89. Once the snickering died down, the investigators did not have to verbalize the implication of the find. "Here's a guy who says he hasn't had sex with his wife for a couple of years, and here's Viagra, condoms, and other bizarre stuff stashed in his garage. We felt it was important," said Foley. "It proved that he was out there doing something with somebody and there was more to this."

Looking around the house one last time just before 1 A.M. Foley was finally satisfied that everything they had wanted to accomplish was done. Where the November 1 search had yielded literally several handfuls of evidence, Foley would list thirty-eight items on his return for the November 12 search warrant, including a large pile of computer equipment.

# 12

WALKING INTO THE WELLESLEY DETECTIVE OFFICE late in the day on Saturday, November 13, Trooper Marty Foley saw Lt. Wayne Cunningham sitting in his office wearing what Foley could only describe as "a shit-eating grin."

"Marty, what was that number again?" Cunningham playfully asked; a copy of the *Boston Phoenix* spread out on his desk. Foley recited the 781–614–3040 number effortlessly, having memorized the telephone number Dr. Greineder called on June 3 and again the day before and the day after his wife's murder. "I found it," said the beaming Cunningham, already sure about his startling discovery before Foley's confirming response. There in the Adult Services section of the November 5, 1999, edition of the weekly alternative newspaper was an advertisement for the Casual Elegance escort service.

Reading the text in the ad, Foley was now all but certain Dr. Greineder had met a prostitute at the Dedham Hilton the previous June 2. "What lies beneath your distinguished exterior would spoil your desire by sensual massage or romantic moments," Foley read. "Very selective 40-year-old possessing taste, refinement, sensitivity. I'll call. Advanced verified appointment. 781–614–3040."

Foley's recollection that the 614 prefix was connected to a pager had paid immense dividends. Now the investigators had to capitalize on it by finding out who placed the ad. "What got us there was it was a pager," said Cunningham. "We [thought it was] an escort. We sent a cruiser down to buy a *Phoenix* and bring it back [to] look in the personals."

Cunningham had been scanning the dozens of sex-related ads in the tabloid newspaper for just ten minutes when he excitedly announced, "Holy shit! I found it." Their initial calls to Casual Elegance with blocked caller identification were not returned. A more concerted effort would be undertaken a little over a week later.

The Friday-night search of Dr. Greineder's home was broadly reported by the Boston media but in New York City, Belinda Markel was unaware police had returned to her uncle's house until she saw *Boston Globe* and *Boston Herald* articles several days later on the Internet. Her surprise quickly turned to anger as she dialed her uncle's telephone number to confront him. "I didn't want it to upset you," Dr. Greineder said defensively. "This is getting embarrassing."

Her uncle's weak reasoning only stoked Belinda's displeasure. "I have to read about this in the paper?" she fired back, the edge in her voice further betraying her fury. "I was pissed," Belinda recalled. "I don't know why it really irritated me as much as it did, but I told him. He didn't have any good reasons for not telling me."

Dr. Greineder had been anxious to get back to work, but had stayed home for a second week to meet with Marty Murphy and gather money for his defense. He would not be surprised if "the bastards" arrested him, he told his niece.

He "never talked about May," Belinda recalled. "Everything was about Dirk. He never said he missed her or how hard it was. He talked about his traveling, how he has to get back to work, he has his research. He went on about how it was impossible for his kids to go anywhere because people were staring at them and he was getting paranoid. He was really interested in just getting on with his life. It was like staying home that second week was an obligation."

As the days rolled toward Thanksgiving, Dr. Greineder returned to his practice and the lecture circuit, but the weight of the police probe began to show. On a business trip to Michigan, he made the first of many "paranoid, rambling calls" to Belinda, convinced he was being followed. "We're at the airport," he told her. "My speech was great but I know I am being followed. I can feel it," he said fearfully.

"Calm down. They're not going to follow you to Michigan," Belinda said, wondering if her uncle had gone "cuckoo." The more Dr. Greineder droned on, the more Belinda found herself trying to analyze his words. He never denied killing May, but Belinda purposely did not ask him.

"I thought about it, and at some point I probably would have been able to, but I realized I needed to keep listening to all these things that were going on," she reflected. "I was the only one who was getting any kind of information, and I wasn't sure why I needed it but it just made sense to leave that line open. If I had confronted him, he would have stopped talking to me. Through this whole thing Dirk thought he was manipulating me. If I changed that, then I wouldn't know anything that was going on. He would have realized he had lost control."

The doctor could not control the police investigation, but whoever had placed the Casual Elegance ad in the *Boston Phoenix* turned out to be elusive prey. The detectives had tried to make contact with the woman, but apparently because she was unable to verify the numbers that appeared on her pager, she never called back. "We felt she was going to be important to be on our side," said Marty Foley. "This woman was cunning . . . and it wasn't going to be as easy as we had hoped, so we had to put some effort into locating her."

Frustrated with not being able to contact the escort, Foley enlisted the help of Trooper Timothy J. Curtin, an undercover drug investigator who had access to a safe house with a telephone number paid under a fictitious name. Late on the afternoon of Monday, November 22, Curtin dialed the number to Casual Elegance. A recorded message from "Elizabeth" instructed him to leave his name and number with a promise she would call back up until 10 P.M.

Within an hour, Curtin's phone rang. "Hi, is this Tim?" the female caller asked. "Yes, it is," Curtin responded. "I'm calling about the Casual Elegance ad in the Phoenix. Is that your ad?"

"Yes it is," Elizabeth replied. "Are you interested?" she asked. "I'm interested, but can you tell me a little about yourself?" Curtin said. "I'm forty-three," she said. "I have short hair, a medium build and height, a good-sized chest and I'm pretty but not a knock out," she described.

"That's good because I'm looking for an older woman like yourself," said Curtin. "Do you work alone? Are you going to be the person who meets me?" he asked.

"I work alone. I run my own operation," Elizabeth responded. "I have clients who are doctors and lawyers with nice cars, and some of them have been using me for several years," she boasted. "That's good because I'm not looking for a young woman," said Curtin. "Can we meet tomorrow night about eight o'clock?" he suggested.

"That's not a good time for me," she responded. "I usually work during the day between ten and two because I have a young child. How about noon in the Foxborough area, we could meet at the Days Inn or the Motel 6," she offered. "That sounds okay," said Curtin. "I'll make a reservation."

"I'll be driving a white Volvo wagon," the woman said. "I'll meet you at noon. Leave me a message in the morning to confirm you are going to be there," she instructed.

"I'll be there," Curtin said, "but I'll call to confirm anyway." Hanging up, Curtin dialed Marty Foley with the good news. With the parking lot under surveillance the next day, Curtin turned off the southbound side of Route One into the Super 8 motel right at noon. Parking in the middle of the mostly vacant parking lot, it was only a few minutes before a woman pulled up in a white Volvo.

Getting out of his car, Curtin walked up to the Volvo to speak to the prostitute and then signaled Foley and the others to move in after her price for sex was set.

Getting out of two unmarked cruisers, Foley approached the woman with Jill McDermott, Kevin Shea, Gerry Mattaliano, and Dermot Moriarty and introduced himself to the petrified woman. "She was a basket case," Foley recalled.

"Elizabeth" was forty-three-old Deborah Herrera. Facing the prospect of turning her eleven-year-old daughter's sheltered life upside down with a prostitution arrest, she readily agreed to Foley's offer to talk at the nearby State Police barracks in Foxborough as long as she could leave to pick up her daughter after school. With the frightened hooker in the back of his cruiser with McDermott, Foley drove to the barracks and got Herrera settled in a conference room, where the detectives gathered around her.

"We're investigating a homicide that took place on Halloween," Foley began softly, trying to put the shaken woman at ease. "We're not aware of any direct involvement by you, but we know about several calls made by the husband of the murdered woman to your number. We think you're running a call-girl operation, which is against the law," Foley continued a shade more sternly. "We found your telephone number in the classified section of the *Phoenix*."

"Should I call my lawyer?" Herrera meekly asked, still believing she was about to be arrested. "We want to talk to you about the murdered woman's husband," replied Foley. "We need your cooperation in the homicide investigation and we would report that cooperation to the district attorney. I can't make any promises, but your cooperation could help you," Foley offered.

The trooper didn't particularly enjoy pressuring Herrera, but she had created her own problem. Foley knew he had to tread carefully with the woman, who lived with her daughter in the upscale town where she was being interviewed. The single mother was deeply fearful for her daughter, who attended the local middle school and took expensive horse riding and ballet lessons.

"She was another fragile soul," said Foley. "We had to handle her with kid gloves because we wanted to get her in front of the grand jury," he explained. "She was really concerned that this would leak out to the local papers and really concerned that her subsidized housing would be taken away because she was making too much money. She was worried her daughter would find out."

Foley tried to assure Herrera the police were more interested in their murder case than busting her for prostitution. "We're more concerned about a customer of yours named Dirk," he said soothingly. "I know who Dirk is," Herrera quickly replied. "He was strange and he had low self-esteem."

She told the detectives she had been self-employed as an escort for two-and-a-half years when she was contacted in early June by a man named Dirk who had seen her advertisement. She never returned calls that would not display on her caller identification or respond to cell phones or payphones, confirming Foley's theory on why their initial attempt to draw out Herrera had failed. She had verified Dr. Greineder's call, however, agreeing to meet him.

"He left a message to return his call and use the name Elizabeth," she said. "I called the number and a woman answered at Harvard Pilgrim Health and I told her I was Elizabeth calling for Dirk. He told me that we needed to be very discreet because he was a doctor and very prominent in the medical profession."

Dirk told Herrera he would meet her in the foyer of the Hilton Hotel in Dedham but she suggested he give her a room number so she could go there directly. "He said that he would rather meet in the foyer," the escort remembered. "That way, I could see him and make sure [in case] I didn't like what I saw. He wanted to make sure he was acceptable to me." There was a discussion about what they would be wearing so they could recognize each other. Herrera said she found the initial conversation odd. "I was amazed a doctor would have such low self-esteem and want to be accepted by someone like me."

When Herrera walked into the hotel through the revolving front door, Dirk was sitting on a couch just inside distinguishably dressed. He seemed awkward and uncomfortable, concerned about Herrera's approval. They went to the room, and the doctor offered her champagne from a bucket of ice. Herrera declined, telling her customer she didn't drink. Dirk left the bubbly unopened and they talked for about thirty minutes until he seemed "to grow more comfortable with himself and me. He told me about another woman he had been seeing named Elizabeth," she continued. Foley took a keen interest in this mention of another person. "He said she was a high-class social escort that he and other doctors and lawyers used, but she moved away and that was why he called me."

Dirk told Herrera he was married. "He had children and loved his wife," she said, "but there was no intimacy between him and his wife." The escort gave her client a condom and they began having sex. "Dirk wasn't kinky or vulgar," she recounted; "he seemed pretty normal."

That is, until he wanted to perform oral sex on her. "I told him it wasn't a good idea, and we talked about Hepatitis A and Hepatitis B, but he still wanted to do it. He told me I looked safe," she said. After their awkward tryst, Dirk thanked Herrera, paying her in cash. "He told me he wanted to see me again and he left a message on my answering service the next day thanking me," she said. "I didn't hear from him again until the end of the summer or early fall. He left me his car phone number and told me to call him back. He said to be careful when I called because one of his children might be with him."

When Herrera reached Dirk in his car, he again was "antsy. He sounded confused and indecisive," she said. "I told him he sounded down and confused and maybe meeting with an escort wasn't the best thing for him right now until he found peace within himself. I told him maybe he should read a book or take a walk on the beach, but I would be available if he needed me."

Herrera would hear from Dirk one last time, she told the rapt detectives. "He left me a message and said he was sorry, but he didn't want me to call him anymore because he couldn't see me," she said. "He said now wasn't the time and that if he needed to see me in the future he would call me. I was kind of upset about what he was saying in these messages, and I talked to a friend of mine about it."

The prostitute never learned Dirk's last name, she said, and didn't know about his wife's murder. If Dirk called her the day before Halloween or again the day after, he didn't leave a message, Herrera told Foley.

The sting to enlist her cooperation had gone as perfectly as Foley had hoped. Before driving away in her Volvo to pick up her daughter, Herrera agreed to testify before the grand jury. "She had made direct contact with him and made direct contact with him recently," said Foley. "That was the most important thing, but she also let us know that there was another person in Dirk's life that he was very close with by the name of Elizabeth. So we knew there were others."

Foley knew he had to somehow find the mysterious Elizabeth the doctor had mentioned to Herrera. She had obviously left an impression on the straying husband, apparently to the point where he had instructed Herrera to call herself Elizabeth. One thing was for certain, Foley thought, tracking down Elizabeth was going to be much more difficult than finding Deborah Herrera.

AS SHE BOARDED A CRUISE SHIP in Fort Lauderdale, Florida, on Sunday, November 21, Belinda Markel knew it was going to be another melancholy Thanksgiving. It had been just before Thanksgiving the previous year that her grandmother had suffered a stroke, commencing the eight-week illness that culminated with her passing. As soon as the family had returned from

May's distressing private funeral, Murray Stark had booked the holiday cruise, looking for a tonic to help ease their grief.

While May's death remained heavy on the hearts of the Markels and Starks, it was the suspicion swirling around Dr. Greineder that dominated their conversations. Belinda and her mother also knew they had a thorny situation to navigate when they returned to New York. With her husband, Greg, acting as an intermediary, Belinda and Ilse had agreed to meet with Trooper Marty Foley and Detective Jill McDermott. The scheduled interview had caused further friction between Belinda and her uncle.

"We knew at that point that we were going to meet with the police, and there was some anxiety about that," she said. "It caused a lot of family arguments. There was anxiety because we didn't know what to expect."

As the cruise wore on, the conversations escalated, with Belinda and her mother slowly coming to the conclusion already reached by their husbands that Dirk had likely killed May. Docking in San Juan on Thanksgiving Day, the two women finally vocalized their revelations while taking a launch to shore with their husbands. "As we're sitting there, this conversation is going on between Greg, my father, and sort of my mother and myself about how the evidence is really mounting and clearly he must have been the one who did it," Belinda recalled.

While the highly regarded corporate attorney and street-smart businessman were all but convinced, Belinda was still holding out slight hope that her uncle had somehow been wrongly accused. Dr. Greineder had talked incessantly about DNA and how the police did not have his, but his claim had waned in subsequent phone conversations. "Even at that point, I'd have to say I was 85 percent convinced that he did it," Belinda estimated. Returning to Fort Lauderdale on Sunday, November 28, Belinda now had another burden on her mind, in addition to her concern with getting her bereaved children back on track with their studies and daily routines.

With the evolving belief that Dirk had killed May, Belinda and Ilse had to be careful in future conversations with their murderous relative, she decided. "By the time we got back, we both knew there was a good possibility that something was wrong and we also had sensed that we were being shut out a little bit more by Dirk and the kids," said Belinda. "I was aware at that point that Dirk was feeding me what he wanted to feed me. When we got back from the cruise, I was almost there with the belief that he had killed May."

Boarding a flight to Baltimore the day after Belinda's return from Florida, Marty Foley had no doubts he had found the man responsible for May's killing. Carrying the first samples to be tested at Cellmark Diagnostics, Foley was hoping the DNA testing would leave irrefutable proof that Dr. Greineder had committed the most reviled form of domestic violence. Chemist Gwen Pino had prepared two swabs from both the hammer and knife, two cuttings from the right-hand brown work glove and three from the left, a sample of May's blood to determine her genetic profile and several of Dr. Greineder's fingernail clippings to identify his.

This "world-renowned doctor" had told anyone who would listen that the police did not have his DNA, but he was badly mistaken in his belief that fingernails would not yield a genetic profile. He was sure to regret granting Foley's last-minute request for his nail clippings the day of the murder.

Foley was also hoping the doctor's computers would help expose his diabolical plot. Meeting with Trooper David McSweeney at the attorney general's office in Boston the day after returning from Maryland, Foley intently listened as the computer investigator outlined how he had started his search of the seized equipment.

Using forensic computers loaded with software called EnCase; McSweeney had first acquired the contents of the seized hard drives by physically removing and downloading them to the forensic system. Creating an evidence file without compromising Dr. Greineder's computers, McSweeney returned the hard drives to the seized equipment before storing it in evidence. The EnCase software allowed the high-tech investigator to copy the information from Dr. Greineder's computers in the precise form in which it was seized.

Once everything was copied and audited, McSweeney could begin searching information by entering key words or phrases the investigators had provided. Using words like *hammer, knife, gloves,* and *nylon rope,* a match would reveal the sentence before and after the word, the investigators having to decide whether the displayed information was relevant. It was impractical to print out all the data because Dr. Greineder's 2.4-gigabyte tower computer would have generated a stack of paper a little more than half the height of the Washington Monument.

McSweeney had started with Dr. Greineder's tower computer on November 17, using the keywords *Estwing, Old Timer, Diehl, Diehl hammer, Diehl gloves, Depot* and *nylon*. "We were actually looking for a laundry list of everything that he had purchased," said Foley.

Later that day, Foley linked up with Jill McDermott for a visit to a motel in Newton where an American Express Corporate account the doctor had opened in the name of "Corporate Physicians" showed a charge from June 8, 1999, his thirty-first wedding anniversary.

Almost simultaneously, Sgt. Dermot Moriarty had gone to the Crowne Plaza in Natick where Belinda's family had stayed during the terrible days after May's murder. The doctor's credit card had rented a room there on February 3, 1998, and the office manager told Moriarty that two telephone calls had been made to the same number from the room. Dr. Greineder had checked in at 1:40 P.M. and left at 4:23 P.M., signing an express checkout receipt for $60.09. Contacting the phone company about the two calls made from the hotel room, Moriarty learned the listing last belonged to a Gilbert Perito doing business as Commonwealth Entertainment.

The doctor's receipts also showing that flowers had been purchased the same day at a florist in Newton, it seemed obvious to the detectives that they were probably given to whoever met him from Commonwealth Entertainment, which had to be an escort service.

The doctor's Am-Ex statements also showed a $212.53 charge at the plush Westin Copley hotel in Boston on February 10, 1998, a week after the Crowne Plaza rental. Another suspicion-raising charge was to People-2People, an Internet dating service catering to nearly two million Boston-area customers.

At the Suisse Chalet motel in Newton, Foley and McDermott spoke to desk clerk Karen Jarvis, who had an engaging sense of humor but no idea how she could find Dr. Greineder's June 8 receipt for the two detectives. The records were locked up in a room upstairs, Jarvis explained, offering Foley the key if he wanted to look himself. "She was funny," recalled Foley. "She gave us the keys and said, 'Go ahead, look.'"

Unlocking the door, the detectives found themselves "in the bowels of this shitty old ragtime hotel," Foley remembered with a laugh. With his background as a white-collar-crime investigator, he was used to dealing with sales receipts and quickly found that the motel's had been stored by month.

"Jill and I looked through the receipts until we found it," he said. Scrutinizing the American Express receipt from June 8, the only imprinted personal information was Dr. Greineder's address for 56 Cleveland Road. It had been signed by a Dr. Thomas Young.

"Who is Thomas Young?" Foley wondered aloud to his partner. Possibly Dr. Greineder just signed the receipt with an assumed name, Foley considered. Or was Dr. Thomas Young real? Thinking back to the day of the murder, when Dr. Greineder signed the consent form, Foley planned to have a handwriting expert examine the two signatures to evaluate whether Dr. Thomas Young's came from his suspect's hand.

In the meantime, they would search for anybody named Tom Young. "We checked every Thomas Young in Massachusetts, every doctor, and nothing came up," Foley said. "That was an unanswered question. Who was Thomas Young?"

Driving to New York City with Jill McDermott on December 1, 1999, to meet with Dr. Greineder's niece and sister-in-law, Foley had been apprehensive. But he was surprised to find Belinda Markel waiting alone, without her attorney husband or other lawyers, and with a friendly plate of cookies on her kitchen counter. "I could tell right away that it wasn't going to be confrontational," he remembered, still wondering if Belinda somehow knew he loved cookies.

Before leaving Massachusetts early that morning for the 1 P.M. meeting, Foley had grown weary of the varying, mostly unsolicited advice he had been given about how to approach May Greineder's niece and sister. District Attorney Bill Keating had warned him to be careful about what he told the women, fearful that, like the doctor's defiant children, they were not going to cooperate and then would pass confidential information to him. Others had expressed similar views, but talking it over with prosecutor Rick Grundy, they both agreed Foley should "play it by ear."

"We were counseled by people who didn't know what they were talking about on what to say, what not to say," said Foley. "I thought that in order for us to get information we would have to give information, and I was willing to give limited information. I was willing to blow it off as well if I didn't think it was going well. We still didn't know May, and we wanted to talk to the people in her family. We wanted to know what was going on before the murder, and we didn't have that information."

But it was not so much information that Foley was seeking as just a sense of how Belinda and Ilse viewed the police investigation. It was unquestionably clear that they would not have the support of Dr. Greineder's children when they put the case before a jury. Foley wanted to know if they could expect the same from May's relatives.

The two detectives were met by a doorman at the entrance to their highrise. Foley's impression that Belinda and Ilse were not average city-dwellers was confirmed by the luxury of their building. "You have to understand," he explained. "You go to Midtown Manhattan on the East River. There's a doorman. There's a security man. There's an elevator man. They all knew Belinda. They all knew we were coming.... These people did not fall off the cabbage truck. They know what's going on. They are obviously successful."

Knocking on the door to Belinda's apartment, Foley may have been nervous but he remained focused. "I was not intimidated, but I went in there knowing there was not going to be a lot of fluff. I think both Belinda and I thought about this meeting beforehand. I felt very confident if we got over that hurdle with the trust issue and gave out some information back and forth that we could develop something."

The detective had felt the same about Dr. Greineder's uncooperative children, but his optimism that they would eventually embrace the investigation never materialized. "I believed if I told Dr. Greineder's kids what I knew, I would have them understanding where I was coming from as well, but they wouldn't talk to us," he said.

Finding Belinda alone without legal representation put Foley immediately at ease. Although, Belinda had wrestled with having counsel there, she ultimately had decided against it. "I made a very conscious decision not to have Greg there or an attorney there," she said. "Greg and I went back and forth about that, basically argued about it, but I decided that I wanted this to be on a different level, and attorneys change things. I figured Marty was expecting to find somebody there, but I wanted to do this my way. I could always get a lawyer involved if I had to."

Sitting down in the family room off Belinda's kitchen, Foley asked about her cruise. Belinda found her stress disappearing with the pleasant detective's gentle demeanor. As Foley recollected the first time he had taken his wife, Cheryl, on a cruise, enlisting the help of his two sons to make it a surprise, Belinda realized how much she had in common with the soft-spoken detective who was trying to solve her aunt's murder. Her girls being the same age as Foley's sons, their shared experiences genuinely propelled their conversation beyond polite small talk, while McDermott quietly listened. Foley and Belinda also found quite a few differences between them. Where Belinda was an only child, Foley was one of seven children, his younger brother Timothy sadly having died when he was a baby.

Easing into the reason for the meeting, Belinda told the detectives she wanted to cooperate any way she could. "May and I had a very close relationship, and I want to help any way I can," she said, locking eyes with Foley. "I've spoken to Dirk, and he knows you're coming here to talk to me and my mother. He said he isn't surprised but I should be careful with you."

Taking notes only infrequently in order to visually engage Belinda while "taking everything in," Foley listened raptly as May's niece eloquently spoke about their special bond. They talked all the time, she explained, but May had grown progressively "preoccupied and tense and seemed more lonely than usual." May had complained about Dirk's long hours away from home resulting from his numerous travel commitments on top of the demanding responsibilities of his new promotion at Brigham and Women's Hospital.

"When I was there for a week last summer, he was gone early in the morning and home late at night. They were renovating the house, and that was distressful to May as well. May and Dirk did everything together, but he was not around to help her with the renovations," Belinda told the attentive detectives.

"Can you describe the relationship between May and Dirk?" Foley asked.

"They did everything together," Belinda said, confirming the description provided by others the detectives had spoken to. She then astutely anticipated Foley's next question: "Did May think there was another woman in Dirk's life? Yes, she did. May was never specific, but last spring she told me she thought there might be someone else in Dirk's life. Through various conversations, May indicated that they did not have a very good sex life. May had a lot of physical conditions that probably didn't help. She had a bad back and suffered from sinus infections, plus she was going through menopause."

Her aunt tried to be romantic with her uncle, Belinda said, but one candlelight dinner erupted into an argument, ruining the evening. "May and Dirk had their share of arguments, and May wasn't the type to let the argument just drop," Belinda explained. "She would keep on talking about it until the other person gave into her side. I would say their marriage has been strained for the last couple of years. I know May was trying to make things work for her and Dirk since the kids left home, but it didn't seem to be working."

Belinda said she had recently been on the receiving end of another of Dirk's "rambling" conversations in which he too indicated there might be someone else in his life. "He said there would be things that would come out that would be an embarrassment and upsetting to me and his children but it was irrelevant," she said. "He said the police were harassing people at work and that they were going after the weakest link — the single and divorced women."

Belinda had pressed her uncle about what he meant, but he had refused to elaborate. "He just said the police were investigating something that had no relevance to this case whatsoever but when it came out he wouldn't be proud of it and it would hurt me and hurt his children very much," Belinda said. Whatever it was, she added, "it was going to hurt this other person too. He was very angry. He kept saying, 'They have no right to do this.' I assumed he was talking about a mistress, but he wouldn't tell me."

"Would May ever divorce Dirk?" Foley asked. "May never discussed divorce with me," Belinda replied. "May had a perfect life. Her husband was a doctor and all her kids were successful, and I don't think May wanted to ruin her perfect life. I think even if Dirk wanted a divorce, May wouldn't give it to him."

Asked about the last time she saw May alive, Belinda told the detectives about her joyous visit to New York in September in which May had spent a fun-filled weekend with Belinda's family and her sister, Ilse. Struggling to check her emotion, Belinda recalled how she learned of May's death from her uncle after returning the phone message left by his daughter Britt. After making the long drive to Wellesley early the next morning, her uncle had first greeted her with a tight hug, his eyes moist with tears, but that would be the only time that week she saw him cry. She recited Dr. Greineder's account of what happened the day of the murder and told how she found it odd that he seemed certain that May had not been sexually assaulted.

Foley was slightly amused to hear Dr. Greineder's complaints about being taken to the police station, where the "police took his clothes and took pictures of him. He was concerned about black and blue marks on his arm," Belinda said, demonstrating with her fingertips pressed to her right biceps. "He was worried they were going to show up in the pictures."

Belinda had also seen scratches on her uncle's neck, which he said had come from shaving, but he had also mentioned having a scratch on his chest. "He didn't show it to me," Belinda said, "but he told me he didn't know how he got it." Foley was interested to learn that two days after the murder, Dr. Greineder was already focused on getting a lawyer and Greg Markel had made the trip to Boston to assist in the selection process.

Belinda was still puzzled by a number of statements her uncle had made, recounting the many strange concerns he had voiced about being inno-cently linked to the murder. Her account of her uncle's nosebleed story and mention of a bloodstained towel he had shared with his wife rocked Jill McDermott, but the young detective remained impassive, as she had throughout the interview. Now wracking her brain to recall her examina-tion of the dirty white towel in Dr. Greineder's Toyota Avalon, McDermott tried to stem her rising panic, thinking she had not seen blood on it.

"She mentioned the towel and I almost died," she admitted. "I had that hot feeling inside like, 'Oh my God, the towel.' I had not thought about it and there was no reason to think about it. I had never mentioned it to anybody, even as an afterthought. She said it was in his car and that Dirk had said he was surprised the police did not take it during the search warrant and now attorney Murphy had it. That concerned me, along with why he was telling Belinda that." McDermott wasn't about to comment in front of Belinda, instead trying to take note of some of the other strange things Dr. Greineder had told his niece.

"Did May have her back brace on?" Belinda abruptly asked.

"She didn't have a brace on," Foley answered. "We found a black brace inside the van," he added.

"She always had that brace on," Belinda replied forcefully, Foley sensing suspicion in her voice.

Hours after the first search of his home, Dr. Greineder had told Belinda the police were looking for work gloves, a hammer, and a knife. "He said he didn't have any of those work gloves but he did own some in the past," Belinda told the detectives. "He said he had worn an old pair of pants that day and was concerned police would find fibers from those gloves. I thought that was kind of strange, and I told him May would have washed those pants a thousand times and there wouldn't be any old fibers on them."

To Foley, it sounded like Dr. Greineder was trying to document reasons for why evidence connected to his wife's murder might be linked to him. He found stunning the news of Dirk's highly unusual commissioning of a second autopsy on his wife, jotting a note to try to identify the doctor, who Belinda believed came from Connecticut.

Still interested in the Greineders' financial status, he asked Belinda if she was curious why they were doing so much work on the home when May had accepted money for her travel expenses to New York.

"I was surprised," Belinda admitted. "I don't know where the money was coming from." Belinda said she was the executor of her grandmother's estate and gave her aunt a partial disbursement of her $43,000 inheritance in May. "The whole family went to England in May, and I know they recently redid their will. They have been doing some estate planning to even out the estate by giving May the house," she added.

"Do you have any plans with the Greineders over the holidays?" Foley asked.

"We had planned to be together over New Years, but now I'm not sure," answered Belinda. "The last I heard from Dirk, he was taking the family to Denmark for Christmas. They are leaving the twenty-second and coming back the twenty-seventh."

Foley found troubling the news that his suspect was planning to leave the country. Dirk had dual citizenship in the United States and Lebanon, where Dirk's father had relocated his family from Germany after World War II.

Without Foley directly acknowledging it, it was clear to him that Belinda knew her uncle was the sole focus of his investigation. Through their mutual flow of information, she learned that there were contradictions between what Dr. Greineder was telling her and what witness statements and the evidence actually showed.

Foley told her Dr. Greineder had provided his fingernail clippings, which he had just delivered with other samples for DNA testing in Maryland. The detective had privately found it comical that Dirk's attorney was saying the police did not have his client's DNA. "I thought Dirk should have known that," he said, before coming to a more logical conclusion. "It could be that he didn't tell Marty Murphy and didn't tell Murphy for a long time."

Belinda offered to escort the two detectives downstairs to her parents' apartment. Foley was inwardly elated at what had transpired between them in just under three hours. May Greineder's niece had provided one bombshell piece of information after another, yet Foley had been touched by the sincerity of Belinda's affection for her aunt as well as her apparent quest for the truth, even if she had to accept that her uncle was responsible for May's hideous demise.

Riding the elevator down to Ilse Stark's floor, Foley tried to prioritize the revelations Belinda had provided, but they all seemed equally important. Dr. Greineder's urgency to hire a lawyer along with his orchestration of a second autopsy on his wife showed a man bent on avoiding the police investigation rather than assisting it. And Belinda was the first person he had spoken to whom May had confided in about her marriage, revealing her suspicion that Dirk was having an affair, which was tragically on the mark.

Belinda's description of the small bruises on Dr. Greineder's right arm had also caught the detective's attention. Shown to his niece several days after the murder, Foley suspected May had struggled and placed a death grip on her husband, perhaps explaining why her right glove had fallen off.

More intriguing were the strange stories Dr. Greineder had told his niece, some of them not unlike the statements he made to McDermott the day of the murder. Foley was still trying to make sense of the whole nosebleed story, wondering about the towel Dr. Greineder had given to

Murphy. "The biggest thing I came out of there with was the towel, and the only reason I say that is because that was something we absolutely did not have," Foley recalled. "We did not have any information about a towel. We also found out about the second autopsy, and we would have had no way of knowing that."

Even more important was the fact that Foley had established a relationship with one of the people closest to the woman he wanted justice for, finding Belinda likable and extremely intelligent. "I wanted to walk out of there knowing I could come back. That was one of the biggest things," he said.

For Belinda, the meeting had been equally enlightening. As she took the detectives down to meet her parents, she felt she was finally getting some information about May's death aside from her uncle's dubious accounts. Still not ready to give Foley her unconditional trust, Belinda had found him, even so, the opposite of what her uncle was saying about him. "I did find that I liked him," she said. "He was not at all what I expected. I felt there was a real person in there. I remember sitting there looking at him in my den thinking, 'Boy, somebody's really underestimated this guy. This guy is really smart.' He was just taking in everything, and I was taking in everything."

Like Foley, Belinda felt willing to meet again. "We were both looking for an ally," she concluded. "We were dancing a little bit, at least on my end, but I thought this was somebody I might be able to trust, and I was beginning to feel a little comfortable with him. I think both of us were taking this in slower steps. A lot of information passed in a short period of time and we had never seen each other before."

At the end of the extended visit, Belinda agreed to testify before the grand jury, a development that was sure to infuriate her uncle. "We ended that meeting with me understanding, without the words being spoken, where he was going, and I think he understood where I was," Belinda said of Foley.

Meeting May Greineder's older sister for the first time, Foley was captivated by Ilse Stark's striking resemblance to her late sibling, almost as if she were a living vision of the cruelly taken woman. Where the detectives' relaxed conversation with her daughter had flowed freely, their interview with her mother was going to be decidedly more structured, with no cookies to nibble.

Contrasted with the casually dressed Belinda, her mother was elegantly clad in expensive clothing with a personality more direct than her daughter's. "Ilse was nicely dressed in this fifteen-hundred-dollar outfit that she had probably just thrown together," Foley laughed. "With Ilse, this was going to be a little more formal. Ilse had an agenda, and she did not mince words, but she was very cordial."

Foley had not expected her husband to be there. Murray Stark had come home from work early to be with his wife. Walking into the couple's apartment, Foley found the Starks were in the midst of a major renovation. The successful couple actually had two apartments, which they were converting into one expansive unit. "The apartment was under construction and there was debris everywhere," Foley recalled. "We had a quick tour of the construction site, and there really was a lot of work going on."

Strangers to city living, the detectives quickly found out what was considered opulent in New York. "I learned there were two balconies," Foley said. "One balcony is good in Manhattan, but two balconies are considered awesome."

Settling into Murray's study decorated "with mahogany and leather everywhere," Foley took a seat in a welcoming leather easy chair overlooking a courtyard with a beautifully manicured garden. Still sizing up Ilse, Foley quickly realized he needed to listen rather than question. "Ilse is a story teller, and you ask her a question and sit back and relax because it is going to last for a while, and it is going to be illustrated verbally," he observed. "She is very eloquent and has a strong vocabulary. She's wealthy. She has a beautiful apartment and she has beautiful clothes. Everything about her is saying that, and if she walked into a room you would know she was there. She had that presence about her."

The grief-filled sister began by offering her cooperation. "I would like to help and assist in any way to help solve my sister's murder," she said, her loss evident. "We have a very small family but we are very close knit."

"When was the last time you saw May?" Foley asked softly. "May came to visit the end of September," Ilse replied. "It was a good visit, very light-hearted," the sister recalled, telling the detectives a story about how she and May had to share the same bed for the first time since they were little girls because of the apartment renovation. "Do you know about any problems May was having or if she had any enemies?" Foley asked.

"No, May was always a fraidy cat," Ilse responded expressively. "If someone was bothering her or if anything frightened her she would let everyone know."

The petite woman illustrated her point with a story about how May had once thwarted a mugging when they were college co-eds by unleashing a shrieking, "child-like, high-pitched scream." About to be accosted on the subway home from Hunter College, the two sisters were saved when the mugger fled at the onset of May's ear-piercing yelling. Ilse described the sound as "unhumanlike," the same word Terry McNally had used to describe the cries he heard at Morses Pond.

Although Ilse remained outwardly impassive, her story nonetheless astonished Foley. "She really had no idea of the meaning of it, but I'm listening to this and I'm thinking, 'What did Terry McNally tell us?' He had heard this 'unhumanlike' scream, almost like a small child the morning of the murder. When Terry said that, I was not even thinking it's May. I'm thinking May died as soon as the hammer hit, but then I'm realizing that it was May screaming. It made Terry McNally a whole lot more important, and it made Ilse Stark a whole lot more important. If she will cooperate with us it will help us later on with the time of May's death," Foley figured.

The scream might also explain the scattering of the odd items around the crime scene, Foley considered. The collection of food storage bags, lighter fluid, and the foil loaf pan containing the surgical gloves clearly indicated that the methodical Dr. Greineder had an elaborate plan for the killing, but Foley was starting to believe his terrified wife's scream had turned those plans awry when the hammer blow failed to kill or silence her.

The detective had spent hours trying to envision what the evidence meant, nearly concluding that Dr. Greineder had intended to clean or burn biological evidence from the murder weapons and gloves with the lighter fluid before bagging them for disposal in the plastic food bags.

Still uninformed about the discovery of the white kitchen bag at the crime scene that everything could have been dumped in, Foley would never discover what the exact plan was, but Dr. Greineder had probably plotted it for weeks, if not months.

It was clear from the autopsy report and now from May's apparent screaming heard by McNally that the hammer blow did not incapacitate May, which forced her husband to ruthlessly improvise his plan by finishing her in a bloody attack with the knife.

Foley envisioned Dr. Greineder probably in a panic after the unexpected struggle ended with the brutish and bloody slicing of his wife's throat, rushing to get rid of the murder weapons, fearful his wife's screams would bring an unwanted eyewitness.

The blood-spotted Ziploc bags looked like they had been dropped where they were found. But Foley suspected Dr. Greineder never got to the loaf pan, latex gloves, and lighter fluid that were hidden in the downed branches and were meant to sanitize the damaging evidence. Spotting Bill Kear ambling down the middle of the access road, Dr. Greineder was further derailed from his multistep plot. Foley believed he was forced into a desperate bid to hide the weapons in the maintenance road storm drain instead of secreting them outside the recreation area.

Refocusing on the conversation, Foley asked Ilse if she was aware of any problems between May and Dirk. "I know things have been more complicated for them since Dirk's promotion," Ilse answered diplomatically. "Dirk has been working longer hours, and I know that bothered May. Dirk wasn't able to give his time to help May with the renovations to the bathroom and the kitchen."

Ilse, like her daughter Belinda, emphasized that the couple normally did everything in tandem. "May and Dirk made all the decisions about the family and the house together," she stressed. "May wouldn't buy a light bulb without asking Dirk first. I could not understand that, but May could not understand how I could buy a couch without asking Murray first."

Asked how she had found out about her sister's shocking murder, Ilse said her niece Britt had called, prompting the family to drive to Wellesley early the next morning. "Were you told what happened to May?" Foley wanted to know.

"We didn't know any details right away," Ilse said. "When we first got there, Dirk basically told us what happened." Like her daughter, she recited the litany of strange concerns expressed by her brother-in-law.

"How was Dirk when you saw him?" Foley inquired.

"It upsets me that Dirk is not more upset about being falsely accused," she replied forcefully. "He doesn't seem upset that the police are looking at him. He seems more intent on finding a lawyer. I've known Dirk and I've seen him get upset. If I was being wrongly accused of something, especially something like this, I would be incensed, and I would be all over you until you found out who did this," she added emphatically.

Foley had observed Murray Stark's patient silence while his wife spoke, the trooper sensing a respectful relationship between the high-powered couple. "I just have one question to ask," Murray said when it was clear his wife had finished. "Did he do it?"

Unprepared for the direct approach, it was the first time Foley had heard that question since his wife asked him in the early morning hours after the first search warrant. "Yeah, I think he did," the detective answered honestly.

"That motherfucker," Murray spat, his disgusted tone indicating he had already come to the conclusion his brother-in-law was responsible. The man's crude response was unexpected, but Foley found he liked him anyway. "I felt good about it because I think he had some confidence in me. I'm looking at Ilse to see what her reaction is, but she says nothing and was expressionless. I'm thinking, 'I like this guy. Maybe he can handle this thing New York style,'" Foley laughed.

Foley was pleased when Ilse agreed to testify before the grand jury. "I had a good feeling when we left," he remembered. Settling into his car, Foley wrote down everything he could remember from the combined four hours of conversation with May's loved ones before steering his way out of Manhattan. Rattling off a list of things they had to do as a result of their newfound information, Foley noticed Jill McDermott was "exceptionally quiet" in the seat next to him.

Still elated with the success of their meetings, Foley didn't dwell on McDermott's silence as he juggled the cell phone with the steering wheel while updating prosecutor Rick Grundy during the drive back to Massachusetts. Although relatively inexperienced, Foley had found his partner to be "a very smart woman. She had gotten thrown into this investigation," Foley explained. "I could not have asked for a better person to work with me. Sometimes the worst partner you can have is someone who is constantly talking, but Jill was good at watching everything and then pointing out something that had been overlooked or should have been done."

Belinda and Ilse were far less exuberant in comparing their conversations with the police. Although they now had an avenue of information outside the rambling lies of Dirk Greineder, the police visit had left them with the bitter final conclusion that he had undoubtedly killed May.

"I felt better knowing," said Belinda. "At that point we were pretty convinced that Dirk had done it, and it was reinforced by the fact that the police were convinced he had done it with some sound reasoning behind it. I had to accept and digest the fact that he had done this. I went through another stage of having to process that information. It's one thing to think it is; it's another to have it pretty much verified for you."

Knowledge brought complications. "The question became, 'What are we going to do about this?'" said Belinda. "How are we going to handle the Greineder family?"

As Connecticut turned to Massachusetts, Jill McDermott was wrestling with her own dilemma. Mile after mile, she had planned to bring up the towel Belinda had spoken of, but her words were choked back by the fear of how the energized Foley would react. Usually even-keeled, her partner had been overly buoyant the entire drive home, most of it spent on the phone to the key investigators in the case.

"I remember sitting in the car, and it was late," McDermott said. "I'm thinking, 'Next exit, I'm going to tell him.' We'd pass the exit and then I'd be thinking, 'Next exit, I'm going to tell him.'" Wracking her memory to recall any hint of blood on the dirty plain towel, McDermott wondered if she needed to say anything at all. "In my head I'm thinking, 'is this as bad as I think it is?'"

With their exit finally approaching, McDermott knew she had to tell her partner before he dropped her off at home. "I have to tell you something," she said at last, Foley turning apprehensive with the correct assumption that her announcement was not going to be good news. "The night of the first search warrant I saw a towel in Dirk's car," McDermott nervously revealed. "I picked it up and looked at it and it was stained, and I thought it was coffee or something like that. I know it wasn't blood. I left it in the car," she said timidly.

"Did you show it to anybody?" Foley asked, already trying to calculate the potential damage from her admission. "I showed it to Terry Cunningham," McDermott replied. "We both looked at it and we didn't see any blood on it. It was just dirt or coffee. He said not to take it," she said.

"All right, it's no big deal. We'll deal with it," Foley told her, trying to ease her obvious anxiety. There was nothing they could do anyway until Dr. Greineder made an issue of it. "What are you going to do at this point?" Foley figured. "What got me more upset was I didn't even know they went into the car. I should have at least been advised. Maybe they told me but I just didn't get it. It might have been at a busy time."

Used to drawn-out, high-stakes investigations, Foley and Grundy expected setbacks. "I told Rick and he said these things are going to come up and we're going to get through it," Foley said. Closing his eyes in bed after the daylong roundtrip to New York, Foley had no idea how much consternation the obscure towel would bring him.

It didn't take long for Dr. Greineder to call, questioning Belinda about what the police had asked in New York. Listening to her uncle for the first time since fully accepting that he had killed May, Belinda felt "very, very uncomfortable" while he ranted.

"They're going after the wrong people," he hissed, as Belinda silently seethed with her knowledge of the truth. If her uncle was upset about Belinda's good words for the police, he could barely contain himself when she told him that she and her mother were being called before the grand jury. He insisted they consult with attorney Marty Murphy to go over what Belinda and Ilse were going to say; his fury surging when Belinda responded that she didn't think it was necessary.

"I need to, I must do what Marty says," he said tensely in his nasally shrill voice. "You have to talk to Marty Murphy about this," he ordered, his upset evident.

"I don't need to. I don't want to and I don't have to," Belinda responded defiantly. "I know what I'm doing." Hardly placated, Dr. Greineder had his attorney call both Belinda and Ilse, insisting they bring someone from his firm to represent them before the grand jury.

"We went back and forth about what I was going to tell the grand jury," Belinda said. "I decided to play it straight and say it's no big deal, but it had turned out to be a really big deal. Marty Murphy called and said I should take one of his people with me and I should be prepared by his people before I went in there. When I said no, that threw out a big red flag. They knew at that point that they had a problem."

# 14

SITTING OUTSIDE THE CLOSED DOOR to the Norfolk County Grand Jury with Marty Foley on December 15, Belinda Markel could not imagine why her mother had been sequestered inside so long. Prosecutor Rick Grundy had told Belinda and Ilse they would both finish long before lunchtime, but as the clock passed 10 A.M., Ilse had been testifying for well over an hour.

"Oh my God," Belinda finally vented. "I'm not going to be in there that long," she vowed with exasperation. The appearance of a crying Ilse with a trail of attending court workers quickly brought her daughter back to the painful reason for their presence before the twenty-four citizens who would decide whether Dr. Greineder should stand trial for May's murder. Enthralling the jurors with her heartfelt memories of May during their upbringing in Queens, Ilse had been overcome with emotion, forcing a break in the testimony.

"She had actually broken down, and they brought her out," Belinda softly recalled. "She was upset that she lost her sister and she was upset with who did it. It was emotional. It's turning a corner. From where we were standing this was a very difficult process to go through," Belinda explained. "This is my family. This is a murder. So just the process of accepting who did it was very, very difficult for her."

Her mother calmed, "we sent her back in there," said Belinda. "They had all kinds of questions, and she had all kinds of answers. She started telling stories and was quite engaging."

Her kids at the neighboring Dedham Mall with Jill McDermott, Belinda had time for another extended conversation with Foley. Interspersing questions for the investigation with frivolous small talk, Foley asked one that could pass for both. "Would you have felt better if May had died of a heart attack," he asked gently, pretty sure what the response would be.

"Yeah, I would still miss her, but . . ." Belinda didn't finish the sentence, but Foley knew what she was saying. "But she wouldn't be here testifying against her uncle for killing her aunt," Foley thought, still clawing for any reasoning that could lead this respected doctor and parent to methodically eliminate his wife in such a vicious manner.

Belinda and Foley continued their conversation, slowly learning more about each other. Belinda frequently got up to pace around the waiting room, occasionally peering out a window at the Dedham Mall next door, where McDermott was trying to occupy her children.

"He had relaxed questions that made sense," said Belinda. "We talked about his wife, Cheryl. We talked about our families, but there were a couple of questions that stuck with me. I'm not the most trusting individual, and I was going through a process of feeling these people out to see who they were. I was now bombarded by all these new players that I would have to get to know pretty fast."

Belinda was touched when Foley told her he had lost his mother when she was just fifty-eight, the same age as May. He could relate to Belinda's cousins' losing their mother because he was about the same age when his mother died, but he could not understand their unconditional support of their father.

Ilse finally finished as the clock spun toward noon, and Belinda took her place. But she was vastly disappointed when she walked into the grand jury room. Expecting more of "an official courtroom setting," she found the grand jurors standing or lounging in mismatched chairs, a worn-looking wooden podium the only piece of furniture that indicated the judicial function of the room. Taking a seat, Belinda saw Rick Grundy casually leaning against a wall in a chair while prosecutor Gerry Pudolsky remained on his feet to start the questioning.

Pudolsky took Belinda through a detailed accounting of everything she had told Foley and McDermott during their groundbreaking trip to New York. True to her words, Belinda's questioning was finished in a fraction of the time her mother had spent before the grand jury. Heading out of the room, she was relieved it was over, finding the process easier than she had anticipated.

One thing the investigators would not have known about without Belinda's cooperation was Dr. Greineder's upcoming Danish Christmas vacation, which had rapidly become a source of sleepless nights for the cops. "That was a huge problem as far as we could see," Foley said. "We have a guy with dual citizenship to Lebanon and he's leaving the country and potentially going to a country where we don't have extradition rights."

Wellesley Police Chief Terry Cunningham was convinced that once Dr. Greineder flew to Denmark it would be the last they saw of him. The immense pressure from the community to solve May Greineder's murder had not subsided, the pointed calls to the chief from Wellesley's elected officials actually increasing as the New Year approached without an arrest.

Belinda confirmed the name of her uncle's New Jersey–based travel agent, who turned out to be a willing godsend to the police. The pleasant travel agent handled all of Dr. Greineder's arrangements and was excited to help the detectives, telling Foley the doctor and his children were round-trip ticketed for the Denmark vacation.

Foley and Grundy were optimistic that their suspect would return to fight for his innocence, but Cunningham was not. Unlike the securely employed prosecutor and state cop, Cunningham faced the real possibility of being ousted as police chief if Dr. Greineder became a fugitive from justice. "I really did not think he was going to come back," said Cunningham. "I remember talking to Rick and Marty about it, saying if he doesn't come back these people are going to fire me."

As Dr. Greineder and his children lifted off from Logan Airport a few days before Christmas, Lt. Wayne Cunningham had already arranged a covert reception for them by Danish authorities to help ease his younger brother's worry. Unknown to the Greineders, with most of the details still protected by the Wellesley Police Department, Danish authorities kept the Massachusetts murder suspect under constant surveillance.

"We knew when he got on the plane and knew when he landed," admitted Wayne Cunningham. "We had someone watching him. We knew where he spent his time, where he was. He was not getting on any other flights. That's what we were concerned with." The relief was palpable when Dr. Greineder returned from Denmark after Christmas.

Over the holidays the State Police detectives had also been working another horrible case of domestic violence that would indirectly lead them to escort service owner Gilbert Perito, who Foley felt could lead them to the elusive woman named Elizabeth whom Dr. Greineder had mentioned to prostitute Deborah Herrera. On the night of December 30, twenty-four-year-old Christine Davis made a terrifying cell phone call to a friend, screaming that the father of her baby was trying to run her car off the road in the city of Quincy.

The friend patched the call to the police, who tried to intercept the maniacal boyfriend, but they could not respond in time to prevent thirty-six-year-old Andrew Clary from ramming Davis's BMW with his Chevrolet Cavalier and hurling Davis head-on into an oncoming vehicle on Quincy Shore Drive. Davis died four hours later at Boston Medical Center. Clary subsequently was charged with second-degree murder. As the investigation progressed, detectives quickly learned that Davis was a prostitute who was once employed by Gil Perito.

On Sunday, January 9, 2000, Sergeants Gerry Mattaliano and Kevin Shea finally located the shadowy Perito driving a bus at Logan Airport. Nearing fifty, he told the two detectives he had gotten out of the sex trade but was the former owner of the Diamond Girls escort service doing business as Commonwealth Entertainment. "I had sixty girls working for me," he boasted, admitting he had been a pimp for many years. "The clients paid a hundred fifty dollars an hour, and the girls paid me sixty dollars," he explained, acknowledging that the phone number Dr. Greineder had dialed twice from the Crowne Plaza on February 3, 1998, belonged to him.

"Did you have an escort with red hair working for you at that time named Elizabeth?" Shea asked.

"Yeah, I remember a girl named Elizabeth," he said.

"What did she look like," Shea said.

"She had red hair, was about five-seven, attractive," Perito answered, recalling more about the woman as he digested particulars of the February afternoon hotel tryst provided by the detectives. "I remember that call," he said, telling the sergeants he had actually driven Elizabeth to the Crowne Plaza. "I remember that job because we didn't get too many clients that called during the day," Perito explained.

"Do you remember the client's name," Mattaliano asked.

"No, I can't remember," Perito said.

"Could his name have been Dirk?" Mattaliano hinted.

"Yeah, that's it," Perito said genuinely. "Now I remember because it was an unusual name. Dirk was his name. He called me a few times afterward looking for Elizabeth even after she left Diamond Girls," he recalled.

"Do you know Elizabeth's last name?" Shea asked hopefully. But Perito couldn't remember. "I'll look through my records and call some of the other girls," he offered. "I know Elizabeth was her real name and I picked her up one time on Common Street in Quincy to take her to a client." Passing the development on to Marty Foley, the case officer was pleased they had confirmed Dr. Greineder had met with a prostitute in February 1998, but the identity of the sultry Elizabeth remained an enigma.

The satisfaction of gaining Gil Perito's cooperation after a five-week search was sweetened the next day when Gwen Pino received the first results from Cellmark Diagnostics. Genetic material gleaned from the knife handle could not exclude Dr. Greineder from being the DNA source, but it was hardly a smoking gun, the crime lab manager explained to Foley.

Studying a faxed copy of the Cellmark report, Foley read that two sources of DNA were found on the knife, with May Greineder being the primary donor and a male being the secondary contributor. DNA from the secondary donor could only be detected on four of nine chromosomal identifying points, but the incomplete profile could not eliminate Dr. Greineder.

Humans share 99 percent of the same DNA, but the final percentage varies. At the time of the Greineder case, most forensic testing focused on thirteen sections, or loci, along the DNA strand in which molecular differences in the chromosomes are measured as "alleles." Cellmark was using a two-pronged procedure that examined the first nine loci with a kit called Profiler Plus. If the genetic sample was large enough, it was then subjected to a testing kit named Cofiler that focused on the last six of the thirteen loci with loci eight and nine overlapping in both kits.

With the knife, a minuscule amount of DNA was recovered, so Cellmark only employed the first test. With the secondary donor showing on only four of nine loci, the pool of potential contributors was almost limitless, but Dr. Greineder could not be excluded, because his alleles matched the four identified. Based on May's blood swatch and the nail clippings Foley had craftily collected from her husband, Cellmark had developed complete DNA profiles of the couple with alleles documented at all thirteen loci.

To try to put the confusing science into terms a jury could consider, Cellmark was instructed to produce a statistical analysis of test results based on human population. A majority of the world's inhabitants might have the same molecular makeup at a particular locus, but the pool of potential DNA donors shrinks as each subsequent locus is identified.

By a tremendously complicated calculation involving the population frequency of particular alleles at certain loci matched with the alleles identified through forensic testing, Cellmark concluded that 1 in every 2,220 Caucasian males could have left DNA on the knife that killed May, assuming that only she and her killer left samples. Running the statistics without limiting the number of DNA contributors, the pool of potential donors swelled to 1 in every 160 white males.

Although an almost infinite number of white men could have been a genetic contributor to the knife, the test data further supported the blocks of evidence investigators were methodically stacking against the highly respected Dirk Greineder. "It was encouraging because we didn't expect to find anything, or not a lot," said Foley. "It was encouraging because the thing is, it's part of Dirk's profile and nobody else's. There is no other DNA there, no other profile there. Even with a population pool that large, there was nothing there other than Dirk."

Only May's DNA had been identified on the hammer, while several cuttings from the right-hand brown work glove failed to yield any genetic material. Other cuttings from the right glove were still being tested, including one Pino had removed from the index finger where the clear liquid had been observed in the proximity of May's blood.

Intrigued by Belinda Markel's account of the second autopsy, and acting on her mother's request to secure May's death certificate, Foley found time to visit the Needham office of the Eaton & Mackay Funeral Home on Tuesday, January 11. Dropping in unannounced, the detective was pleasantly greeted by funeral director, Kevin Green, who had coordinated May's memorial services and cremation after taking a telephone call from her daughter Kirsten the day after her mother was killed.

"I remember it was kind of strange because she told me she would be handling the funeral arrangements for her father because he was tied up with his legal counsel. I thought it was strange she would be discussing her father's legal matters with me so soon after the death," the funeral director admitted.

Handling the arrangements for the Greineders was odd from the start, Green said. "I never met face-to-face with the family until the day of the funeral," he recalled. "We usually have the family come in, sign all the paperwork, and discuss the arrangements in person. There were several things we needed Dr. Greineder to sign, but he didn't sign them until the day of the November three memorial service."

"Do you know anything about a second autopsy that was performed on Mrs. Greineder?" Foley asked the undertaker.

"I was made aware on Tuesday, November two, that Dr. Greineder wanted to have a second autopsy done," Green replied, looking up from his records. "His daughter Kirsten came to the funeral home that Thursday to bring clothing for her mother's private viewing and said her father had made arrangements to have a doctor do a second autopsy on Saturday. He had contacted a doctor in New York City or possibly Connecticut and she gave me an envelope to give him when he did the autopsy."

When the doctor arrived around 2 P.M. on Saturday, November 6, he introduced himself to Green, but the funeral director could not remember the man's name. He brought the doctor to May's remains, where the rare extra postmortem was performed.

"Did anyone witness the autopsy?" Foley asked curiously.

"Mr. Eaton and Clint Paddock, the embalmer, were there," Green said.

Funeral home owner David Eaton and Paddock were both at the Needham office that day, and Foley invited them into the conference room to join the impromptu, yet astonishing, interview.

Paddock said he arrived at the funeral home shortly after two o'clock to help Eaton embalm May but found a doctor performing an autopsy on the woman. "I said very little to him," Paddock remembered. "I think he was from Connecticut. He drove a Volvo."

Eaton could also not remember the doctor's name, recalling that the physician had spoken into a tape recorder and had taken pictures using a disposable camera, which was left slicked with blood. "I remember thinking, 'who was going to develop that film?'" Eaton said. "Who would want to touch it? The camera was covered with blood."

The watchful undertakers said the doctor collected "six to eight" tissue samples from the deceased woman, including some from her vaginal area. "He put them into separate test tubes," said Eaton. The medical examiner had spent about ninety minutes with May, leaving with his samples as Eaton and Paddock finally began to embalm her body.

Because of the five-day delay in preparing the remains, Dr. Greineder had inquired about the possibility of his family still viewing his wife. "He was concerned about the appearance of May," said Eaton. "He was concerned about the ability of the funeral home to make her presentable. I told him I knew he had found her body and he should know what we would be working with. We finally decided the body would be prepared for viewing," Eaton added with irritation, which Foley sensed came from Dr. Greineder overruling the funeral home owner's opposing recommendation.

"We had the viewing at the Newton Cemetery chapel," Eaton concluded. "All the family members viewed the body except for Dr. Greineder. He stayed in the background."

Later thumbing through copies of the funeral home's paperwork, Foley noted the Greineders had paid slightly more than $5,400 for May's arrangements, a modest sum as funerals go. Scanning some of the itemized charges, the detective paused at a line denoting "casket or other receptacle" with a price of $275. He wondered what kind of casket you could get for that price.

A call several weeks later from a victim/witness advocate at the attorney general's office would leave the detective further perplexed about the Greineders' handling of May's cremation. The family had contacted the AG's office to see if May's funeral expenses could be paid by a fund to assist the victims of violent crime. Victim advocate Cheryl Wilson asked Foley if the Greineders qualified.

"They have insurance. They wouldn't qualify for that. Besides," Foley bluntly told Wilson, whom he had known for years, "the husband's a suspect."

Foley would later identify the coroner who had performed the second autopsy as Dr. Edward McDonough, a deputy medical examiner for the state of Connecticut. McDonough expressed no interest in helping Foley with his murder probe or providing information about the autopsy, including whether the samples he collected were turned over to Dr. Greineder.

If Dr. Greineder's financial records were slowly exposing his secret extramarital wanderings under an assumed name, his computers were proving just as enlightening. Frequently joining Trooper David McSweeney to assist in the forensic searches of their suspect's tower unit and laptop, Marty Foley and Wayne Cunningham had been at the attorney general's office when a keyword search turned up an incredible series of Internet correspondence.

Using the keyword *nylon rope* based on an unopened package of white rope seized from the search of Dr. Greineder's van, the three cops found themselves reading sexually explicit electronic conversations between a "Tom" and a "Paty Peres." Seeing the name Tom, Foley and Cunningham instantly thought of Thomas Young from the doctor's American Express Corporate Card receipts.

Because the EnCase software had retrieved the messages from deleted or temporary Internet files still stored on the hard drive, words and characters were missing from the text, but the detectives recovered a complete e-mail sent by tyoung<cosmic_jockey@yahoo to Patricia Peres<portugues _baby_1999@yahoo.

"*Hi baby,*" the message began on Thursday, October 21, a little over a week before May Greineder's slaying.

*It is still thursday but by now its friday in lisbon. I hope you got my message from yesterday and i am still sorry that we did not get to chat. I was hoping to get an email from you tonight but I guess you did not send one (yahoo seems to be working ok from here). hope everything is ok with you and that*

*you are not too lonely. I wish you were here with me. i have a nice hotel*
*room all to myself and it would be so wonderful to have you here to share it*
*and to make hot wonderful love with you. I have restarted my story (forgot*
*the original one on my home computer) and will send you some tomorrow.*
*sure wish you were here — send me an email so that i know you still care.*
*Miss you meu amor Able Tom."*

From fractured correspondence lifted from other e-mails, it appeared
Paty Peres was writing from Portugal. "Based on the e-mails they were
sending back and forth, he had met this woman with screen name of Paty
Peres at some type of convention in Colorado and they had rekindled
an old relationship. They had apparently known each other before," said
Cunningham, who would go to obsessive, but unsuccessful lengths, to
identify the woman.

"There were these strange sex stories he had written involving Tom and
Paty, and looking at this e-mail I'm thinking, 'Is all this real or is this part
of his imagination?' He's obviously e-mailing someone who is real, but is
the fact that she's supposed to be living in Lisbon all part of the fantasy?"
Cunningham wondered.

The detectives were amazed to discover a batch of neatly typed hardcore
sex stories apparently penned by Dr. Greineder, which were retrieved from
slack space on the hard drive and later found hidden under passwords on a
floppy disc in innocuously titled documents like "asthma.to.add," "asthma.
dog," and "asthama.tom." The lurid, often deviant depictions mostly centered on the sexual exploits of a character named Tom.

One fantasy, entitled "A Nurses Story," involved a patient named Tom
being seduced by a nurse named Cathy. Darker, more disturbing tales
involved Tom delving into sadomasochistic bondage with a "nylon rope,"
painfully binding his genitals while his dominant "Mistress" degraded
him with unusual sexual acts.

Other pornographic missives flavored with fetishes had characters
named John, Doyle, and Jeff involved in a series of raunchy encounters
with women named Jean, Cindy, and Cathy. Judging from their correspondence, Dr. Greineder was sending Paty Peres the kinky stories that
had filled more than twenty single-spaced pages.

Sorting through the scrambled, cryptic displays of the EnCase scan, the detectives found one garbled e-mail, sent by cosmic_jockey to portugues _baby_1999 the day after May's murder, decidedly more chilling: "i have had a tragedy in the family and cannot email now. Maybe in 2 weeks i can email again. I will do it at this address. love Tom," the detectives read silently. "Tom Whatever is happening i am with you. Courage Tom! a lovely kiss paty," was the reply.

The e-mails showed that Dr. Greineder had messaged Paty Peres in the days before his wife's murder and the day immediately after. "We found the Paty Peres e-mail had been sent early on the morning of November one," said Cunningham. "We had known he called Herrera the day before and the day after the murder, and now it appeared we had the same situation with e-mail to Paty Peres." Fearful the information might not be retrievable again, the detectives repeatedly clicked the forensic computer's print symbol.

"We kept printing screen after screen," said Foley. "We knew we wouldn't be able to sit down with Grundy and explain this. We needed to show him copies. A lot of it was a jumbled mess that had to be read through. Page after page was printed out."

With most of the incriminating content dredged from deleted and cache files, the detectives quickly found that Dr. Greineder was prone to trolling Internet porn sites like hornypony.com, big-bondage-celebrity.com, and oral-delight.com. The staid Wellesley town fathers would quietly acquiesce to Chief Terry Cunningham's request that filters be removed from his brother Wayne's computer so the detective could survey the hardcore sites frequented by their suspect.

Matching the findings from the computer searches with Dr. Greineder's financial records, Foley was sure the doctor had met with a prostitute only a week before his wife's murder while attending a conference in Mahwah, New Jersey. According to records provided by the Sheraton Crossroads Hotel, Dr. Greineder used his room phone to log his laptop onto the Internet at 1:56 A.M. on Saturday, October 23, spending the next fifty minutes online.

The computer search revealed that Dr. Greineder had spent most of the time browsing sites for New York–area escort services. A 2:46 A.M. telephone call made from his room indicated he had selected a prostitute.

The listing came back to Marilyn's Escort Service in Brooklyn, leaving Foley convinced that four $100 ATM withdrawals Dr. Greineder had made in the hotel lobby before going online ended up in the hand of a hooker from the escort service. The amused but somewhat perplexed investigators also noted a $16.95 charge for an adult movie at 3:56 A.M. that Saturday morning, which was paid along with the doctor's other incidentals by his American Express Corporate Card.

After returning to Wellesley, Dr. Greineder used the Corporate Card he had issued in the name of Thomas Young to join People2People, the online dating service owned by the *Boston Phoenix*. Match.com, another Internet matchmaking firm that *USA Today* reviewed as "on pace to change the way mainstream Americans find their romantic partners," was bookmarked on his computer. The People2People subscription was charged on October 24, 1999, exactly one week before Dr. Greineder killed his wife.

The luck in recovering the doctor's voluminous cyber wanderings was not lost on the computer-savvy Cunningham. "We were fortunate that we were able to get this information," he said. "It was just luck of the draw that it hadn't been overwritten." Cunningham would not be as lucky in his attempt to identify Paty Peres through her Internet Protocol address, the unique sequences of numbers Internet providers use to designate an individual's computer.

Tom and Paty were using a free Yahoo account, tossing a huge obstacle in the path of Cunningham's search. "Because it's free, there's no billing information," he explained. "The best way to track an IP number is through billing information."

Undaunted, Cunningham ran a search using special software to identify the IP address through the network it used at the time. "You plug the IP number into the software and it actually goes out on the Internet and finds the root to that software and will show you graphically on a map where that IP address is assigned on the Internet," he said. "I did that and it showed Portugal."

Unfortunately, it was too late. "The IP address we were looking for was a dynamic IP address and it had been issued to someone else," said Cunningham. "We had the date and time for Paty Peres, but by the time we got to them the records hadn't been maintained and there was no way to check for previous users."

The Portuguese connection still intrigues the detective. "Why he killed May and who Paty Peres is, are the two questions that linger in my mind," Cunningham said. "I think we were so close to finding Paty Peres. Paty Peres could share some insight."

# 15

AS JANUARY TURNED TO FEBRUARY, the investigators and prosecutor Rick Grundy were under increasing pressure from District Attorney Bill Keating to arrest Dr. Greineder. In no hurry to begin turning over their evidence to the doctor's attorney through the mandated discovery process criminal charges would bring, they resisted the DA's heavy-handed overtures, seeing no sense in rushing the grand jury investigation. "Keating was worried Dirk would kill himself or flee the country," Marty Foley recalled. The district attorney felt there was more than enough evidence to win a conviction, but Grundy vehemently disagreed. The doctor's stature in the community and the support of his children were not to be taken lightly, Grundy rightly believed, leading to many squabbles with his anxious boss. Grundy, who had grown up on the tough streets of Newark, New Jersey, and was prone to bouts of anger, often kept the details of his quarrels with Keating private.

"The tension was building in that office with Rick and Keating," Foley observed. "Rick wanted to complete the grand jury investigation. The grand jury was in the middle of it, and he wanted them to complete it. If we shut the grand jury investigation down, time would no longer be on our side, it would be against us."

The long, drawn-out process of trying to locate the elusive prostitute named Elizabeth was perhaps the strongest argument to hold off on an indictment. There were several false starts, but finally Foley and Jill Mc-

Dermott were able to locate her at her mother's condominium in the South Shore community of Weymouth.

Elizabeth was twenty-seven-year-old Elizabeth Porter, who, a computer check revealed, was wanted for violating probation. When Foley called her mother's condo from the building lobby intercom, Mary Porter tried to shoo away the determined detectives, as she had successfully done the day before. After wasting a day chasing down the mother's bogus information about her daughter's whereabouts, Foley realized he had been tricked.

"Elizabeth doesn't live here," the mother lied again. "I know she's living there," Foley said hotly into the phone, still miffed at being given the run-around the day before. "If I have to, I'll get the condo association president involved," he bluffed, mindful of the nosy woman who had wanted to know why the police were visiting her building.

Mary Porter buzzed the detectives through the lobby door. "She let us right in," grinned Foley. "She obviously didn't want that woman to know why we were there."

Taking the elevator to the fifth floor, Foley and McDermott were let into the Porter condo through a door opening from the kitchen. Walking inside, the dimly lit unit reeked of cigarette smoke. Cautiously striding toward a sunken living room, Foley finally came face-to-face with the woman the detectives had spent three months intently searching for. He immediately noticed Elizabeth Porter's striking auburn hair, but the natural beauty described by Gil Perito was far from evident. Appearing obviously ill, she looked like she hadn't shampooed her hair in a while and was clad in a rumpled bathrobe.

A shady character, apparently her boyfriend, hovered nearby. "She looked like she was living on the couch," said McDermott. "She was sick-looking." Perito having told them Elizabeth was a drug-user, Foley thought she might be going through the ravaging cold turkey process of cleansing herself from powerfully addictive heroin. "She looked like a junkie," he said. "She looked strung out."

Foley went right to the reason for their visit. "We're investigating a homicide and we think you might be able to help us," he told the gaunt woman. "We know you used to work as an escort and you once worked for Gil Perito."

"I was a prostitute," Elizabeth admitted, "but I got diagnosed with AIDS when I was in Framingham," she said, meaning the state prison for women. "I used to work for escort services, but I stopped after I got sick. I got it sharing a needle," she revealed.

"Do you remember a customer named Dirk?" Foley asked, still pondering Elizabeth's AIDS admission.

"Do you have a picture of him?"

Foley handed her a photograph.

"Yeah, I remember him," the ailing woman said, scanning it. "I saw him once through Gil and once on my own because he offered me more money. But I don't remember his name being Dirk."

"Did you know him as Tom?" Foley asked. The persona of Thomas Young was turning up ever more frequently with the unmasking of Dr. Greineder's secret sex life.

"Yeah, he told me his name was Tom," Elizabeth said, her response seemingly truthful. "I remember he was some type of doctor. He said he was a research doctor and that he was from California. He said he traveled back and forth to Boston a lot for his research," she recalled.

"What did you tell him about yourself?" Foley asked, now certain Porter was the woman named Elizabeth Dr. Greineder had told prostitute Deborah Herrera about.

"I told him that I was a nursing student at Boston City Hospital. He thought I was educated, but there isn't even a nursing school at that hospital," she said bemusedly.

"Do you remember when you met Tom?" Foley asked.

"I can't remember exactly," she said. "I think it was a couple of years ago. I remember it was cold out."

"Do you remember the first time you met Tom?" Foley said, trying to jog her memory.

"The first time I met him through Gil," she said positively. "I don't remember where I met him, but he got me roses. After I left him, he paged me the next day. I called him back and he said he wanted me to know that he had a good time — that I had really thrown him for a loop," she described expressively. "He said it was the best time he had ever had and he wanted to see me again. He didn't care what it cost. He offered me more money to meet him on my own without Gil, so I gave him my pager number," Elizabeth said, reciting the number for the detectives.

"How much did Tom offer you?" Foley asked.

"Five hundred dollars an hour," Elizabeth said, easily recalling the inflated price over what she typically collected.

"Did you meet with him again?" Foley pressed, aware of the charge from Boston's Westin Hotel on Dr. Greineder's credit card five days after he had sex with Elizabeth at the Crowne Plaza in Natick.

"Yeah, he paged me."

"Where did you meet the second time?" Foley asked, hoping she could remember.

"I met him at an exclusive hotel in Boston," she said as if still impressed by the setting. "I think it was the Westin Hotel. I remember he had champagne and roses," she gushed. "I think they were pink roses and he had chocolate-covered strawberries for me, which no one had ever done before. He also got me these expensive lotions and oils — the good stuff — I think it was the Neutrogena lotion."

"Did Tom have any specific requests for you?" Foley asked, intrigued by the lavish accompaniments Dr. Greineder had waiting in his pricey hotel room.

"Yeah, I was actually thinking about that the other day," Elizabeth replied. "He said he liked the way I dressed and he wanted to take a rose and run it all over my body. He wanted to take a shower with me, but I wouldn't let him," she said, telling the detectives she let her client watch her shower instead. "He also wanted to do oral sex on me, which is strange because most guys don't want to do that with an escort. I wouldn't let him," Elizabeth added impassively.

"Had anyone else ever requested that?" Foley recalled that Dr. Greineder had wanted to do the same thing to Herrera.

"I had never been asked that from a client," Elizabeth stressed.

"Is there anything else you remember about Tom?"

"I remember the first time I met him he wore a wedding ring and I asked him if he was married, why he was doing this," Elizabeth recounted. "He told me he wasn't married, but I asked him why he was wearing a wedding ring. He said it was habit and that he was separated and hoped to be divorced soon."

When she met with Tom the second time at the Westin Hotel, he had made a point to show her his bare ring finger. "He said, 'See, I don't have a wedding ring on now,'" she told the detectives.

"Did he say anything about his wife?" Foley queried.

"I got the impression that he didn't want to be married. He seemed to be embarrassed to be married. He didn't seem like he wanted to be with his wife, like he just wanted to get away from her. He said he was no longer attracted to his wife because she had grown old and soft and there was no more passion in their marriage."

Asked if her client spoke about his children, Elizabeth recalled him saying he "had great children and they were in college."

"How did Tom treat you?" Foley continued.

"He treated me like a queen, but he was weird," Elizabeth said emphatically. "He gave me an uncomfortable feeling. He was seedy and he was too excited." Turned off by his exuberance, Elizabeth said she rebuffed Tom's subsequent attempts to meet again. "I had a bad feeling about him," she said. "I thought it was weird he only wanted to see me. He paged me all of the time but I ignored them. I didn't see him again."

Foley told Elizabeth he knew about the warrants for her arrest and handed her a grand jury subpoena, doubting she would actually show up in Dedham to testify. But right on time two days later, Elizabeth did show up, and repeated everything she had told him for the twenty-four captivated grand jurors.

Driving to Vermont on Friday night, February 19, 2000, for a well-deserved weekend of skiing with his family, Marty Foley was preoccupied with Dirk Greineder. He had taken a call from Belinda Markel, who had told him her uncle was planning a family trip to Bryce Canyon in Utah. Dr. Greineder was scheduled to attend the fifty-sixth annual meeting of the American Academy of Allergy, Asthma and Immunology in San Diego on March 3, and he had just told his niece he would extend that trip with the visit to the canyon.

The authorities were already aware of the doctor's scheduled Southern California trip through Foley's clandestine relationship with his travel agent, but Belinda's confirmation that he intended to meet his family in Utah forced a simple, albeit explosive conclusion. It was time to arrest Dr. Greineder.

With Mexico just south of San Diego, Foley was not about to allow his prey another chance to escape, possibly after a final good-bye visit with his children. "We were closing in and we were not going to let him get anywhere near Mexico," Foley said. "He was going to have to be arrested before he left on that trip."

Put between both sides again, Belinda began the delicate dance of keeping track of her uncle so she could report back to Foley. "It started this chain where Marty was trying to keep tabs to make sure Dirk didn't leave early, and I was staying in touch with Dirk," she said. First thing Monday morning, the travel agent cheerily gave Foley the Greineder family's entire itinerary, unaware the detective was about to spoil an expensive vacation.

With Rick Grundy poised to formally indict Dr. Greineder for his wife's murder, crime lab manager Gwen Pino delivered exciting news from Cellmark Diagnostics on Friday, February 25. A cutting from the right-hand brown work glove had yielded a secondary genetic profile that matched Dirk Greineder's on eight of thirteen loci where DNA was profiled. Having more genetic matter to test than they had with the knife, Cellmark put the glove cutting through both the Profiler Plus and Cofiler kits, and the statistical analysis of the collected alleles skyrocketed the probability that Dr. Greineder's DNA was on the glove worn by his wife's killer.

The calculations would eventually show that only 1 in 170 million white males, including Dr. Greineder, could have left their DNA on the glove. Foley's recollection of the man's runny nose had likely paid enormous dividends. The "through-and-through" cutting from the right glove's index finger had contained May Greineder's blood and secondary genetic matter, possibly nasal discharge her husband had subconsciously wiped with his clothed finger.

Pino had removed the fabric sample from the top of the finger down to the palm, so it was also possible that she captured DNA left by sweat, from Dr. Greineder being overheated by the protracted efforts of killing his wife

Dirk and May Greineder wed in 1968 and had what others thought the perfect marriage and family. Mark Garfinkel, *Boston Herald*

May had tried to rekindle her relationship with Dirk, but he was deep into a secret life of phone sex, Internet porn, prostitutes, and swingers. Investigation photo

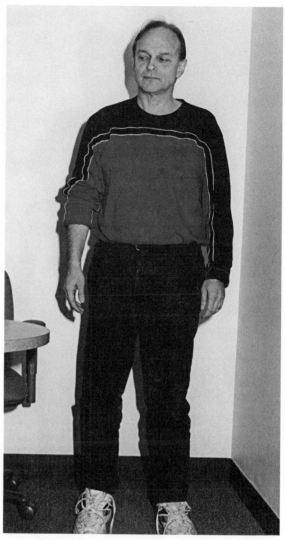

Hours after telling police he had found May horribly murdered, Dirk was oddly composed as he volunteered his bloodstained clothing and sneakers, which would yield incriminating evidence against him. Investigation photo

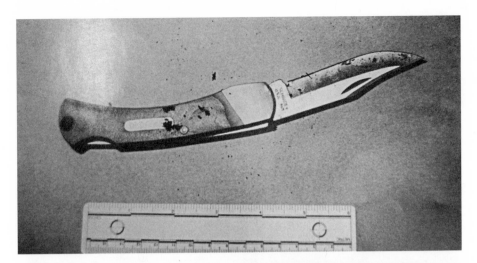

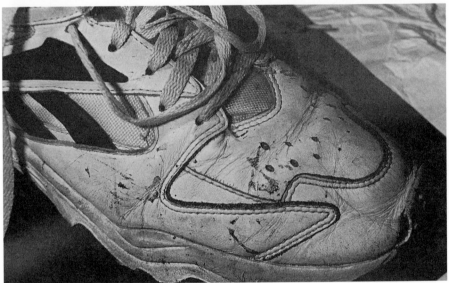

TOP The folding knife Dirk used to kill May was found by investigators within hours of the murder. Investigation photo

BOTTOM Blood spatter found on Dirk's white Reebok sneakers showed that he had been within "inches or feet" of May when she was killed, and proved to be a critical piece of evidence in convincing the jury to convict him. Investigation photo

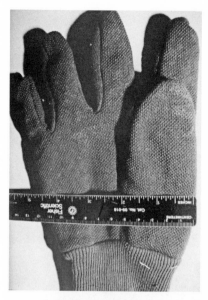

The distinctive dotted brown work gloves worn by Dirk to keep his hands free of blood could be found only at Diehl's Hardware in Wellesley. The gloves provided investigators with incriminating DNA evidence against him. Investigation photo

Dr. Greineder refused to turn over his eyeglasses, but photographs coaxed by Sgt. Marty Foley would clearly show the bloody swipe on the left lens left by the distinctive dimpled work gloves he wore when he killed May. Investigation photo

Sgt. Marty Foley leads Dr. Greineder to his Dedham Superior Court arraignment on March 1, 2000, after working for four months to expose the evil he perpetrated on May. Matt Stone, *Boston Herald*

Judge Paul Chernoff presided over the Greineder case from pretrial proceedings through Dr. Greineder's unsuccessful attempt to win a new trial following his conviction. Mark Garfinkel, *Boston Herald*

Wellesley Detective Jill McDermott, suddenly thrust into her first murder investigation, partnered with Marty Foley to expose Dr. Greineder's lies. Courtesy of Jill McDermott

Kirsten, Britt, and Colin Greineder were unconditionally behind their father for the entire trial no matter how distressing the testimony, and their support never wavered. Nancy Lane, *Boston Herald*

Belinda Markel and Ilse Stark's support of the case against Dr. Greineder caused irreparable estrangement from the Greineder family. Patrick Whittemore, *Boston Herald*

Sgt. Marty Foley shows the jury the condoms discovered along with self-prescribed Viagra in Dr. Greineder's garage during the second search of his home, which gave investigators the first indication of his sordid secret life. Patrick Whittemore, *Boston Herald*

Prosecutor Rick Grundy shows the jury how Dr. Greineder used a folding knife and distinctive brown work gloves to kill May. Nancy Lane, *Boston Herald*

Defense attorney Marty Murphy questions FBI analyst Lorie Gottesman about the Estwing two-pound hammer used in May's murder. Gottesman's testimony about food storage bags linked to the Greineder household would be far more damaging to Dr. Greineder. Ted Fitzgerald, *Boston Herald*

Rick Grundy used every opportunity to show the jury the clean hands Dr. Greineder claimed he used to check May's bloody wound and lift her bloody body, in contrast to his clothing, which was coated with her blood. Associated Press

Dirk Greineder grimaces as jury foreman Stan Smith delivers the
guilty verdict following six grueling weeks of sensational testimony.
Patrick Whittemore, *Boston Herald*

Jurors, the strain of the trial evident in their demeanor, discuss their verdict after a searing six-week experience none of them will ever forget. From left, Michael Paul, Jeffrey St. Armand, Jahon Jamali, Tony Najjar, Cheryl Nixon, Dr. William Giesecke, and Stan Smith. Ted Fitzgerald, *Boston Herald*

After exposing Dirk Greineder's guilt, there was nothing but profound sadness for Belinda Markel, Ilse Stark, Rick Grundy, and Marty Foley over May's senseless killing. Ted Fitzgerald, *Boston Herald*

Massachusetts Trial Court Officer Bill Weed handcuffs Dr. Greineder after a jury of his peers found him guilty of murdering May, sending him to prison for the rest of his life. Patrick Whittemore, *Boston Herald*

after the initial hammer blow had failed to incapacitate her and then hurrying to discard the evidence. Regardless of how the murderous husband had left his cells on the glove, the powerfully incriminating results were going to be hard to discount. "I was excited because it was so much better than the first one," recalled Foley. "I was more excited because it wasn't anybody else. He couldn't be excluded."

Foley dialed Belinda Markel on his cell phone on Monday, February 28. The conversation was short, Foley not needing a lot of words to explain what the next day's events were going to do to Belinda's family.

"We plan to do this tomorrow, but I'll call you first," he said of Dr. Greineder's impending indictment. Hanging up with a nervous acknowledgment, Belinda took a deep breath, knowing that once her uncle was arrested her relationship with his children was bound to change forever.


# 16

REPORTING TO THE NORFOLK COUNTY GRAND JURY, Marty Foley anticipated that Tuesday, February 29, 2000, would be one of the more memorable days of his police career. It would certainly turn out that way, but not for the reasons Foley expected. Being the final witness to appear before the investigative panel that had been sitting for four months, the detective sensed that the twenty-four grand jurors were anxious to complete their work. "The grand jury was ready for this," he said. "They were ready to wrap this thing up. They had had questions for every witness, and they had been very interested."

Prosecutor Rick Grundy had wanted to use Foley's final testimony to join the investigation's loose ends for the grand jurors while providing an overview of the mounting evidence against Dr. Greineder. After Foley walked out of the grand jury room, Grundy then made the formal request that the men and women who had digested weeks of secret testimony indict Dr. Greineder for the murder of his wife. He left the grand jury to make its vote, confident it would result in an indictment.

But his satisfaction would be short-lived. Unbeknownst to the core investigators, the apprehension of Dr. Greineder was being ripped away from them by District Attorney Bill Keating, who was orchestrating a grandiose operation to arrest the doctor culminating with a press conference timed for live coverage on the evening newscasts.

Foley was surprised, and then annoyed, to learn that Dr. Greineder's office in Brookline was surrounded by plainclothes officers who had a standing order to arrest the doctor if he left the building. "It seemed like a lot was going on, and I didn't know everything that was going on," Foley said. "For some reason at this point, everyone was concerned that Dirk was going to run or do something, and I had no concerns along those lines."

Dr. Greineder was seeing patients, giving no indication he planned to abandon his public contention that he was a man falsely accused and eager to prove his innocence. He could have run beginning the afternoon of his wife's murder, but for the past four months he had made no move to flee. If the doctor wasn't at his office, Foley assumed he'd just drive to his house and arrest him there. "I had no problem going any place to arrest him, and I conveyed that," he said, the frustration still evident. "Other people were concerned. I had learned that we had two lieutenants sitting on the office in Brookline and four or five of our guys were there and four or five of Wellesley's people were there. I didn't understand why this was all happening."

The instructions to arrest Dr. Greineder if he left before the grand jury handed up the indictment only confused Foley more. "I thought that was ludicrous," he said. "I have arrested high-profile people and I would have handled this a lot differently." Foley had probably spent more time than anyone battling to expose the evil perpetrated by Dr. Greineder, and now there was a good chance he was going to be elbowed out of the way by confidants of the district attorney who had little involvement in the case.

"There are few satisfactions you get doing this job, and one of the things you do get that is satisfying is arresting people that you have been hunting at this point for four months," Foley said bitterly. "That would have pissed me off. It pissed me off that people were even thinking like that."

Informed by a downcast Jill McDermott that she had been ordered to join the police posse deployed at the doctor's office near Fenway Park, Foley defiantly told her she was going to wait until the grand jury returned its indictment as they had originally planned. "I said, 'That's not going to happen,'" Foley said with an impish smile. "I told her, 'This is what's going to happen. You and I are going to get the arrest warrant together. We're going back to Wellesley to drop your car off, then we're going to drive back down Route Nine and go to Dirk's office and arrest him.'"

If Foley was annoyed about the unwarranted meddling of the district attorney and his underlings, Grundy was near apoplectic when the detective passed along a directive from a grand jury clerk to call the DA's office. The county worker, who was closely tied to Keating, had somehow been designated as a liaison to the DA's office, thrusting him into the already chaotic management of the indictment. After guiding this complex, high-stakes investigation for four months, Grundy was now answering to a politically connected court worker.

Standing in one of the grand jury waiting rooms, Foley and McDermott could hear Grundy around the corner having a heated argument on his cell phone, presumably with someone at the district attorney's office. Suddenly filling the doorway with his strapping frame, the former college outfielder hurled the phone as hard as he could, the black plastic whizzing by McDermott's head before smashing into a wall and ricocheting in pieces off a window. "Fuck them," the infuriated prosecutor yelled, his face near purple with rage. "Who the fuck do they think they are dealing with? If they want to try this fucking case let them try it," he railed before storming out of the building.

"He basically said he quit," said Foley, still upset over what happened. "Rick actually left the building."

Almost beaned by Grundy with no explanation, McDermott also wisely opted not to intervene. It was funny in retrospect, but all she could think of then was how close the phone had sailed by her head. "I could tell he was pissed," she understated. "I don't think he said good-bye. He got off the phone and whipped it by my head and he left. Nothing was said and I wasn't going to ask any questions."

After giving Grundy time to ventilate, Foley got him on the phone. The past four months had taught him how to approach the impassioned prosecutor. "This isn't fair to Ilse and Belinda. We can't do this," the detective reasoned, sure that Grundy would place the hurt caused by May Greineder's death over his bruised feelings. "At least indict him," Foley implored.

"All right, we'll get the indictment," Grundy grumpily agreed, eventually returning to the brick building where the grand jury was completing the first step of bringing Dr. Greineder to justice. Foley sympathized with Grundy's plight, the detective fully agreeing with the star prosecutor that getting a guilty verdict against the upstanding doctor was far from a lock. Unfortunately, most others in their office, including the district attorney, thought otherwise.

"They saw this completely different than Rick and I saw this," Foley explained. "I really believe they thought this was a slam-dunk and we were going way overboard by obtaining all this information and doing it the right way through the grand jury. It seemed like they had been talking about this amongst themselves and they had made decisions without consulting us. At this point, Rick just had enough. There were people Rick hated in that office because they were political hacks, and they were actually making decisions that were clearly Rick's decisions to be made."

The Norfolk County Grand Jury handed up the indictment against Dirk Greineder around 3 P.M. While Foley was supposed to alert the police contingent encircling Dr. Greineder's office as soon as the indictment was delivered, he instead drove with McDermott to Dedham Superior Court, where they obtained an arrest warrant. On the way, he had called Belinda Markel to give her the news before anyone else. "We got it," Foley said wearily, the untold events of the day thick in his voice. "We're going to take care of it."

Talking to Foley earlier, Belinda had noticed an element of stress she had not seen in him before. "He was tight in the first conversation I had with him," she said. "I had known Marty from a number of conversations we had to this point, and I knew something was bothering him. He was quick to get off the phone." His second call with the update that Dr. Greineder had been indicted was equally brief. "He was in a zone," Belinda said. "A zone where you have yourself focused."

Taking a deep breath with the realization that her uncle was formally charged with May's murder, Belinda made a telephone call. "I called my mother to tell her they were going to arrest Dirk," she said softly. "Let me know when it's over," Ilse Stark had replied.

Heading down Route Nine toward Brookline, Foley finally called his superiors to report he was holding the arrest warrant. Dwelling on the day's tumultuous events, Foley could still not decipher what was happening. "This investigation was running very, very smoothly until we hit this day," he reflected. "I felt I was losing control of it."

The absurdity of the situation grew more evident when the veteran state trooper saw the concealed perimeter of cops around Dr. Greineder's Brookline Avenue building. "I was amazed," said Foley. "There's no doubt he's a bad guy, he's killed someone, but he's in there looking at patients. Jill and I could have gone up there and I could have walked this guy out in handcuffs, into my car and back to Wellesley like I had done many times before with people of his stature, and it wouldn't have been a big deal. Nobody in that building probably would have known I had done it."

Instead, Foley and McDermott were going to make the arrest with a half-dozen other cops, including McDermott's father, Brookline Lt. Bill McDermott. In spite of the overkill, Foley thought the father-daughter involvement "was a nice touch."

Taking the elevator to the fifth floor, the police contingent silently marched through an empty lobby past a young man at a reception desk. "Can I help you?" the worker offered feebly. Foley ignored the receptionist and instead led the pack down the hallway to Dr. Greineder's office, where Foley had searched the day after the murder.

Almost as if he had been waiting for them, Dr. Greineder sat meekly behind his desk. "You have been indicted for the murder of May Greineder and you are under arrest," Foley said sternly, standing the expressionless doctor up to pat him down. "We're going to bring you back to the Wellesley Police Station," Foley said, handcuffing the doctor's arms behind his back. "You're going to be booked and you can make any phone calls you want from there."

He read Dr. Greineder his Miranda rights and picked up his briefcase from the desktop, but was stunned when a superior told him to leave it. "He doesn't need that," the supervisor said. Foley did not believe what he was hearing. "We'll take it. We're not coming back here," Foley protested.

"No, he doesn't need that," the supervisor persisted. Foley dearly wanted to take the briefcase, but he would have been forced into a confrontation with a superior far outranking him in front of officers from other departments.

Foley grudgingly laid the briefcase back on Dr. Greineder's desk. "There was a reason to take his briefcase. It was part of his belongings, and it was right there under his control," Foley said bitterly. "It could have contained all the information about the missing Corporate Physicians American Express cards and Tom Young that we had been chasing for three months," he added, only half sarcastically.

While eschewing something potentially important like their murder suspect's briefcase, they were nevertheless going to tow Dr. Greineder's Toyota Avalon back to the police station. "There was no reason to take the car," Foley said. "It was secured in a garage with an attendant and was not part of the arrest. If he had the car when he was arrested, then they could search it and inventory it but they decided to tow it back and search it anyway."

While Foley escorted the compliant Dr. Greineder out of the medical building, his captive's eyes darted toward several people who now had noticed the police activity, but the doctor remained silent. To Foley, he seemed almost resigned to his arrest. "I think he knew it was going to come," Foley speculated. "Marty Murphy had probably told him he was going to be indicted, and I think Marty even asked Rick to let him know if he was going to be indicted." Grundy had not extended the courtesy to his friend-turned-adversary.

With a seat belt securing Dr. Greineder in the front of his green Crown Victoria and Jill McDermott riding in back, nothing was said on the drive back to Wellesley, but Foley could not stop thinking about the day's upsetting events. "I am fit to be tied at this point," he recalled. "This was a bad day. I wanted to get this day over with and it was absolutely not going to get better. They never consulted with me about how we wanted to do this. They just had their plans all set and ready to go."

The same situation existed for Grundy. "Nobody's telling Rick how to do anything, and now they're going to tell him when and how," Foley said. "It's a difficult case as it is, and you've got this guy who's prosecuted thirty or forty homicide cases and he knows what he's doing and how he's going to do it and these guys have no idea. This is obviously a huge case. It's probably the biggest case to come out of this office since Sacco and Vanzetti, and it could have been handled correctly if Rick was just left alone."

Parked in front of Manhattan's Asphalt Green at York Avenue and Ninety-First Street where her kids were swimming, Belinda Markel heard her cell phone ring about 4 P.M. "It's over. We got him. I love you guys," reported a subdued Rick Grundy before hanging up.

"He sounded spent," said Belinda, who would not learn until months later that Grundy had briefly quit. "I got on FDR Drive, went home, and told my mother and waited for the phone call."

With her uncle in jail, Belinda knew it was only a matter of time before his attorney learned of her family's cooperation with the police. The stress mounting as more time passed without a call from her cousins, she anxiously waited in her apartment for the phone to ring. "Now I'm getting tense," she recalled. "Those last couple of weeks I was dancing a lot. I'm talking to the Greineder family. I'm talking to Marty Foley. I [knew] where things were going but there was a certain amount of tension."

Despite their disagreements over the police investigation, Dr. Greineder had kept in close communication with his wife's relatives from New York, mostly because he needed their help. "Things had changed, but some of it stayed the same. I was in constant contact with them," Belinda said. "We knew that they were going to need help. We knew there were bad feelings, but they needed money and that's what a lot of this came down to. We knew they would call."

Taken into the cellblock at the Wellesley Police Station, Dr. Greineder said nothing beyond answering questions for his booking form. The prominent family man was photographed and fingerprinted before being locked in a jail cell for the first time in his life.

Ordered held without bail by a clerk magistrate, he would have to spend the night until his Dedham Superior Court arraignment the next morning. Watching the booking process from the periphery, Lt. Wayne Cunningham observed that Dr. Greineder was almost morose in contrast to his resistive behavior during the searches of his house.

"He was flat," Cunningham said. "He wasn't as whiney as he had been. I expected more of that."

Hanging up his office telephone, Chief Terry Cunningham could hardly contain his anger. Preparing to announce Dr. Greineder's arrest with a press conference in front of the police station, Cunningham was incensed to hear that District Attorney Keating had instead invited the media to Keating's office in neighboring Dedham.

Like Foley and Grundy, Cunningham had been unaware of the heavy-handed manipulation of Dr. Greineder's indictment by Keating's office until it was too late to react. Cunningham had also assumed that the arrest would be low profile with Foley and McDermott joined by one or two supervisors, not the dozen cops garrisoned in Brookline. "We didn't know of the DA's plans," the chief said with irritation.

"These were the people who early on in the meetings were saying all you have to do is steer this one in," Cunningham continued. "It's a ground ball. This case is a slam-dunk, they said. But there was no smoking gun. These people didn't know what they were talking about."

Cunningham was especially galled at Keating's decision to host the press conference because the issue had been discussed only a few weeks before. Another area police chief had complained that the DA's office had undercut his department in a highly publicized case, forcing the Norfolk County Police Chiefs Association to make Keating promise future press events would be held at the local police station. "We had entered into an agreement with the DA," Cunningham said. "I went over to Keating's office with three or four chiefs and said when there's a high-profile case, it's our town and the people who live there want to see our police in the background. It's not an ego thing. It's just the way it should be done. Three weeks before the indictment Keating said no problem."

Cunningham couldn't believe it when he took the call informing him the media would not be gathering in Wellesley. "No, we're going to have the press conference here at Wellesley PD," he argued. "No, we've already made the decision," the chief was told. Unwilling to back down, Cunningham threatened to have his own press conference, but Keating would not be deterred. "I said we're going to have two press conferences because I'm going to have one here, and do you know where the press is going to come? They're going to come here," Cunningham said.

Already fed up with the goings on in his office that day, Grundy offered to make a stand with Cunningham. "I get on the phone with Keating and have a discussion and Rick's here and Rick says, 'I'll be here, wherever you want to do it,'" said an appreciative Cunningham. Realizing that "the DA wasn't moving," the police chief decided it would only hurt the case against Dr. Greineder to make the dispute public. "I thought, 'Do we really want to do this?'"

With Dr. Greineder booked and settled in a jail cell, Marty Foley had no desire to attend a press conference, wherever it was, until he was instructed to return to Dedham. "I had no intention of going there, but I was told to go back," he said. Walking into the DA's office, Foley found it a beehive of activity with a throng of media setting up cameras and lights in the law library. Bill Keating was nothing short of giddy as he told the Wellesley and State Police investigators what he planned to cover during the press conference.

"I've got it all set. I've got charts. I've got pictures," he told a surprised Terry Cunningham. "You've got to be shitting me," thought Cunningham. "He was like a kid in a candy store."

Overhearing Keating repeatedly mentioning a backdrop, Foley was shocked when he realized the DA wanted to display a detailed map of Morses Pond that Foley had marked with undisclosed information important to the investigation. "I had already talked to him and said you can't use that," Foley remembered with annoyance. "There were things on there that I had written. I told him you have to use something else."

Adamant that the map was not going to be displayed to every media outlet in greater Boston, Foley retreated to his office where he had another depiction of Morses Pond. "It was a smaller map and I said if you want to use something, use this," he suggested to the district attorney. Frowning over the downscaled, less expressive map, a crestfallen Keating consented to the switch. Before Keating could change his mind, Foley snatched his working copy and squirreled it in his office.

The DA had already been advised not to use Foley's map by Terry and Wayne Cunningham. The brothers were far more troubled when they read the press statement Keating excitedly handed them. "He was like a little kid," said an appalled Terry Cunningham. "He was running all around the office talking about how he was going to talk about this and talk about that. He laid out the whole thing."

The Wellesley chief tried to dissuade Keating from revealing too much of the evidence against Dr. Greineder but he was impervious to the recommendation. "You can't do that," Cunningham counseled. "Oh yes I can," Keating said royally, arguing that the information was going to be revealed in court the next day where the press would hear it anyway.

When Keating enthusiastically thrust his prepared statement at Foley to read, the trooper was aghast at the breadth of information the county's top law enforcer wanted to disclose. "I thought, 'This is outrageous,'" Foley said. With the DA ignoring the Cunninghams' advice and unsure if Grundy was still employed, Foley had no way to save the politically motivated Keating from himself.

"In the past, when issues started spinning out of control, I could count on Rick to restore an element of common sense. But this time was different," said Foley, who found Grundy fuming in his office, still incensed over his boss's heavy-handed meddling.

The detective vented his frustration, but Foley realized that Grundy was done arguing with Keating, who was clearly bent on making a public relations splash at the expense of investigative integrity, regardless of who counseled him against it.

"I talked to Rick and said this is fucked up. I felt like I had lost control," recalled Foley. "This guy hadn't even been arraigned yet and the DA is going to talk about hookers and secret double lives with the press."

Foley asked Grundy if he had read Keating's overexposing media statement. The prosecutor nodded that he had, dejectedly tossing open his hands as if to say, "What are you going to do?" At least it looked like Grundy was still on the team, Foley thought, unaware that Jill McDermott had given her chief a briefing on the day's tumultuous events. It was Terry Cunningham and, to a lesser extent, prosecutor Gerry Pudolsky who bluntly told Grundy he had to reconsider his hasty decision to quit.

"Rick, you can't walk away from this," Cunningham had challenged the exasperated prosecutor. "Look, Terry, I've got other issues," Grundy began before the police chief cut him off. "No, I trusted you. I put my faith in you," Cunningham hotly countered. "Now you're going to walk away from this? You can't do this to me."

Pudolsky, who had seen Grundy walking down the street after his angry exit from the grand jury, took a more personal approach. With a wife and a baby daughter to support he owed it to them to stay, the older, respected attorney had reasoned.

It was approaching 6 P.M., and the law library was now jammed with more than two dozen journalists who had scrambled to Dedham on an hour's notice for the Greineder story that immediately had topped the Boston newscasts and would land again on page one of the morning newspapers. The dormant Greineder case had unexpectedly burst back into the news.

Easing into the jammed law library, Foley found a spot behind the row of steel tripods manned by fidgeting photographers, confident there was no way he could be caught on tape. Glancing back at Bill Keating settling at a podium in front of the TV cameras, Foley cringed when he saw McDermott with the Cunningham brothers standing near the DA. He tried to get his partner's attention so she could duck out of the camera shot, but McDermott ended up being another unsuspecting backdrop to one of Massachusetts' more memorable press conferences.

"Thank you for coming," Keating began cheerily as the television stations took the press conference live. "Last Halloween morning, October thirty-first, at the Morses Pond area in Wellesley, Mabel 'May' Greineder was brutally assaulted and murdered. Today, a Norfolk County Grand Jury, after investigating this since the first week of November on a weekly basis indicted Dirk Greineder, also known as Thomas Young, for the murder of his wife."

Huddled against a wall, Foley recoiled at the mention of Thomas Young even though he knew the disclosure was coming. Turning his attention back to Keating, the DA was just getting started with his jaw-dropping presentation.

"Let me first go through the crime scene analysis and I'll try to detail this," Keating said, using a pointer on the map provided by Foley. "This is Morses Pond in Wellesley. This purple road is the access road to Morses Pond," he demonstrated, then went on detailing how witness Bill Kear had seen the doctor emerge from where his wife lay and then detour down the paved maintenance road where the weapons were found before finally approaching Kear and asking if he had a phone.

Keating then revealed the discovery of the second glove in the catch basin near Dr. Greineder's van before moving to more incendiary evidence. "But in reviewing the background of her husband, looking at business documents, looking at credit cards, looking through computer material, we were able to determine that Dirk Greineder had a focus on pornography. He had a focus on and a frequency in engaging with prostitutes, and he had even adopted the fictitious name Thomas Young, which he used on the credit card and on documents of the like to try and create a second identity that he followed through his secret life. This background information clearly demonstrated that, in terms of the relationship, there were difficulties and there was some strain."

Across Boston's newsrooms, Keating's synopsis of Dr. Greineder's adulterous alter ego struck like a thunderclap. Already a major story because of the successful suburban professionals involved, the depiction of the murderous Harvard Medical School professor cavorting with hookers under an assumed name fully injected the story with sensationalism.

Feeding off the buzz of the bombshell revelations, Keating moved to the final topic in his prepared remarks, highlighting the forensic evidence collected against Dr. Greineder. The cat now almost fully out of the bag, Keating unveiled more prosecution secrets. "We were looking at him from the beginning because of the circumstances we described at the crime scene," Keating finally admitted publicly. "We conducted forensic testing and we wanted to pursue that as soon as possible because he had blood on his jacket, on his eyeglasses, on his sleeves, on his sneakers. But interestingly enough that blood stopped and there was no blood at all on his hands."

Taking questions from the frenzied reporters, Keating agreed that Dr. Greineder had modeled his wife's killing after the sinister unsolved murders of Irene Kennedy and Richard Reyenger.

"Do I think he anticipated that people would make a link, another woman dead by a pond in a suburban town that begins with W? Do I think that maybe he staged the scene to look like those killings? The circumstances were such that you have to wonder if he didn't try to point things in that direction," Keating answered candidly.

Foley could barely contain his disgust when Keating predicted victory over Dr. Greineder's defense. "What matters is not a quick arrest," the DA said, contradicting his own previous urging. "What matters is not making the public feel better," he added, also contrary to his private position. "What matters is where you end up, with an arrest that leads to a successful prosecution. We will convict him."

Astounded by the district attorney's bombastic comments, defense attorney Marty Murphy would soon fight back with a motion to sanction Keating. The extraordinary press conference mercifully over, Foley wished he had been able to duck into his office as Grundy obstinately had after observing the start of it from the doorway to the law library.

"I wasn't very proud with what was going on," Foley said soberly. "People were taking all this credit and nothing spectacular had happened. It was just another event in the investigation of May Greineder's death. From here on in, time was no longer on our side," he explained. "Nobody seemed to get that. Rick got it, but nobody seemed to get that we now had to start turning over everything and Marty Murphy can start pushing us. I remember Rick saying he's going to be throwing paper at us left and right. And he did. Rick predicted this would happen, down to the Greineder children never coming to our side."

Watching the live television coverage in his Newton home, Steve Rosenthal was stunned to learn that his college roommate living the next town over had been charged with his wife's murder. As a freshman at Yale in 1958, Rosenthal had shared a block of dormitory rooms with Dirk Greineder and Tom Young, a likable fellow from Baltimore who kept the group chuckling with his delightful sense of humor. He had been aware that his former friend had been under a cloud of suspicion but found it illogical that the man he knew could commit such a crime.

"I never had any suspicion there was a dark side to him or that he could be at all capable of doing something like this," Rosenthal reflected. "When I heard the news of the murder I had no reason to believe at all that he was involved in it. When I heard his computer had been seized and his rights were being violated I was really kind of up in arms and I was really surprised by that. I thought the police were being overzealous about it. I was giving him any benefit of the doubt."

Rosenthal had known Dr. Greineder was living in Wellesley, having followed the swimming exploits of his three children in the newspaper. They were just like their father, he had thought, as he fondly remembered watching Dirk swim the butterfly for the powerhouse Yale swim team.

The son of a doctor, Rosenthal became a highly regarded photographer of architecture while his Yale friend continued his medical studies with a grueling duel doctorate program at Case Western Reserve University. "I remember him as being kind of tightly wound up, tightly strung. That was the impression I had of him," said Rosenthal. "Other people said he had a lighter side and was really kind of humorous. I never really saw that."

Both sons of German parents, Dirk Greineder and Steve Rosenthal shared vastly different upbringings. While Dirk's father was a doctor in the German military, Rosenthal's father was not allowed to practice medicine because of his Jewish heritage. His parents left Germany in 1936 before Adolf Hitler unleashed the full carnage of the Holocaust, and Rosenthal's family was able to secure his grandfather's release from the Buchenwald concentration camp before the Nazis began their methodical extermination of six million European Jews. Two of Rosenthal's aunts would not be as fortunate, the family never seeing them again after their internment in Nazi death camps.

Despite what could have led to a contentious relationship given their contrary circumstances, the two men became friends, hardly discussing the raw wounds still festering thirteen years after the end of the war. Following the media coverage of May Greineder's murder, Rosenthal was squarely behind her embattled husband.

Hearing the allegation that Dr. Greineder had used Tom Young's name to veil his adulterous roaming, however, Rosenthal felt his loyalty waning. Young, a successful attorney in Baltimore, was well liked by his Yale classmates, and the assault on his name was distressing for Rosenthal. Digesting DA Keating's incredible revelations, Rosenthal considered for the first time that his Yale roommate might be complicit in his wife's slaying. Talking it over with his wife, Rosenthal wrestled with his responsibility to call the Wellesley police about the true identity of Tom Young. After watching the continuing coverage later on the 11 P.M. newscasts, Rosenthal decided he would sleep on it before making a decision in the morning.

Sleep was delayed in coming for Belinda Markel. The call she had expected earlier finally came from Britt Greineder about 7:30 P.M. "The bastards have arrested him," her cousin wailed, running on incoherently about a car being towed. "You need to come up here," Britt pleaded. "We have to get together with Marty Murphy. We have to get him out of there," she sobbed over the image of her father locked in a jail cell.

"All right," Belinda agreed. "I'll come up with my mother in the morning," she promised, hanging the phone up with a feeling of dread. Her fiendish uncle was not going to be allowed to cash in on the support of Belinda and her parents, but she empathized with her cousins. "I was still looking for a way to have a relationship with them and try to help them," Belinda said sincerely. Waiting for sleep before rising early to drive to Wellesley, Belinda wondered if her relationship with the Greineder children could survive her abandonment of their father.

Tossing in bed, Marty Foley could not shake the rare depression that had enveloped him. That morning he had risen with the purpose of arresting Dirk Greineder, never thinking his head would be full of bitterness and confusion when he laid it on his pillow that night. Bringing Dr. Greineder to justice certainly would not have been celebrated festively, but Foley and his colleagues had craved a taste of satisfaction for being able to expose his cold-blooded charade.

"I didn't expect to go home feeling shitty," Foley said simply. DA Keating's meddling aside, Foley was concerned the day's amateurish events would harm the relationship he and Grundy had nurtured with Belinda Markel and Ilse Stark.

"This is not a guaranteed win. That was the biggest thing here," Foley said passionately. "We were developing a relationship with Belinda and Ilse and that was getting harder. They had to put themselves out there, and they were trusting us to do a good job in the investigation; and look what we had to show them."

Always striving to remain emotionally level, Foley tried to purge the day's negative happenings from his thoughts, instead focusing on what had been accomplished. The overriding goal of indicting and apprehending Dr.

Greineder had been reached. The doctor would have to formally face the consequences of his treacherous act with an arraignment in the morning. "It didn't go as planned, but it went fine," Foley conceded. The end result was Dirk Greineder spending his first of many nights in jail.

ARRIVING AT THE WELLESLEY POLICE STATION at 7:30 A.M., Marty Foley was surprised to hear that Dr. Greineder had slept so soundly overnight that he had to be woken not long before Foley's arrival. Mentioning it to Jill McDermott, the detectives concluded their suspect's arrest had probably come with an odd sense of relief after weeks of waiting for the police to come.

"This guy hadn't slept much, probably not in the last four months," said Foley. "It's tough to kill somebody and then put your head down on a pillow. This was probably the first good night's rest he had in a long time."

Feeling decidedly better than he had the upsetting night before, Foley and McDermott were going to take Dr. Greineder to his Dedham Superior Court arraignment, but the detectives were told not to get him there until the early morning work of the court was completed, after 10:30. The media were already positioned around the massive granite courthouse, Foley was told.

Rising after his own fitful night's sleep, Steve Rosenthal had made his decision. Telephoning the Wellesley police, he was quickly transferred to the detective office after explaining he knew the identity of Thomas Young. Less than thirty minutes later, Detective Bill Vargas was on Rosenthal's Newton doorstep clutching a Polaroid camera.

Showing Vargas a Yale alumni directory bearing the names of Dirk Greineder and Thomas Young, the detective took pictures and hastily offered Rosenthal his thanks as Vargas hustled back to his cruiser to confirm the Yale connection for his superiors.

Loading Dr. Greineder back into the front seat of his cruiser, not a word was spoken while Foley and McDermott took him to Dedham. The media now had practically surrounded the historic courthouse that operated as one of the oldest in the Commonwealth. The hulking Greek-style granite courthouse was dedicated on July 4, 1825, replacing a wooden structure built in 1796 from a design by post-Revolutionary architect Charles Bulfinch complete with a bell made by Paul Revere.

The main courtroom in Dedham was the setting for most of Norfolk County's major criminal cases, none more famous than the trial of Nicola Sacco and Bartolomeo Vanzetti.

Charged with the April 1920 robbery and murders of a Braintree shoe company paymaster and his bodyguard, a crime many scholars believe the Italian immigrants and self-professed anarchists did not commit, Sacco and Vanzetti were found guilty following a sensational seven-week trial that drew hundreds of protesters.

After a series of failed appeals, they were executed at the Charlestown State Prison on August 23, 1927. The designation of the main courtroom on the second floor as the "Sacco and Vanzetti Room" surely gave little comfort to the defendants who have appeared there since.

Seeing the media ringing the courthouse as he came down Dedham's High Street, Foley turned down a side street and made a hard right to park behind the building. Glancing toward the expansive stone stairs where prisoners were brought inside, Foley saw that it was lined with reporters and cameramen now scrambling to record the disgraced doctor's first public appearance.

"I'm going to walk around the car and get you out and walk you in," Foley told the doctor. Before Jill McDermott could get on the other side of the celebrity defendant, a court officer grabbed the dazed doctor's right arm as soon as Foley helped him from the cruiser, and the two men led the handcuffed doctor up the stairs through the gauntlet of media. Dr. Greineder, tastefully clad in a tailored beige sport coat, slacks and a white dress shirt open at the collar, ignored several shouted questions about whether he had killed his wife.

Trailing behind with a phalanx of court officers, McDermott had been bumped out of one of the murder case's more memorable photographs. "I was okay with that," she said. "TV adds ten pounds, right?" she joked. "I remember pulling up and was like, 'Whoa, there's a lot of media.' The press was really interested in this. I thought there would only be a couple of reporters, but it was kind of unreal. I was grateful to have Marty there."

Led into the crowded courtroom twenty minutes later by two white-shirted court officers, a shackled Dr. Greineder turned toward his distressed children and future son-in-law, trying to flash them an encouraging smile, but his teeth remained buried in a frozen grimace.

Appearing bewildered and continually blinking as if trying to make his reality disappear, Dr. Greineder could utter only the words "not guilty" throughout the proceeding. Providing Judge Malcolm Graham (a former Boston Celtic), with photographs depicting May Greineder's grievous wounds, prosecutor Rick Grundy unveiled more tantalizing revelations in asking the judge to hold Dr. Greineder without bail.

The doctor had telephoned a listing for a prostitute on the day before and the day after his wife's murder, the prosecutor said, the allergist telling another hooker his wife "was getting older . . . soft." Reciting the other evidence breathlessly revealed on live TV the night before by District Attorney Bill Keating, Grundy told the judge he could link Dr. Greineder to the murder through DNA and physical evidence collected at the crime scene.

Detailing the doctor's sensational second identity of Thomas Young, which investigators had just confirmed, Grundy disclosed that Dr. Greineder had used the name of his Yale classmate to fraudulently obtain an American Express Corporate Card to pay for his sexual encounters with prostitutes. No one, possibly not even his slain wife, was aware of the doctor's adulterous lifestyle, the prosecutor added. "None of these individuals know anything about Thomas Young," Grundy emphasized with a glance toward the doctor's tormented children behind him.

Opposing Grundy's contention that Dr. Greineder was a flight risk because of his dual citizenship and expertise with four languages, defense attorney Marty Murphy urged Judge Graham to set his client's bail at $100,000. "He's in a fight for his life," said an impassioned Murphy. "At the end of this fight, he is confident he will be vindicated." Dr. Greineder could have run during a Christmas trip to Denmark or during business engagements across the country, Murphy argued, but did not despite "waiting for a knock at the door" to be arrested.

Introducing the judge to the doctor's three children, still tearfully huddled together on the hard courtroom bench with Kirsten's fiancé Aleks Engel, Murphy pledged that Dr. Greineder would never run from his family, who were vouching for his innocence.

"The consequences of fleeing would be to break off contact with his family. There is no basis to believe he is prepared to do that," Murphy said assuredly. "They are totally in support of him," Murphy continued, turning to the doctor's children seated behind him. "They will not waver in that support. They love him very deeply. They are confident in every fiber of their body that their father did not kill their mother."

Rejecting Murphy's recommendation without explanation, Judge Graham ordered Dr. Greineder be held without bail, his two daughters quaking with grief as the court officers led their manacled father past them. "We love you," they chorused, their words garbled with emotion. A satisfied Marty Foley stood poker-faced in his dark suit as the defendant was led out the main door at the rear of the second-floor courtroom toward the holding cell directly across the hall.

If there was one thing that fascinated the public about the Greineder case, it was the unyielding support of the disgraced doctor's children; it might have topped even his secret sex romps. How could such three intelligent, accomplished young adults stand behind a man who mounting evidence suggested ruthlessly killed their mother?

Foley had been skeptical of Grundy's proclamation just after May's murder that her children were never going to condemn their father, but Grundy had seen it just the year before in the retrial of David Magraw, whose original conviction for killing his wife, Nancy, had been overturned on appeal. As they had during the first trial, the slain woman's son and two stepsons had stood by their accused father even as Grundy won a second murder conviction against him in the retrial. The support of Magraw's sons, ranging in age at the time from nineteen to twenty-seven, had not been lost on both juries. Grundy expected Dr. Greineder's three handsome, successful children to have the same influence at their father's trial.

Confronted with the unimaginable assertion that their model father was a serial adulterer, the Greineder children met the incredible disclosures with a furious denial. In the early afternoon Belinda Markel arrived with her mother at 56 Cleveland Road, where her cousins were still reeling from the avalanche of loathsome revelations unleashed by their father's indictment and arraignment.

With their prior knowledge of the damning evidence of Dr. Greineder's culpability, Belinda and Ilse Stark mostly listened as the traumatized children debated the credibility of the detestable allegations unfurled at the theatrical press conference the night before and again during the morning's circus-like arraignment. "It's all lies," was the consensus from the doctor's children, younger daughter Britt typically the most animated.

It was clear to Belinda, listening to the quizzical banter among her cousins, that they had no inkling of their adored father's sexual dalliances. Even though Dr. Greineder had cryptically warned the family that "something bad" would come out, his children had been blindsided by the portrayal of the ultimate family man as a homicidal philanderer.

Ensconced in the Norfolk County Jail, where he was only allowed to make collect calls, Dr. Greineder phoned home in the midst of his children's suffering confusion. "Daddy, we love you. We love you, Daddy," Kirsten gushed after accepting the call. "It's okay, Daddy," she soothed. "We're here for you. We love you. Yeah, Belinda's here," Kirsten said, sitting on the living room ottoman and looking toward her cousin.

Only hearing one side of the conversation, Belinda watched for her cousin's reaction after she asked her father if the unsavory accusations were true. Stiffening higher on the ottoman, Kirsten asked a follow-up question. "Do you think Mom knew?" she asked solemnly before her shoulders deflated. Grabbing a pen, Kirsten began jotting down a list of instructions from her father before yielding the phone to her siblings.

Being hurried off the payphone at the house of correction, Dr. Greineder exchanged only quick words of encouragement with Britt and Colin. Asked what their father had said in response to her pointed questions, Kirsten recited his answers. "He said some of it's true," she said sullenly. "He said, 'I'm not proud of it.'"

"Did Mom know?" Britt asked. "I think so," Kirsten replied quietly, echoing her father's response. The understated admission of his infidelities sparked an impromptu debate on sexuality among his children that left Belinda inwardly shaking her head. Who was to say what was right and what was wrong when the family had never discussed sexual intimacy, one of the daughters offered in trying to account for her father's behavior.

To Belinda, her cousins' naiveté was genuine. Beyond the mandatory warnings parents give their young adult children, Dirk and especially May never spoke candidly about sex, particularly near their children. "This conversation they were having was all very clinical," Belinda recalled. Admitting there were cracks in their parents' storybook marriage, the children's debate exposed the fact that they had intended to confront their father about his increasing hours away from home when the family was together for Thanksgiving. The death of their mother had made the family meeting unnecessary.

"Their mother had talked to them, and they were going to read him the riot act about spending more time at home," Belinda remembered. Dejectedly detached from the discussion, Colin abruptly dissolved to tears. "I should have known something was wrong," he sobbed. "I was on his computer one day and I found some of it, porn and stuff." Sitting next to him to offer a comforting back rub, Belinda asked how he reacted. "I closed it up," he said forlornly. "It wasn't too hard to find. I literally tripped on it."

Living at home after graduating from Yale in May 1997, Colin used his father's computer up to three times a day to e-mail friends and play chess on the Internet. Going into the history folder one day he was met with a list of sex sites his father had apparently visited. Investigating further, he found a file containing downloaded hardcore images. Trying to swallow the disappointment of stumbling upon his admired father's cyber sex sessions, Colin felt embarrassed for him, pondering whether he should ask his dad about the activity.

As the days and weeks passed, Colin could not bring himself to confront his father, he regretfully told his stunned relatives. Instead, he continued to check the history folder to monitor what his father was doing. The spying son was relieved when several weeks went by without any porn showing up on the home computer. Leaving for a month-long trip to Costa Rica in August 1997, Colin was feeling better about his father, but the relief was short-lived when he returned.

Dr. Greineder had resumed his Net surfing for porn, sometimes taking a break for a couple weeks before returning with a flurry of activity. "A month or so later I went back and it was there," Colin lamented. "I wondered if Dad knew I had seen it and tried to hide it," he speculated with his sisters. Still not having the nerve to approach his father, Colin instead began erasing the history folder when he found porn, lest someone else find it, especially his mother. His confession completed, Colin sadly leaned back into the couch where his cousin continued comforting him.

Kirsten ended the ensuing silence. "He said all this isn't true," she said defensively. "Regardless of what they said, that's not the kind of person he is," she asserted. "It's all exaggerated. People make mistakes."

Having been briefed on the full extent of her uncle's proclivities, Belinda could see his children had still not grasped the scope of his involvement. "They seemed to be focusing on the porn aspect of it and that the rest of it was not true," she said, her cousin Britt repeatedly driving home that "we know him better than anyone else, and none of this is true." Feeling helpless and beyond their considerable abilities, the Greineder children wondered aloud "what are we going to do?" The sibling concurrence was they were going to try to get their father out on bail.

Belinda's cousins asked about her intentions. "I will always be here to support you," she responded, leaving it at that. Throughout the afternoon, it failed to dawn on her cousins that she was not behind their father. "I know it didn't get through to them," she said. "When we left, my cousins had a list of instructions from Dirk of things that had to be taken care of."

About that time in Maryland, a confused Tom Young was sizing up the Baltimore County homicide detective in his downtown law office and wanting some answers before he said anything about Dirk Greineder. Earlier he had taken a surprise telephone call from Detective Al Meyer. Young said the detective had inquired "who I was and if I knew Dirk Greineder." He invited the officer to his office, where he had some questions of his own.

"I don't like to be asked questions when I don't know why," said Young, whose heart problems had forced his recent retirement after thirty-six years as a trial attorney practicing business and insurance law. A Trooper Marty Foley from Massachusetts had called Meyer's boss that morning, Meyer politely explained, adding that Foley was investigating the murder of Dirk Greineder's wife and had arrested him the day before.

From what little Foley had told the Baltimore police, the husband had used Tom Young's identity to hide his association with prostitutes and pornography. The detective watched the affable lawyer's concerned curiosity turn to shock.

Young told Meyer he attended Yale University with Dirk Greineder from 1958 to 1962. "We roomed together for several years until Dirk took a single room his senior year because of his caseload. I'm shocked by these allegations," Young said candidly. "I have never known Dirk to have a propensity for violence."

"When was the last time you talked to him," Meyer asked the shaken lawyer.

"The last time I actually saw him was in the late sixties or early seventies when he was living in the Washington area," Young replied, searching his memory about a man he hadn't heard about in thirty years. "He was working at the National Institute of Health and possibly also the Bethesda Naval Hospital. I believe I went to a couple of Christmas parties he had."

"Was there anything unusual that happened at these parties?" the detective asked in light of the sex allegations.

"No, no," Young said quickly. "They were just typical cocktail parties. I never really had a chance to talk to Dirk's wife or get to know her." He said that he had not spoken to Dirk since 1970, but they "may have exchanged Christmas cards for a few years. Dirk was born in Germany and grew up in Lebanon," Young added, almost thinking out loud. "He used to stay with me and my family during the Christmas vacations here in Baltimore because he had nowhere else to stay."

Sitting afterward in the office he would soon turn over to a younger, trusted associate, Tom Young tried to make sense of the dastardly way his former friend had resurfaced in his life.

Young met Dirk their freshman year. He found the studious foreign student very likable "but eminently teasable. He didn't take himself seriously but he took everything seriously," Young recalled.

Dirk's mother, he told his friends, came from a prominent Lebanese family, and he had lived in the Middle East most of his life. Where Young might have been a candidate for class partier, Dirk was all business when it came to his studies and athletics. They nicknamed him "Grinder" because of his unrelenting dedication to his class work. Dirk was an accomplished swimmer, too, who was sought out by legendary coach Bob Kiphuth to compete for the powerhouse Yale swim team.

"He was a championship swimmer and had the medals to prove it," Young said admiringly. "The coach liked Greineder and he wanted Dirk to be on the team and pushed him very hard. Dirk could do the butterfly and they wanted him to do the butterfly, but it began to conflict with his pre-med studies so Dirk quit the swim team."

By the time of their senior year, Dirk had grown almost consumed by his studies. After he took a single room away from his buddies, they still saw him often but the lightheartedness they had seen freshman year had diminished with each passing semester. If there was one thing that could distract the disciplined Dirk Greineder, however, it was female companionship.

"Dirk was a ladies' man," Young said. He "was very attractive to the gals and very attracted by them. He was very interested in sex. When he would come back for the school year after summer vacation in Lebanon we would vicariously live through his stories for at least until Thanksgiving." Young had given Dirk nary a thought until he received the jarring telephone call from the Baltimore County Police.

With unanswered questions of their own about Dirk's arrest, Belinda Markel and Ilse Stark bought every local newspaper they could find in the gift shop of the Crowne Plaza in Natick. They took the elevator to their room, and Belinda turned on the television set, eager to monitor reports on the arraignment, since his children were still dutifully imposing Dirk's media blackout in the Greineder home. Ilse and Belinda were still mystified by the denial exhibited by the Greineder children of the emerging truth that their father had heartlessly killed their mother.

"It was so overwhelming," Belinda said somberly. "There was no anger at their father. I didn't understand that. I would have been angry with my father but there was no anger at all. It was just incredible."

Other than disbelief and unconditional support, the only other emotion from her cousins was Colin's shame over finding his father's pornography along with his regret for not saying anything about it. The truth about what happened to their mother seemed secondary to pleasing their father, Belinda thought ruefully. Finished with the papers and the early newscasts,

Belinda and her mother rode the elevator down for a bracing drink and dinner. Watching the late news, snuggled under the blankets, they watched with some amusement Marty Foley leading Dirk into his arraignment.

A little earlier that evening, the detective had to stifle some amusement of his own. Calling Tom Young after getting home from work, Foley could tell right away that he was going to like Dirk Greineder's college friend. "Leave it to an Irish cop from Boston to wait until I had a couple of martinis in me before calling," Young had boomed good-naturedly over the phone. Being careful with what he told the victimized attorney, Foley felt confident that Young would help him.

"He sounded like a pretty good guy and he sounded somewhat receptive," Foley recalled. "He was going to talk with us and give us some information. He was a little upset his name was being used in the way it was. He was pissed at all that."

# 18

LISTENING TO HER MOTHER'S SIDE of the telephone conversation with Britt Greineder, Belinda Markel could see the day was turning bad before they had even left their hotel room for a Thursday morning meeting at the Greineder home with attorney Marty Murphy. "I've been reading the papers and I have a lot of questions for him," Ilse Stark replied when Britt called with the meeting time. This stoked her niece's ire. "You may not read the newspaper and you may not watch the television," Britt barked at her aunt, almost like a mother punishing a toddler.

"Excuse me?" Ilse countered, taken aback by the harsh words from her niece. "You heard me," Britt replied defiantly. "We do not read the papers. We do not listen to the news. You are not allowed to do that." Having held her tongue too many times before, Ilse unloaded her fury on her disrespecting niece. "Nobody is going tell me what to do," she screamed into the phone. "I'll read the goddamn papers if I want to. If you don't want to read them that's your business."

A short time later when Ilse and Belinda walked into the Greineder home, Britt acted like nothing had transpired. Settling into the basement family room for their meeting with Murphy, the attorney innocuously began with a call for family unity, unaware — as the Greineder children still were — that Belinda and her mother were not allied with them.

Ilse quickly took control of the conversation. "I will do whatever it is I need to do to help my nieces and nephew, but that will be the extent of my help," she proclaimed firmly, snapping Murphy's focus. Tentatively searching the faces around him, the attorney tried to shake off the comment by returning to his agenda. Telling the expressionless relatives from New York what it would take to get Dr. Greineder out on bail and what his fee entailed, Murphy tried to rally their support. "This is a man who has been treated terrible," Murphy implored. "The police have framed him with this, and he needs your help."

He did not get the reaction he wanted. "I am now presented with a person that I don't know," said Belinda, referring to the sexual allegations swirling around her uncle. "Did you know about this?" she pointedly asked the lawyer. "I found out a little while ago," Murphy replied sheepishly, "but this is the same man he has always been. Dirk did not kill May."

Staring at the attorney, Ilse was more frank in stating her position about her jailed brother in law. "I will pay for tuition for these kids," she began. "I will make sure they have a roof over their head and food to eat, but I will not put one penny toward his defense." Reading the expressions on Murphy and her cousins, Belinda was surprised that they still did not grasp the New York family's defection. "I thought Ilse was pretty clear but I don't think they got it," Belinda said with amazement.

Watching the rattled attorney, Belinda realized her cousins had probably told him he could count on their full support. "The wheels were turning really fast in Murphy's head because he thought he was going in there to find this united front with outrage over Dirk's arrest," said Belinda. "He was panicking. You could see that look like 'I'm losing this.' But he wasn't convinced we were both lost. He sort of left my mother alone after a while then he started with me."

Delving back into his agenda, Murphy explained when his client's court dates would be and how they could try for bail. Kirsten pulled out her calendar book in an effort to get everyone on board but Belinda and Ilse were unresponsive. Belinda felt their scrutinizing stares as the realization of the divisiveness finally dawned on the Greineder children.

"Now everyone was uncomfortable that we were still there," Belinda remembered. "Now they are looking like they are waiting for us to leave, but I wasn't going anywhere." Murphy finally spoke up, informing the New York relatives that he had scheduled a series of media interviews with the children, including an inquiry from *People* magazine. "Oh, really," Belinda said, somewhat surprised that her cousins were going to host the hated press after strictly following their father's instructions to avoid media coverage of his case. With the first reporter due to sit down with the children in less than an hour and already waiting outside, they spread out to prepare the house.

Belinda felt their eyes boring into her. "Everybody was looking at us," Belinda recalled with a mixture of amusement and disappointment. "Marty Murphy didn't know what to do. My mother was sort of fascinated watching them get ready, but I was busting chops."

Belinda sat contently on the couch, "waiting to see what he was going to do. I wanted to see how far it was going to go," she said of Murphy. Turning toward the two women, Murphy finally asked them to leave. Belinda feigned ignorance. "Oh?" she questioned, fully aware she and her mother were unwanted there.

"We have reporters coming and it would be best if you weren't here," Murphy said, none of the Greineder children doing anything to overrule him.

"Okay," Belinda agreed.

Ilse, now aware of the tension caused by their presence, looked at the disheveled Murphy then back at her daughter. She realized Belinda had purposely antagonized the attorney. "You made that man crazy," she whispered to her daughter. Saying their good-byes, the two women left for New York, their outrage rising with each step closer to Belinda's Expedition parked in the driveway.

"We got in the car and we were pretty pissed," Belinda reminisced icily. "A decision was made at that point. If we were not going to help them financially, then they had no use for us." But Belinda had no regrets in denying financial support for her accused uncle. "I was worried Dirk would get out on bail," she said. "If he got out on bail he would have been gone."

Her cousins faced a daylong stream of reporters. Dedham District Court Judge Gerald Alch had armed the press with a few more explosive questions when he lifted the impoundment on more than a hundred documents connected to the case. Most of the material involved the Greineder search warrants and affidavits penned by Marty Foley, including the revelation that the doctor had prescribed Viagra to himself, which electrified the already frenzied media coverage.

Reporters and editors had chuckled over the disclosure and the affidavits' other salacious details, much like the detectives had after finding the erection-enhancing drug in Dr. Greineder's garage. The *Boston Herald* listed the other contents of the cardboard box, including the package of Trojan condoms "with one missing, a knotted length of nylon rope, and other items."

Once resolute in shunning what they felt was unfair coverage of their mother's murder, the Greineder children spent most of the day using the Boston media to hype their steadfast support of their father. With Murphy shuttling in reporters and photographers every thirty minutes for "one-on-one" interviews at their quaintly decorated dining room table with a prominently displayed bowl of fruit, the wholesome children repeatedly answered the same questions, never wavering from their message.

"My father did not commit this crime. My father did not kill my mother," Kirsten said sternly. "The process that is going on now is an absolute travesty of justice. People keep using that word 'denial.' We don't think we are the ones in denial. Denial is denying the judicial system has the wrong man. Instead of being made to find the person who did this, the district attorney is motivated to get this case solved. He doesn't want an answer, he just wants the case over," Kirsten accused.

"We don't know who did it," Britt echoed, "but we absolutely know it wasn't him. It was some violent, dangerous person. It was not my father. Our father is innocent and we'll do whatever it takes to tell everyone that. I never questioned as to whether my father was responsible for my mother's death."

"We have a strong will and will do whatever it takes to bring to light what we know," Colin stressed. "I'm feeling outrage and I'm feeling frustration in a system that I feel has failed us. A system that we attempted to trust in and it has failed miserably with putting on trial and indicting an innocent man."

Asked about their father's reported infidelities, they skirted the questions. "We do have feelings and frankly, our dad's answers to this will come out at a later time," said Colin. "This is not the time. We love our father and we know he is innocent."

Their slain mother, Kirsten added, would be the most vocal in support of her accused husband. "She was the strongest fighter of anyone you ever met."

Murphy would tell one columnist "this is what they thought their mother would have wanted them to do. All along they felt the investigation was unfairly focused. They thought their mother would have wanted them to speak out now."

Proudly pointing out family photographs lining the living room mantel, the Greineder kids told reporter after reporter that their parents had a loving relationship, always putting their children's needs first. "We're very lucky that not only did we have a stay-at-home mom, we obviously had a very intimate relationship with her, and yet, we had just as close a relationship with our father," Britt gushed. "Despite being a very successful doctor in the community, despite the fact he had to work, he made an effort to be actively involved in our lives," Britt added, describing her father as never missing a swim meet or soccer game with time to build them piñatas on their birthdays. "He was just as involved as my mother was," agreed Colin.

When the Greineder children were asked to describe their mother, the accolades seemed slower in coming. "We lost someone we can never replace," Kirsten said stoically.

With Dr. Greineder safely locked up in the county jail, the investigators turned to a treasure trove of new evidence provided by the return of more than two-dozen grand jury subpoenas. American Express provided copies of the doctor's July 12, 1998, application for the Corporate Card issued to Corporate Physicians, the deceitful Dr. Greineder having listed a third, unnamed employee of his phony business in addition to the fraudulently identified Thomas Young. The account was billed to his Wellesley home, and the doctor had claimed Corporate Physicians had been in business for ten years.

A week before killing his wife, Dr. Greineder had joined ultimatelive. com, a hardcore adult Internet site based in Fort Lauderdale, Florida, that discreetly billed its customers through a service generically named provider.com. The $24.95 thirty-day membership, paid with the Corporate Card issued to Thomas Young, allowed Dr. Greineder his choice of streaming pornography, live chat, interactive chat with nude women in Amsterdam, and the option to trade pictures. Required to provide an e-mail address, he gave the user name pussyryder@yahoo. Ten days after his wife's brutal slaying, Dr. Greineder inexplicably cancelled his membership.

More eye-opening was the material returned by People2People, the *Boston Phoenix*-owned Internet dating service that catered to some two million customers of all sexual persuasions. Dr. Greineder joined under the name of Thomas Young the same Sunday night he signed up for ultimatelive.com. He provided the user name casual_guy2000@yahoo before putting his personal information in the "Men Seeking Women" section, knocking ten years off his age:

> "*49 years old, 5 ft. 10 in., smoking: never, drinking: occasionally, ethnicity: caucasian, body type: average, education: doctorate, children: children who are grown, hair color: light brown, eye color: brown, employment: full time.*" As for what he wanted in a woman, casual_guy2000 filled in, "*35 to 60 years old within 30 miles from Boston, Massachusetts; ethnicity: caucasian, body type: slim, slender, athletic, average to a few pounds overweight, education: high school, some college, bachelor's, master's, or doctorate.*"

Logging out of People2People shortly before midnight on October 24, 1999, Dr. Greineder was back on the site less than six hours later. At 5:42 A.M., casual_guy2000 read a posting from macp143sum, which Marty Foley understood to mean "Massachusetts couple for threesome."

> "*White couple in their early 30s looking for average to chunky white men for sexual times. We enjoy peek booths, adult theaters, rest areas, dark*

*bars and most things public. We drink, he smokes and we occasionally*
*party. Not looking to entertain as we have kids but could if we really liked*
*someone. I'm 5'4", 145 pounds, 38D, tight butt, long muscular legs, long*
*brown hair, brown eyes and unfortunately a bit of a tummy from having*
*kids. Happily married but he enjoys me in a group situation and to be*
*honest, so do I."*

Dr. Greineder's reply showed his appetent interest.

*"I am white, married but she does not play so I am looking for a very*
*discreet couple with whom to play. I am also very oral, both give and receive*
*and would love to exchange emails to see if we can fit. I am a few pounds*
*overweight; (really only a few), love big breasts to suck and love group*
*activities. I'm basically straight but can be flexible in group situations. I*
*cannot host but would be willing to arrange for hotel accommodations if*
*we got along. I'm 49, clean, disease and drug free, college grad, managerial*
*type. Please email me."*

Macp143sum quickly responding, Dr. Greineder was instructed to e-mail
them back that night.

Turning to an ad from a woman named misstressrk, Dr. Greineder sent
a reply to her offer of rough sex. "I am mature, 59, white, a few pounds
overweight, athletic, doctorate degree, looking for discreet relationship,"
he wrote. "Interested in your offer, but would reject anything leaving permanent marks. Please e-mail if you are available."

At 5:51 A.M. that Monday morning, Dr. Greineder read a posting from
bkalleycat, a woman claiming she was forty-five years old, five-feet, and
four-inches tall with an average body. She wanted a man "49 to 60 years
old" who lived within a hundred miles of Pelham, New Hampshire.

*"Classy, intelligent, warm, compassionate, sexy, sensuous, playful, fit,*
*active, down-to-earth with a wild and crazy sense of humor, loves to dance*
*and make romance (with right man I am a very attentive lover, wonderfully*
*uninhibited and wickedly open to most anything, so what do you have in*
*mind?). Extremely liberal in most areas of life, including politically . . . so*
*what more could you be looking for? Oh yes, in case you are wondering,*
*kids are grown but on their own . . . so let's do it, what have you got to lose??*

Interested in bkalleycat, Dr. Greineder messaged, "Hi, I'm 49, white, clean,
healthy and fit. Looking for mutual petting and more . . . I'm very open-
minded, and I live in the greater Boston area—where are you? Let's e-mail."

The documents showed Dr. Greineder was back in the Men Seeking
Women site the next day. Just before 9 A.M., he sent an inquiry to daisy-
may828, who was seeking a man "41 to 49 years old" living within thirty
miles of Boston who was a moderate drinker. "I'm interested in an un-
complicated intimate relationship," the doctor messaged. "I'm very clean,
educated, good-looking, athletic, DD free, sincere, but not ready for long-
term relationship. Email for more."

The subpoenaed records provided the identities of the doctor's contacts.
Foley was particularly interested in macp143sum because they had replied
to casual_guy2000. If Dr. Greineder had met the couple for group sex
right before killing his wife, it would be more damaging evidence to pile
against his weakening reputation as a loving family man wrongly accused.
Ringing the doorbell of Amy Page's East Bridgewater home unannounced
at suppertime on Monday, March 6, 2000, Foley and Jill McDermott were
greeted by a woman in her late twenties. Stepping into the house, the two
detectives could see three young kids in the kitchen delightfully dining
on SpaghettiOs.

Following the woman to the living room where they could talk away
from the children, the detectives quickly learned she was the babysitter. She
said Amy was still at work. Foley left his page number and got a response
a little over an hour later.

Employed in Boston, Amy Page agreed to meet the detectives at 12:30
the following afternoon at the Hard Rock Cafe on Clarendon Street. Calling Foley the next morning, Page asked if she could bring her husband,
Harry. Foley agreed, suggesting they meet in Boston's Copley Square at
the majestic Trinity Church, where Clarendon intersects Boylston Street.
Page informed Foley that she would be wearing a white sweater and shoes
with a black skirt.

The weather was springlike that Tuesday afternoon. A dark-haired woman approached the detectives as soon as they got out of Foley's cruiser. "We called you about an e-mail you sent on People2People," Foley explained, trying to put the nervous woman at ease. "Are you macp143sum?" Foley asked. After Amy Page had considered the trooper's question for a minute, her brief confusion cleared. "Oh that's not me," she said. "That's my husband, Harry. He does this sometimes," Amy said with a trace of annoyance. "Where's Harry?" Foley asked. "He's right there," Amy replied, pointing to a nearby bench where a hulking man in a long black leather coat was sitting. She walked over to confer quickly with her husband, and the couple returned to the detectives.

"That was me," Harry Page sheepishly admitted about macp143sum's provocative e-mail. "Sometimes I play around and I speak like I'm Amy. I might be in a little trouble with her for using her name online," he confessed with a guilty glance at his wife. Putting aside the humorous image of Dr. Greineder thinking he was communicating with a woman when it was the portly Harry Page at the keyboard, Foley decided to go only where he needed and asked the couple if they had actually met with casual_guy2000.

"No we never met," Harry said, having only a vague memory of casual_guy2000. "I put in an ad looking for average to chunky white men for a sexual time, and I know I got some replies but I can't remember the names. We never met anyone in person as a result of that ad. I screen the people for drug use or weird stuff and we always exchange e-mails and meet for coffee before we meet," he explained.

"Do you know anyone named Dirk Greineder or Thomas Young?" Foley asked.

The couple did not recognize either. "I'll check on my computer when I get home," Harry offered. "I think I might still have some e-mails that were sent to me and I'll take a look to see if there is anything else I can remember," he said helpfully.

Three hours later, Foley got a call from the accommodating Harry Page. "I found some e-mails he sent me," he cheerily told the detective. "We sent him some pictures and he also sent me a picture. Do you want me to send that too?" Page asked.

"A picture of Dirk? Yeah, I'll take that," the detective said, hiding his eagerness.

Page unable to send the e-mails to Foley's computer at the DA's office, he forwarded the correspondence to Lt. Wayne Cunningham in Wellesley, then faxed Foley the text of the messages. Reading the e-mails from casual_guy2000 as they slid out of the fax machine, Foley found that Dr. Greineder seemed consumed with meeting the kinky couple in the days leading up to his wife's murder. He tried contacting the Pages at their free Yahoo address at 8:13 P.M. on Monday, October 25, 1999, but discovered he had been given the wrong user name. Reaching the couple on the People2People site, casual_guy2000 was told to use peepbooth@yahoo, not peekbooth, as he was originally told.

With the miscommunication happily resolved, Dr. Greineder remained enthusiastic about meeting the couple for sex. "Hi Amy — thanks for responding and also for sending me a new address. I thought I was typing wrong!" he wrote, and added the message he had previously tried to send.

*Here is what I tried to send this morning: Hi — I am terribly pleased that you are interested and that we might be able to meet. I am open to your suggestions — maybe a good way to start is to exchange pictures (I have scanned ones with and without clothes though not very good since I had to take them myself). In general, i think the only way to proceed that makes much sense is to plan to meet in discreet public place where we can talk and exchange ideas. That cuts through much of the rest of the crap since everything is so much clearer once one is face to face. I would love to meet for a drink (after a few more emails or phone calls) with the option to stay and play together right after if we are compatible. Obviously, it can also be separated into two separate events but I will be impatient if we find we are indeed compatible. Let me know what you think — you can email me back here. My special interests are to please my partners in any way possible. As i told you I am very oral and I certainly love dual penetration activities, whether oral/vaginal or double anything in fact. I think I have dabbled with almost anything you can think of, though my preferences remain pretty vanilla if you call threesomes vanilla!!) Hope to hear from you soon. Tom*

After viewing a half-dozen sexually explicit pictures of Amy the couple had sent him, Dr. Greineder excitedly replied just after midnight on Tuesday, October 26, with an e-mail headlined "Lets talk!"

*Loved your pics! Looks like you're into some B/D too. I have had some interest/*
*experience with this though I have given up all my toys. Maybe you still have*
*some! But mostly, I liked the images and i am sure that I will love to play with*
*you. Since you were so quick to send provocative photos I will attach a nude*
*one of me. Hope you like it and will be interested in meeting soon. Maybe its*
*time to talk. Call me if you can. I noticed that you were online really early*
*this morning so maybe you can call me early Tuesday. Best would be between*
*7 and 8 AM if that works for you. Otherwise, call anytime but i may need to*
*ask you to call back or give me a number to call you because I may be in a*
*situation where i cannot talk freely. I am excited by your cooperation and*
*candor! Look forward to hearing from you by phone or email. Tom*

Realizing after waking five hours later that he had neglected to give *peep-booth* his phone number, Dr. Greineder e-mailed the couple again at 5:25 A.M. Tuesday with a number to call.

After receiving his photograph, peepbooth responded to casual_guy2000 several hours later, indicating that they were reluctant to talk by phone. "We'll see," Harry Page typed, pretending to be his wife. "Had bad experience using phone as anything other than a guarantee to meet in the past. Loved the pic! I prefer the cocks I suck to be trim but I can make an exception. I rarely gag even when deep throating and when I do it's because of too many hairs. Amy ps Still looking for a good Halloween party Saturday."

Not talking on the phone was fine by casual_guy2000. "No problem," Dr. Greineder wrote.

*Email has revolutionized this process. I would like to know a few more*
*things but they can be discussed in person. I am a bit worried about the sig*
*which suggests you may use rest areas — how careful are you about who/*
*how you interact? What about meeting for a few hours on Thursday this*
*week? I cannot stay the night but could meet after 6 and stay until 10–11*
*pm? If not this week, it would probably be 2 weeks off b/c i am out of town*
*part of the following week. let me know. Tom.*

It seemed to Foley, scanning the final e-mail Page had faxed, that casual_guy2000 had upset Page with his inquiry about their sex partners. At 10:16 A.M. on Wednesday, October 27, Dr. Greineder asked:

*did i say something offensive? "i know that asking about your behavior is provocative, and it is difficult to do via email, but i apologize if i offended. I find it better to do that over the phone and in person, but since i felt that i would not be talking on the phone, i asked anyway and may have overstepped. Forgive me if thats it and lets communicate some more anyway. I really am not offensive. If its merely that you have been busy — well thats ok. Thanks for listening. Tom.*

Reading the e-mails on his computer screen in the Wellesley detective office, Wayne Cunningham was also bowled over by Dr. Greineder's cavalier behavior just days before murdering his trusting wife. Opening the photo attachment casual_guy2000 sent the Pages, Cunningham had to wait for the image to appear line by line. Like an electronic strip tease, the smirking doctor's head and face were exposed in front of a white background; Cunningham transfixed as the color picture enlarged to show Dr. Greineder's bare chest and abdomen.

Perched in anticipation as the image developed lower, Cunningham let out a hoot when Dr. Greineder's genitals appeared, the full photograph showing him completely naked, standing in front of a white louver door. Collecting himself, the giddy Cunningham recognized the door from an upstairs bedroom in the Greineder house. Calling Foley, a snickering Cunningham suggested it would be worth the trooper's time to drive over to Wellesley.

Showing the photograph to his brother Terry and the other Wellesley investigators working on the case prompted another round of "hooting and hollering." Cunningham printed out a copy of their naked murder defendant and prepared it for viewing by the virtuous Jill McDermott. "I took a small yellow sticky note and put it on his picture like a skirt," Cunningham revealed with a twinkle. "I showed it to Jill and said if you want to see him all you have to look under the yellow sticky. She got tortured by that whole thing, the poor kid. We took a lot of enjoyment out of that photograph and the whole relationship with Harry and Amy and what Harry had planned for him," the detective gleefully confessed.

The nude Dirk Greineder would become the bane of the good-natured

McDermott's existence. "That crazy picture kept popping up everywhere. I'd be going through paperwork and Rick Grundy would slip it in there and there it would be." For the proper McDermott, Dr. Greineder's twisted sex life was getting to be a little much. "First we had Deb Herrera, then Beth Porter, and then this whole lifestyle," she said. "He's looking for a threesome online and he's this world-renowned allergist forwarding full-length nude pictures of himself, and we know it was taken in his house. Every time I thought it was bad, it would get worse," she recalled. "He was just not getting enough."

Foley's viewing brought another encore of frivolity, leaving the trooper amazed by Dr. Greineder's audacity. "There in all his God-given talent was Dirk," chuckled Foley. "Was there laughter? Yes," he smiled. "There were a lot of phone calls like, 'You're not going to believe what we just grabbed up. You're not going to believe what this guy just gave us.'"

Examining the photo, the detectives theorized it had been taken with a digital camera, perhaps the one Dr. Greineder's credit card receipts showed he had purchased but one they never found. Weighing the evidentiary value of the picture, Foley decided it depicted a man losing control. "Were we surprised, absolutely, but it was a feeling that this guy was getting tighter and tighter and more wound up," Foley said. "He's losing control, and he did. He lost it." Like his partner, Foley could not grasp the doctor's addictive quest for sex. "I'm thinking fifty-eight or fifty-nine years old, get over it pal. I mean really," Foley said. "This guy had an obsession, and he couldn't fulfill it. That's the thing. I don't think he could fulfill it."

Starting with the tryst with a hooker in New Jersey, Dr. Greineder spent the week before his wife's death on a sleepless sexual rampage, logging onto People2People late at night and early in the morning. "We could see the progression of behavior, and it started to escalate," Foley said.

The investigators also noticed similarities in the e-mails Dr. Greineder had sent the Pages and the stories of kinky sex he had composed for Paty Peres. "Some of the things he had mentioned in the e-mails went back to the ramblings we had gotten off his computer that went toward the dark side a little bit," Foley explained. "This guy was wound up and out of control. We already know at this point that he was with a prostitute in Mahwah. He's doing these things online. He's trying to meet these people. He's not sleeping. These things are happening, and it's building up and building up."

While on a short hiatus from her contact with Marty Foley and Rick Grundy, Belinda Markel was in constant communication with her estranged relatives in Wellesley. Her uncle was writing her letters from the Norfolk County Jail, and Belinda's cousin Britt telephoned almost daily in the initial weeks following her father's arrest. The big issue was the Greineders' need for money.

Belinda finally made a decision to expedite the remainder of her cousins' inheritance from their grandmother's estate. "I went over to the attorney and told him to draw three checks for what their balance was," she said. "I walked away with three checks for about sixty-seven hundred dollars apiece. I left mine, my mother's, and May's in there. You don't usually do it this way, but they wanted the money and my grandmother would have wanted them to have the money. If they were going to hand it over to their father, that would be their choice," she decided.

Stopping into a Manhattan bank, Belinda also withdrew $2,000 in cash for Colin, tired of hearing that her cousin wouldn't be able to afford to eat when he returned to Yale Medical School. She called her cousins and told them they could expect her in Wellesley the next day.

Gathering around the new dining room table their slain mother never got to see, the Greineder children silently accepted their inheritance checks. Turning to Colin, Belinda pressed the wad of bills she had withdrawn into his hand. "This should get you through the rest of the school year," she said. The discomfort in the room was obvious, and Belinda was then asked the inevitable question: "how I felt about their father."

"He's somebody that I don't know anymore," she explained, trying to soften her defection, "and I don't think you and I are in the same camp regarding him."

"How dare you!" Britt roared. "How could you!"

Belinda tried to reason with them. "Look, I don't feel the same way as you do."

"You can't be part of our family if you feel that way!" Britt interrupted.

"Look, I love you guys," Belinda said with some irritation. "I'm obviously here with good intentions. I'm trying to help you."

Acting as a peacemaker, Kirsten told her younger sister that Belinda was entitled to her opinion. "I appreciate her being honest," Kirsten said, her disappointment evident.

Colin echoed Kirsten's stance, and the conversation turned to the Greineders' financial situation and what could be done to augment it. They were having trouble getting the company to pay their mother's life insurance Belinda was told, as a result, meeting the monthly mortgage looked dicey.

Going through the numbers, Belinda could not understand why her cousins were poverty stricken. "I couldn't quite figure out why they couldn't do this, but Dirk was feeding them bits and pieces of information about where money was. I'm not sure they knew the actual amount of money that was available to them."

Funding for Dr. Greineder's defense was always the overriding concern, and Belinda's cousins told her they had considered trying to take out a second mortgage on the home until they discovered an obstacle resulting from estate maneuvering before their mother's death. "They couldn't do it because the house was actually in May's name," said Belinda. "They couldn't get the life insurance money. They were coming up with all sorts of ways to try to raise funds, and none of them were any good."

Belinda suggested they check with their father about retirement accounts the family might be able to tap into, which ended up infuriating Dr. Greineder. "That created a real ruckus with Dirk because Dirk hadn't told them about the retirement money," recalled Belinda.

Immersed in their discussion about finances, Kirsten surprised her cousin with an invoice pulled from a pile of statements. "We have a real problem with this," she said, handing Belinda the bill for May's funeral expenses. "I applied for the victim's fund at the attorney general's office and they just told us that we are not entitled to those benefits. We planned this funeral within a dollar of that. They told us that they wouldn't pay more than that and we were very careful how much we spent and now they are not paying at all," Kirsten complained to her dumbfounded cousin.

"Why wouldn't they pay," Belinda asked, unsure why the Greineders would even seek governmental assistance to pay for May's funeral.

"They said it was because my mother had life insurance," Kirsten answered. "We can't pay this bill. I don't know what to do. I talked to the man at the funeral home, and he said we could pay on an installment, but I told him I would talk to you. Can you take care of this?" she asked, pushing the $5,408.85 bill at Belinda.

Some of the bizarre events surrounding May's funeral were explained by the Greineders' penny-pinching attempt to have it paid by a public victims' fund, but Belinda could still not overcome her bewilderment at the family's callous handling of May's cremation. "How could you not have five thousand dollars?" she asked. "Didn't your father think of paying this bill?"

"We can't do it. We just don't have the money," Kirsten replied curtly, avoiding Belinda's question.

Silently tucking the invoice in with her other paperwork, Belinda decided any further discussion would be fruitless. She hugged and kissed her cousins before getting in her car and heading back to New York. It would be her last visit to 56 Cleveland Road.

# 19

IT WAS RAW AND RAINING on Tuesday, April 4, 2000, when Belinda Markel and Ilse Stark braced themselves and stepped onto the trail in the pine tree forest at Morses Pond. In Massachusetts for an appointment with District Attorney Bill Keating the next day, May Greineder's niece and sister wanted to walk the recreation area she had loved so much, hoping it would somehow have an answer for the unexplainable.

Flanked by Marty Foley and Rick Grundy, with a pack of Wellesley cops trailing behind, it was the first time Belinda or Ilse had been to Morses Pond since May's death. "It was raining. It was miserable out," Belinda said solemnly, the unpleasant weather bolstering the bad memory.

Slowly making the circuit that Dr. Greineder claimed he and his wife had walked that day, Foley and Grundy respectfully explained the significance of each area, pointing out where the civilian witnesses in the case had been positioned. When the grieving women were approached by a resident asking if they knew May or her family, Foley politely shooed the woman away. Why Dr. Greineder would perpetrate such an act was still mystifying to all, and they bounced ideas off each other at each stop on the sad tour.

"As we were going, we were talking about what could have happened or why May maybe didn't go one way or the other," Belinda recalled. "We talked about the scream when we were on top of the sandpit. We were all asking questions and listening to each other, and in some ways we were answering their questions."

The group of Wellesley cops still respectfully trailing behind, Foley and Grundy stopped at the spot where May died on the tree-covered trail. Lowering his already softened voice, Foley described how May was ambushed with the hammer, furiously killed with the knife, and then dragged off the trail where her husband of thirty-one years continued his attack with knife thrusts to her head and lifeless body. The detective could see the emotional pain welling up in the two women with their understanding of each horrifying detail, but they had wanted to see for themselves.

Foley completely understood why. "Belinda was a little upset but Ilse was really, really distraught," he said soberly. "I think a lot came back. To really put the whole story into perspective, you have to be there. You have to see the sandpit. You have to see the traffic circle. You have to see, for this to happen, it could have only happened in this one area. To be at the spot where she was killed, to me it's always emotional. I couldn't imagine what the family members felt."

As the women privately reflected in the place where their adored May was taken from them, their obvious heartbreak inspired the investigators in their pursuit of justice. "Going through that scene again it was kind of an emotional thing for me as well," Foley admitted. "For us it was the need to do a good job with this case. He's hurt these people so much and they are true victims in this crime, and it was emotional to me and I'm sure to Rick as well to see what these people had gone through. It was energizing for us," Foley revealed. "Maybe the kids are calling us bastards, but we were doing this for a reason. It was very emotional. It's still very emotional when I think about it."

"We still had all these questions going back and forth," said Belinda, who despite the upset, found the pond visit beneficial. She would later take time to write Foley a thank you note, a gesture that touched the state trooper. "I knew how hard it was," Belinda said. "He had told us it was a long road, and I was glad he was going to be there."

Belinda and her mother were still trying to salvage their relationship with the Greineder children, but the underlying conflict was always there. Ilse was distressed to hear that May's ashes were in a storage closet at the Newton Cemetery awaiting payment and pickup. After speaking with her niece Kirsten, Ilse agreed to pay the outstanding balance, arranging to have May's ashes sent to New York to be placed in the family niche.

When Kirsten and her fiancé stayed with Ilse and Murray for two days to shop for a Saks Fifth Avenue wedding gown Ilse had offered to pay for, "not much was said about the case," Belinda recalled. Britt was still regularly telephoning, while Belinda "periodically" talked to her cousin Colin. Their jailed father continued his fervent letter writing to Belinda. Meanwhile she was talking to Foley and Grundy, so it was "beginning to get a little complicated," she understated.

The investigation got another boost on Monday, April 10, when Jersey City Detective Bob Potter called with news of the prostitute who had gone to Dr. Greineder's New Jersey hotel room the week before the murder. A few days earlier Marty Foley and Wayne Cunningham had spent most of a long day in New York City where they had tracked down Marilyn's Escort Service with the help of Detective Gerry Neville of the New York Police Department. It was located in a dingy three-decker in Brooklyn. Hesitant employees of the escort service had identified the hooker as "Leaha" from Jersey City once they realized the cops had no interest in shutting them down and just wanted the woman's name. They spent the rest of the day and night in Jersey City with Potter, trying to track down Leaha, but Foley and Cunningham finally had to return to Massachusetts empty-handed, until the diligent Potter called with the news that she had been found.

Foley and Cunningham made a return trip down to New Jersey. Leaha, whose real name was Nora Lopez, remembered meeting a john in Mahwah, but unlike Elizabeth Porter and Deborah Herrera, Lopez had only a faint recollection of Dr. Greineder. Still, she agreed to cooperate.

The developments were not all positive on April 10, however. Appearing in Dedham Superior Court to address Marty Murphy's motion on the district attorney's press conference, Rick Grundy could only watch while Judge Charles F. Barrett lambasted his boss for violating the state's disclosure rules. "There can be little doubt that the disclosure rules in criminal matters were flagrantly violated by the District Attorney," Barrett would later write in a ruling. "It is not possible at this time to determine if these disclosures will materially prejudice the defendant."

Saying the trial judge should decide "at the appropriate time" whether Dr. Greineder was entitled to relief from the DA's public comments, Barrett also declined to rule on whether Dr. Greineder deserved a change of trial venue to another county because of adverse publicity. Despite the setback, Grundy managed to convince the judge that Dr. Greineder should not be released on bail.

Unknown to the media, Murphy, responding to a prosecution subpoena, had turned over to Grundy a bloodstained towel bearing a Ritz-Carlton logo that Dr. Greineder said he had shared with his wife to stem their strangely simultaneous nosebleeds.

After this opening salvo in the defense of Dr. Greineder in the motion to sanction the prosecution for the district attorney's public comments, Murphy then launched a major offensive aimed primarily at Marty Foley and his search warrant affidavits. Murphy filed a fifty-page memorandum on July 10 seeking the exclusion of evidence collected from Dr. Greineder's house, vehicles, and computers, heaping much of his argument on the innocuous typo in Foley's first affidavit wrongly indicating he had been assigned to the Norfolk DA's office for fourteen years. The memorandum all but called Foley, now promoted to sergeant, a liar willing to do anything to pin the murder on Dr. Greineder.

The first hearing on the motion was scheduled before Dedham Superior Court Judge Paul Chernoff, who would see the case through trial, and Foley knew Grundy's defense of the search warrant affidavits was critical. "It was primarily the first search warrant," Foley said. "If we lost that search warrant we would lose every search warrant because that affidavit was attached to each and every search warrant from there on in."

Even though the mistaken implication of Foley being at the Norfolk DA's office for fourteen years was corrected on subsequent affidavits, Murphy had targeted the ambiguously written sentence.

Beyond the typo, Foley knew Murphy well enough to know the practiced attorney would focus on his relative inexperience investigating murders. "I think he would have attacked that anyway," Foley speculated. "The thing is, I had only done homicide investigations for nine months, and he knew that. We were not going to attempt to mislead him, but any police officer at that scene could have written the affidavit," Foley stressed.

Approaching the dapper, gray-haired man with the matching close-cropped beard at T. F. Green Airport in Warwick, Rhode Island, on Thursday, August 10, 2000, Marty Foley thought Rod Englert looked more like a traveling magician than a crime scene expert. He was standing next to a pile of luggage and hard-sided trunks containing a multitude of high-intensity lights and other devices to examine evidence. Englert would be a key, if somewhat controversial player in the prosecution of Dr. Dirk Greineder.

A police officer for thirty-eight years, Englert had retired in 1995 as the deputy chief of the Multnomah County Sheriff's Department in Portland, Oregon. He had risen through the ranks there after spending a brief stint as a cop in the Los Angeles suburb of Downy. Early on, Englert had been fascinated with the burgeoning science of blood pattern interpretation, studying in the 1970s with Dr. Herbert McDonald, a pioneer in the field.

Involved in "several thousand" homicide investigations throughout his career, Englert had won his expertise from practical experience, not a college classroom. Where the majority of the experts in the field were scientists with the accompanying degrees, Englert's schooling was more suited to his police career. He held a bachelor's degree in police science and police administration from California State University and had taken some graduate level courses at Portland State University and the University of Virginia. Like the Cunningham brothers, he was also a graduate of the prestigious FBI National Academy.

For twenty-five years, mostly part-time when he was a police officer, he had operated Englert Forensic Consultants, hiring out his expertise at $375 an hour. Qualified to testify as an expert in twenty-two states and military and federal courts, Englert had built a reputation as a highly skilled, innovative authority on the re-creation of bloodshed at a crime scene.

He had testified in or consulted on hundreds of cases around the country, including the unsuccessful murder prosecution of O. J. Simpson. He had also lectured all over the United States, at Britain's New Scotland Yard, and before police chiefs in Russia. As a staff member of the National College of District Attorneys, Rick Grundy had heard Englert speak at a convention and was impressed with the polished expert's presentation.

Although he was more than satisfied with the work of State Police Lt. Ken Martin, Grundy decided that another expert was needed to move the Greineder case along. The investigators had considered hiring noted forensic expert Stuart James of Florida until they learned defense attorney Marty Murphy had beat them to that scientist, whose writings on blood spatter interpretation were considered the standard in the field. Crime lab manager Gwen Pino had reservations about Englert, with his lack of any scientific degrees, but eventually warmed to his participation.

"I made the mistake of listening to Grundy on picking out the expert," she said candidly. "Grundy had seen Englert do a presentation that he thought was really good, so he wanted to use this guy. I'm like, fine, we'll bring him in and see what he does. He worked with us and he was pretty good."

After taking Englert to Morses Pond to familiarize him with the crime scene, Foley drove him to the Sudbury crime lab for a preliminary look at the Greineder evidence. The prosecutor had sent Englert just about everything in the case file in advance, the expert's philosophy being there can never be too much information or opinion in trying to re-create a crime scene. At the lab, he unpacked some of his sophisticated tools of the trade, using hand-held lights to scrutinize Dr. Greineder's bloodstained clothing and other pieces of evidence recovered near May Greineder's savaged body. He would be back the following morning for a full day of work, but as it was late, Englert took the Greineder investigators out to dinner, Grundy not finding out until later that their expert was still charging them $375 an hour.

Meeting at the crime lab Friday morning, the core group of investigators, including Pino and Martin, gathered around Englert for a closer look at their evidence. Agreeing with Martin, Englert determined the small bloodstains on Dr. Greineder's jacket, pants, shirt, sneakers, and backpack were medium-velocity spatter that was deposited when his wife was killed. Likewise, the blood smears on the sleeves and left shoulder of the yellow windbreaker were deemed transfer patterns, as Martin had asserted. The blood was likely deposited when Dr. Greineder dragged his dying wife off the dirt trail. Aiming the special lighting at the shoulder of the nylon swim-team jacket, Englert concurred that the distinctive fine swirls in the bloodstain could only have come from May's bloody hair.

Next he examined stains above each wrist that showed areas unsoiled by blood, Englert pointed out what he believed were "grab patterns" left by Dr. Greineder pulling at both sleeves with the bloodstained brown work gloves. It was late afternoon by the time one of the last items was brought out — the blood-spotted Ziploc bag containing the two other bags. Laying the bag on the black countertop, the investigators let out a collective gasp.

"All of a sudden, we saw all these dots," said Foley. Clearly visible on the dark background, there was only one thing that could have left the dimpled impressions in the bloodstain. "We brought the gloves back out," said Foley. "We thought, okay, these dots are being made by the gloves. It was grabbed with the gloves on."

As the rest of the evidence was pulled out, the excitement mounted with the realization that the distinctive rubber dimples from the gloves had left bloody impressions elsewhere. "We found dots patterns on the hammer, knife, jacket, glasses. It was my thought and Rod's that those dots came from those gloves," Foley said. "Whoever was wearing those gloves touched the hammer, touched the knife, touched Dirk's jacket, the Ziploc bags, the glasses. That's the case as far as I was concerned."

Watching with the others huddled around the examination table, Gwen Pino had to agree. "There are the dots and Grundy goes hysterical," she recalled. "Once we found them on the bag we started to find them every-where."

"We all started saying what else did we miss?" Foley said. "Why didn't we see this before? I think Rod Englert said if it wasn't these gloves, what else could make these marks everywhere? If it's not the gloves what is it? It has to be the gloves. Once we saw it, then we knew what to look for and we saw it everywhere."

Foley and Englert were convinced that the brown work gloves sold exclusively at Diehl's Hardware in Wellesley would be their smoking gun at trial. "Seeing it nine months later, the evidence was really starting to make sense," Foley said. "When we were talking evidence before, we were talking about little tiny bits and pieces. We were not talking about the whole picture."

On September 20, Marty Foley and Rick Grundy traveled to Maryland on a two-day trip that would turn out to be extremely productive. At the FBI Crime Laboratory in Washington, they were introduced to Lorie Gottesman, a scientist in the lab's questioned document section. In addition to being an expert in comparing and identifying documents such as counterfeit checks, anonymous letters, and ransom notes, Gottesman was an authority on plastic bags made from blown polyethylene. Taking the three Ziploc bags found near May's body and several boxes of food storage bags seized from the Greineders' kitchen pantry, Gottesman would later make a sophisticated analysis of the bags to see if they had been manufactured together.

Made from large vats of melted plastic with additives to prevent it from sticking, the liquid polyethylene is blown through a narrow slit called a die into a mold under high heat. Air-dried into long sheets, the plastic is then run through a conveyer system much like newspaper coming off a printing press, with the filmlike plastic eventually folded and heat-sealed into bags. Plastic bags made from the same mixture usually contain particles that haven't completely melted that can be compared, while the dies often leave lines or striations in the plastic that can be observed with special lights and filters.

Bags made from the same sheet would have identical striations from the stress of being pulled through the machinery. Most of the time, molten plastic collected on the edge of the dies will produce identical patterns, allowing Gottesman to further conclude that particular bags came from the same sheet of plastic. Slicing open the three bags from the Greineder case, Gottesman determined that the one spotted with blood and another bag found inside were both Ziploc heavy-duty gallon freezer bags. The second bag found inside the bloodstained one was a Ziploc heavy-duty half-gallon freezer bag. Turning to a box from the Greineder pantry containing twelve of the Ziploc half-gallon bags, Gottesman sliced all the bags open and compared them side-by-side with the crime-scene bag. Not finding many striations or individual characteristics, Gottesman could not make a conclusion other than the dies had probably been cleaned before the bags were made.

Picking up a box containing seven of the original fifteen gallon-sized Ziploc bags, Gottesman repeated the process with far different — and potentially devastating — results for Dr. Greineder. The seven bags in the box and the two from the crime scene all came from the same sheet of plastic, Gottesman concluded. Studying the creases from where the bags had been folded together in the box, Gottesman took it a step further with her determination that the two bags found near May's body had been taken consecutively from among the seven still left in the box.

Claiming he knew nothing about the plastic bags found at the crime scene, Dr. Greineder was going to have a hard time explaining how storage bags from his own kitchen ended up in the bloody gloved hand of his wife's killer.

On Wednesday, October 18, Judge Paul Chernoff ruled the prosecution could keep the bulk of its evidence. He eliminated just about all of the material gathered from the search warrant the previous February for Dr. Greineder's computers, which was prompted by the quest to find Paty Peres. Since Dr. Greineder was not read his Miranda rights the morning of the murder, Chernoff limited testimony on his statements to Marty Foley to the first five minutes of their conversation.

While there was some "embellishment" by Foley in his search warrant affidavits about his experience investigating violent crimes, the judge concluded the detective did not intentionally misstate how long he had been assigned to the Norfolk DA's office. While the November 12 search warrant allowed for the seizure of Dr. Greineder's computers and an initial search of their contents, the detectives were navigating uncharted legal territory when they delved deeper with the February 7 search warrant.

Unless a keyword used by the investigators was mentioned on a search warrant affidavit, Chernoff ruled any evidence gleaned by their use was inadmissible. Because the word *nylon*, which had turned up the sexually explicit stories apparently written by Dr. Greineder and the e-mail correspondence with Paty Peres, was not listed on any search warrant document, the prosecution would not be able to present the material at trial.

In all, Chernoff rejected thirty-five keywords, including "Paty" and "Peres," only the kinky e-mail between Dr. Greineder and Harry and Amy Page survived, because "People2People" had been mentioned in a search warrant affidavit. The ruling set a Massachusetts legal precedent, and Chernoff made five recommendations for the future police search of computers.

Issuing another pretrial ruling on February 5, 2001, Judge Chernoff limited the admissible scope of Dr. Greineder's extramarital activity to the week before his wife's murder, saying "this evidence enables a near snapshot view of the 'defendant's entire relationship' at a relevant time with his wife." The decision was privately considered a stinging defeat among the investigators, who wanted to admit all the doctor's deviant behavior going back to 1997.

Chernoff ruled that including the whole history of Dr. Greineder's extramarital activity "might derail into an improper assessment of his character" by a jury. Saying he had to "separate the wheat from the chaff," the judge ruled the jury should still hear evidence that could go to the doctor's motive to murder.

As to the phone sex and trysts with prostitute Elizabeth Porter, the prosecution "failed to demonstrate how this type of activity, conducted well before the time of the murder, has a bearing on the defendant's desire to murder his spouse," the judge concluded.

Even though Grundy would still be able to present evidence that Dr. Greineder used Tom Young's identity to join People2People, solicited the prostitute in New Jersey, and sent a nude picture of himself along with the raunchy e-mails to the Pages, the ruling was received with great disappointment. "We were getting our ass kicked," Marty Foley bluntly assessed. "The judge was bending over backwards for the defense."

For Wellesley Police Chief Terry Cunningham, the ruling brought a resurgence of unhappiness from the town's elected officials and residents, who had been temporarily placated by Dr. Greineder's arrest. "I was getting heat," he said, "because we were losing motions and the folks here thought, 'Oh my God, you guys screwed up the investigation. It took you so long to charge him and now you are losing all this stuff. You had the whole investigation and all you got was a week.'"

The investigators could not comprehend how the judge could not allow the entire progression of Dr. Greineder's proclivities culminating with a week of furious activity before he killed his wife. "We felt that was important to show to put things in perspective," said Wayne Cunningham. "Trying to show how crazy he was with only a snapshot of a week was unfair and extremely difficult."

Even Marty Murphy was not happy with the ruling. "For reasons I described in the motion, we tried to have it excluded in the first place," the defense attorney said. "If that evidence was introduced at trial, I thought it would be difficult for the jurors to concentrate on the facts of the case. Dr. Greineder had the advantage of being a good citizen with a supportive family and [permitting this evidence] couldn't [allow me] to portray him as a remarkable and outstanding citizen."

Murphy would also be unhappy with the judge's ruling that, despite his contention that rabid media coverage and statements by the district attorney had "poisoned" the county's jury pool, Dr. Greineder's trial would not be moved out of Norfolk County unless selecting a jury proved troublesome. He had been optimistic that he would reap some benefit from Judge Barrett's harsh rebuke of Bill Keating's press conference, but Murphy would end up receiving no compensation.

With the trial looming just two months away, the effort to expand the evidence against Dr. Greineder continued at a feverish pace, the tight deadline only magnifying the stress. Based on the recommendation of hired forensic expert Rod Englert, Foley and State Police Lt. Brian O'Hara flew to Seattle to meet with Michael French, an expert in latent fingerprints at the King County Sheriff's Department. Englert's advice was to have the bloodstained windbreaker and black pants Dr. Greineder had worn the day of the murder treated with a chemical called amido black, which binds protein to make biological stains more pronounced for analysis. Foley hoped the treatment would better illuminate the blood patterns, especially the ones suspected of coming from the rubber-dimpled brown work gloves. After getting Murphy's permission to treat the evidence with amido black, Foley and O'Hara worked late into the night on March 21 at the state police lab in Agawam in western Massachusetts conducting tests on Dr. Greineder's pants before flying to Seattle early the next morning.

A photography expert who had been to thousands of crime scenes in his twenty years as a forensic investigator, O'Hara sprayed the pants with fluorescein hoping to expose bloodstains on the dark material under alternate light sources. Wearing special glasses to enhance the process, the two officers were startled when a handprint appeared above the right pants pocket where Foley later theorized Dr. Greineder had secreted the knife after killing his wife. As they scrambled to photograph the luminescent image likely left by the bloodstained right work glove, the distinctive handprint suddenly faded before O'Hara could snap a picture.

"You could see an area where he would have put his right hand on his pocket," said Foley. "You could see it clear as day, but by the time we tried to photograph it, it was gone and we could never duplicate it. It would have been a bloody handprint on his jeans."

Dejected, Foley and O'Hara left the lab at 11 P.M. for the two-hour ride home. They had to be at Logan Airport three hours later to catch their flight to Seattle.

Taking the clothes to Seattle turned out to yield more fortunate results. Mike French dipped Dr. Greineder's windbreaker in amido black, and the investigators left it to dry overnight. Looking over the jacket in the morning, Foley and O'Hara made another surprising discovery. Previously unseen on the white panel on the back of the jacket between the shoulders were a series of small, acutely shaped stains that could have only come from one thing — blood cast from a weapon being drawn above Dr. Greineder's right shoulder.

Technically classified as castoff, this kind of spatter is produced when centrifugal force causes blood to fall away from the weapon when it is brought to a halt before being thrust back downward. The tails of the resulting spatters will point in the direction where the blood was deposited. Even though the rear white panel of the jacket had been scrutinized for stains under a variety of high-intensity lights, the nylon had repulsed the blood, leaving no visible trace until the enhancing amido black brought the signature stain into the view.

"Both O'Hara and French said it was castoff, probably from a knife blade," said Foley. "The blood did not stick enough to see with the naked eye but there was enough protein left to show the stain with the amido black."

Bringing the jacket back to Massachusetts, the investigators had a major decision to make. To prove the castoff stain was blood, it would have to be removed and tested, then sent to Cellmark for DNA analysis. "Do we destroy that pattern to extract DNA and test it to conclusively prove it's blood, or do we leave it the way it is and call it castoff?" said Foley, explaining the dilemma. "We thought it was better to keep the pattern." The choice would end up being the wrong one.

The forensic investigation had other low points. Meeting at the Sudbury crime lab on April 26, Rick Grundy went ballistic when he found out a report that had been completed more than a year before linked fibers from Dr. Greineder's nail clippings to the brown work gloves. Reading his own copy of trace evidence analyst Beth Fisher's report as Grundy scanned his, Foley knew his more volatile colleague was going to erupt. Grundy did exactly that, ripping Fisher in front of lab manager Gwen Pino with an expletive-laced tirade.

Fisher had microscopically examined the cotton fibers from Dr. Greineder's nails against material taken from the work gloves to compare the diameter, appearance, and color. Using a comparison microscope, Fisher observed that the fibers taken from the brown work gloves had the same "light beige to light green" coloring as the fibers recovered from Dr. Greineder's fingernails. Fisher could not say the fibers came from the same source, but concluded they were comparable and could have come from the same origin.

Grundy could not believe Fisher had gone some seventeen months downplaying her own results. "The fibers are the same, and you don't think that's important?" Grundy screamed at her. Pino could muster little sympathy for her underling. "They were ready to kill Beth," she said.

Confronted with the development just a month before trial, the investigators scrambled to exploit the fiber evidence that could further connect Dr. Greineder to the gloves worn by his wife's killer. The next morning, Foley was on the phone to the FBI lab in Washington. "I was pleading with them," he laughed, able to smile about the situation now. "I told them I was going to bring the gloves and the sample slides and I needed someone to evaluate them. . . . And I need it in three weeks."

The FBI supervisor was not sympathetic. "He said it was impossible," said Foley. Refusing to take no for an answer, Foley told his FBI contact his tale of woe, finally convincing the man to help him.

Flying to Washington on May 2, Foley hand-delivered the material to FBI analyst Sandra Koch, who was also asked to compare the left-hand brown glove worn by the killer with a glove found in the doctor's dog house and one purchased by police at Diehl's Hardware. Koch's primary instruction was to examine the construction of the three gloves, including how they were made, if they were knit or woven and how many different fabrics were used. All of the gloves were cotton, with Koch noting that they were made with three different colored fabrics.

Taking cuttings from the gloves, Koch found they were stitched the same way. Counting the gripping dots, Koch concluded the three gloves had the same number. The glove found at the murder scene and the one taken from the doctor's dog house were identical, Koch concluded, while one of the fabrics used to make the glove purchased at Diehl's had a slight color variation from the other two. In Koch's opinion, the storm drain and doghouse gloves were made together, while the gloves from the hardware store came from a different dye lot.

Taking the slides containing the fibers from Dr. Greineder's fingernails and samples from a crime-scene glove, Koch made her own glove cuttings to put under a comparison microscope. The FBI expert noted that the fibers from Dr. Greineder's fingernails "exhibited the same microscopic properties" and were consistent with the fibers taken from the storm drain and doghouse gloves. Defense attorney Marty Murphy would bitterly contest the findings from both Koch and Beth Fisher.

Murphy was also making the prosecution's life miserable over the towel Dr. Greineder claimed to have used with his wife to stem their simultaneous nosebleeds. Served with a grand jury subpoena to hand over the mysterious towel, Murphy had insisted the blood-spotted towel be sent to Cellmark Diagnostics for DNA testing.

Of the sixteen bloodstains on the towel, seven showed the complete genetic profile for Dr. Greineder, while an eighth matched him on seven of thirteen loci. One cutting matched only May Greineder's profile, while another seven showed mixed results, with her as the primary donor. The secondary donor on the mixed results was male, and Dr. Greineder could not be excluded from one cutting; for the other cuttings it was undetermined as to whether he could be included.

Murphy had also demanded cuttings be taken from May's blue fleece gloves, Pino sending four cuttings from each to Cellmark on February 22, 2001. On one cutting taken from the top of the middle finger on the left hand blue glove, the testing developed five alleles at one locus, meaning there was likely DNA from three contributors. It would become a so-called "mystery allele," because it could not have come from Dirk or May. Although it was one allele from just one of thirteen loci and May's glove could have come in contact with a host of innocent people before her death, Murphy would seize on the development for all it was worth.

Murphy would not glowingly endorse the Cellmark testing, however. During the course of the different rounds of testing, Cellmark had raised its computer threshold for analyzing the electronic results. Cellmark's testing on the Greineder evidence had produced a series of visible peaks on a graph known as an electropherogram. The vertical height of a peak indicates the relative amount of DNA at the designated loci within the DNA molecule, which is reported in Relative Fluorescent Units or RFUs. The results interpreted from numerical peaks generated by the complicated process, threshold basically tells the computer to record anything above a certain height as a peak. At lower thresholds, like the 40 RFUs Cellmark used to analyze the Greineder evidence, the peaks become muddied, prolonging the process of the DNA analysts in reaching conclusive results.

For that reason, Cellmark had boosted its testing threshold in the spring of 2000 to 60 RFUs to streamline the process, but the higher threshold would not have returned results that included Dr. Greineder's DNA, as did the first tests conducted on the knife and brown work gloves tested at 40 RFUs. As Rick Grundy would correctly explain, once DNA is identified, it is there. Murphy planned to attack that contention with everything he could muster.

# 20

TYPICALLY RUNNING LATE, Belinda Markel had the added stress of not knowing what to expect once she and her mother finally arrived in Dedham on Thursday, May 24, 2001. They had never been to the affluent suburban home of Norfolk County's Superior Court. Upon arriving, they nervously glanced at the tangle of television equipment on the courthouse lawn, festively covered with a sprawling white tent. Skipping up the double-tiered rows of wide granite steps, the unsuspecting women were not even sure the TV setup was there for Dirk's case, since they had not been there to see the frenzied coverage accompanying his previous appearances in the Dedham court.

Belinda had more trepidation about what waited inside. Although she had still periodically spoken with her cousins as well as defense attorney Marty Murphy, she thought she had made it known that she and her mother "would not be with" Dr. Greineder's defense. "I thought I had been clear all along, especially with Kirsten, about what my views were concerning Dirk's guilt," she said. "It was very, very difficult to walk into that courthouse that morning having absolutely no idea what to expect."

The tented outdoor television studio would prove to be one of the first hints that Belinda and Ilse were clueless about what they were in for. Assembled for Court TV (now truTV), the open-air studio had been put together overnight, looking from a distance like a tented party was planned on the courthouse lawn. The scandalous details of the case were to be broadcast around the globe starting that Thursday.

Rising to prominence during the 1991 West Palm Beach rape case of William Kennedy Smith, Court TV had lured millions of new viewers four years later with its gavel-to-gavel coverage of the nine-month O. J. Simpson trial. While the Greineder coverage would not reach the astronomical viewership of the Simpson case, ratings from the case of *Commonwealth of Massachusetts v. Dirk K. Greineder* would make the network executives smile.

With the main courtroom on the second floor in use for another murder trial, Judge Chernoff would oversee opening arguments in the smaller

Courtroom Ten near the back of the courthouse where the shackled Dr. Greineder was brought in every morning. Now nineteen months after May's frightful murder, the electricity in the overflowing courtroom was unmistakable as pent-up anticipation felt by longtime case observers peaked with the realization that the high-stakes trial was finally going to commence.

Confidently striding into the charged courtroom where the only empty seat stood reserved for him, Dr. Greineder looked like a man determined to prove his innocence. Noticeably thinner since his dramatic arraignment fourteen months before, he would grow increasingly more gaunt as the trial progressed.

In what would become a habit, particularly during difficult testimony, Dr. Greineder turned to smile at his three children sitting in the front row diagonally behind him. His expression toward Belinda Markel and Ilse Stark was decidedly different when they were brought timidly into the crammed courtroom, the overflow of spectators unnerving them. "It appeared that he was trying to be intimidating as opposed to angry," remembered Belinda. "I almost felt he was trying to manipulate us at that point, or at least me, like if he made me feel uncomfortable enough, he would make me change my tactics even up until that moment."

As the two women followed victim advocate Pam Friedman to their designated front-row seats on the prosecution side of the room, the Greineder children made it instantly clear with their hostile stares that Belinda's pretrial conversations with Kirsten had failed to enlighten her cousins that the New York relatives stood against their father. "It was at that specific moment that it was absolutely clear to everybody when Pam sat us down," Belinda recalled softly. "The glares were just unbelievable. It was very, very uncomfortable. There was a tremendous amount of stress and anger from the other side of the room."

Her only knowledge of criminal court proceedings from old "Perry Mason" reruns, Belinda, like her mother Ilse, had had no idea how the system worked. Trying to look around without being noticed, Belinda slowly realized that the obvious separation from where her cousins were seated had created a charged dynamic in the cramped courtroom. "It took me a while to realize the impact of that, having never done this before," she said. "I didn't really understand what kind of statement it was going to make, but when we sat down in that first row away from them I think it was clear to everybody."

Making their first-ever court appearance since Dirk had been charged, Belinda and Ilse could feel the examining eyes of the courtroom audience, particularly reporters eager to interview them. "I remember sitting there trying to take in everything I possibly could as to who these people were because I had no idea," said Belinda. "I was trying to figure out all the people sitting to the left. I didn't know it was the press."

One person who would not be attending the doctor's trial was Aleks Engel, Kirsten's fiancé, who had made it clear to the defendant's closest supporters that he believed Dirk was likely guilty of killing May. Nevertheless, the August wedding was still on, and since they could only count on Kirsten's support in the courtroom until then, in three months, Dr. Greineder was anxious for the trial to begin. For that reason and because he remained jailed pending his trial, Dr. Greineder did not press Murphy to seek a continuance to consult additional experts to counter the prosecution's DNA evidence.

Just two months before trial, major issues emerged involving the defendant's DNA expert, Dr. Christy Davis, when an Australian court slammed Davis following her nineteen days of testimony in an evidentiary hearing. The court ruled that Davis "lacked integrity, was incompetent, and lacked sufficient training and experience to interpret electropherograms accurately or to testify as an expert." Additionally, Murphy had discovered a California case in which the judge all but dismissed an affidavit filed by Davis based on prior testimony and criticism of her work by judges in other cases.

Rick Grundy was well aware of the issues surrounding Davis, and Murphy clearly could not put her on the stand to refute the prosecution's DNA evidence prepared by Cellmark Diagnostics. But Dr. Greineder still wanted Murphy to go to trial without seeking a continuance. Murphy would be criticized later for doing so.

Before seating the jury, Judge Chernoff met with the lawyers at sidebar, almost like an umpire going over the ground rules before the first pitch. At sixty-two, he had been hearing criminal and civil Superior Court cases for fifteen years, having been elevated after nine years as a justice at Newton District Court. Chernoff's legal career was highly regarded. The diminutive judge could infect a courtroom with his enveloping good nature, almost like a teddy bear in black robes, handing out pieces of hard candy during recesses. More apt to talk to reporters about his adored Boston Red Sox during breaks in the proceedings, the judge carried a baseball onto the bench autographed by Sox fireballer Pedro Martinez for inspiration.

Enveloped by a huddle of lawyers at the sidebar, Chernoff revealed his final interpretation of where the first five minutes of Marty Foley's conversation with Dr. Greineder ended during his initial interview the day of the murder. "I drew the line on the Miranda issue with the defendant saying that he checked the carotid artery," Chernoff told the attorneys. "It may go further on re-examination depending upon evidence that is presented."

Signaled to proceed with his opening statement, Rick Grundy settled in front of the jury box as the jammed courtroom held its collective breath. The prosecutor opened with words from the man he was determined to send to prison for life.

"Is she dead? Am I going to be arrested?" Grundy began, reciting the questions Dr. Greineder had asked Officer Paul Fitzpatrick in the minutes after his wife's murder. "Thirty to forty minutes after this defendant called the Wellesley police to say his wife had been attacked," Grundy continued, "he stood in that circle area that we visited yesterday with Officer Paul Fitzpatrick, a uniformed Wellesley police officer, and those are his words. This physician," Grundy pointed accusingly at the defendant calmly taking notes as if he were at an asthma seminar.

"Is she dead? Am I going to be arrested?" Grundy repeated, firing the first salvo in what would be an exhaustive effort to discredit the outwardly respected doctor. Mocking Dr. Greineder's claim that he had checked his wife's carotid artery when she was obviously dead, the contrast between the doctor's clean hands and his blood-covered clothing spoke the real truth, the prosecutor asserted.

"Ladies and gentleman," he stressed, "unfortunately, you will see pictures of May Greineder's carotid artery, of her entire neck area. I want you to think of this defendant telling individuals that he checked her carotid artery as he stood there with Officer Paul Fitzpatrick and those clean hands."

Taking the jury through an overview of his voluminous, yet varied evidence, Grundy told the jury Dr. Greineder's arrest resulted from "elaborate plans gone awry. Too elaborate, too thought out," he said. "Items left behind, items that will have a link, as you will see, to this defendant."

Telling the jury that May "was a mother and a dedicated wife" who "loved, cared for and nurtured her children," Grundy tried to persuade the jurors that her husband was not the respected family man he seemed, but instead harbored "deeply and closely held secrets."

Taking a more measured approach, Marty Murphy opened his shorter statement by telling the jurors they had to put aside whatever sensational details they had heard about the case and decide Dr. Greineder's guilt or innocence based on the "real stuff," the evidence. "Whoever it was that smashed the back of May Greineder's head with a two-pound drilling hammer, that cut her throat, that stabbed her twice in the chest and stabbed her five times in the head, whoever that is, it's not this man," Murphy said, glancing at his client distinguishably posed at the defense table.

Hitting the sex allegations head on, Murphy for the first time publicly admitted Dr. Greineder was unfaithful to his wife. "This case is not about whether Dirk Greineder committed adultery," Murphy began, eyes in the courtroom shifting to see the reaction from his client's children.

"If the charge here was that Dirk Greineder committed adultery, the evidence will show that Dirk Greineder is guilty of that charge. If the charge here was that Dirk Greineder used the Internet for sexual gratification in ways that you might find very distressing, if that were the charge, the evidence will show that Dirk Greineder is guilty of that charge. But Dirk Greineder is not charged here with adultery or infidelity or use of the Internet for sexual gratification in ways you might find disturbing, he is charged here with the murder of his wife. All of those things had nothing to do with the murder of May Greineder," Murphy implored.

Instead of searching for the person who had killed May, the police focused right away on Dr. Greineder, Murphy accused, yet never tested his hands for the presence of blood. Attempting to cast more doubt on the prosecution's case, Murphy dramatically revealed the discovery of DNA on May's fleece glove that came from someone other than the victim or her husband.

"What that means, members of the jury, is that the state's own DNA experts found DNA from an unknown stranger at this crime scene," he said, his voice rising for effect. "Who is that stranger?" Murphy grandly inquired. "Well, the answer is, members of the jury, we don't know. We don't know because the state, the police, and the prosecutors did not conduct a fair and objective search for the truth."

As Murphy finished, Kirsten rushed from the courtroom, the admission of her father's sordid dalliances perhaps being too much for her. But returning to her front-row seat a short time later, the doctor's oldest child forced a reassuring smile when her concerned father craned his neck to look back at her.

The divide between Dr. Greineder's children and their relatives from New York did not go unnoticed by the jury, even though they would adhere to Judge Chernoff's instruction not to discuss the case or follow it in the media. The panel had yet to learn the names of the two obviously grieving women sitting away from Dr. Greineder's children, or their relationship to May, but it was clear they had come to a conclusion about the defendant's guilt different from the one his three impressive children had chosen.

"From day one we noticed a family was on one side and his kids were on the other, and we all knew they were not looking at each other," said juror Mike Paul. "There were obviously issues."

From their front-row seats in the jury box, Sara Barbera and Dr. Bill Giesecke saw nothing strange in the Greineder children's support, even though they knew that the attractive young adults were strategically positioned by Murphy for their benefit.

"They were there for us," said Giesecke. The dentist, thinking of his own grown children, couldn't imagine what they would do if thrust into the same nightmarish dilemma dropped on the Greineder siblings. "To imagine your mother being murdered is one thing. To imagine your father being the murderer is just incomprehensible," he sympathized. "I don't think it can be done."

To Barbera, who was pregnant with her first child, the Greineder children had no other option but to support their disgraced father. "I totally understand where they were coming from," said the expectant mother. "If you believe he's guilty, you have no one. You don't have a mom. You don't have a dad."

Determined to decide Dr. Greineder's fate based on the evidence, the jurors would notice May's relatives every day in court, but the divisive emotions resulting from her death were put aside. "We were going to look at this without being influenced by some of those obvious ploys," said juror Cheryl Nixon, an English professor at Wellesley's Babson College. "That was something we tried to uphold."

The reporters made their first run at Belinda and Ilse at the lunch break as they uncomfortably walked out of the courthouse. Ilse sternly rebuffed the approaching journalists, telling them only that she might have something to say after the trial. Her daughter gently tugged at her as they quickened their pace out the front door. "Walk," Belinda had ordered her mother upon seeing the advancing reporters.

Alone in the sanctity of Belinda's big SUV, the two women tried to decompress. "We were like, 'Holy shit,'" Belinda recalled. "I didn't expect the media presence that was there, and it was overwhelming. I had to get out of Dedham for those forty-five minutes at the lunch break. We had to get out of there. We both needed some breathing room to regroup. It was almost like every part of your body hurting from being tense."

Just because Rick Grundy was now putting witnesses on the stand didn't mean the evidence gathering against Dr. Greineder had ceased. In the community room at the Wellesley Police Station, several officers sat around a long table sorting through a mountain of sales receipts from Diehl's Hardware.

Shortly before Dr. Greineder's arrest in February 2000, Sgt. Mike Price had arranged for the busy hardware store to deliver a pallet-load of their sales receipts from the previous three years. It took the Greineder investigators 1,800 man-hours to sort through the receipts, bundled in rolls collected from the cash registers each day, in search of the Estwing two-pound hammer, the distinctive rubber-dimpled work gloves or any credit card numbers from Dr. Greineder's accounts.

Matching the receipts with sales records from Diehl's, the investigators concluded that forty pairs of the brown gloves were sold during the first ten months of 1999 with only four of the hammers being purchased. With the trial approaching, Chief Terry Cunningham agreed to Grundy's request for a second examination of the receipts in spite of the enormous overtime cost to his department.

As Grundy called to the stand some of the first responders to Morses Pond on Halloween 1999, the medically trained Kirsten and Colin were mostly able to keep their composure during the graphic depiction of their mother's ghastly injuries, but Britt was reduced to tears every time her mother's savaged condition was mentioned.

The rules of testimony generally prohibiting a witness from revealing what other people said, juror Stan Smith felt like he was "trying to watch a movie one actor or actress at a time. You're not sure what the whole story line is going to be," said the CEO of a high-tech company. "It's only when you are allowed to think about it all that you understand what was happening."

As the trial went into recess for the long Memorial Day weekend, it didn't mean the two sides took time to relax. For Grundy and the core group of investigators, the trial would be a marathon of sometimes twenty-hour workdays with weekends used as preparation for the coming week's testimony. As they sorted through evidence at the Dedham courthouse on Sunday, May 27, Grundy, Marty Foley, and Terry Cunningham made an incredible discovery. Rechecking the Diehl's receipt from September 3, 1999, found on Dr. Greineder's work bench against the sale of work gloves and two-pound hammers, the lawmen couldn't believe it when they realized a hammer was sold just two minutes after Dr. Greineder paid $6.76 for nails.

No one had to verbalize that they had a devastating piece of circumstantial evidence. Lynne Mortarelli, a University of Rhode Island student working her second-to-last day at Diehl's, had handled the 8:55 A.M. cash sale for the six packages of nails that generated the receipt Foley had collected from Dr. Greineder's workbench during the second search of the Greineder home. The next sale Mortarelli rang up moments later at 8:58 was the $31.49 cash purchase of an Estwing two-pound hammer displayed just behind her register at the front of the store. Although Mortarelli would not be able to identify Dr. Greineder as the customer in either of the sales, the inference that a hammer was sold just moments after someone in the Greineder home bought nails could have a swaying effect on the jury.

Returning to court on Tuesday, May 29, the jury would be engrossed by Terry McNally's testimony about the childlike scream he heard from the ridge above the sandpit. The defendant listened stoically, but he would show some emotion with another witness, however, appearing to cry while dabbing his eyes with a handkerchief as Grundy played his cell phone call to police dispatcher Shannon Parillo. With Parillo standing impassively on the witness stand, Dr. Greineder turned repeatedly to his sobbing children who mostly covered their faces in grief upon listening apparently for the first time to their father's call.

With only Marty Foley left to testify from among the core group of witnesses who encountered Dr. Greineder the day of the murder, Grundy moved his case to the complex forensic evidence collected against the accused husband. Putting Trooper Julia Mosely on the stand, the jury heard that all the evidence gathered from Morses Pond was devoid of fingerprints. The diminutive Sgt. Deb Rebeiro followed Mosely with her damaging testimony about the crime-scene footprints left by Dr. Greineder's white Reebok sneakers.

Grundy using photographs to highlight Rebeiro's impressive testimony, Dr. Greineder's children turned away when images projected on a large screen included their mother's body and legs jutting grotesquely into the dirt trail. Equally distressed, Belinda Markel and Ilse Stark bravely scanned the disturbing images along with the jury, tears streaming down Ilse's face.

When crime lab manager Gwen Pino took the stand on Monday, June 4, Grundy took her through a detailed accounting of mostly bloodstained evidence and samples sent for DNA testing. The unveiling of May's bloody, knife-slashed clothing rattled her relatives despite Judge Chernoff's advance warning that "very sensitive evidence" would be shown from "the victim in this case, some with some stains."

Still, some of May's loved ones and several of the jurors recoiled as Pino identified the sliced, soiled garments that so graphically conveyed May's violent demise. When Pino lifted May's blood-soaked T-shirt, Dr. Greineder turned to his distressed children mouthing silent words of comfort before choking up himself then blowing his nose into a handkerchief.

Giving the jurors a hint of the gradually emerging reason the attorneys were bitterly locked over a towel filched from a Ritz-Carlton hotel, Grundy made a point to have Pino testify that no trace of blood was found on the tissues in May's jacket pocket. Blood was confirmed on the towel turned over by Murphy, Pino told the puzzled jurors, who had yet to hear about the improbable simultaneous nosebleed Dr. Greineder claimed he had with his wife.

Putting Pino through a lengthy cross-examination, Murphy scored some points by having the chemist reveal that no blood was detected inside Dr. Greineder's small red backpack, making it highly unlikely he stashed the weapons and gloves there before ditching them in the storm drain. Counterattacking Grundy's repeated screening of a photograph showing the defendant's pristine hands, Murphy asked Pino if any requests were made to test Dr. Greineder for blood there the day of the murder. "No, they did not," Pino simply replied.

Using Chief Terry Cunningham to identify evidence seized during the two searches of Dr. Greineder's home, Cunningham also identified the clear food storage bags taken from the Greineder's pantry. The jurors would have to wait to hear the damning conclusion of FBI scientist Lorie Gottesman linking them to the plastic bags at the crime scene. Of more interest to the jury was his gripping testimony about finding the identical pair of brown work gloves in the doghouse behind the Greineder home. Cunningham recounted how he was unaware the roof was hinged until Kirsten had pointed it out, all eyes in the courtroom shifting to the sheepish woman.

Grundy sent Marty Murphy copies of the Diehl's receipts that night, knowing his friend would do whatever possible to have them barred as evidence. Marty Foley tried not to laugh the next morning when Grundy told him Murphy's reaction to the revelation that a hammer had been sold a couple of minutes after someone from the Greineder family had bought the six packages of nails.

"Can you believe the guy that murdered May was in the store the same time Dirk was?" the defense attorney had said. It seemed an attempt to put on a brave face at all costs.

# 21

FEELING RELAXED as he raised his right hand to be sworn in on Tuesday, June 5, Marty Foley would remain standing on the witness stand for the rest of the day and most of the next morning. After a description of his training and experience, prosecutor Rick Grundy then took the detective to the events of Halloween morning 1999 and his first face-to-face meeting with Dirk Greineder, using the opportunity again to highlight the bloodstained doctor's clean hands.

Foley recounted his conversation with Dr. Greineder almost verbatim, staring at the note-writing defendant while reciting his conflicting accounts of what happened that morning. "Any time they asked me what he said, I either pointed at him or looked right at him," said Foley. "He was constantly taking notes. I'd love to see what he had written down there."

Since Judge Chernoff's pretrial ruling prevented Grundy from taking Foley past the point where Dr. Greineder said he checked his wife's carotid artery, Grundy shifted the testimony to the Wellesley Police Station, where Dr. Greineder had turned over his clothing and nail clippings and allowed the police to walk through his home.

Foley's testimony played well for the TV-viewing audience. The confident witness's riveting testimony about the Greineders' loveless sex life had viewers enthralled. "The courtroom TV star so far has been Sgt. Martin Foley, the State Police detective who first grilled Dr. Greineder at the crime scene," wrote *Boston Herald* television critic Monica Collins. Court TV analysts described him as a "hard-nosed cop" and a "Bostonian version of Sgt. Joe Friday." "Court TV executives must have been high-fiving during that testimony," Collins opined. "The Greineder trial provides a string of the real-life-is-stranger-than-fiction moments that play so vividly on TV."

Except for the pressure of millions of viewers watching the attorneys' every move, the prosecution team was generally happy that Court TV had decided to broadcast the entire trial. "It was the best thing in the world having Court TV do it live," said Chief Terry Cunningham. "Without seeing the evidence it would be easier for people to say Dirk had been railroaded.

They didn't get to see the evidence going in, and they were glued to the TV in this town watching it."

With Grundy turning to the events of the second search of the doctor's home, Foley told the jurors about the $6.76 receipt from Diehl's Hardware he found on Dr. Greineder's workbench. The clock now approaching 3 P.M. after a long day on the witness stand, Foley was handed the cardboard box found in the doctor's garage.

Donning latex gloves as other witnesses had done when handling certain evidence, Foley pulled out the small plastic vial of Viagra and the bright-colored box of Trojan condoms.

"And does it indicate, sir, to whom that prescription is prescribed?" Grundy asked.

"It is prescribed to Dirk Greineder," Foley replied.

"And does it indicate by whom it is prescribed?" the prosecutor continued.

"Yes," Foley stated, privately enjoying the moment, "Dr. D. Greineder."

Finally given a chance to question Foley, Murphy tried to make the witness pay for a misstatement he had inexplicably made during a pretrial hearing the summer before when Foley said blood had been observed on the towel found in Dr. Greineder's car by Jill McDermott and Terry Cunningham. Grundy had apparently missed hearing the misstatement, which ended up in the transcripts of the hearing.

"And on the night of November one, you were told by other investigators that two investigators looked into Dr. Greineder's car and there was a towel in that car that appeared to have bloodstains on it, true?' Murphy grandstanded.

"False," Foley replied forcefully.

With the jurors riveted by the exchange, Murphy read back Foley's words from the July 2000 pretrial hearing, making effective use of the detective's error. "Did I read your answer correctly?" Murphy emphasized.

"That's correct," said Foley.

"And that was your testimony last July eighteenth under oath in this courtroom, correct?" the defense attorney prodded.

"That's correct," Foley restated without elaborating.

The whole issue of the towel still rankles Foley, especially how Murphy originally gave them one towel then replaced it with the blood-spotted towel the doctor said he swiped from the Atlanta Ritz-Carlton during a business trip. "We didn't attack it, and I got slammed hard during pretrials," Foley said with frustration. "Murphy really got after me hard, and we should have gone after him and Grundy didn't. Grundy took the high road and didn't go after him."

The mysterious towel had been a constant source of concern for the detective. "We were like, 'What the hell is with this towel?'" Foley said. "It was just another red herring that popped up, except there was a drop of blood from both Dirk and May. Where did that blood come from?" Foley rhetorically asked, still fairly certain the second autopsy Dr. Greineder commissioned on May provides the answer.

For the defense, the towel was a critical piece of evidence. "Dr. Greineder had told a number of people about this event that occurred the morning of the murder," said Murphy. "Each of them had nosebleeds and used the same towel to stop the bleeding. It was important to show that blood came from both [Dirk and May]. It corroborated statements he had made to people, which the prosecution was trying to debunk as fiction on his part."

The towel was also important to the defense's DNA transfer theory. "If [Dr. Greineder] was telling the truth, [the towel] would have been in the Avalon," said Murphy. If the investigators had not seen a towel, "it would undercut the defense, and it would reinforce the Commonwealth's theory that it was a crazy story," he explained. "It would suggest he was fabricating evidence. It would suggest he was lying to members of his family."

Approaching Belinda Markel in the ladies' room during a break, Britt violated the cousins' self-imposed silence to inform Belinda that Wolf, the older of the family's two beloved German shepherds, had been put down that morning. "Wolfie died," Britt said with her typical strong emotion. "I figured you would want to know."

Walking up to Kirsten in the courtroom, Belinda offered her sympathy. "I'm very sorry to hear of Wolfie's passing," Belinda said sincerely. "I know it must be hard. Please pass my condolences to Colin," she requested.

Only expressing her thanks, Kirsten would later call her cousin at the Crowne Plaza in Natick, where a week of hostility boiled over. "They wanted absolutely nothing to do with us," Belinda wistfully recalled. "They couldn't believe that we're doing this. She told me her father was innocent and basically what a horrible person I was."

Belinda got the same lecture when she bumped into Nancy Gans in the first-floor ladies' room. Belinda and her mother subsequently found another bathroom to use in a vacant jury room to avoid further confrontations. Kirsten's angry telephone call would be the last time that Belinda spoke to any of her cousins during the trial. They did leave several birthday gifts for Belinda's children on her courtroom bench, with a note saying that the packages had come from "Uncle Dirk."

Rick Grundy would have to wait until after the next day to correct the damage from Foley's pretrial misstatement about the towel, but more fireworks would ensue before then. They started during a recess bench conference when the jury was not present. Murphy, after months of battling to limit what Foley could say about his lengthy conversation with Dr. Greineder the day of the murder, suddenly wanted the detective to address questions beyond the first five minutes set by the judge's ruling.

It was only days before that the defense had thought it a major victory when Judge Chernoff ruled where the first five minutes of the conversation ended, but after Foley took the stand the defendant and his attorney realized they had made a tactical blunder. With testimony portraying the defendant as covered in blood, the ruling prevented any mention of Dr. Greineder's claim that he had tried to lift his wife, thus leaving no explanation for the bloodstains on his clothing.

"It would be our view that where the conversations were excluded as a result of the officer's violation of the defendant's Miranda rights, that as long as we aren't offering an incomplete conversation we have the ability to essentially stop the clock where we want to stop the clock," Murphy insisted to Grundy's shock. "And we would like to stop the clock after all the conversations at the pond are finished. That's what I would intend to do," Murphy added aggressively.

By this time the jury had returned and Foley had once again taken his place on the witness stand. Asked for his opinion, Grundy blasted his rival.

"Your Honor, I find it outrageous, quite frankly, with all due respect, that the defense would come to the judge with the jury sitting in the box after a half day of this officer's testimony, after the judge made a ruling as to the precise statement where that would kick in, and instruct the judge that he has decided where he will end that questioning," Grundy said, his fury evident. "The fact of the matter is the court issued a ruling. The Commonwealth has presented this witness through that ruling and obviously is extraordinarily prejudiced in a way that can't be addressed before this jury."

Grundy stressed that such a move at this point would leave "an impression that the Commonwealth chose not to elicit some testimony because they felt it damning to their case" and would imply that the prosecution had "attempted to hide something from the jury." Grundy added, "Mr. Murphy obviously wants that testimony because he feels it benefits his client. Your, Honor, it goes beyond that."

Murphy countered that he "should be able to waive those rights and stop the clock at any point." He agreed with the judge that he had no case law to back this position but suggested that the judge could explain to the jury that the extension of the testimony was just a procedural process under the rules of evidence. Murphy said he wanted "to make it absolutely clear that I'm not accusing Mr. Grundy of trying to hide the ball in front of the jury," which only fueled the prosecutor's pique.

"Your Honor," Grundy appealed, "that's the outrageous part. Mr. Murphy asked for this, and he got it. He put his towel in the water. He let the Commonwealth go all the way through it. Now he doesn't like the temperature of the water and he wants to change it. It's just not appropriate or fair. It's very simple judge," Grundy continued, trying to keep his rising voice from the jurors now seated nearby. "You cannot have your cake and eat it, too."

With the jury patiently waiting for the resumption of testimony, Judge Chernoff cut the discussion short, telling the lawyers he was going to allow the disputed testimony but that Grundy would elicit it first on redirect before Murphy questioned Foley about it. The compromise was unacceptable to the prosecutor. "Again, the Commonwealth is far more prejudiced than that can come even close to addressing. We're going to look like a bunch of fools who have no idea what we're doing," Grundy challenged.

"I'm going to stand on the ruling," Judge Chernoff said. But he stressed to Murphy that if he was going to waive the Miranda objection, then all of Dr. Greineder's statements on Halloween 1999 were admissible. "I would not let the clock be stopped and started," the judge warned. "It goes all the way through."

Standing on the witness stand for the resumption of Murphy's cross-examination, Foley had no idea what was being heatedly discussed just a few yards away in the huddle around the judge, but the detective could clearly see that Grundy was upset.

Testimony finally got under way, Foley answering a series of questions from Murphy concerning his law enforcement experience, agreeing with his one-time golf partner that he had been investigating homicides only nine months before May Greineder's murder. The testimony was mostly mundane. Murphy asked if Foley had been aware of the similar Walpole and Westwood murders, a question he had passionately fought to be allowed to ask. But Foley's affirmative answer seemed to make little difference to the jury. Apparently still unconvinced the only store in the area selling the brown work gloves was Diehl's Hardware, Murphy then asked Foley a series of tedious questions about the other stores that were checked.

After Grundy asked some follow-up questions, he indicated to the judge that it was time to give the jury instruction regarding the new testimony about the day of the crime as mediated at the sidebar. Judge Chernoff told the jurors that the "time-honored and rather technical rules of evidence, which might not seem to make sense to laypersons," had forced him to limit the prosecutor's line of questioning until the redirect.

Grundy then had the detective recount the full extent of his dealings with Dr. Greineder the day of the murder. He told how the doctor had claimed to have tried to pick up his wife after checking her carotid artery and how he had kept asking to go make a call and to take care of his dogs. Hammering home the image of the defendant's clean hands, Grundy had Foley testify that Dr. Greineder denied washing them or had reached the pond before turning back to find his wife.

Murphy then countered with a number of follow-up questions, finally asking, "You never asked Dr. Greineder for his consent to have his hands tested for the presence of blood, correct?"

"That's correct," Foley agreed before being excused from the stand. Pleased with his performance, Foley felt he had blunted Murphy's "Harvard Law School intimidation," his tactic of standing right next to the witness when confronting them with evidence. Foley had felt in command as he stood on the stand looking down on his questioner.

Walking out of the humid courtroom, Foley knew there was a good chance he might be recalled before the trial was over. His instincts would prove correct.

There was one person who had a direct connection between *Commonwealth v. Dirk K. Greineder* and the O. J. Simpson case: Dr. Robin Cotton. Dr. Cotton, who had spent six days testifying against Simpson, had almost become a household name during the celebrity-studded trial that captivated the nation for nine months. In the Greineder case, Cotton took the stand just after lunch on June 6, and her testimony would be among the most engrossing, and the most downright boring, that prosecutor Grundy had to offer. Complicated, but dangerously incriminating, her testimony was a sort of preview of the fight to come over the blood pattern analysis of Ken Martin and Rod Englert, and defense attorney Murphy would do everything he could to attack it.

The forensic lab director for Cellmark Diagnostics, Cotton came across as the brilliant, refined scientist she was, never failing to answer with polite consideration, regardless of how Murphy tried to discredit her. "My impression of her is I expected her to be pruning roses," said juror Sara Barbera.

Grundy first had Cotton explain the process of collecting and extracting DNA, reserving her more damning testimony for the next morning. In a direct examination that could only be described as superb, Grundy concisely guided Cotton through the complex evidence and how it was gleaned. Almost in checklist fashion, the bespectacled scientist identified one sample after another, effectively outlining its connection to Dirk or May Greineder, oftentimes to both.

In the analysis of the combination of alleles that could not exclude Dr. Greineder's DNA from the gloves and knife, juror Elaine Miller, a Massachusetts Institute of Technology mathematician, had her first sudden recognition of the defendant's guilt. "It was so overwhelming," Miller recalled, already impressed with the forensic expert testimony of witnesses like Gwen Pino and Deb Rebeiro. "The technical aspects just blew us away. What amazed me was I had no idea the State Police had that kind of technical expertise."

Sitting in the row in front of Miller, Dr. Bill Giesecke, surprisingly, was not nearly as impressed with the DNA evidence. The Walpole dentist, the only member of the jury medically and scientifically trained, found the amount of matter Cotton had talked about just too minuscule. "When I hear they are doing samples run with five or six cells, that is too small a sample for me," Giesecke explained. "I'm not going to put too much weight on that because I feel five years down the road somebody is going to say they shouldn't have done this and I'm not going to base my decision to put a man in jail for life on that."

By the time he turned his witness over to his opponent just after the morning break, Grundy had taken five hours over two days to present a voluminous amount of potentially devastating DNA evidence. With the courtroom temperature soaring into the usual nineties as the lunch hour approached, the opening of Murphy's grueling, highly technical cross-examination was a harbinger of more sweltering tedium to follow.

The defense attorney scored points with Cotton's testimony about the mystery DNA on May Greineder's glove and Cellmark's mid-case elevation of the computer-programmed threshold from 40 to 60 RFUs that wouldn't have shown DNA results on the knife and gloves. But the bulk of Murphy's nine-hour cross-exam consisted of technical nitpicking and having Cotton provide an overly clinical lecture on testing for DNA. Just two hours into his questioning of Cotton, jurors Stan Smith and Jahon Jamali began dozing in their top-row seats, while other jurors were clearly disengaged. It would only get worse in the blistering heat of Friday, June 8, as Murphy's onslaught of technical questions about the Cellmark data consumed nearly the entire day's testimony.

Unable to get Cotton to agree that a second mystery allele was detected on May's left-hand blue glove based on his interpretation of the Cellmark results, Murphy felt evident frustration. "You know there's a lot at stake here, Dr. Cotton?" Murphy admonished, drawing an objection from Grundy. The judge sustaining the prosecutor's objection, Murphy returned to his complicated cross-examination.

When Murphy finally gave Grundy back his witness late Friday afternoon, it was obvious to everyone watching in the broiling courtroom — particularly the defendant, who was furiously scribbling on a notepad — that Murphy's marathon cross-exam did little to diminish Dr. Cotton's powerful testimony for the prosecution. In the end, the DNA testing included parts of the doctor's profile with certain evidence, and more importantly, it did not exclude him.

"The DNA evidence did not eliminate him at all," said juror Stan Smith. "And you can argue the one or two places where Marty Murphy tried to say there was DNA evidence of other people, some of it looked like it could have been from exterior parts of May's clothing. I'm sure a lot of us carry DNA from other people from walking around somewhere. At no time did it ever exclude Dirk. If it had eliminated him, it would have been a big piece of the defense case."

## 22

ILSE STARK'S LONG AWAITED APPEARANCE on the witness stand finally arrived first thing on Monday, June 11. She delivered everything expected and more. Having previously announced that she was "going first" when it came time to testify against Dirk Greineder, she got no argument from Belinda Markel. "I didn't want to go on the stand anyway," Belinda said. "This was something that was weighing on me. I thought I was going to be sick thinking about it, and it was made worse by not knowing when we were going on."

Prosecutor Rick Grundy had told May Greineder's sister the night before that she would be facing her accused brother-in-law as the new week's first witness. Trial observers, particularly the media, were eagerly awaiting to hear what Ilse had to say. The assertive New Yorker did not disappoint.

Taking the stand in an elegant black outfit with a string of pearls draped at the top of her dress, Ilse unexpectedly tried to address the jury before Judge Chernoff quickly interceded. "For the sake of clarity, may I just make a statement?" Ilse said suddenly. "My sister . . ."

"No, no, please. You have to respond to questions," the judge interrupted. "My sister has been referred to as Mabel and May and I just want the jury to know why," Stark explained, ignoring the judge's admonition, to her daughter's hidden amusement. "Well, perhaps the lawyer will . . ." Judge Chernoff began before Murphy quickly interceded with a request they go to the sidebar.

Well aware that May's sister had already captured the attention of the jury, Murphy complained that Grundy had violated the judge's order by not telling him a day in advance what Ilse would say with regard to conversations she had with May. "I think the court's prior order said that I was supposed to get twenty-four hours' specific notice if any of those statements were going to come in, and I have not received any such notice," Murphy complained.

Grundy calmly countered that everything Ilse had to say was contained in her grand jury testimony that Murphy had for months. Still, the judge scolded the prosecutor, who had constantly pushed the limits of Chernoff's rulings. "I understand that," Chernoff said testily. "But I wrote an order recently which said we wanted a day's notice on this so that I could, in fact, exercise these issues and not have the jury sitting in the box or the jury room, which is what I think is something to be absolutely avoided."

For Murphy, knowing what May's sister and niece were going to say was critical to his defense of Dr. Greineder. Both had talked with May on a regular basis, and Murphy was very concerned that their testimony would open the door to hearsay comments that May thought her husband was having an affair or that all was not as it appeared in their outwardly happy marriage.

"I didn't want the Commonwealth to offer hearsay statements of May's sister and her niece," Murphy would say later. "It was a major objective to keep the hearsay statements from May Greineder to Belinda Markel and Ilse Stark out. There were a number of witnesses who would have testified that the Greineders seemed happy and that May expressed happiness about her marriage, but we didn't want to [put them on the witness stand and] open the door to statements she had made to Ilse and Belinda [that indicated otherwise]. Prior to trial we thought the better part of the argument was to keep Mrs. Greineder's comments out."

The jurors were thirsting to know more about May than just the circumstances of her grotesque death, and they listened raptly as her older sister described how they had grown up in New York City the best of friends. Ilse eloquently recounted how May had the "vision" to pursue a master's degree in nursing at a time when women were expected to be housewives.

Wistfully recalling May's last "wonderful" visit to New York the month before she died, Ilse told the jurors her sister sounded "stressed" when they spoke by phone two days before her murder. Her relationship with her husband "was very strong," Ilse described, "although it struck me as being a different type of relationship. Whatever decisions were made for the house, no matter how major or minor, or in their life, it was something that had to be done with Dirk," Ilse said emphatically, frequently speaking directly to the jury while avoiding the hostile staring of her brother-in-law.

Recalling how she learned of her sister's death through a phone call from her niece Britt, Ilse kept her composure while Britt wept openly sitting behind her father. Periodically glancing at her brother-in-law, Ilse still found him glaring at her, his anger evident. Bringing Ilse to the morning after her sister's murder, Grundy had her describe Dr. Greineder's account of what happened to his wife.

When Ilse was asked if she was aware of any medication prescribed to the Greineders' German shepherds, her answer had Grundy's intended effect on the jury. "Wolfie, the older male, was on Prozac," Ilse said. Juror Bill Giesecke said he was "getting a hint that Zephyr may have been drugged with Wolf's Prozac" to keep the dog from interfering in Dirk's attack on May. What the defendant did with the dog before he killed his wife remains one of the many unanswered questions in the case, as many feel Zephyr surely would have come to May's aid.

Answering another nagging question for the jury, Ilse said her brother-in-law "always" carried a cell phone, though it was inexplicably left at home the morning her sister died. The jurors attentively jotted notes when Ilse told of Dr. Greineder's insistence that her daughter Belinda be the one to identify May at the medical examiner's office, recounting their argument when Ilse defied his wishes that she not go. "At any rate, he was adamantly opposed to it, as he was to his children going," Ilse testified, revealing for the jurors that it was the first time in more than three decades that she ever had "a cross word" with Dirk.

Recalling Dr. Greineder's oddly serene living room account of what happened to her sister, Ilse indirectly revealed why the attorneys seemed locked over the towel examined by Wellesley police in the defendant's Avalon. "They were going to the pond," Ilse recounted. "They simultaneously had a nosebleed as they were walking up the driveway from the house, and they used a tissue that May had. As he passed his car he opened it up and there was a towel there, which didn't surprise me because Dirk was very fastidious for the dogs and so forth, and they took a towel and they shared the towel to clean up their nosebleeds." Still confused about the relevance of the towel, the jury found that the circumstances of the strange account would remain murky.

Grundy steered Ilse to testimony about Dr. Greineder's desire for the second autopsy, which delayed May's family funeral. Murphy's objection returned the lawyers to the sidebar, where the defense attorney again tried to block the jury from hearing the testimony. "I think that has no relevance," Murphy argued. "What has happened here, I would suggest, is very clear," he added with an edge. "The Commonwealth is essentially sending the message to this jury that the defendant was not only prepared to cut his wife up the first time out at Morses Pond but then he was prepared to pay to have somebody else do it again."

Disagreeing, Judge Chernoff ruled the jury could hear the reason the private family funeral was delayed as well as testimony about Dr. Greineder's request for money from his sister-in-law, another conversation Murphy wanted barred. The sinister implication Grundy was trying to make that Dr. Greineder may have obtained his wife's blood from the second autopsy to create the bloodstained towel to bolster his DNA transfer defense would again escape the jury.

Trying to show Dr. Greineder had far greater concerns than grieving over his slain wife, Grundy had Ilse tell the jurors that her sister's cremated remains went unclaimed for months, but a flurry of objections from Murphy blocked testimony that Ilse ultimately paid the funeral home bill.

"You did a great job," Belinda whispered, when Ilse returned to her seat after being excused from the stand. But Ilse was still silently seething over the menacing looks sent her way by Dirk.

Switching back to the forensic case built against Dr. Greineder, Grundy put trace analyst Beth Fisher on the stand to explain the significance of the fibers recovered from Dr. Greineder's fingernails that she had not found important until Grundy's crime lab meltdown. But the following testimony from Diehl's Hardware employees Lynne Mortarelli and Beth Murphy would be far more enrapturing for the jury.

The college-bound cashier taking the stand first, Mortarelli set up Murphy's bombshell testimony that a two-pound Estwing hammer was sold at Mortarelli's register less than three minutes after someone from the Greineder household bought nails. Grundy projected the hammer receipt next to the $6.76 Diehl's slip seized from Dr. Greineder's workbench, while the jurors soberly studied the exhibits with interest. As much as defense attorney Murphy tried to explain away the incriminating receipts as pure coincidence, the jurors could not shake the incriminating images looming on the large screen behind the witness stand.

"This guy would have to be like a phantom," juror Stan Smith concluded of the murderer, if Dr. Greineder was truly innocent of killing his wife. "He was always right there, and Dirk was always right there. He would have to be the luckiest guy in the world and Dirk would have to be the unluckiest. He just happened to be behind Dirk in line at Diehl's and in the park at the same time to kill his wife while Dirk left with a German shepherd?" Smith asked sarcastically.

Watching the lawyers return to the sidebar for the umpteenth time after Beth Murphy's damaging presentation, Belinda Markel had no idea she was the topic of conversation. With one of his witnesses unable to make it to court that day, Grundy wanted permission to put May's niece on the stand without the court-ordered twenty-four notice.

Timidly taking the stand in a sleeveless print dress, Belinda outlined the special relationship her small family enjoyed, describing her only aunt as being "like a second mother to me and a grandmother to my children." As her mother had so effectively done to start the day's testimony, Belinda directed her answers to the jurors, who were eager to hear more about the woman who had been reduced through testimony to a body at the Morses Pond crime scene.

The unspoken estrangement between the New York relatives and Dr. Greineder's children was completely illuminated for the jury members, who heard the same pain in Belinda's words as in her mother's testimony. "I was sitting there, the same age roughly as May, with children the same age as those children," reflected juror Elaine Miller. "It was a family that seemed not much different, and I saw the children on one side of the aisle and Belinda and her mother on the other, and you can't believe this."

For juror Mike Paul, sitting in the first row of the jury box, it was clear that the decision by the New York women to testify against Dr. Greineder had come at great emotional cost. "I had a lot of respect for them," the publishing company ad salesman said. "They both came to the decision that they believed he did it and they knew it was going to cost them this family, no doubt about it. They said to themselves that they were going to do what was right whether they lost those three kids. They did what they had to do. I thought that was terrific."

Testifying on live television against a man she had once admired for three decades, Belinda found the experience painfully uncomfortable. Despite her aunt's idyllic lifestyle, cracks had formed in her marriage, Belinda told the attentive jurors.

Quietly recalling how she learned of her aunt's death, Belinda went on to chronicle her uncle's strange behavior and odd comments after her arrival in Wellesley. His first statement when they sat down in his home office to talk had nearly left Belinda speechless, she told the jurors. "He said that they had had intercourse that morning but there is nothing wrong with that because they're married," she recounted. "I was shocked because I never really had that kind of conversation with him, and then he went on to tell me what happened in the park, that May had been hit and killed."

In later conversations, Belinda continued, her uncle became increasingly concerned about fibers on his pants, also worrying that his blood may have been transferred to May's killer as a result of their bizarrely coincident nosebleeds. Like her mother, Belinda also felt her uncle's glare throughout her testimony. "He just stared straight at me," she remembered. Her cousins also tried to make eye contact as they constantly swayed on their court bench to keep the squirming Murphy at the defense table in front of them from blocking their view. Grundy, Belinda said, was "the only person who wasn't looking at me." For support, she fixated on the sympathetic face of her mother.

Other parts of Belinda's account of the Greineder home in the days following May's murder were decidedly more enlightening, especially regarding her uncle's behavior under the growing weight of police suspicion. He was concerned about whether scratches on his neck and bruises on his arm showed up in police photographs, the jurors diligently noted. Belinda also highlighted his fear that he would be innocently linked to May's murder through the dog's spongy ball or the bloody towel.

The jury was rapt hearing Belinda testify that Dirk told her "there would be things that would come out that would be an embarrassment and upsetting to myself and his children, but it was irrelevant." Finally she was excused after parts of two days on the witness stand, but Belinda was destined to make a return trip.

The rest of Tuesday was a blur of corporate witnesses confirming Dr. Greineder's financial transactions masquerading as Thomas Young. The defendant declined to look at his former college buddy when he raised his right hand just after lunch. "My name is Thomas G. Young," the affable Baltimore attorney stated from the witness stand. Head down, overly engrossed with his pad and pen, Dr. Greineder would not make eye contact with Young.

Philip Boucher, a sales representative for Norman Librett's, testified that the only store in eastern Massachusetts that purchased the distinctive brown work gloves from the New York product distributor was Diehl's Hardware in Wellesley. Shown gloves recovered from Morses Pond and later the doghouse behind the Greineder home, Boucher agreed that they matched the ones he sold to Diehl's.

FBI trace evidence examiner Sandra Koch, who had agreed to help the frantic Grundy and Foley near the eve of trial, testified how the gloves from Dr. Greineder's doghouse had the same manufacturing characteristics as the bloody gloves found at Morses Pond. Complementing the work done by Beth Fisher, Koch agreed there were similarities in the fibers stuck to Dr. Greineder's fingernails and samples taken from a crime-scene glove.

If Tuesday's mix of testimony had its memorable moments, Grundy's lineup for Wednesday, June 13, would be a show-stealer. Three grueling weeks into the sensational trial, the testimony that most had been waiting for was poised to take center stage in all its breathtaking audacity.

Glancing at the distraught woman in the front seat next to her, Jill McDermott could already tell her twenty-seventh birthday would be one to remember. She was driving a BMW luxury sedan that had been seized during a drug investigation, but her excitement had dimmed when she realized the air conditioning didn't work. Shuttling witnesses to the Dedham courthouse was one of McDermott's main responsibilities during the trial, and she had risen early to pick up prostitute Deborah Herrera, who was on the verge of panic during the entire ride from Foxborough to Dedham. "She was a mess," McDermott said of the fearful single mother. "There was a lot of appeasing her and keeping her calm. She was so concerned her daughter would find out what she did, as well as her family." McDermott tried to keep the conversation away from Herrera's televised date with the witness stand by talking about herself. "She was very interested in me and my job as a detective, so I tried to keep her going with that," McDermott recalled.

The reporters — and some members of the jury — were overly anxious for the sex testimony, but no one noticed when Marty Foley walked New Jersey hooker Nora Lopez through the front door of Dedham Superior Court. "We were dying to see the hookers," admitted juror Sara Barbera. Lopez, who had met Dr. Greineder for sex a week before the murder, was almost a perfect image of the stereotypical prostitute, and Marty Murphy had certainly noted her flashy presence in the courthouse. But the jury would not see her. The defense attorney saw no benefit in putting the woman before the jury to personalize the tryst she had with the defendant, and Murphy and Grundy agreed on a written stipulation of their meeting in lieu of testimony. While spared this indignity, it would still be a long, disturbing day for the doctor and his relatives, and particularly for the men and women sitting in judge of his innocence.

The trembling Deborah Herrera timidly taking her oath, the jurors were surprised when the respectfully dressed, soft-spoken woman answered that she was the only employee of the Casual Elegance escort service. Speaking so softly that one juror told the judge she couldn't hear the witness just feet away, Herrera nervously recounted her involvement with Dr. Greineder leading up to his wife's murder. "We never would have picked her for a hooker," admitted juror Elaine Miller.

Pointing out the defendant, Herrera almost in whispers testified about the telephone conversations she had with Dr. Greineder subsequent to their June 1999 encounter at the Dedham Hilton. With courtroom observers straining to hear her words, Herrera revealed how Dr. Greineder was "very confused and indecisive" at the time, a month before he brutally murdered his wife. She said she had advised him that "seeing an escort wasn't the best thing to do for him until he found some peace within himself." The testimony reduced Ilse Stark to sobs, while the doctor's children sat grim faced on their bench across the aisle. The defendant seemed to be the only one unaffected by the witness's sincerity. Acting oblivious to the distress his humiliating secret sex life was causing his family and ignoring the pained expressions of many of the jurors, the defendant frequently turned to his children with reassuring looks that were not acknowledged.

It was the woman's public humiliation that had made Ilse break down in tears, incredulous that she could choose such a way to provide for her daughter. Belinda Markel was not nearly as compassionate. "I didn't feel sorry for her," she recalled coldly. "This is how you are supporting your child? I felt absolutely no pity for her whatsoever."

The testimony would grow more salacious as the day progressed, but one witness would have far more impact on the jury than any of the people Grundy called to expose Dr. Greineder's kinky dark side. Glass contractor Luis Rosado, who had comforted a distraught May Greineder the Friday before her death in the midst of her problem-filled home renovation, testified about overhearing Dr. Greineder ask his wife if she had used his computer. Rosado's inference was that she may have inadvertently seen indications of her husband's pornographic wanderings.

For Belinda and Ilse, Rosado's description of May's breakdown over problems with the bathroom work was illuminating. Even if she had known about Dirk's deviant activity, they reasoned, May still would have tried to turn a blind eye to keep the peace for Kirsten's wedding. "She was totally dedicated to the children, and she wouldn't have done anything to upset her wedding," said Ilse.

Rosado's testimony also jolted Murphy to the extent that he had to change his trial strategy. "Luis Rosado testified differently than the police report suggested he would testify," Murphy recalled. While the police report noted that Rosado had overheard Dr. Greineder ask his wife if she had used his computer, Rosado's trial testimony described it as an "angry exchange," leaving the jurors to wonder if May had discovered her husband's various sexual activities.

Up until Rosado's testimony, Murphy added, "our plan was not to mention May Greineder's knowledge. [But now] the jury could draw the conclusion that Mrs. Greineder might have discovered Dr. Greineder's use of the Internet for dating services or pornography a couple of days before the murder. After that testimony, we decided to have Colin say she might have been aware of that activity for some months or longer."

Riveted by any testimony about the couple's relationship, the jurors would grow more disgusted with the defendant as the temperature rose in the stuffy courtroom. Some were clearly repulsed when Bob Gifford proudly explained the various services provided by his ultimatelive.com Internet smut site that Dr. Greineder had subscribed to. He testified about live chat with "nude models" in Amsterdam, trading naked pictures, and "streaming movie-type things." Murphy, leaving most of the lurid testimony uncontested, had Gifford state that pussyryder, the customer who paid with a credit card in the name of Thomas Young, was one of up to 35,000 daily browsers who visited the site.

Decidedly more mainstream, Peter Brennan from the People2People Internet dating service would shatter Dr. Greineder's previous persona as a devout family man. Shortly after joining on October 24, 1999, casual_guy2000 tried to contact customers for sex at a furious rate, Brennan testified. Hearing the explicit contents of Dr. Greineder's e-mails to misstressrk, bckallycat, daisymay828, and Harry and Amy Page at macp-143sum, the jurors had no doubt the defendant was a serial philanderer, but the extramarital activity did not convince them he was a killer.

"I was disgusted because his children were there," said juror Elaine

Miller. "You keep putting yourself in that place. I kept thinking how could anyone have done this to their children? It was beyond comprehension."

It would only get worse when the recipients of those e-mails embarrassingly took the stand to acknowledge their postings that attracted casual_guy2000. Listening to Harry Page's hesitant narration of his kinky electronic conversations with Dr. Greineder, the jurors couldn't help noticing the wounded demeanor of his children. "I thought I saw signs of cracks in Kirsten," remembered Dr. Bill Giesecke. "I thought she was showing signs of doubt."

The jurors were strictly following Judge Chernoff's instruction not to discuss the case, but Colin's distress over his father's sordid dalliances briefly surfaced in the jury room. At one point he was observed rolling his eyes before resting his chin on his clenched hands and shaking his head. "I think it crushed him when it was brought to light," said juror Stephanie Vitzthum. "That was the first time I noticed his head hung. We did not discuss the case. We know a lot about each other, let me tell you, but we did at one point say, 'Did you see that poor kid hang his head?'"

# 23

DR. DIRK GREINEDER WOKE UP in excruciating pain in the early morning hours of Thursday, June 14, suffering a bout of diverticulitis. The day's testimony from Lt. Ken Martin would do nothing to make him feel better. The fast-talking Martin's interpretation of the blood covering Dr. Greineder was far easier to understand than Dr. Robin Cotton's dense DNA testimony. The jurors were spellbound by Martin's conclusion that the defendant was "within inches or feet" of his wife when she died.

Rod Englert, however, would not have the same effect on the jury, even though much of his testimony mirrored Martin's. Unable to effectively block Martin's devastating testimony, Murphy would be far more confrontational with Englert. But before the defense attorney could get to the polished expert, he had to watch the jurors soak up his opinion drawn from prosecutor Rick Grundy that the flow of blood on Halloween morning in 1999 pointed to the defendant as his wife's killer.

Frequently interrupting Grundy's questions with objections, Murphy finally asked the judge if the lawyers could confer at sidebar. Grundy fought not to laugh when Murphy objected to the mannequin that the prosecutor planned to dress with Dr. Greineder's bloodstained clothes.

"The mannequin is a male mannequin that has a bald or shaved head, has a very high eyebrow ridge and has painted brown eyes," Murphy said excitedly. "I would ask the court to step down and take a look at this mannequin because I believe it would be very difficult to imagine a more sinister looking mannequin," Murphy said in all seriousness. "I know there are mannequins available that are much less featured than this mannequin and, you know, to dress up a mannequin in the defendant's clothes, especially one that has facial features that make him look like a vicious killer is incredibly prejudicial. I think whatever this witness wants to do can be done just by an examination of the clothing itself," Murphy concluded with a shot at Englert.

"Mr. Grundy?" Judge Chernoff asked, shifting his bemused expression to the smirking prosecutor.

"Briefly, your Honor, the vicious killer is a mannequin from a tuxedo rental store," Grundy explained while trying not to laugh. "And he has the same exact expression as he did when he was attempting to get people to rent tuxedos."

Judge Chernoff decided the mannequin could stay, but not directly in front of the jury box, so the "menacing" figure was moved to the middle of the courtroom. Murphy would have died had he known about another statue the prosecution had commissioned that looked exactly like the defendant. "It was Dirk," laughed Marty Foley. "We had it made down to every detail. It was on wheels and must have weighed three hundred pounds. It's still in the basement over at Wellesley PD."

Finally getting a chance to question Englert after lunch as the temperature in the humid courtroom again soared toward ninety degrees, Murphy wasted no time in trying to discredit the expert's methods and conclusions. "Now, you've said on occasion, sir," Murphy mockingly began, "that a crime scene speaks to you?"

"I have and that's a terminology used to let crime talk to you," Englert answered affirmatively. Scrutinizing the determined defense attorney from his first-row seat in the jury box, Dr. Bill Giesecke had a sinking feeling Murphy's expertise was going to put him back on the fence again. He had been impressed with the "scientist" he had been waiting for to explain the physical intricacies of how blood is shed, but now Giesecke correctly sensed Murphy was about to expose some warts on cross-examination.

Englert was a certified hypnotist, he admitted, but had not used the controversial technique in a criminal investigation since the 1970s "when it was the trend." When Englert was asked questions about "the surface tension of blood" and the properties of viscosity and gravity, it become blatantly clear to the jurors that he held no scientific degrees.

"And, sir, is it fair to say that you have no degrees in any of those subjects?" Murphy asked.

"No sir, I do not," Englert acknowledged. The paid expert's confirmation that he had already collected $17,000 for his work on the case was also duly noted by some of the jurors. The stellar advocacy by both attorneys was frustrating the jurors' instincts to lean one way or the other over Dr. Greineder's guilt.

"I would see Rick get up there and rip [the defendant] apart and then all of a sudden Marty would get up and defuse everything," said Dr. Giesecke. "They were really good."

On this sweltering Friday afternoon, Murphy had scored more points with the scientifically trained dentist. "I thought he was a quack, and that really upset me," Giesecke said of Englert. "I'm listening to this and I finally got what I needed, a scientist, and then Marty blows him out of the water by asking what the specific gravity of blood is and the guy has no idea what the specific gravity means. It blew it for me. I have to discount this guy's testimony."

If absorbing the scope of Dr. Greineder's sexual obsession had been wrenching, there was no description for what Dr. Stanton Kessler's testimony did to May Greineder's loved ones. The gray-bearded medical examiner taking the stand as Monday, June 18's first witness, Kessler's clinical but horrifying description of May's wounds agonizingly drove home the savageness of her murder. Almost as if running down a checklist, Kessler described the ten stab wounds and two blows to the head he observed on the petite middle-aged woman. Prosecutor Rick Grundy saved the "rapidly fatal" neck wound for last.

Listening to Kessler's exact description of May's savaged condition was one of the few things Belinda Markel was unprepared for. "It was very, very rough," she said, her voice still thick with emotion.

While the defendant stared down grimly at the defense table, his children expressed a contrasting agony behind him. Britt, typically, was in tears. Kirsten gripped the edge of the heavy court bench with both hands, her eyes clenching tighter as Kessler recited the anatomical devastation to her mother's throat.

The medical terms, unfamiliar to most in the courtroom, only magnified the terrible images for emergency room doctor Kirsten and her medically trained brother, who sat distraught but dry-eyed between his sisters. Kirsten pushed her face into her hands and slid her palms up to wipe tears from each eye, while her sister Britt's silent sobbing percolated into gasps, prompting Colin to lean over and rub her back. At one point, their father turned to mouth "I love you" in a feeble effort to comfort them. Later, as Dr. Greineder wiped his face with his hanky, his eyes were devoid of tears.

The gruesome depiction of how her sister died finally proved too much for Ilse Stark. Her face flushed and her eyes misted by tears, she left the courtroom clutching a tissue. She would be spared Kessler's blunt assessment about why her adored sister was unable to fight back. There were no defensive wounds, Kessler stressed, offering his opinion that the loving wife of thirty-one years "was taken by surprise." Clearly affected, several of the jurors cast furtive glimpses toward Dr. Greineder.

Shocked by the testimony that May had briefly struggled for her life after being struck by the hammer and had taken a fracturing blow to her face before her husband employed the knife, Belinda was horrified with the realization that her death did not come as instantly as she had believed. Dr. Kessler's theory that there could have been two thrusts of the blade into May's neck filled her niece with the nightmarish image that her aunt had time to realize her approaching death at the hands of her betraying soul mate.

"Those were things we didn't know," Belinda recalled softly. "It was tough for both of us. When he said she very well could have been alive when this was going on because there could have been movement by the neck, that it looked like a struggle, that was one of the rougher moments, if not the roughest."

Grundy ended his case with the jaw-dropping testimony of FBI analyst Lorie Gottesman. Her delivery flat and technical, the jurors were still mesmerized by Gottesman's conclusion that two of the food storage bags found near May Greineder's body came from a Ziploc box in her kitchen pantry. The implication aside, Belinda found the technology spellbinding. "I thought it was absolutely fascinating that they could do that," she said.

Sitting for seventeen days trying to ward off Grundy's compelling case against Dr. Greineder, Marty Murphy's first witness in his defense was a show-stealer. Taking the stand in a gray blazer and matching print dress, Dr. Kirsten Greineder took her oath smiling at the transfixed jurors next to her.

Acknowledging her dazzling credentials dating back to her graduation with honors from Wellesley High School, the jurors could see for themselves the rare combination of beauty, brilliance, and athleticism bestowed upon a single person. The thirty-year-old emergency room resident engaged the jury with every answer, appearing almost too eager to describe the perfect American family.

"I truly had a wonderful childhood," she gushed. "It has really been as I have gotten older that I realized how blessed I was. I had two parents — or continue to have two parents — who loved me, supported me, and allowed me the opportunity to do everything I wanted and supported me in my educational pursuits, my athletic pursuits, and let me have fun."

Swimming was the family passion, Kirsten continued, her upbeat demeanor dimming when she identified the bloodstained yellow and white New England Barracudas swim team jacket her father was wearing when her mother died.

Looking like a nervous father at one of her swim meets, Dr. Greineder leaned on his right elbow, fidgeting his fingers along the frame of his eyeglasses. Confident and oddly clinical, his daughter appeared perfectly comfortable on the witness stand. When Murphy respectfully began addressing his questions to "Dr. Greineder," the witness assertively interrupted. "First off, call me Kirsten," she ordered, her beaming smile not enough to defuse the demanding way the words came across.

Using projected photographs depicting the Greineder walking route at Morses Pond, Kirsten brought the jurors along on an enthusiastically narrated tour of an average family outing. "Why would you walk this way in the winter months if the beach house was closed?" Murphy asked for his client's benefit.

"Because when the beach is closed to people, it's open to dogs," Kirsten chirped, almost on cue.

"And what was your goal in going down there?" Murphy led.

"Our goal was actually to be able to throw the ball for Zephyr in the water," the witness confidently told the jury, a not so subtle combination of the key claims in her father's Halloween morning story. "She is also an avid swimmer," Kirsten added, "and swimming is the best way to exercise dogs, from my understanding."

Unsure of what she had expected from her oldest cousin, Belinda Markel couldn't believe how Kirsten was almost ignoring her own mother. "It was the real smack in the face that they had truly, truly abandoned their mom," Belinda said.

Murphy finally did ask Kirsten about her accomplished mother. When Kirsten told the jurors about her mother's nursing career, interrupted for twenty-two years so that she could be home with her children, the daughter's description again was noticeably emotionless. The young doctor's description of her mother's various ailments was even more clinical, confirming that she suffered from a bad back and nosebleeds.

"When your mother had that kind of back pain and you were in a position to see, what typically did she do?" Murphy asked.

"She had to lie down, typically," Kirsten replied. "She had to stop what she was doing and lie down."

Already upset over Kirsten's testimony, Belinda and Ilse were further enraged when Kirsten explained why her mother sometimes neglected to wear her back brace. "It was a combination," she said placidly. "I mean, she was stubborn and also she was forgetful. She didn't like to be dependent on anything to do whatever she wanted. She saw the back brace as something that made her dependent, and she didn't like that."

The description was noticeably unsympathetic, considering that Kirsten was describing her murdered mother. Asked about her mother's computer prowess, Kirsten all but called her highly educated mother a moron. "I gave up on my mother," she said with exasperation. "When I was in Germany, I really wanted my mother to get online so she could check my e-mails. I would write every night so that they would have an e-mail for them in the morning, but she refused to get online," the daughter complained. "I used to ask my dad to print them out so she would have them at the kitchen table to read in the morning during breakfast."

Kirsten showed a little more attachment when recalling her mother's diligent planning for her wedding, her voice slightly cracking when she recited how she learned of her mother's unthinkable death. But the sentiment quickly dissipated when she described how "devastated" her father looked when she returned home from Michigan.

Ignoring again the beastly way her mother had been attacked and killed, Murphy led his witness through a series of questions that aimed her ire instead at the police investigation that had quickly targeted her father.

Her account of her father's attempt to check for a pulse in his horribly injured wife tried to portray the defendant, who was looking on nervously, as beside himself with terror. "He came up and he knew something was terribly wrong. . . . He said to me, 'Kirsten, I was shaking,'" she said descriptively. "He says, 'I was shaking so much I couldn't even tell if she had a pulse.' I remember that was the thing that struck me because our relationship has been somewhat of doctor to doctor to some degree."

Her answer to another Murphy question stoked Belinda's fury. "Kirsten, did anyone forbid you to go to the medical examiner's office?" Murphy asked. "No, never," Kirsten replied with spiteful emphasis.

Belinda deflected her rage at her uncle. "What kind of person are you who actually gets your children to go up and outright lie for you in a court of law?" she asked with revulsion. "I mean straight out. That just really disgusted me. I don't think my kids could do it and I don't think I could ever ask them to do it."

Expecting his adversary to query about the implication of heartlessness in her mother's cremated remains being left in storage, Murphy finished his direct examination with a series of questions that inadvertently exposed some of the darker workings of the Greineder family.

"And did different members of your family have different views about what to do?" Murphy asked about her mother's ashes.

"My sister, brother, and I did not agree as to what to do," Kirsten admitted. "We're a very opinionated, very intense family, and we definitely have our times of disagreement."

Kirsten had wanted some kind of permanent memorial, while "my sister Britt felt the entire opposite," she testified. Her perkiness vanished with the upsetting topic. "My mother never really wanted any land of any sort, whether it be a small plaque or a grave, never wanted anything to be taken up with her remains," she explained, so Britt "felt that my mother would have wanted her ashes to be strewn in nature." Her brother, Colin, was torn between his two sisters' wishes, leaning more toward Kirsten's stance.

"And what about your dad?" Murphy asked. "My dad, I think, was really comfortable with whatever we wanted. I think he was right along the lines with my brother in that he felt somewhat torn between two ends," Kirsten softly told the jurors. The only thing the family could agree on, Kirsten said, was that the ashes would not go to New York for placement with May's deceased parents.

"We all felt that we wanted my mother to stay nearby to us," Kirsten told the jury. "If, in fact, we were going to have anything, we wanted it to be nearby because we don't go to Queens very often. If we were going to have the opportunity to visit her, we wanted it to be nearby in a place where we would have easy access."

An agreement finally resulted, Kirsten explained, whereby after six months, a decision would be made about her mother's final resting place. "That would give us a little bit of time with breathing room, and the crematory was willing to hold on to her ashes for free for a year," Kirsten testified, an explanation that came across to some in the courtroom as uncaringly cheap.

When her father was arrested four months later, "the added new issues that we were dealing with" resulted in accepting their aunt Ilse's offer to take their mother's remains to New York, Kirsten concluded, not mentioning the unpaid funeral bill.

Rick Grundy then began his cross-examination. He would be criticized by some of the TV commentators for his surprising aggressiveness with the slain woman's daughter.

"During that four months your Aunt Ilse had indicated to you on numerous occasions that she was concerned that her sister was in Potter's Field, is that correct?" Grundy accused.

"I actually don't even know what Potter's Field is," Kirsten protested. "I never heard the reference to Potter's Field. I did hear from my aunt that, at least on one and perhaps on two occasions, that she wanted to take my mother's remains to New York, and we all four felt very strongly due to wishes expressed by my mother to us that she should not go there."

Ilse looking on with an expression of disbelief, sometimes shaking her head in disagreement with her niece's testimony, the prosecutor was unrelenting. "Well, your aunt's concern was the fact that they were being held by a business, isn't that correct?" Grundy probed.

"They were in what essentially is storage, from my understanding," Kirsten agreed.

Again demonstrating that the "issues" connected to her father took precedence over finding a final resting spot for her viciously slain mother, Kirsten defensively sparred with the prosecutor over his interpretation of Ilse's offer to pay the funeral bill. "She offered to pay them if they went to New York," Kirsten said, contrary to Ilse's testimony that the Greineders could keep the ashes.

"And ultimately she did pay that and receive the ashes?" Grundy pressed.

"Absolutely," Kirsten agreed.

"During that same four-month period, you traveled to Denmark with your father, yourself, your brother?" Grundy suddenly tossed at the witness, the unspoken inference being that the Greineders had prioritized the Christmas trip over paying the funeral expenses. "And your family was planning a trip just prior to your father's arrest to San Diego and Las Vegas, is that correct?" Grundy piled on.

"Before my father's arrest?" Kirsten asked meekly. "Yes," she had to agree again.

Grundy asked Kirsten about her parents' relationship, how the thought of marital infidelity by either of them was unfathomable until she learned the lurid details of his secret sex life. "And Doctor, you then asked your father if your mother knew, isn't that correct," Grundy inquired about her father's call home from jail.

"I actually remember that, and I remember him not answering me," Kirsten began before Grundy quickly cut her off.

"Your father told you, 'I think so,' didn't he?" Grundy interjected aggressively.

"On that conversation?" Kirsten replied, stalling her answer. "My memory of that phone conversation is my dad curtailing the phone conversation very quickly," she said.

"Do you recall telling other people present that your father said, 'I think so,' in response to your question as to whether or not your mother knew?" Grundy repeated, challenging her again to dispute her cousin Belinda's account.

"I don't recall it," Kirsten stammered.

Belinda was floored by this particular lie, mystified as to why Kirsten would make such a claim when the full scope of her father's vast infidelities had already been fully exposed. "I was outraged because that was such utter bullshit," Belinda said of Kirsten's dubious testimony. "I couldn't understand why she would lie about that. It didn't make any sense to me. He had admitted it."

Before anyone could fully digest Kirsten's expansive, yet riveting testimony, Murphy astonished the court audience with the announcement of his next witness. "The Commonwealth calls Dirk Greineder," his misstatement likely attributable to Murphy's former role as a prosecutor, this being his first major trial as a defense attorney. But the slip-up was mostly overlooked because of the excitement generated by the revelation that the doctor would take the stand.

Wearing a dark suit coat and blue tie, a frail-looking Dr. Greineder apprehensively took his oath as the anxious spectators looked on. Answering in his high-pitched, nasal twang with a hint of a foreign accent, Dr. Greineder started by spelling his name. Murphy then had him tell the jurors the history of his life, beginning with his 1940 birth in Berlin.

The defendant mostly focused on his friendly questioner. Calmly, almost as if he were lecturing at an asthma seminar, he recounted the academic and professional successes of the Greineder family. The doctor's children looked almost bored, only Britt rocking between her siblings on the bench trying to keep her father in view and focus on his answers.

Occasionally sneaking glances at the jury, like a child on the first day of school too nervous to leave his mother, Dr. Greineder would quickly return his gaze to Murphy, as if he were afraid of the jurors' rejection. It would only get worse as the questions became tougher from his lawyer. "Doctor, in the mid-1990s, did your relationship with your wife change in any way?" was the first difficult one.

"Around that time," he answered uncomfortably, "she seemed to progressively lose interest in sex and subsequently also apparently developed some discomfort and pain, which led to our stopping having sexual relations sometime in the mid-1990s."

"I know this is difficult to talk about in public," Murphy soothed, "but was that your choice or hers?" he asked.

"No, I'm afraid it was her choice," the defendant said half-convincingly.

"And how did that sit with you," Murphy continued.

"I was disappointed. I guess I would say that," Dr. Greineder said.

Leading his client into his extramarital wanderings, Murphy clearly wanted the jury to believe Dr. Greineder reluctantly cheated on his wife, but the avalanche of kinky activity would overwhelm most on the panel. Now outwardly uncomfortable and retreating from the limited eye contact he had made with the jury, Dr. Greineder frequently looked down with fluttering eyelids.

Starting with his introduction to phone sex, Dr. Greineder testified that he branched out to Internet pornography. His children listened with pained expressions. Colin leaned on the arm of the court bench, looking embarrassingly downcast. Ilse Stark could only shake her head in apparent disgust.

The defendant didn't help himself by embarking on long dissertations about how to pay for phone sex with a credit card and the intricacies of navigating a chat room, his rambling preventing Murphy from halting him with another question.

"Is this something, Doctor, you have difficulty talking about?" Murphy finally asked, trying to get his client to refocus.

"Yes, it's embarrassing," Dr. Greineder replied. "It's embarrassing," he repeated after a pause, unable to expand on his answer. The strategy was a risky one for Murphy. By having Dr. Greineder reveal the full extent of his deviant activity, he in effect forfeited the pretrial ruling he won to limit the sex testimony to the week before May's death.

The decision to reveal the full extent of his extramarital activities was one that had been fully thought out and agreed to by Murphy and his client. "My view from the start was that there was no relation between the sex evidence and a motive to commit murder. If we stuck with the sex evidence in the seven days before the murder, it would make it appear there was an unprecedented explosion of activity and the jury would think this unprecedented activity [resulted in the murder]. We wanted to show the jury that Dr. Greineder's conduct had stretched back for a number of years and show the jury the Commonwealth's use of the sex evidence was a desperate act to show motive — that it was a desperate effort to sully up the defendant's character. I said in my opening statement that if he was on trial for being an unfaithful husband he would be guilty, but it doesn't show that he was guilty of murder. I wanted to show the jury that this [testimony] did not bother us at all."

Asked about things he did with his family, Dr. Greineder stammered, then lost his train of thought. "I'm sorry. I guess I'm under a little bit of stress here," he understated.

"During those years, Doctor, were you happy with your family?" Murphy recast, his sympathetic delivery contrasting with the defendant's stiff demeanor.

"Very much so," Dr. Greineder began slowly, the words sounding almost forced. "I felt very blessed to have the family that I had."

"Can you explain to the members of the jury, Doctor, how it is you can say that you felt happy when you were going on phone sex lines and going to pornographic websites. Can you explain that?" Murphy lobbed back, almost like a parent exercising some tough love.

"I can try, and it's hard simply because it seems so silly," the witness offered unconvincingly. "What the family meant to me, and means to me," he said correcting himself, "is so much more. And you know," he continued, becoming emotional, "my wife was the most wonderful person I ever met. She made me a better person," he now wailed, but without tears. "She helped my family become what we became. I was a better doctor because of her, and I was a much better father because of her. And in hindsight, it seems so silly," he sniveled. His nose was now running freely but still without tears in his eyes. The odd condition was not lost on the jurors, who could see firsthand how the police said the doctor had appeared at Morses Pond.

Colin and Britt were openly crying, while Kirsten watched her father with an approving smile. "My family really was, and is the most important thing in my life to me," their father continued.

"So, how do you explain what you were doing," Murphy restated, giving his client another try at explaining himself to the men and women sitting two steps next to him sworn to decide his fate.

"It wasn't central; it was a side activity," Dr. Greineder responded. "I was, I guess, gratifying a secondary need," he added, the explanation doing little to answer the question. "I did it and I'm not proud of it."

Murphy strategically asked the judge to recess for the day and gently patted his client on the shoulder as they walked back to the defense table, where the doctor glanced at his children behind him, Colin and Britt still dabbing tears.

It was far from a disastrous performance, despite his tepid demeanor. The predominantly defense-leaning commentators on Court TV graded Dr. Greineder's testimony with rave reviews, one calling it an "A-plus job." Belinda could not completely disagree.

"He wasn't so bad the first day," she said. "After the first forty-five minutes I remember thinking he might be able to do some damage. I was concerned." While Belinda and her mother were able to see the many flaws in the defendant's testimony, they worried the jury had not. "I didn't think he was great," said Belinda, "but we both walked away thinking there was a possibility he could sway some of the jury."

The reviews of Dr. Greineder's testimony were not all positive, however. Leaving the courtroom, Ilse Stark concurred with *Boston Herald* columnist Peter Gelzinis that there had been a decided "chill" in the sweltering courtroom when both the defendant and particularly his older daughter were on the witness stand.

"The chill in the air of Dedham Superior Court was not solely a result of Dr. Dirk's economy of emotion," the longtime street reporter would write. "There was the testimony of his first born, thirty-year-old Kirsten, who has interrupted her residency in emergency medicine to see her Dad through what they would classify as an 'issue.'"

The "issues," Gelzinis noted, "took precedence over her mother's unclaimed ashes down at the funeral home. Such 'issues,' no doubt, as the revelation of her Daddy's secret sex life, to say nothing of his infidelity. 'Issues' about the kind of things they were taking out of their Wellesley home and finding in the woods around Morses Pond."

Uncharacteristically opening up to the perceptive, soft-spoken journalist, Ilse agreed she had been mystified by the testimony. "Issues, indeed," she concurred. "Yes, that is the perfect word, isn't it," she said softly.

"This was their mother. What issues can there be? If it were your mother, wouldn't you at least take her remains home, put them in a cupboard, instead of allowing them to gather dust in Potter's Field? That's the problem here. Everything was an issue." Regardless, the grief-stricken aunt was not prepared to disown her adored sister's children. "I think of Jesus' words," she told Gelzinis. "Forgive them, for they know not what they do."

Resuming the stand in a more casual beige suit jacket with a brown and black patterned tie the following morning, Dr. Greineder would be feeling anything but relaxed. Murphy didn't mince words with his first question to the nervous defendant. "Did there come a time, Doctor, when you made a decision to contact a prostitute?"

Unhesitating, Dr. Greineder simply answered "yes," before detailing his February 1998 tryst with Elizabeth Porter.

"Did you do anything? Did you bring anything to the hotel?" Murphy set up in anticipation of Grundy's cross-examination.

"I felt extremely awkward and uncomfortable about what I was doing," the witness said haltingly, "and I brought a bottle of champagne, thinking that by making it a little more social, it wouldn't be quite as awkward." He met with the prostitute again six weeks later at the Westin Hotel in Boston, Dr. Greineder told the jurors, stating that she was the first woman other than his wife that he had had sex with since his marriage thirty years before. Watching quietly across the courtroom, Belinda Markel and Ilse Stark harbored serious doubts.

As his children silently listened, Dr. Greineder admitted to his rendezvous with Deborah Herrera and Nora Lopez, also revealing that he had sex with two women he had met through Internet chat rooms. After meeting with Porter in the winter of 1998, the philandering husband, concluding that his name "was just too unusual," decided to fraudulently obtain a credit card in the name of Thomas Young.

"And why did you pick Mr. Young's name?" Murphy asked.

"It was a screen name I started using," the defendant tried to explain. "It was a name that was common and I didn't think it would embarrass or bother anyone."

The jury was visibly repulsed by the doctor's almost carefree explanation for his sordid roaming, but his reason for prescribing himself Viagra left nearly everyone perplexed.

"Viagra was, I believe, released in 1998, and I felt it might be helpful in light of my awkwardness, even with these commercial encounters, to try out some Viagra," the defendant offered illogically, noticeably avoiding eye contact with the jury. His reason for writing a second prescription in the summer of 1999 was equally as disturbing to the jurors, along with his wife's shell-shocked loved ones.

"The day of June second I was in the hospital area when I realized I was to meet with Ms. Herrera that afternoon, and I had not brought my Viagra with me. So I stopped at a local drug store and obtained a second prescription since that was easier than going home," he casually recounted.

As he was turned off by his "very uncomfortable and crass encounter in Mahwah" with prostitute Nora Lopez, Dr. Greineder turned to People-2People, he testified. Summing up the bad encounter with Lopez as a "New York experience," the defendant said it "just wasn't something I wanted to do again," and it pushed him toward the likes of swingers Harry and Amy Page.

The kinky bondage-laced e-mails he sent the couple were an "exaggeration," the doctor unconvincingly explained. Realizing that "the People-2People avenue was less desirable than the escort-prostitute approach" because "it was more likely to lead to more entanglement and complications than I was willing to get involved with," Dr. Greineder said he decided to return to prostitute Deb Herrera, whom he had unsuccessfully called the day before and day after May's murder. "I began to recognize that if I wanted just a quick sexual encounter that probably my best bet was actually a commercial prostitute."

Belinda and Ilse fully aware of the extent of her uncle's kinky dalliances, were left speechless with his next revelation. Asked if his wife knew of his "activities," Dr. Greineder replied he was "not sure," but sensed that she did after she found Viagra in his travel kit. "My wife was an incredibly intelligent and intuitive person, so I actually wondered if she couldn't feel it," Dr. Greineder prefaced before dropping his bombshell.

"She called me one day at work and said that she had accidentally opened my travel shaving kit and had found a bottle of Viagra and did I have an explanation. I couldn't think of anything other than to say that I had bought them to experiment with," he said, stupefying the courtroom. "This is, of course, when Viagra was new and there was a lot of noise about it on the Internet — I mean, in the news and the TV," he corrected. Hearing May's purported response, Belinda again didn't believe her uncle.

"She didn't say much more," he stated evenly. "She said, 'Oh, well, I'm sorry I was prying, I didn't mean to. I opened it by accident.'" Within "a day or two," the defendant continued, his wife apologized to him again "for opening my travel kit and prying into my private affairs. And after the summer of 1998, we never talked about it again. I never really knew what she knew, but I felt she probably had some idea," he concluded timidly.

The fantastic account still roils Belinda. "May would not have apologized for that crap," she said scornfully. "She wouldn't have been embarrassed, especially at that point of where she was."

Still unconditionally supporting their father, the three Greineder children dissolved to tears when he steadfastly rejected any consideration of seeking a divorce. "Never. I couldn't imagine living without her," he said, renewing the tearless wailing he had exhibited the afternoon before. "My wife was a wonderful person. She was truly the best person I have ever known. I still wanted a sex life and obviously I was pursuing that," he said, "but life with May was so much more than a sex life. It was all about sharing, it was about caring, it was about little things, like doing a crossword puzzle on Sunday mornings with her because she wanted to after we walked the dogs," he choked.

Kirsten, perched between her siblings, offered her sister Britt a tissue while her brother Colin dabbed his eyes and comfortingly rubbed his oldest sister's leg.

Bringing the witness to the weekend of his wife's murder, Murphy dramatically grabbed the hammer, knife, and gloves used to kill May, showing Dr. Greineder each item before asking if he had brought them to Morses Pond "to kill his wife." Gripping both sides of the witness stand, Dr. Greineder either looked down or at his lawyer with every denial. It was a moment he could have engaged the jury and professed his innocence, but it was lost.

Murphy moved on to the confusing story of the nosebleeds and the mysterious blood-spotted towel. Here the doctor added a new twist to the account. He said that while he was struggling to get Zephyr into the minivan and fumbling to loop a choke collar around her neck, the German shepherd's head "banged" his nose. "Not real hard, but I guess hard enough to give me a nosebleed," he offered with hesitation.

To Belinda, the incredible new version was a sign of desperation, and she hoped the jury would see it as such. "He's falling apart," she thought. "As his testimony went on I felt confident that he was doing more damage because he kept changing so many bits and pieces."

Looking almost bored sitting at the prosecution table, Rick Grundy was in fact studiously jotting notes on a legal pad. He was jolted by the audacity of the doctor's sudden witness-stand revelation that Zephyr had caused his nosebleed. Now he was incredulous to hear Dr. Greineder indicate that his wife may have brought the Ziploc bags from their pantry to Morses Pond.

"May used them to garner different kinds of berries to bring home to feed the birds," the defendant boldly testified, after having told police he knew nothing about the bags. "She was convinced that the berries would add something to the bird seed we were buying and that some birds were fruit-eaters and we should provide for them."

Ilse Stark also shook her head in disbelief. She remembered that her brother-in-law had admitted that he never actually saw his wife with the bags that morning. Murphy now brought Dr. Greineder on a photographic tour of Morses Pond, which he had also employed with his daughter Kirsten. Turning to view the hanging projection screen behind him, the witness was forced to make some eye contact with the jury.

Turning to a picture of the stone footbridge leading to the beach, Dr. Greineder suddenly stepped off the witness stand to point out the fence along the footpath. "This is the berry patch, if you will," he said excitedly, trying to bolster his testimony about May having the Ziploc bags unprompted by a question from Murphy.

After the morning break, the resumption of testimony began with Dr. Greineder's discovery of his slain wife. At first he thought she was just resting, Dr. Greineder said, but he quickly realized something was terribly wrong. "I just expected any moment that she would turn her head and look at me," he cried, tears finally squirting from his eyes.

His voice cracking as he recounted trying to take his wife's pulse amid his rising panic, Dr. Greineder again made a drastic change from what he had initially told Jill McDermott and Marty Foley. He had tried to pick up his wife not once but three times, he said, vividly describing the event. His children recoiled in horror with his description of their mother's head "flopping back" and him "straightening her out to keep her airway straight. All I could think of at the time was scoop and run, scoop and run, which is what we used to say in the emergency room," he whimpered, the graphic testimony leaving juror Sara Barbera in tears.

"I couldn't scoop her out of there," Dr. Greineder added, his tears replaced with a flow of nasal discharge he tried to wipe away. Unable to halt the runaway account, Murphy could only stare with his jaw clenched as Dr. Greineder rambled on with his eyes fixed on the top of the witness stand until he finally looked up to field another question.

Now composed but still looking down, almost talking into his chest, Dr. Greineder's avoidance of the jury was painfully obvious. "He didn't look us in the eyes," said juror Mike Paul. From his top-row seat, Stan Smith could see Murphy trying to signal his client to look at the jury with quick movements of his eyes or nods of his head. "I don't think he ever, ever looked our way," recalled Smith. "He might have looked above us a couple of times. It was almost like there was a hand on his head and he couldn't bring himself to turn and look at us."

The engaging testimony of other witnesses made Dr. Greineder's avoidance all the more pronounced. Smith could not understand how a man "fighting for his life" could not make simple eye contact with the people charged with deciding his guilt or innocence. "For a guy who was known to be arrogant and cocky, it was pretty hard to believe that he couldn't look strangers in the eye," said the juror, who was also not convinced by the defendant's breakdown on the stand. "He tried pretty hard to cry, but it didn't seem that genuine," Smith remembered. "When Dirk said he picked her up three times, Murphy just shook his head as if he couldn't believe it."

Making a notation in her notebook, Stephanie Vitzthum wrote, "Dirk doesn't even look at us." The defendant's demeanor was disconcerting, but the jurors were still not ready to form an opinion about his guilt. All Sara Barbera could think of was the close relationship she had with her own father as she wiped her tears away. "It was very hard for me when he was up there," she admitted. "I think that maybe it was because I was about to become a parent. You reflect a lot on your childhood when you are pregnant, and you think about how your family worked. I had this father who cared so much about me. I saw Dr. Greineder crying and I just started crying. It made me cry."

When the defendant gave his recollection of Britt arriving at the Wellesley Police Station, Britt got up and left the courtroom red-faced and crying, her older sister following moments later when the anguish of Britt's heaving sobs filtered through the heavy double doors at the back of the courtroom.

Continuing his disputing of key prosecution witnesses' testimony, Dr. Greineder said he never told his niece he had sex with May the morning of the murder. "I'm pretty sure that what I told Belinda was, 'Can you believe it? The first thing the policeman asked me was did I have intercourse with my wife that morning,'" her uncle testified.

Belinda was not amused. "I think he just called me a liar," she whispered wryly to two Boston newspaper reporters sitting in front of her, the humor hiding her bitterness.

Rounding out his direct examination as the 1 P.M. lunch hour approached, Murphy asked his client about the Diehl's Hardware receipt the police had scooped from his workbench. Admitting it was "conceivable" he had purchased the six small plastic boxes of nails just moments before someone bought an Estwing two-pound drilling hammer, the doctor was adamant that "I really have no memory of such an event." He certainly would have remembered buying a hammer, he added with contrasting surety.

Throwing one last series of questions at his client, Murphy had the accused reiterate his innocence. "Doctor, before October 31, 1999, did you form an elaborate plan to kill your wife?" Murphy asked.

"I did not," the defendant replied.

"On October 31, 1999, did you go to Morses Pond with gloves and a hammer and a knife and a loaf pan and other gloves and lighter fluid with the intention of killing your wife?" Murphy expanded.

"I did not."

"How did you feel about your wife, Doctor, on October 31, 1999?"

"I loved my wife, and I loved her on October 31, 1999."

"How did you feel about your family, Doctor, on October 31, 1999?"

"It was the most important thing to me in life, more than work, more than fame, more than money," Dr. Greineder responded with forced animation.

"Doctor," Murphy finished, "did you kill your wife?"

"I did not," the defendant said again, his attorney finally ready to rest.

Before Murphy could even lift his notes off the podium, a pent-up Rick Grundy sprang from his chair theatrically bombarding Dr. Greineder with questions before Judge Chernoff could signal the lunch break.

"Doctor, on October 31, you had Britt call Kirsten to inform her of the death of her mother, is that correct?" Grundy fired just out of his chair. "Yes, sir," Dr. Greineder replied defensively.

"And you had Britt call Colin to inform him of the death of his mother?" the prosecutor continued, his voice still rising.

"I don't recall exactly how we tried to reach Colin," the confused defendant responded in a precursor of failed memory to come. "He was not in his room when we called him," Dr. Greineder ultimately offered.

"And you had Britt call Belinda Markel to inform her of the death of her aunt?" Grundy pressed aggressively.

"I don't think so," the defendant disagreed, apparently forgetting the message his youngest daughter had left on Belinda's answering machine. "I don't recall who called, but I believe that fell to me. But again, I can't remember."

"And who called May's older sister to inform her of the death on October 31, 1999?" Grundy attacked.

"To the best of my recollection, Britt, a member of my family," the doctor conceded.

"And on October 31, 1999, you loved May?" Grundy asked doubtfully. "I loved May, and now," the doctor replied.

"And Britt was making those calls?" Grundy asked as more of a statement, continuing his rapid questioning before the witness could reply. "And on November first, you loved May too, isn't that correct sir?" Grundy continued, his question dripping with sarcasm.

"I love her now," the tense witness responded. "And you called who on November first?" Grundy concluded forcefully. "I called Ms. Herrera," Dr. Greineder said quietly, referring to the prostitute, "to cancel . . ."

"Thank you," the prosecutor interrupted, now ready to have the jurors eat with the contentious exchange fresh in their mind. "Can we take the lunch break, your Honor?" Grundy requested triumphantly. Neither the judge nor especially Murphy was overly pleased with the prosecutor's dramatic proceeding with questioning a witness outside of the usual protocol of respectfully asking the judge first.

After the lunch break, Grundy's cross-examination, which had been hotly anticipated from the moment that Dr. Greineder took the witness stand, could only be described as withering. Juggling one question after another, Dr. Greineder appeared indecisive and evasive. The more the defendant babbled, the more Grundy seemed to catch him in small lies.

After one long go-round, Dr. Greineder finally admitted he had purchased a pair of textured brown work gloves at Diehl's similar to the ones worn by his wife's killer.

Moving right to the vivid evidence that he had repeatedly shown the jurors, Grundy projected the damning image of Dr. Greineder's clean hands displayed below the blood-soaked cuffs of the yellow windbreaker. Grundy then addressed the question of whether the doctor had washed his hands. After another evasive series of answers, the defendant again had to answer the question to Grundy's satisfaction. "Do you recall telling Sgt. Foley that you hadn't washed your hands because the police had been with you the whole time?" Grundy repeated for the third time.

"I believe so," a begrudging Dr. Greineder finally acknowledged.

"And today, we hear that you actually tried to pick up your wife three times, isn't that correct sir?" Grundy added.

"That's correct."

"You never told the police that prior to today, did you sir?"

"They never asked," Dr. Greineder responded defiantly.

Unrelenting, Grundy confronted Dr. Greineder about his stories that continued to change from the witness stand, accusing the defendant of tailoring his testimony to rebut the incriminating evidence presented by Grundy's damaging witnesses. "Oh, you believe that you actually told an investigator who has testified here in court during the course of your trial that you were on your knees and you backed up on you knees into a pool of blood?" was one typical Grundy query.

"No, I'm sorry. You have managed to make me misspeak," the harried witness replied. "I remember backing up. I don't remember whether or not I told Sgt. Foley that," Dr. Greineder countered.

"And you never said that before you heard Deborah Rebeiro talk about your heel mark, did you?" Grundy slammed back.

Stone faced, Dr. Greineder's children sat with their arms crossed, almost as if mentally trying to ward off the punishing cross-exam. Raising one inconsistency after another, Grundy wondered how Dr. Greineder could say it was only after making his frantic telephone call for help that he realized his wife had been set upon when he had already told dispatcher Shannon Parillo "someone attacked her. It's definitely an attack."

"Are those your words, sir?" Grundy pressed. "They may be," Dr. Greineder said feebly.

Never giving Dr. Greineder a chance to recover from one damaging exchange to the next, Grundy kept the rattled defendant on edge. "Do I understand your testimony to be that your wife, not once, but twice, came to you and apologized to you for looking in your shaving kit and finding your Viagra after the two of you had been sexually inactive for over a year? Is that your testimony?"

"That's correct," the doctor said, waiting for the inevitable follow up.

"Did you accept her apology?" Grundy asked.

The doctor seemed unprepared for the question. "It didn't seem . . . I don't know what I . . . I can't recall exactly what I answered her," he stammered.

Grundy also hammered Dr. Greineder on his sudden witness-stand revelation that May might have taken the Ziploc bags to Morses Pond. "Again sir, you have no knowledge of your wife taking these items that day. This is pure speculation that you offer to the jury, is that correct?" Grundy taunted.

"I have no specific knowledge," the defendant agreed.

"And we now know that, in fact, these bags came from your house, is that correct?" Grundy prodded.

"I believe that's slightly true," Dr. Greineder responded dejectedly.

"And you never told Belinda that the dog jumped on you and caused the nosebleed, did you sir?" Grundy asked, again suddenly shifting topics on the befuddled defendant.

After sparring with Grundy over the semantics of his question, Dr. Greineder finally admitted he never told his niece that Zephyr bumped his face, only that he and May had simultaneous nosebleeds.

"And is it fair to say that as you testify to this jury today charged with murder, you realize that sounds ridiculous and you changed the story?" Grundy accused.

"No, that's not true," Dr. Greineder protested.

After a torturous give-and-take concerning Dr. Greineder's varying accounts of how May hurt her back at Morses Pond, Grundy asked the doctor why he just didn't escort his stricken wife out to the traffic circle, since he was walking that way anyway. "You decided to leave her in the sandpit instead of going in the same exact route you were both going?" Grundy posed logically. "That was the decision you made, correct?" he challenged.

"I guess," the defendant answered lamely, the absurdity of not helping his wife to the traffic circle not lost on the jurors. Unwilling to leave it at that, Grundy tried unsuccessfully to have the doctor explain why he went ahead of his injured wife.

"Mr. Grundy," Dr. Greineder said sternly, "it's the worst decision I ever made in my life."

"Perhaps, perhaps not," Grundy shot back before Judge Chernoff ordered the exchange stricken.

Dr. Greineder's evasiveness reached its peak when he was asked about his venture down the paved beach road, where the murder weapons were recovered. "How far down the path did you go?" Grundy simply asked.

"I don't know," was the defendant's familiar response.

"Did you go from here to the end of the courtroom?" Grundy gestured with exasperation.

"It's impossible to answer that today," the doctor stonewalled.

After this uncooperative performance, Dr. Greineder would have one final chance the next day to redeem himself in front of the jury. Not quite ready to decide his guilt based on his evasive testimony, some of the jurors were troubled nonetheless. "His mannerisms were not those of a person that was feeling confident about what he was saying up on the stand, and that didn't help him," said Stan Smith.

"I saw a man who cried a lot without a lot of tears," agreed Dr. Bill Giesecke. "I was watching closely to see how many tears he was shedding, and he wasn't shedding many tears but he was crying a lot."

But the defendant seemed to be able to recover quickly. "I watched him pick up the pitcher at one sidebar and pour a glass of water and pick it up and he didn't shake at all," Giesecke had observed. "That shocked me. That showed me a man who could probably be capable of just about anything."

Although repulsed by the depths of Dr. Greineder's sexual obsession, Elaine Miller was still holding out hope that the defendant had been wrongly accused. "I wanted him to be innocent," she said, "because those children had lost their father and their mother in the most terrible way. I didn't want that poor woman who died in such a horrible way to have as her last thought that this man to whom she had been married for thirty-one years had killed her."

The defendant looked refreshed as he took the stand again on Wednesday, June 20, returning to the dark blue blazer with a red power tie. If

Grundy was fatigued after working long into the night readying for his second day with the defendant, he didn't show it as he resumed his aggressive cross-exam. Obviously coached overnight by Marty Murphy after his shaky performance the day before, Dr. Greineder was more confident in his answers, finally trying to speak directly to the jury.

His new persona became frayed, however, when Grundy commenced on an extended line of questioning concerning his changed testimony that he had tried to lift his wife three times. Squatting on his haunches on the floor in front of the defendant and jurors, Grundy was prepared to physically demonstrate all of the doctor's lifting movements.

"Were you kneeling in such a fashion as I am now sir?" was a typical query from the demonstrative prosecutor.

"I'm not completely sure," was a typical response.

Unrelenting, Grundy asked question after question while constantly changing positions on the floor in a vain attempt to mimic the doctor's clouded recollection of trying to pick up his wife. After ten excruciating minutes, the defendant was still unable to give the jurors an account of how he thrice tried to lift his grievously injured wife.

"You are again asking me to speculate," Dr. Greineder complained.

"I'm asking you to answer as truthfully as you can to this jury about your wife," Grundy countered hotly.

"I know what I know," the defendant shot back. "I don't know exactly what you are asking me," he whimpered. But the questions were quite understandable to everyone else in the courtroom.

After more contentious exchange Dr. Greineder finally provided some semblance of how he lifted his wife, only to be ambushed by a Grundy inquiry that ripped the hush of the courtroom. "Did you make a concerted effort to place your wife's heel back at the direct end of that drag mark," Grundy unloaded, the implication clear that Dr. Greineder could not have lifted his wife three times without her heel moving from the end of the furrow in the dirt that led from the blood pool on the path.

"I made no concerted effort whatsoever at that time," was all Dr. Greineder could say.

Grundy delivered a second barrage. Once again projecting photographs of the defendant's clean hands "as we've all been forced to see for the last month," Grundy had the witness reconfirm for the jurors that they were the same hands he had used to lift his blood-soaked wife three times. "Prior to ever washing your hands, correct?" Grundy followed.

"Prior to washing my hands," Dr. Greineder agreed, not haggling over indisputable answers as he had done the day before.

Grilling Dr. Greineder about why he had his daughter Britt make the notifying calls about May's death to the family, the defendant's daughter was being watched almost as closely as her father. Inexplicably wearing a white cocktail dress reminiscent of Sharon Stone's memorable outfit in *Basic Instinct*, Britt was perched on the court bench, unconsciously pumping her right leg like a nervous piston. The demonstrative daughter would grow more distressed as Grundy steered the testimony into her father's far-reaching infidelities.

The doctor had remained mostly dignified so far, clearly following the advice of his attorney, but he slipped back into his bad habits as Grundy pelted him with more questions about his character. Growing argumentative, the defendant tried to spar with the prosecutor despite the poor results from the day before. Forced at times to prod the evasive defendant for just "yes or no" or "true or false" answers, Grundy pressed his attack on Dr. Greineder's credibility.

The prosecutor, jumping from topic to topic, left the struggling defendant unguarded, and Dr. Greineder admitted that he had discussed a second autopsy for his wife after telling Belinda Markel how he had found May's dilator. The defendant finally explained that he wanted the second autopsy because he was fearful the state's autopsy would reveal that his wife was unable to have intercourse and he wanted the condition further documented in case the authorities used it against him.

"And by Monday, after the experience of the night before," he said about the first search warrant, "I did feel a concern about the direction of the investigation. I felt that if the police felt that I had not been having sexual intercourse with my wife . . . that it would further encourage their efforts to look at me."

Asked if he knew if blood was taken from his wife, Murphy objected before his client could respond.

"Where are you going with this?" Judge Chernoff asked Grundy at sidebar. The prosecutor, like Marty Foley, had long suspected that Dr. Greineder had spotted the Ritz-Carlton towel with his wife's blood and created the crescent-shaped stain on the front seat of his Toyota Avalon to bolster his nosebleed-DNA transfer alibi.

Sensing where his rival was going, Murphy was appalled. "Are you really legitimately suggesting," Murphy prefaced, "that you think Dr. McDonough from the medical examiner's office took blood and gave it . . .'"

"Absolutely," Grundy interrupted, not letting Murphy finish.

"You can't legitimately have a good faith basis to believe that the Deputy Chief Medical Examiner of the Connecticut Medical Examiner's office took blood from the victim and gave it either to me or the defendant?" Murphy repeated incredulously.

"I don't know. I haven't been able to speak to Dr. McDonough," Grundy replied, neglecting to tell the judge that the medical examiner had rebuffed Marty Foley's attempt to interview him.

"I'm going to sustain the objections to this question," Judge Chernoff ruled without elaborating. The defendant continued to deny having any memory of what was done at the second autopsy or whether he even read the report, and the testimony would not benefit either side. Confused over the relevance, the jury would ultimately disregard the murky testimony.

They would clearly understand the implication of the defendant leaving his wife's remains in storage when Grundy asked Dr. Greineder if they had been held in a cardboard box. "I believe so. I'm not exactly sure," he admitted with a trace of defeat.

"You're not exactly sure," Grundy pounced, "because you never went to see them. Correct?" he demanded.

"That's correct," the defendant confirmed.

Taking square aim at the defendant's credibility, Grundy embarked on a long series of questions about Dr. Greineder's infidelities to show how he had hid the activity until after his indictment, callously allowing his children to ignorantly testify about the strength of his marriage before the grand jury.

"We did not actually discuss the specifics of their testimony," Dr. Greineder offered weakly.

"Did you tell your attorney what you'd been doing before your kids went in there and testified?" Grundy inquired.

"Not in any detail," the defendant admitted, confirming Belinda's suspicion that he had also misled his lawyer.

"And yet what you were doing in that marriage, you testified to this jury, was a side activity, correct?" Grundy continued.

"I may have used the word 'side,'" Dr. Greineder reluctantly agreed.

"And you were concerned because if something happened to that marriage it was going to affect the relationship with your kids. Correct sir?"

"It was going to affect the relationship with my wife May and my kids," Dr. Greineder quietly agreed.

"Sir, you didn't know what the FBI could do with those Ziploc bags, did you?" the prosecutor asserted with his next question.

"I didn't know that they were Ziploc bags," the defendant replied uncooperatively. "At the time I was only asked about plastic bags," he added defiantly.

"Let me ask you something sir," Grundy restated, circling back for a counterattack. "You didn't know the FBI could hook those up to the original box they came from, did you sir?" Grundy forcefully restated.

"Specifically, of course not," Dr. Greineder answered.

"And they would have been in the storm drain [with the other evidence] if you had, wouldn't they?" Grundy taunted.

"It wouldn't have done much good, would it?" the defendant defiantly lobbed back, his brazenness charging the courtroom.

"I guess not," Grundy agreed with obvious satisfaction.

Put off by some of Grundy's confrontational tactics, the jurors still found his cross-exam highly effective, particularly the repeated questions about the defendant's immaculate hands. "That is what made me think he was guilty right away," recalled Elaine Miller. "He used it well," agreed Dr. Bill Giesecke.

"If you look at the blood as to where it was on his sleeve, it goes all the way down to the end of his sleeve and stops right where his hand begins, perfectly in a perfect line," said juror Jahon Jamali, who was home on summer break from his studies at Johns Hopkins. "That on a [guilty] scale of one to ten, that's getting close to a nine."

Dr. Greineder's testimony did little to sway the jury toward exonerating him. "They needed him to tell a compelling story," said Cheryl Nixon. "He had to get up there and kind of sell us, and he didn't do that. The difficulty of the case was really . . . you are staring at what is the American dream. You're looking at it and it looks back at you and reveals something horrible underneath that. None of us wanted to believe that — that . . . under the perfection and the accomplishments [something] could happen like this."

Murphy's remaining witnesses that week provided none of the drama of his client and also would do little to buttress his claim of innocence. Finishing Wednesday with testimony from the doctor's insurance agent and tax attorney, the two men detailed Dirk and May Greineder's estate planning. Hearing that Dr. Greineder's estate totaled almost a million dollars, Belinda Markel and Ilse Stark reacted with surprise, then anger, as they mulled the defendant's desperate pleas for money in the days after May's murder.

Thursday, June 21, would be filled with testimony from two defense DNA experts, Dr. Dan E. Krane and Marc Scott Taylor, who would be mildly effective in theorizing that genetic material Dr. Greineder left on his wife could have been transferred to her killer. Murphy called his last expert the next day, but the testimony of Stuart James, the Fort Lauderdale-based authority on blood pattern analysis, did little to tarnish the damaging presentations by Lt. Ken Martin and Rod Englert.

Reaching the end of its fifth week, the grueling trial was taking a toll on all its participants. The sensational testimony already beyond most observers' expectations, the final week would far surpass everything the Court TV executives had hoped for.

SEATING THE JURY on Monday, June 25, for what would be the final day of testimony, Judge Paul Chernoff had no idea the high-stakes trial he had managed so effectively would nearly spin out of control. Promising the jury they would get the case before the day's end, the judge fully expected the attorneys to make their final arguments sometime around the lunch hour.

For prosecutor Rick Grundy, the jury could not get the case fast enough. He was physically and mentally exhausted from five weeks of pitched battle against his equally skilled opponent, and the lack of sleep and proper eating was getting to him. Perhaps mentally steeling himself for the worst, he had convinced himself, in some cases correctly, that the jurors did not like him. Still confident and effective in the courtroom, he was downcast outside it.

"Everything was black," recalled Belinda Markel. "You had to pump him up or you were going to jump off the roof." Belinda constantly reassured Grundy, but the emotional prosecutor could not be convinced. "Nope," he would reply, "the dentist hates me. The old lady hates me," he said of the jurors.

His game face in the courtroom masking the self-doubt raging within, Grundy took his seat at the prosecution table that Monday morning wrongly assuming he had one final obstacle to cross. The last witness for the defense, Colin Greineder confidently took his oath, already commanding the jury's attention as Marty Murphy settled at the podium facing him.

Pleasantly accepting the attorney's good wishes on the witness's twenty-sixth birthday, Colin was noticeably more personable than his older sister had been exactly a week before as he colorfully illustrated his Wellesley upbringing in the Greineder family. Watching nervously from the defense table, the defendant ran his fingers over his lips and chin while listening to his only son's engaging testimony.

"My mother, she was the person I felt closest to in the whole world, without a doubt," the traumatized son touchingly told the jury. "She was a wonderful person. It's hard to just sum her up with adjectives. There are so many, but she was warm and caring. She was funny and she was fun to be with," he gushed with genuine tribute. "She was fun to be with if you were a little kid. She was fun to be with if you were an adult."

His sisters Britt and Kirsten sat listening to their younger brother's heartfelt words with pride. Talking about what it was like to grow up in the Greineder household, the witness's voice cracked as he praised his parents, but like his father, he stemmed the flow of tears. "You felt like you had two parents that cared for you, no matter what," Colin said emotionally. "They loved you no matter what."

There was one condition about being a Greineder, Colin revealed. "You had to be willing to be part of the family," he explained. "As long as you signed up and you were there and you were emotionally involved, it was fine."

Steered into testimony about finding his father's computer saturated with pornography, the animated witness fell downcast. "I . . . I felt . . . I felt embarrassed and I was just sad," he stuttered, his voice cracking again as he ran on about how he had wanted to confront his father but couldn't.

At the attorney's prompting, Colin testified that he asked his mother if she was happy in her marriage, her purported answer another trial shocker. "She said, 'Our sex life could be better,'" Colin told the hushed courtroom, implying he too was left speechless by his mother's frankness before finally asking her if she had talked to his father about it. "She said, 'Oh, yeah. Yeah, we've talked about it,'" Colin said theatrically, 'but I think your dad has his own way of dealing with that now.'"

While Colin's testimony came as a surprise to most in the courtroom, it had been carefully prepared by Murphy and the defendant to counter the damaging testimony of contractor Luis Rosado, who had described an agitated Dr. Greineder asking his wife two days before her murder if she had used his computer.

Fearful the exchange would lead the jury to believe that Dr. Greineder killed his wife just after she discovered his extramarital activities, "we decided to have Colin say she might have been aware of that activity for some months or longer," said Murphy. "I thought that had the potential to blunt the notion [that] she had just discovered the defendant's use of the Internet a few days before the murder and that it led to a violent event."

The sensational testimony would be taken at face value by the TV commentators, touching off another round of analytical blather about whether May knew of her husband's cheating, but Belinda Markel was certain May wouldn't have told Colin so casually, if at all. Colin surprised Belinda again when he testified that he had overheard Belinda's first conversation with his father after she arrived in Wellesley. "There's a sliding glass door between the kitchen and the study," he claimed "and I was sitting right outside the door." Following the family trend of calling her a liar, Belinda was incredulous when her cousin said he never heard his father state he and his mother had sex the morning of the murder. And as she was still digesting this upsetting testimony, he called Belinda a liar again when he told the jurors no one had prevented him from going to the medical examiner's office to identify May. "Was there some discussion? I guess," was all he would acknowledge. "I didn't want to go and everyone seemed to think that was okay."

Halfway through Colin's testimony it was clear to Belinda that her cousins were willing to push the boundaries of perjury to save their father. "It didn't surprise me at that point that Colin was going to say anything different from what his siblings said," she remembered. "I was getting used to it."

But Belinda had yet to see the pinnacle of the supportive son's audacity until he suddenly testified that he might have purchased the six small packages of nails at Diehl's hardware on September 3, 1999. The $6.76 receipt found on his father's workbench being a damning piece of circumstantial evidence, Colin did everything but confirm that he might have been in Diehl's two minutes before a two-pound Estwing hammer was sold. Testifying he had purchased nails to replace ones taken from his father, Colin said he left them in a cylindrical container in the middle of his father's workbench. Unfortunately for the defendant, his son could not remember exactly when or where he made the replacement purchase.

"I'm pretty sure I bought them in Wellesley," Colin said as if trying to convince himself. "And when you shopped for hardware in Wellesley, Colin, where did you shop?" Murphy helped. "I almost always go to Diehl's," the witness replied. Handed the Diehl's receipt confiscated by Marty Foley, Colin was emphatic that he could not say for sure that it resulted from his purchase. Studying a projected picture of his father's workbench, Colin pointed out several containers on the bench top that could have been the nails he bought, but he remained noncommittal. "I can't tell you that those are the specific ones," he said helplessly.

Sitting impassively just steps away at the prosecution table, Rick Grundy was going to make Colin pay for his noticeably suspect testimony about the nails, but retribution would not come with the defendant's son on the witness stand. Handling Colin much more respectfully than he had his older sister, Grundy was still able to expose problems within the all-American family.

"Sir, was there any conversation amongst yourself and your siblings as to sitting down with your folks at Thanksgiving to talk to them about your dad spending more time at home, or his new work schedule with his new responsibilities?" Grundy politely asked. "Yes," Colin answered, only elaborating that a "family meeting" was planned.

Grundy turned to the dispute between Britt and her parents over her decision to delay going to medical school. Colin's analysis was eye-opening after he touched on his own clashes with Britt when he tried to tutor her. "For a brief period of time Britt decided that she didn't want to be involved, and that's a big decision," Colin said cryptically, his sister once again in tears.

Returning to his sisters behind the defense table, Colin was greeted with a warm hug and kiss from Kirsten while his father turned with a toothless smile of approval. Murphy then rested his case, but observers were caught off guard when Grundy called Britt Greineder as a rebuttal witness.

As Britt was obviously a bundle of emotion taking her oath, Grundy trod carefully with the fragile witness during an abbreviated direct examination in which he asked only a handful of questions about her father's statements of when he first saw May's fatal neck wound. The defendant, sitting perched with his hands folded in his lap, studied his younger daughter with the aid of his eyeglasses, the rapid blinking of his eyes betraying his nervousness.

Britt was given a few moments to compose herself while the lawyers conferred at sidebar about a picture of the family in Germany that Murphy wanted to introduce. Her shaky demeanor completely changed when he asked her to identify everyone in the snapshot for the jury. "Sure," she said cheerily, bounding off the witness stand toward the enlarged image projected behind her.

Having now heard from all of the Greineder siblings, the jurors were mostly disappointed with their incomplete portrayal of their slain mother. "They didn't give her much," observed Dr. Bill Giesecke. "I was disappointed," agreed Mike Paul. "They obviously loved her, but I thought they would bring her more to life and talk more about the things she would have done for them or did for them. It was obvious to me they were saying what they were told to say," Paul added.

"May got lost in the testimony," said Elaine Miller, the juror closest in similarity to the murdered woman. "May's brilliance never came through."

For juror Stan Smith, the children made a connection. "I think I saw more of May through her kids than anyone else," he said. "I think they all spoke highly of her. Anybody would love to introduce their kids as all having gone to Yale. I think they were a close-knit, driven, focused family." It would only be later that Smith realized that "the only three character witnesses Dirk had were his three kids."

Marty Foley had just climbed the marble stairs to the second floor when a court officer opened the main courtroom door in search of him with word that he was needed on the witness stand. Having no idea why he was being recalled, Foley sensed it had something to do with Colin's testimony. "I'm thinking Colin's got to be lying about something," he recalled.

Projecting a picture taken during the second search of Dr. Greineder's home showing a pegboard hanging over his workbench, Grundy asked Foley to once again identify the $6.76 receipt from Diehl's Hardware as he commenced a methodical dismantling of the dutiful son's testimony that he could have purchased the nails. "And sir, did you have an opportunity to correspond those nails listed in that receipt with the packages that were in that tool bench area?" Grundy asked sternly, fully aware of how Foley would respond.

"Yes," replied the methodical witness. Standing in a half crouch with a laser pointer directed at the projection screen bearing the blurry image, Foley, still not knowing what Colin had said, pointed out the various containers of nails denoted on the receipt.

"And that would be a total of six boxes of nails, is that correct?" Grundy asked, further cementing the certainty of Foley's testimony.

"Yes, sir," the witness answered confidently. Strolling out of the courtroom, Foley had no idea his rebuttal had left many of the trial observers — most importantly some of the jurors — speculating that the dutiful Colin had lied for his father.

Conscious of the emotional sideshow involving the children, the jury would give little weight to their testimony. "We basically dismissed their testimony," said Dr. Bill Giesecke. "We didn't analyze their testimony, number one, because we didn't want to do so. We didn't want to say they were lying," he admitted. "We didn't need that."

Colin's apparent stretching of the truth regarding the nails had upset Belinda far more than anything he had said to disparage her personally. "The nails had a greater impact on me than the fact that he was backing up his father's story about what I had said and calling me a liar," she said. "With the nails, it was out and out where he could be proven wrong, and the fact that Dirk just sat there encouraging him to do that angered the hell out of me."

Grundy summoned Belinda back to the witness stand to refute the contradictory testimony of her uncle and cousins. But joining Murphy at Judge Chernoff's sidebar, the prosecutor had no idea how the impeccably run trial was about to implode into a near travesty.

Contacted by the court clerk's office minutes earlier, Murphy told the judge a Wellesley resident had called reporting that "they saw someone at Morses Pond" the day of the murder. "I've just gotten a cryptic message," the defense attorney began ominously, "that she wrote a letter to the Wellesley police and that the information has been in the possession of the Wellesley police and they've never followed it up."

The stunning implication of the woman's "two urgent calls" to the courthouse still shielded by the privacy of the sidebar, Murphy told the judge that if such a letter existed, he had never seen it. "I would simply request that if that information is available at the Wellesley Police Station that a search be conducted," he asked.

Still assuming the attorneys would deliver their final arguments so the jury could finally begin deliberations after five grueling weeks, Judge Chernoff sent the panel to an early lunch to give Grundy and Murphy a little extra time to prepare. But after finding out more about the mysterious message, the judge unhappily realized he would be postponing his scheduled instructions to the jury.

The letter faxed to the courthouse at 10:43 A.M. that morning was addressed to the Wellesley Police Department from "Richard Acheson and

Jacqueline Swerling, 1 Ingleside Road, Wellesley." Dated "November 2, 1999," it appeared to have been typed by Swerling, who referred to Acheson has "my partner."

The couple had driven to Morses Pond to walk their dogs the day of the murder and were told by a police officer "that something terrible had happened," Swerling wrote. Sensing "it was either a murder or suicide," the couple had driven home, where they encountered "a man standing at the foot of our driveway with his back toward us staring at the house and yard."

The man, clad in jogging clothes, walked away when he noticed the couple in their car, leaving Swerling and Acheson uneasy. "He was clearly studying our home and yard," the letter read. "His face was distorted due to his breathlessness and he was perspiring profusely."

Hearing later about the murder at Morses Pond, "we thought again about this man and felt this information could be useful," Swerling wrote, providing her telephone number "if you would like to discuss this further with us."

The judge indicated he wanted to hear from Swerling before he let the attorneys make their closing arguments, which threatened to send Grundy into a deeper tailspin as he put the word out for Chief Terry Cunningham to return to the courthouse immediately. Cunningham was eating a crabmeat sandwich at a downtown deli with his brother Wayne and Jill McDermott when his pager blared with the urgent message to call Grundy. When he called him moments later Grundy wouldn't tell Cunningham what was wrong, but the distress in the prosecutor's voice was obvious. "Just get back here," Cunningham was told.

The chief hustled through the first-floor door of the district attorney's office minutes later. "Have you ever seen this before," Grundy said with foreboding, handing Cunningham a copy of Swerling's letter.

"Rick, I've never seen this," Cunningham replied, the disastrous implications needing no elaboration.

"You swear, you've never seen this before," Grundy said again, exaggerating his calmness to control his anger.

"Rick, I've never seen it," Cunningham repeated. "Well, Chernoff is taking a look at this," the prosecutor finally blurted.

"Are you serious? He's really taking a look at this?" Cunningham asked incredulously.

"Yup," the morose prosecutor replied, clearly distressed by the development.

The names on the letter did not immediately register with the police chief, but his brother Wayne's familiarity with the address brought everything flooding back for Terry Cunningham. Since 1993, the Wellesley department had had "at least twenty" responses to Swerling's home for incidents ranging from her involuntary commitment to the psychiatric unit at Newton-Wellesley Hospital to "three possible overdose attempts" involving pills and alcohol. In between, department records showed at least two drunken driving arrests and a host of domestic disputes involving Swerling and Acheson.

"They had called me back from the station and said this is the woman that lives at One Ingleside," Wayne Cunningham recalled. "I said, 'Oh my God, I know exactly who they are talking about.'" Knowing the judge wanted to see the police chief before deciding whether he needed to hear from Swerling, Grundy instructed Cunningham to stay secreted in the first-floor office.

"Chernoff doesn't know you're in the court," Grundy told the chief. "He's looking for you. Don't go upstairs," the prosecutor ordered. Cunningham felt foolish sitting alone in the DA's office, but his spirits soared when he heard closing arguments were about to start. Then his optimism crashed when a court officer knocked at the door moments later to inform the secluded chief he was wanted by the judge.

With the courtroom still full in anticipation of closing arguments, Judge Chernoff finally revealed what had happened, the unspoken ramifications echoing like a thunderclap. "We were thinking mistrial or something else is coming up," said Belinda Markel. "We were all so strung out at that point and we didn't know who she was. We were pretty upset."

Deciding he would put Swerling on the stand for a voir dire hearing away from the jury as soon as she could be brought to the courthouse, the judge first had Terry Cunningham sworn. Taking in the capacity audience as he glided toward the witness stand, Cunningham was not relishing his inquisition from the judge. "I didn't want to go up there," he admitted. "He was going to be the one asking the questions and I didn't know what he was going to ask."

Trying to gauge if the Wellesley police had actually received Swerling's letter, the judge had the chief explain how the department's mail is handled, particularly letters from the public. It was he himself, he told the judge, who personally reviewed those letters after they were opened but not read by his secretary. "If it had to do with this case," the chief stressed, "I would have personally given it to the person in charge of detectives."

Handed the letter written by Swerling, Cunningham was emphatic he had never seen it before. Queried about the contacts his department had documented with Swerling, Cunningham didn't hold back. "I'm aware that she's had at least twenty to twenty-five individual contacts," Cunningham said. "I know of, I believe, three possible overdose attempts. I think there were two [for] operating under the influence. It's been a multitude of calls between domestic situations with the individual she lives with. I believe there was even a missing person's report," the chief concluded.

Racing back to Wellesley, Jill McDermott was still trying to figure out what had just happened. "They had me go back to the station to go through all the records," she recalled. Fearing she was about to unseal a Pandora's box, McDermott wondered who else might come forward after seeing the attention Swerling's claim had garnered. "I thought this was going to be never ending," she said. "I thought every loon was going to come out of the woodwork and say they saw this and they saw that."

The incredible development quickly turned into the day's top news story, the reporters easily seeing the urgency in the police as they scrambled to investigate Swerling's inflammatory accusation. "Wellesley PD went wild," described Marty Foley. "They were telling Jill to go back and check her notes and all our reports. Our biggest concern was did we miss anything."

When Jacqueline Swerling took the stand, the heavy-set woman with short blonde hair seemed thrilled to be the center of attention as she plopped into a seat on the witness stand. Standing to look down on the witness from the bench, Judge Chernoff began his questioning after Swerling was sworn. The jurist took an overly cautious approach, much like an adult meeting a young child for the first time.

Shown the letter faxed earlier to the courthouse, Swerling readily agreed that it was the one she wrote two days after May Greineder's murder. The man she saw in her driveway, she testified, left her uneasy.

"He was in a daze," she said quickly. "He was in a total daze and he was blocking our driveway." She had been diligently following the media-hyped trial on Court TV, Swerling said, and she had checked her computer for the letter. But pressed about her memory of sending it to the Wellesley police in 1999, Swerling admitted, "I just can't. In all honesty, I don't know your honor."

Delicately shifting to Swerling's mental health issues, the judge asked her if she ever had "negative contact with the Wellesley Police Department."

"Yes, I have," she quickly admitted.

Waiting near the rear door of the courthouse for State Police to drive her home, Swerling told two Boston newspaper reporters she thought Dr. Greineder was innocent. "I'm totally partial to him to this point," she said. "I've always doubted whether or not he did it based on what happened to us." Watching the end of testimony on Court TV that morning, Swerling realized it was her last chance to find out why the Greineder investigators did not respond to her letter.

"Why didn't the Wellesley police get in touch with me?" she accused. "They never did. Shame on me for letting it go so long. Everyone had this man found guilty long before he went to trial," she said defiantly, seemingly not fully aware of the uproar that she had inflicted on the professionally run trial. "If you had some weirdo in your yard like we did that morning, you'd have doubts too."

Meeting at the sidebar after Cunningham testified that a search of the police station had failed to turn up Swerling's letter, Murphy indicated he might want to put Swerling in front of the jury but needed to consult with his client. Waiting for Swerling's mental health records "from three different places," the judge said he would not rule on the matter until morning.

# 25

DAYLIGHT BROUGHT another spectacular summer day in New England on Tuesday, June 26, and the lunacy that had filled the sweltering main courtroom at Dedham Superior Court the day before had dissipated with the rising sun. Apparently deciding the negatives of putting Jackie Swerling before the jury far outweighed the potential benefit, Marty Murphy told Judge Paul Chernoff at the morning sidebar his client would not call the Wellesley woman.

It would prove to be a smart move for Dr. Greineder because hours later the mystery jogger observed panting in Swerling's driveway introduced himself to the Wellesley police. Patrick Libby, now a resident of the city of Somerville bordering Boston, had grown up in the Ingleside Road dwelling, and had stopped there during a run on Halloween 1999 to check the place out. Bent over in Swerling's driveway catching his breath, the twenty-seven-year-old Wellesley native had sensed a car behind him, and sheepishly jogged away after the male operator tooted the horn.

Seeing the blanketing media coverage of Swerling's misguided intrusion into the smoothly running trial the next day, Libby was aghast when he realized he was the mystery jogger and immediately called the Wellesley police. "I was kind of astonished I was connected to something like this," Libby told the *Boston Herald*. "It was pretty surprising."

Murphy was slated to make his closing argument first. The defense attorney knew he needed a perfect finish if he had any hope of weakening the wall of evidence Rick Grundy had stacked against his client. Stepping to the plate for his last chance to make a direct appeal to the jury, Murphy belted a home run. Coming across fresh and rejuvenated, Murphy provided the jury with a passionate eighty-minute oratory, dramatically highlighting the key points favorable to his case.

Before Dr. Greineder deserved to be branded "with the horrible label of being a murderer of one's own wife, the murderer of the mother of one's own children," Murphy reminded the jury, his client's guilt had to be beyond a reasonable doubt. Before they could do that, he cautioned, there were three questions they needed to consider. Did Grundy ever give them proof that Dr. Greineder wanted his wife dead? Did they ever hear a reason for Dr. Greineder to kill his wife? And most importantly, Murphy stressed, did Grundy give them any "real evidence" that Dr. Greineder had the capacity for pure evil? "Because there is no other word to describe what happened out there in Morses Pond on October 31, 1999," the attorney rightly surmised.

"Guesswork, conjecture, and speculation," Murphy would repeat throughout his animated address, is what police had used "to fill the holes, plug those gaps, and connect those dots" to make a case against Dr. Greineder, all the while aware of two other unsolved murders in the county.

Grundy had "mocked Dr. Greineder" about the simultaneous nosebleed with his wife, but the blood-spotted Ritz-Carlton towel was a key piece of evidence for the defendant, Murphy stressed. Regardless of whether the jurors believed the absurdity of the story or not, it still contained DNA from Dirk and May. "Mr. Grundy wants you to believe that somehow, by some means, that towel was created after the fact," the defense attorney correctly stated.

Murphy asked the stone-faced men and women before him to use plain old common sense in reaching their decision about Dirk Greineder. "You can use it to decide whether it made any sense at all that Dirk Greineder put on this yellow jacket, went out to the pond that morning with a plan to kill his wife with a hammer, a knife, work gloves, latex gloves, a loaf pan, lighter fluid," Murphy listed. "Can you really conclude that an intelligent man, a doctor, a PhD in pharmacology, would choose this way to kill his wife?"

Judge Chernoff called a five-minute recess after Murphy's tour-de-force performance, and even observers convinced of Dr. Greineder's guilt offered congratulatory words in the marbled second-floor foyer. "Marty had become the complete opposite," Marty Foley concurred. "It was like he and Rick had reversed roles. He became the demonstrative guy, raising his voice, flailing about the courtroom."

Expecting a similar delivery from Grundy, the audience was surprised when the fiery prosecutor came out with a low-key, almost private talk with the jury. The distressing sideshow orchestrated the day before by Jackie Swerling had not helped the exhausted attorney, who was already consumed with self-doubt about his ability to convince the intelligent panel that the prominent physician had maniacally killed his wife. Belinda Markel struggled to hear Grundy in the cavernous courtroom, fearful that his subdued demeanor was playing poorly for the jurors, but the humbled lawyer had already made a connection.

"As I told you in my opening, the only experts of this case would be yourselves," Grundy began quietly, standing right at the rail separating him from the jury. "And no matter what flurries around this case," he added in an obvious reference to the media sensationalism, "this case is about one thing and only one thing. May Greineder," he announced, holding up a picture of the slain woman. "This is what this case is about. A life taken, this woman," Grundy said, flashing the picture again.

Marty Murphy had put forth a pretty good argument, the prosecutor acknowledged, but he took each item of evidence "in isolation" instead of connecting them together. "I was reminded of something my father used to say to me," Grundy reflected. "He told me, 'Rick, you can explain anything. You can't explain everything.' Perhaps that's somewhat of a theme for this case."

Speaking more softly, Grundy thanked the jury "for your kind attention" during the "enormously long trial" and apologized for his sometimes confrontational style. "I know I can be brash at times," he genuinely conceded, "and that may not help at all in your discerning information. But forgive me my trespass and please take note of the information that was gotten from the stand," he asked.

Placed together, it showed Dirk Greineder was the only person who could have murdered his wife. "Everywhere the defendant went at the pond that day, a killer left pieces of evidence behind," Grundy reminded them. "Everywhere the defendant went at the pond that day, he left the defendant's DNA behind."

Dirk and May were no longer the "team" their children thought they were, the prosecutor continued, but any alteration in that perception was sure to tarnish the cherished relationship the defendant had with his grown kids.

It was true he did not have to prove motive, Grundy reminded the jury, but even if he did, "what's a motive for murder?" he asked. "What's a possible explanation for killing people? It certainly is the ultimate exercise of control over a person," he suggested. Either way, Dr. Greineder had surely been remorseful when he was on the witness stand. "I'm sure that life that he had doesn't look so bad right now," the prosecutor snidely asserted.

And remember Dr. Greineder's clean hands, Grundy instructed. The defense attorney had made a big deal over the defendant's hands never being tested, but no trace of blood was ever found on the phone he used to call police or the rear door handle of Paul Fitzpatrick's cruiser he had repeatedly pulled while trying to get out.

"That's not conjecture. That's real," the prosecutor said in retort to Murphy's closing. In fact, Dr. Greineder began making excuses for damaging evidence within minutes of killing his wife, Grundy said. He told Belinda Markel he had sex with May that morning then concocted the incredible story about the simultaneous nosebleeds with the shared towel.

"That's important, ladies and gentlemen, not just to be kicked to the curb," Grundy advised. "It's the inception of the transfer theory of the DNA, and the defendant's DNA is all over her. How many married couples have had simultaneous nosebleeds?" he mocked. "Is it just another lucky break for the killer in the woods, with the gloves following the same path as the defendant? Buying the same gloves, dropping them off by his van, dropping them off down the paths he goes down? Putting his DNA on them, running around with all kinds of crazy stuff, creating problems in his marriage?" Grundy listed with skepticism. "The killer did it all," he goaded.

Yes, the DNA evidence may have been tedious and susceptible to different interpretation, the prosecutor sympathized, but the end result "is once it's there, we know it's there. There can be a question as to the amount of it," he conceded, "but the [DNA] transfer theory that was put forth in this case would have been novel to the science at this point in time," Grundy said of the opinions espoused by defense experts Taylor and Krane.

If the DNA was too complicated, all the jurors had to do was focus on the blood-spatter testimony of Ken Martin and Rod Englert, Grundy offered. "I'll ask you one favor," he requested. "Each and every morning you find the brightest light in that deliberation room. You look at the inner left lapel area here," he pointed on the yellow windbreaker. "See these dots. If they mean anything to you, you give them the weight that they deserve. These are consistent with the dimples on those gloves."

The testimony of Dr. Greineder's children, Grundy warned, was slanted toward their father. "I hope and believe he did buy some nails at some point," he said, referencing Colin's eye-raising testimony. "As much as Mr. Murphy would like you to rely upon judgments of both the victim's and the defendant's children, I would suggest to you that obviously they are clearly biased. They have only one parent left. They have a reason to want to believe what they want to believe."

Grundy expressed sympathy for the unenviable position the men and women before him were in, but they had to put their feelings aside. "I suggest to you that the defendant's greatest defense here is that you don't want to believe that an upstanding physician, with good standing in his profession, loved by his children, could commit such a crime, as Mr. Murphy said, that was pure evil. And if we could gauge pure evil, see pure evil, hear pure evil, it would make all of our jobs a lot easier. I wish I could tell you exactly how a person gets to that point in their own life. I can't," he admitted. "I can't tell you how a person gets to the point where he's doing as many things that this defendant was doing, but because of who he is we cannot shut our eyes from the facts in this case," the attorney softly instructed.

"I suggest to you ladies and gentlemen," Grundy concluded, "that this defendant, on October 31, 1999, killed his wife. It's the ultimate act of control. I would ask you to do one thing," he said quietly. "Return a verdict that speaks the truth, a verdict of guilty."

Meeting with the attorneys at sidebar, Judge Chernoff informed them of his decision to make Stan Smith the foreman of the jury, with neither Grundy nor Murphy objecting. Hearing his name announced, the corporate CEO almost verbalized his total surprise. "I almost said, 'Oh, shit,'" he remembered with a laugh. "Up until that point I was thinking how was anybody going to get a bunch of people that had very dissimilar backgrounds and different attitudes — different as could possibly be — to come to some type of consensus?"

After twenty-three days of testimony, seventy-five witnesses, and a Norfolk County record of 473 trial exhibits, the seven men and five women tasked to determine Dirk Greineder's fate retired to the jury room at 2:15 P.M., finally allowed to discuss the mind-bending things they had silently gathered in for five weeks.

Casting his eyes around the second-floor jury room, Smith could feel the weight of responsibility filling the eyes of the eleven men and women looking back at him. Up to now, in their private sanctuary away from the courtroom the time had been spent with lighthearted chatter and arguments over how the Red Sox would do that year, but the silence now permeating the room only underscored the seriousness of the conversation to come. Using his business experience of meeting important decisions head on, Smith laid out the ground rules, making it absolutely clear that all twelve jurors would speak with equal voices.

"Stan was excellent," said juror Stephanie Vitzthum. "He stood up and said every question will be answered, every witness will be gone through." The process for that, the CEO softly announced, would be an examination of every piece of evidence introduced from the beginning of testimony when paramedic Jason Harris was first called to the stand.

Freed from the pressure-filled confines of the oppressive main court-room, a spent Rick Grundy walked out of the courthouse and plopped down on one of the granite steps facing busy High Street. While defense attorney Murphy would remain ensconced in a small air-conditioned courtroom, Grundy would bide the long hours of jury deliberations on the sun-splashed stairs of the imposing courthouse to the media's delight. Sure to be one of the first notified of a verdict, Grundy was a like a pied piper drawing the reporters and trial spectators to the front of the courthouse where the busy intersection of High and Court streets took on the look of a carnival.

"I sat out there with my sunglasses on watching the world go by," mused Belinda Markel. Everyone was in the same predicament of waiting, and the bored conversation ranged from the endless speculation over when the jury would return a verdict to mundane comments about the beautiful weather. The huge satellite trucks lining Court Street and the white-tented Court TV studio expanded across the spacious lawn of the Dedham courthouse caused motorists to slow down and gawk as they drove by. Some honked their horns, while others yelled "guilty" or "he did it" from their car windows.

Tucked away in their second-floor jury room, the twelve jurors were conscious of the media siege outside, but they had determinedly gone to work on what Judge Chernoff had rightly labeled the awesome task before them. Shuffling through the first exhibits and scanning their notes of witness testimony, the jury began what Marty Foley had started so many months before.

Taking the large charts and aerial photographs of Morses Pond, they tracked the movements of the civilian witnesses there that horrible Halloween morning against the testimony of the defendant.

Using sections of string and thumbtacks to measure the movements of Bill Kear, Rick Magnan, Duncan Andrews, and Terry McNally, the jurors would eventually come to the same conclusion reached by Foley. "When we finally put that map up on the wall and put push pins where people were, we said, 'Ah, he wasn't there,'" Smith said of Dr. Greineder. "It became clear he wasn't seen in certain places and he was seen in others. None of that testimony made much sense to me until we put that up on the board and connected the dots."

Far from convinced the doctor was guilty beyond a reasonable doubt, the jury spent long hours on the timeline, which left them with serious doubts about the defendant's account of what happened at Morses Pond. "We played it straight at first because we were assuming he was innocent," said Dr. Bill Giesecke. "Then we said, okay, how's it work if Dirk is guilty? He was the only one seen," the juror concluded. "Dirk didn't see anybody and Dirk would have had to have seen someone."

To Stephanie Vitzthum it made no sense for the killer to dump the weapons and one glove in the lower storm drain then travel back up the long access road to drop the second glove in the catch basin near Dr. Greineder's van. "How was 'Shadow Man' going to loop back around and put the second glove in the Turner Road storm drain?" she asked skeptically.

As their deliberations moved into a second day, Dr. Greineder's conflicting statements about how he found his lifeless wife also troubled the jury. The male jurors sparing the women in the room the trauma of reviewing the autopsy photos, Paul decided there was no way a trained physician with experience working in an emergency room could overlook the gruesome wound on his wife's neck the first time he saw her. "From the pictures I saw, it's impossible to not to see she was dead immediately," he said emphatically. "Even from twenty feet, thirty feet, I mean you could tell."

Agreeing with prosecutor Grundy, the jurors would come to believe the accused husband had not behaved how they would have upon finding a savaged loved one. "Wouldn't you be screaming bloody murder?" asked Sara Barbera.

"He didn't say my wife's been murdered, watch out, there's a crazy murderer in the area," agreed Paul. "Instead, he says my wife has been attacked; I have to go up and use the phone. It didn't make any sense."

Still, early conclusions of guilt expressed by some of the jurors were quickly neutralized by the objections of those far from decided. "I was pissed," said juror Charles Salvi. "How can you people presume guilt?" the postal worker had asked his more pragmatic colleagues.

"I voted not guilty," Bill Giesecke said of the first straw poll on Wednesday morning. "And I was going to vote not guilty until I was the only one. I was compelled to hear everything," he recalled. "I couldn't imagine an intelligent man going out on a Sunday morning in a busy park in a yellow rain jacket to kill his wife with a knife. I mean, it made no sense at all."

A methodical scrutiny of Sgt. Deb Rebeiro's footprint testimony continued to slant the panel against Dr. Greineder's innocence. To foreman Stan Smith, the impressions left by the defendant's white Reebok sneakers did not correspond to his impassioned testimony of trying to save his dying wife. "It looked like he just sort of walked away," the juror recalled. "It didn't look like he had run around and done all that he could have but it put him there. There were a few prints that looked like they were going backwards and he was dragging her."

Making sure that every juror was satisfied with their interpretation of the evidence before moving on to the next witness, the wall of guilt that prosecutor Grundy had urged them to stack was slowly taking form. "The footprints were kind of a building-block approach," said Smith. "It looks bad for him again. He shouldn't have been at all these places but he was, and now he is going backwards with her. It didn't convict him, but it said he wasn't doing anything you would expect a husband to do if he came across his wife who was in distress, especially an emergency room doctor."

After another anonymous straw poll first thing on Thursday, June 28, it was obvious the jury still had a lot of work to do. Counting the secret ballots, Smith noted that two jurors still considered Dr. Greineder "not guilty," while several others remained undecided. In an ominous sign for the defendant, the majority had signaled a finding of guilt.

One area of evidence that would have no bearing on the jury's decision was Dr. Greineder's mind-boggling secret obsession with sexual gratification that had filled hours of testimony. "It bothered me for the character," admitted Stephanie Vitzthum, "but it did not change my opinion about his guilt or innocence."

The jury taking Grundy's advice to carefully scrutinize the blood-spotted clothes worn by Dr. Greineder, particularly the distinctive yellow swim team jacket, their conclusion would be irrefutable. Smith and Giesecke took the gloves with the other jurors crowded around them, and they attempted to align dots on the gloves with blood patterns on the windbreaker. "We said let's just see if we can line up the gloves with the jacket, and they were a perfect match," said the foreman.

Taking a break for lunch, Charles Salvi was wearing the gloves while handling a banana he intended to eat when the juror made a stunning discovery. There in the bruised skin of the banana was the distinctive dot pattern they had found on the windbreaker. Rubbing a gloved finger along another section of the banana, Salvi created a sweeping pattern on the fruit identical to one blotting the defendant's jacket.

Giesecke, who had returned to maneuvering the gloves against the bloody fabric of the windbreaker, was suddenly interrupted by a gasp behind him. "Holy shit, look at this," Salvi said, handing the dentist his banana. Giesecke was jolted by the dimpled dot patterns on the blemished banana skin identical to those on the windbreaker.

"There was a sweep in the bruise and we matched that to the sweep on the jacket," he said, still bemused by the event. Experiencing the same phenomenon that the investigators had the summer before at the crime lab, the jurors found the distinctive dot patterns jumping out at them from all the evidence.

"We started picking up the dots on other things," Giesecke agreed, with a begrudging compliment for controversial prosecution expert Rod Englert. "His testimony called me to it," the juror admitted. "I couldn't accept his testimony, but when I could look at it in front of my eyes and prove it to myself I believed it."

Poring over every inch of the bloodstained evidence, the jurors made another startling discovery on the back of the nylon windbreaker that they had heard no testimony about. Discussing what could have caused the small, circular stains highlighted by amido black, they could come to only one conclusion. It had to be blood cast from an upraised weapon. Not knowing Marty Murphy had convinced the judge to keep the incriminating pattern out of evidence because Grundy could not prove it was May's blood after deciding not to remove the stain and have it tested, the astute jurors had found it anyway.

The simple touching of the banana had helped yield irrefutable, yet catastrophic results for Dr. Greineder. "When we put the dots on the jacket, now we could say Dirk was there," said Smith. "The murderer was wearing the gloves and Dirk was wearing the jacket and nobody is arguing those points. Now we know the glove has touched Dirk and that means either he was there when she was murdered and saw the murder, which he never claimed, or was wearing the gloves and touched his sleeve. The weight was pretty heavy, and I think that removed any doubt from anybody."

The wrenching conclusion was a pivotal moment in the jury room, leaving all but one juror convinced beyond a reasonable doubt that Dr. Greineder had heartlessly killed his wife. "We kept a list of all the coincidences that would have had to have taken place for it to have been anyone else," said Elaine Miller. "When we looked at this list of coincidences that we would have had to accept, we couldn't do it," she revealed.

"We kept saying 'coincidence or not,'" agreed Sara Barbera, one of the jurors swayed by the blood-pattern evidence. "Ken Martin absolutely convinced me," she said.

"The thing that disturbed us the most," added Stephanie Vitzthum, "was we didn't know what time he arrived at the pond. We knew what time she died. We know what time he made that call, but we don't know when they got there."

The jurors had Vitzthum, roughly the same size as the defendant, model his windbreaker, in another demonstration that would have eye-popping results. When handed the two-pound Estwing hammer, Vitzthum cradled the head in her palm with the handle running up the sleeve, exactly as Rick Grundy had carried the weapon every chance he got. "You couldn't see it," Vitzthum said, the other jurors realizing it would have been hard to spot by Bill Kear who was focused on the defendant's German shepherd as he warily watched Dr. Greineder cross behind the traffic circle. "Bill Kear was not going to be looking for that," Bill Giesecke said. "He's not going to see it from seventy-five feet away."

Murphy had been emphatic that Kear surely would have seen the weapon. The jurors also dismissed the defendant's testimony that he and his wife had suffered the simultaneous nosebleed. "I didn't buy it," juror Mike Paul said with annoyance. "The towel, I didn't buy it. It was one of those coincidences that didn't make sense," he added.

"We thought that the towel was bizarre," concurred Elaine Miller. The jurors also found unbelievable the defendant's account of Zephyr bumping his face. "He was trying to make it show how his DNA got on the things, but I don't think anybody weighed that very much," said Stan Smith. "They didn't do a compelling job of creating real uncertainty from that. They didn't distance Dirk at all from the evidence."

The defendant's sudden testimony that his wife may have brought the Ziploc bags to the pond that morning also insulted the jurors' intelligence. "He said he didn't know anything about the bags until he got on the stand and brought up the berries," said a skeptical Jeff St. Armand, who, like the rest of the jury, had been captivated by the incriminating plastic bag testimony of FBI expert Lorie Gottesman that linked them to the doctor's kitchen. With the bags completely free of fingerprints, the jurors found the defendant's speculation that his wife had carried them preposterous. "Her fingerprints were nowhere to be found," said Smith.

The foreman taking his fourth, and final, secret poll of his deliberating peers before the jury was bused to their hotel Thursday night, the vote stood eleven to one in favor of the defendant's guilt, with only juror, Jennifer Flynn, not fully convinced of the defendant's culpability.

# 26

WORD THAT THE JURY HAD A REACHED A VERDICT filtered from their second-floor refuge in Dedham Superior Court during the Friday lunch hour. Energized with nervous excitement, Marty Foley felt confident they had come to the right conclusion. "At that point I knew it wasn't going to be a mistrial," he recalled. "My gut feeling was he was going to be guilty."

Belinda Markel had just seen her mother off to recline in the car when Pam Friedman delivered the long awaited news with a call to Belinda's cell phone. "My mother had a terrible headache and I put her in my car," Belinda vividly remembers. "I went back to get her and she was asleep." Frantically dialing her husband and father while trying to help her groggy mother back to the courthouse, Belinda, unlike Foley, could not stem the fear welling inside her. "The tension was unbelievable," she said. "I thought he was going to be found not guilty."

Inside the jury room, the wrenching result of their first open vote just after ordering lunch had sapped the appetite of the overwhelmed panel. The morning had been spent addressing the lingering doubts still held by New York University student Jennifer Flynn; the young woman had ultimately come to a tearful conclusion she could no longer dispute. The accomplished, admired family man standing accused before her was indeed responsible for the reprehensible, senseless execution of his trusting wife.

As Stan Smith recorded the unanimous verdict on his first official polling, many of the jurors broke down with the overly distraught Flynn. "Oh, my God," a choked-up Sara Barbera had silently gulped.

"It made us sick. It was horrible," said Elaine Miller. "We didn't want him to be guilty. I didn't want those children to be sitting there and having their father guilty. We in our own minds didn't want to believe it."

Despite the dire ramification for the Greineder family, there would be no wavering during the jury's last empaneled lunch together. The evidence had been examined exhibit by exhibit with every question answered, while the jurors had gone to the limit of affording the defendant every chance for reasonable doubt. "What we ultimately all felt was there was just so much evidence; whether you liked one thing or the other thing, there was something for everyone," said college professor Cheryl Nixon.

When each item of evidence had been rated as either "probable, possible, or unlikely," the stack toward the defendant's guilt left the others in its shadow. "It was just so overwhelming," Miller said of the evidence of culpability, "that and the list of coincidences." Presiding over the sacred but humbling civic process that decides a citizen's guilt or innocence, foreman Smith was overcome with admiration as he scanned the faces of the men and women around him.

Together for thirty hours over four days, holding a man's life in the balance, the jury had kept its deliberations more professional than some business meetings the Wellesley CEO had chaired. "It was extremely positive," Smith said. "When it got down to the discussion part, it was very serious, very thorough, and everybody took it very seriously. Nobody was talking over each other, and nobody was insulted." The respectful give-and-take had ultimately illuminated the doctor's indisputable guilt for all twelve jurors.

"It just all added up," agreed Barbera, one of the jurors holding hope for Dr. Greineder's innocence. "There were so many things." It was only after they held the evidence in totality, as the prosecution team had hoped, that it was distressingly clear what the verdict would be, said Stephanie Vitzthum. "Until you put it together there is always that shadow of a doubt," she explained. "For whatever reasons we all chose, we were able to say he was guilty."

Little was said as they nervously waited to announce their verdict. The jurors could see the terrible fallout that would come from their still secret consensus. "I looked outside, and the media was just flying into the courthouse. It was just a zoo outside," said Mike Paul.

"Talk about putting a tent over the circus," acknowledged Terry Cunningham, "all you needed was a grinder to sell some popcorn." Taking a seat with the other case investigators alongside Belinda Markel and Ilse Stark in the courtroom, the Wellesley chief braced himself for the worst. Expecting an acquittal, on the basis of Grundy's pessimism, Cunningham tried to console himself with the belief that he had done everything he could have to expose Dr. Greineder's guilt. "At least all the evidence came out," he thought while the squirming capacity audience in the Sacco and Vanzetti Room awaited the defendant's arrival.

With a reinforced phalanx of white-shirted court officers lining the main aisle and others positioned around the courtroom for added security, Dirk Greineder was led to his seat. His jaw clenched and eyes aflame with alarm, the defendant cast a fleeting glance toward his children without making eye contact or flashing his signature reassuring smile. Taking his seat, Marty Murphy leaned over to offer his client a hasty handshake. A half minute later Dr. Greineder instinctively sprang to his feet with the rest of the audience at the electric announcement of "jury entering."

Murphy fidgeted while the jurors shuffled to their double row of seats, while Rick Grundy stood ramrod still, stoically convinced they were about to tell him he had failed to deliver justice for the deliberate taking of an innocent life.

His seat closest to the defendant, Mike Paul, like most of the other jurors, could not bring himself to look at the anxious Dr. Greineder. "I was going to do what I always do. I was just going to walk in the same way and turn around but I'll tell you, my knees were shaking," he admitted.

Studying the determined faces of the incoming jurors, Marty Foley was encouraged to see their avoidance of the hopeful defendant. "They weren't looking at him, and that was a pretty good sign."

The Greineder children had joined hands, clasping each other in an anxious chain, as soon as their father entered the courtroom. Across the aisle, their relatives from New York sat just as expectantly, but with far different hopes for the outcome. "I think at that point I wasn't breathing," recalled Belinda Markel.

The Boston television stations broke into regular programming for live coverage of the verdict that was also being beamed worldwide by Court TV as the historic courtroom vibrated with tension. Judge Paul Chernoff addressed the stone-faced jurors and told them, "We are all very, very indebted to you," the heart-stopping anxiety turning almost comedic when the judge added that their service would exempt them from jury duty for at least three years. "It's probably likely we'll see you sometime in the next decade, and we will be waiting for you," the judge said with admiration.

Turning the proceeding over to clerk Michael Hulak, Judge Chernoff reclined in his chair while Hulak explained to foreman Stan Smith how the jury's verdict would be unsealed. Marty Murphy stood with Dr. Greineder. The defendant fixed his stare on the tall foreman standing in the top row of the jury box.

"Mr. Foreman, members of the jury, have you agreed on a verdict?" Hulak formally asked.

"Yes, we have," Smith responded, his confident reply only intensifying the paralyzing anticipation in the stuffy courtroom.

"May I have the papers, please?" Hulak requested.

The verdict slip was passed over for the judge's viewing. Confused about the process, Smith had assumed Judge Chernoff would reveal their decision until he saw the white verdict slip coming back to him. "I thought my job was done," Smith chuckled. "This was not supposed to be happening. I felt like saying, 'Your honor, I'm done.'"

Handed the verdict slip again, Smith made a snap decision that would sear the memory of everyone transfixed on the jury foreman. Turning to face the desperate defendant, Smith locked eyes with Dr. Greineder. "I didn't know what I should do," he admitted. "Do I look at the judge? Do I look at the courtroom? No, I should look at Dirk," Smith had instantly decided. "I felt if I'm reading the verdict, I had to look at him. I had one or two seconds to think about it, and that's what I did. I had no idea it would have that kind of effect on people."

In a straight line behind the foreman and the defendant, Marty Foley felt a rush of confidence as he searched the distinguished juror's face. "I knew as soon as he stood up and looked at him that there was no question this guy was guilty. I thought he's going to tell him right here and now."

Dr. Greineder's children still clung to each other nervously behind their father, Kirsten's eyes nearly squeezed shut, her face pale with worry as the clerk's practiced voice broke the stomach-churning silence.

"What say you, Mr. Foreman as to indictment number 108588, Dirk K. Greineder; is the defendant guilty or not guilty?" Hulak boomed with Dr. Greineder still staring expectantly at Smith.

"Guilty," Smith assertively answered as Dr. Greineder dropped his head with an abbreviated grimace but showing no other emotion. "Guilty of what sir?" Hulak loudly continued.

"Murder in the first degree," Smith responded strongly. "With deliberate, premeditated and malice aforethought." Wincing at each of the juror's devastating words, Kirsten Greineder slumped back in her seat, her body wracked with anguish. Britt, incredibly composed in contrast to her typical courtroom histrionics, sat motionless with her eyes closed, the three siblings still holding hands. Staring straight ahead with defeated resignation,

Colin's dark eyes conveyed his devastation as he watched Court Officer Bill Weed bind his father's wrists with handcuffs.

Her eyes filling with tears across the aisle, holding on to her equally affected mother, Belinda Markel was overcome with gratitude for the twelve people she didn't even know by name who had seen through her uncle's diabolical lies. "I thought, 'Thank you, God,' and I just fell apart," she said. "I was glad that the right thing had been done, but let's face it, the whole thing was tragic."

For Foley, even greater than the sense of relief was the satisfaction that justice had been served. He was hardly surprised with the guilty verdict, but Foley had worried more about what an acquittal would have done to Belinda and her mother. "I was very pleased," he said, "but I was happier for Belinda and Ilse after everything they had gone through."

Terry Cunningham was not prepared for the flood of emotion he felt upon hearing the verdict. "I started to well up," he said. "There was some relief, but sitting there with Marty and Rick day after day and Rick would have that picture of May there, that's what this was really about," he realized. "We never lost focus on what this whole thing was about, and we spent eighteen months of our lives on it. I wasn't prepared for the way I was going to feel. I wasn't prepared for the people around me and how they reacted. It was very, very hard not break down, to be honest with you."

Burying his face in his arms just steps from the jurors, Rick Grundy was powerless to hold back his surging emotion. The tough city kid mouthed his thanks to the jury before dissolving into tears. The judge signaled a ten-minute recess before sentencing, and a placid Dr. Greineder was led out of the courtroom still showing no expression. "I love you," he said to his children as the court officers hustled him back to the holding cell. "We know," Britt calmly replied.

As the Greineder children and the supportive Nancy Gans were escorted out of the courtroom by a group of court officers, the heartbreaking magnitude of the jury's decision showed the most on May Greineder's oldest child. Deathly pale and rubber-legged from grief, Kirsten staggered behind her siblings out a side door. And then from behind it came her heaving, wailing sobs.

"It was horrible," Belinda recalled softly. "No matter what our relationship was, to hear them howling on the way out was heart wrenching." Belinda took solace in the consequences to their father. "To see Dirk's face realizing he was not going to see the light of day again, that was satisfying."

Conscious of the unfathomable suffering they had heaped on the Greineder children, the jurors, bound to the truth, understood how it was that the doctor's loved ones had sought to escape it. "They didn't sit down the way we were able to . . . after taking notes for six weeks and analyzing it," said Stephanie Vitzthum. "Nobody wants to believe it," said Mike Paul. "Love is blind. They were in denial. That's all it is. They were in complete utter denial."

As Judge Chernoff left the bench to have one final conversation with the jury, Grundy made his way toward Belinda and Ilse. He stopped to meet Foley with a crushing hug of admiration and a round of male back slapping. Then he gathered the women from New York into his arms for an emotion-filled embrace.

"It's amazing how many lives were affected by this," Belinda sadly recollected. "As I go through it again it's amazing how many lives became intertwined."

Exchanging embraces with her smiling older partner from the State Police, Jill McDermott found the whole experience surreal. "It was hard to believe it was over," she said. "It was very satisfying to see Belinda and Ilse hugging Rick and Marty. It was emotional for all of us."

When the verdict was announced over the public address system at the State Police crime lab in Sudbury, Gwen Pino felt a little uncomfortable as a cheer echoed throughout the building. "Normally, it's not like that," she said. "We have to be impartial, but this was a big case for the lab because it involved so many of us."

Reflecting on the brutality of May's death, Pino felt nothing but contempt for the now-convicted doctor. "He was so caught up in being a doctor and his kids' loyalty to him and the way they worshipped their father. He didn't want to lose that by getting divorced from their mother because they also loved their mother," Pino speculated. "I think he was so selfish that it was enough to murder her. She would have wrecked his reputation, and the kids would have looked at him in a different light, and she would have been the heroine. He wasn't going to allow that. He wanted to be the center of the universe in that family."

The immense weight of failure removed with the guilty verdict, Rick Grundy took his seat at the prosecution table to await the judge's sentencing, reflectively laying his forehead on his folded hands until he felt someone gently touch his back. He turned to see the familiar face of his good friend and adversary, and Grundy rose from his chair to envelop Marty Murphy in a hug. After offering a private congratulation and another pat on the back, Murphy sat down at the defense table, where he nervously tapped the tabletop in anticipation of the judge's return. Surprisingly, among those filing in to take their seats were most of the jurors, who had invested so much in the sensational trial. Meeting one last time with Judge Chernoff, he had invited them to watch Dr. Greineder's sentencing. Brought in moments later for the final time, Dr. Greineder stared straight ahead.

Apprehensively following her mother to the witness stand where she placed a comforting hand on her shoulder, Belinda Markel stood quietly while Ilse Stark poignantly explained that there was no sentence that could reverse the incurable hurt inflicted on her family. "Your Honor, I have not prepared anything," she apologized before speaking directly to the humbled jurors sitting beside her. "Ladies and gentlemen, I'm speaking from the heart, so please forgive me if I'm not eloquent," Ilse told them. "But listen with your heart, rather than your ears," she instructed. "I think we have already been sentenced. A sentence has been imposed upon myself, my daughter, our family, nieces, nephew, grandchildren, and so forth. And we have been sentenced to a life without my sister, who as a human being had her foibles and baggage, as we all do," Ilse perceptively noted. "But as a human being she was also an extremely special person who had a sense of humor, a wit, and such a profound sense of right and wrong, and helped you see it without being judgmental about it. And my grandmother used to say, 'When a person dies, a library burns.' With the loss of my sister, the Smithsonian is gone," Ilse eulogized. "I thank you for everything," she told the jurors, her voice thick with gratitude. "God bless you," she implored before stepping away from the witness stand.

Still showing no expression other than a brave resignation, Dr. Greineder stood to receive his punishment. "Dirk Greineder," clerk Hulak, began, "the court in consideration of this offense sentences you to be imprisoned to the Massachusetts Correctional Institute at Cedar Junction for a term of your natural life and you stand committed pursuant to this sentence." Handcuffed again, Dr. Greineder was removed to spend the rest of his days in a prison cell.

Leaning against the wall in the first-floor corridor of the courthouse, Belinda finally had a sense her aunt was at peace. "I think she knows," she quietly told a reporter. "Nobody will ever know how much I lost. Justice has been served." Asked if the estrangement with her cousins could one day be healed, Belinda had no idea. "I can't even begin to think about where that goes," she said sadly. "We have no other family."

As the jurors filed out the back of the courthouse, they were stunned to see several dozen adoring spectators offering applause and shouts of encouragement. The reaction was mixed. "I couldn't believe that they were applauding and cheering for us," said Dr. Bill Giesecke. "That made me sick," disagreed Elaine Miller. Not looking for "anyone's justification," Mike Paul still appreciated the gesture. "It felt good," he recalled. "By those people staying and waiting for us, I felt like it was reinforcement for the job that we did."

Dr. Greineder would receive a vastly different reception from the mob a short time later when he was led out the back door to spend the first of many nights in state prison. In something reminiscent of the old west, some in the crowd screamed threats and obscenities at the convicted murderer, a bespectacled Dr. Greineder blinking nervously as his only response.

As for May's relatives, the end of the trial was the beginning of a search for understanding. Still grasping to collect her thoughts, Belinda Markel set out on an aimless walk in the tree-lined neighborhood surrounding the courthouse, a journey for understanding that still remains painfully uncompleted. Taking her own stroll down Dedham's Court Street, Ilse Stark found herself at the door of the towering St. Paul's Episcopal Church. Inside the majestic, stone house of worship, Ilse settled into a wooden pew in the darkened sanctuary for her own personal reflection. Whatever she whispered there remains to this day between sisters.

# epilogue

THE VICTORY CELEBRATION, if justice can be called a victory, ended just after last call at Desmond O'Malley's, a short walk down Route Nine from the Crowne Plaza Hotel. The extended prosecution team had retired to the Natick hotel for a lighthearted banquet following the guilty verdict, District Attorney Bill Keating buying the steak dinners and a festive Ilse Stark supplying the champagne. Then they moved the party to the pub.

Although the pints of Guinness and Bass Ale were flowing freely that night, the emotional toll caused by Dirk Greineder's treachery still rippled like a cold undercurrent beneath the boisterous revelry. For those directly involved in the case, May Greineder's senseless murder had left an indelible mark that will always be felt.

Many of the jurors would return to Morses Pond bearing flowers for May in the coming days. Almost a month after coming to the conclusion that the upstanding family man had indeed viciously snuffed out the life of the mother of his children, juror Sara Barbera gave birth to a baby girl; the proud parents named her Maeve Hazelton "May" Barbera. Deeply affected by their role in the Greineder case, most of the jurors have stayed in touch since delivering their verdict.

After eighteen months of almost constant preparation of the case against Dirk Greineder, Chief Terry Cunningham, his brother Wayne, and Jill McDermott returned to the normalcy of being Wellesley police officers, although McDermott eventually retired to marry and have a family.

Less than three months after the Greineder trial, terrorists unleashed the devastating attacks of September 11, 2001. Antiterror concerns moved to the forefront and Sgt. Marty Foley's demonstrated investigative expertise resulted in his immediate transfer to the office of State Fire Marshal Stephen D. Coan, where he was later promoted to lieutenant and put in command of the elite State Police Fire and Explosion Investigation Section. His exemplary service was further recognized in November 2004 when he was promoted to the prestigious rank of detective lieutenant. Foley retired from the Massachusetts State Police in May 2007.

Like Foley, Belinda Markel is still consumed by the unanswered questions surrounding Dirk Greineder's murderous behavior. After researching the children of Nazis and speaking to noted Northeastern University criminologist Jack Levin, Belinda reached the conclusion that her uncle was a murderous sociopath of the likes of Scott Peterson or Charles Stuart. "He thought he was going to be good at this because he was good at so many other things," she said sadly. Belinda and her family still live in Manhattan. Her aunt's ashes remain with those of May's parents in Queens.

A startling DNA match in June 2003 would bring more bad news for Dr. Greineder's continued claims of innocence. District Attorney Keating announced that Martin G. Guy, a former Walpole resident Rick Grundy had sent to prison for life just before the Greineder trial, had been genetically linked to the gruesome December 1998 slaying of Irene Kennedy. Guy had been convicted for the September 1999 stabbing death of Christopher Payne at their Norwood rooming house and Guy's DNA was later entered into a criminal database where authorities genetically linked him to the Kennedy murder.

A cornerstone of Dr. Greineder's defense was that his wife was slain by a mysterious madman much like Irene Kennedy and Dick Reyenger, but Guy's subsequent conviction of first-degree murder on September 20, 2006, for the Kennedy killing further eroded his shattered credibility. Guy has also emerged as a prime suspect in Richard Reyenger's August 1999 murder investigated by Marty Foley, but the lack of physical evidence has so far prevented the authorities from bringing a third murder charge against him.

Following a series of six extensions granted by the Massachusetts Supreme Judicial Court for Dr. Greineder to file his automatic appeal beginning in July 2003, Greineder's appellate lawyer, James L. Sultan, instead filed a multipronged motion for a new trial in July 2005. On January 26, 2006, Dr. Greineder made his first public appearance since his June 2001 conviction, standing again before trial Judge Paul Chernoff for a hearing in Dedham Superior Court. It would be the first of many evidentiary hearings on the motions before Judge Chernoff over the course of 2006 and the first half of 2007.

On October 31, 2007, eight years to the day that Dr. Greineder had so horribly killed his wife, Judge Chernoff denied his bid for a new trial in a far-ranging ruling in which he made many findings of fact in support of the prosecution's case. On October 9, 2009, the doctor's attorneys appeared before the Supreme Judicial Court to argue his final state appeal. Just over a year later, on November 4, 2010, the SJC upheld Dr. Greineder's conviction for good, despite a vigorous appeal effort by his legal team. Throughout Dirk Greineder's years-long appeal process, his three children have supported his innocence every step of the way.

Dirk Greineder now spends his days among the general population at the state prison in Norfolk, Massachusetts. From all reports, he has adjusted well to prison life. He has taken a leadership role in a lifers group and advocated on behalf of inmates who, like himself, will die behind bars.

Still, he clings to his severely tarnished assertion that he is an innocent man. Those affected by May's death still desperately search for reasons why. Maybe someday Dirk Greineder will finally share the answers, but for now, that seems highly unlikely.

# authors' note

THE SENSELESS SLAYING OF MAY GREINEDER is one that has garnered
intensive media coverage for more than a decade, but at its core, it is one
example among the thousands of domestic murders committed every
year, most of which although not receiving the attention of May's case are
no less tragic and devastating to the families involved. The unimaginable
loss felt by May's family has touched us personally, and we hope to bring
attention to ending the scourge of domestic violence.

This book would not have been possible without the support and friendship of Ilse Stark and Belinda Markel. We are grateful to Belinda for sharing
her intimate experiences involving May's death despite the pain she and
Ilse will always carry.

We would also like to thank a number of others involved in *Common-
wealth v. Dirk K. Greineder* who took time out of their busy schedules and
lives to share their experiences and thoughts with us, including: Jill McDermott, Terry Cunningham, Wayne Cunningham, Gwen Pino, Tom Young,
Steve Rosenthal, Brian O'Hara, Stan Smith, Michael Paul, Sara Barbera,
Dr. Bill Giesecke, Cheryl Nixon, Elaine Miller, Stephanie Vitzthum, Jeff St.
Armand, Charles Salvi, and Jahon Jamali. Thanks as well to Northeastern
University Brudnick Professor of Sociology and Criminology Jack Levin
for his unique insight into the minds of killers.

Our gratitude also to editor Richard Pult for seeing the potential of this book and allowing us the chance to tell this story. Our thanks as well to Gary Hamel for taking our manuscript and making it so much better. We would also like to thank Francisco Stork, Bethany Wood, Anna Reppucci, Laurie Rizzelli, Eric Gedstad, Deepak Karamcheti, Joel Brown, Brian MacQuarrie, Todd Shuster, Stephanie Schorow, and Laurel J. Sweet for their help, advice, encouragement, and support of this project.

We are very pleased to include the photographs of *Boston Herald* photographers Ted Fitzgerald, Mark Garfinkel, Nancy Lane, Matt Stone, and Patrick Whittemore and our gratitude as well to *Herald* chief photographer Jim Mahoney for allowing us to use their superb images and share their amazing talents in helping us illustrate this story.

Finally, without the love and support of our families, who put up with our long hours away from home and the incessant demands of our professional lives and of the writing of this book, this project would not have been possible. Our thanks and our love to Sandi, Dan, and Ellen, and Cheryl, Tim, and Dan. You make us who we are.

*Tom Farmer and Marty Foley*

# bibliography

LAW ENFORCEMENT AGENCY REPORTS

*Commonwealth of Massachusetts Department of State Police Case No.*
 *1999-112-0340*

Trooper Martin T. Foley interview with Dr. Dirk Greineder, October 31, 1999

Trooper Martin T. Foley interview with Wellesley Patrolman Paul J. Fitzpatrick,
 October 31, 1999

Trooper Martin T. Foley interview with Wellesley Detective Jill McDermott,
 October 31, 1999

Trooper Martin T. Foley interview with Trooper Kenneth Rudolph,
 October 31, 1999

Trooper Martin T. Foley interview with William Kear, October 31, 1999

Trooper Martin T. Foley interview with Lt. Kenneth Martin, October 31, 1999

*Wellesley Police Department Investigative Report Case No. 99-5-IV*

Detective Jill McDermott interview with Dirk K. Greineder, October 31, 1999

*Wellesley Police Department Officer's Narrative Report Incident No. 99-1044-OF*

Sgt. Peter T. Nahass crime scene events and recovery of weapons and glove,
 October 31, 1999

*Commonwealth of Massachusetts Department of State Police Case No.*
 *1999-112-0340*

Trooper Julia Mosely Crime Scene Services Section Report of Investigation,
 February 15, 2000

*Commonwealth of Massachusetts Department of State Police Case No.*
 *1999-112-0340*

Lt. Robert H. Friend Jr. conversation with Attorney Terry Segal

*Wellesley Police Department Officer's Narrative Report Incident No. 99-1044-OF*

Sgt. Michael F. Price interview with William Kear, October 31, 1999

Sgt. Michael F. Price interview with Richard Magnan, October 31, 1999

Sgt. Michael F. Price interview with Britt Greineder, October 31, 1999

*Wellesley Police Department Incident Report Incident No. 99-1044-OF*

Patrolman Paul J. Fitzpatrick interview with Dr. Dirk K. Greineder

*Commonwealth of Massachusetts Department of State Police Case No. 1999-112-0340*

Sgt. Dermot P. Moriarty interview with William E. DeLorie, November 1, 1999

*Commonwealth of Massachusetts Department of State Police Case No. 1999-112-0340*

Trooper Martin T. Foley and Wellesley Lt. Wayne Cunningham interview of
    Wellesley Patrolman Paul J. Fitzpatrick, March 27, 2000

*Commonwealth of Massachusetts Department of State Police Canine Section
    Incident Report*

Trooper Kenneth Rudolph with Canine Arek at Morses Pond, October 31, 1999

*Wellesley Police Department Officer's Narrative Report Incident No. 99-1044-OF*

Detective William Vargas interview of Richard Magnan, October 31, 1999

Detective William Vargas and Sgt. Michael F. Price interview of Sammy Sit,
    November 7, 1999

*Commonwealth of Massachusetts Department of State Police Case No. 1999-112-0340*

Trooper Martin T. Foley interview of Richard Magnan, November 6, 1999

*Commonwealth of Massachusetts Department of State Police Case No. 1999-112-0340*

Trooper Martin T. Foley and Wellesley Detective Jill McDermott interview of
    Duncan and Patricia Andrews, November 6, 1999.

*Massachusetts Trial Court Affidavit in Support of Application for Search Warrant*

Trooper Martin T. Foley for 56 Cleveland Road, Wellesley, MA, November 1, 1999

*Commonwealth of Massachusetts Department of State Police Case No. 1999-112-0340*

Trooper Martin T. Foley on search warrant, 56 Cleveland Road, Wellesley, MA,
    November 1, 1999

*Massachusetts Trial Court Search Warrant Return*

Trooper Martin T. Foley for 56 Cleveland Road, Wellesley, MA, November 1, 1999

*Commonwealth of Massachusetts Office of the Chief Medical Examiner Autopsy
    Report*

Mabel Greineder, 56 Cleveland Road, Wellesley MA

*Commonwealth of Massachusetts Department of State Police Case No. 1999-112-0340*

Sgt. Dermot P. Moriarty on search warrant executed for Greineder dogs November
    2, 1999 at 56 Cleveland Road, Wellesley, MA

*Commonwealth of Massachusetts Department of State Police Case No. 1999-112-0340*

Sgt. Dermot P. Moriarty on hotel records from the Hilton at Dedham Place,
    November 8, 1999

*Massachusetts Trial Court Affidavit in Support of Application for Search Warrant*
Trooper Martin T. Foley for 56 Cleveland Road, Wellesley, MA, November 12, 1999
*Massachusetts Trial Court Search Warrant Return*
Trooper Martin T. Foley for 56 Cleveland Road, Wellesley, MA, November 12, 1999
*Commonwealth of Massachusetts Department of State Police Case No. 1999-112-0340*
Trooper Timothy J. Curtin interview with Deborah Herrera, November 23, 1999
*Commonwealth of Massachusetts Department of State Police Case No. 1999-112-0340*
Trooper Martin T. Foley interview with Deborah Herrera, November 23, 1999
*Commonwealth of Massachusetts Department of State Police Case No. 1999-112-0340*
Sgt. Dermot P. Moriarty interview with John Davey, Crowne Plaza, 1360 Worcester
    Road, Natick, MA, November 30, 1999
*Cellmark Diagnostics Case No. F991579*
Report to Gwen Pino, Massachusetts State Police Crime Laboratory, January 6, 2000
*Commonwealth of Massachusetts Department of State Police Case No. 1999-112-0340*
Trooper Martin T. Foley and Wellesley Detective Jill McDermott interview with
    Belinda Markel, December 1, 1999
*Wellesley Police Department Investigative Report Case No. 99-5-IV*
Detective Jill McDermott and Trooper Martin T. Foley interview with Ilse Stark,
    December 1, 1999
*Wellesley Police Department Investigative Report Case No. 99-5-IV*
Detective Jill McDermott interview with Terence McNally, November 1, 1999
*Commonwealth of Massachusetts Department of State Police Case No. 1999-112-0340*
Sgt. Gerard R. Mattaliano and Sgt. Kevin Shea interview of Gilbert Perito, January 9,
    2000
*Commonwealth of Massachusetts Department of State Police Case No. 1999-112-0340*
Trooper Martin T. Foley interview with Kevin Green, January 11, 2000
Trooper Martin T. Foley interview with Clint Paddock, January 11, 2000
Trooper Martin T. Foley interview with David Eaton, January 11, 2000
*Wellesley Police Department Investigative Report Case No. 99-5-IV*
Detective Jill McDermott and Trooper Martin T. Foley interview with Elizabeth
    Porter, February 16, 2000
*Cellmark Diagnostics Case No. F991579*
Report to Gwen Pino Massachusetts State Police Crime Laboratory, February 23,
    2000
*Baltimore County Police Department Report of Investigation*
Detective Allen Meyer interview of Thomas G. Young, March 1, 2000
*Commonwealth of Massachusetts v. Dirk K. Greineder Superior Court Criminal No.*
    *108588*
Judge Paul A. Chernoff Memorandum of Decision and Rulings on the Defendant's
    Motion to Suppress Physical Evidence and Statements, October 18, 2000

*Commonwealth of Massachusetts v. Dirk K. Greineder Superior Court Criminal No. 108588*

Martin F. Murphy Motion for Hearing and Relief to Remedy the Commonwealth's Violations of Court Rules Concerning Prejudicial Pre-Trial Statements and Grand Jury Secrecy, March 20, 2000

*Commonwealth of Massachusetts v. Dirk K. Greineder Superior Court Criminal No. 108588*

Judge Paul A. Chernoff Memorandum of Decision and Order on the Defendant's Motion in Limine to Exclude Prior Bad Acts Evidence, February 5, 2001

*Wellesley Police Department Investigative Report Case No. 99-5-IV*

Detective Jill McDermott interview with Luis Rosado, November 12, 1999

*Commonwealth of Massachusetts v. Dirk K. Greineder Superior Court Criminal Action No. 2000-108588*

Judge Paul A. Chernoff Findings of Fact, Rulings of Law and Order on Defendant's Motion for New Trial Based on Jury's Exposure to Extraneous Information, May 5, 2006

*Commonwealth of Massachusetts v. Dirk K. Greineder Superior Court Criminal Action No. 2000-108588*

Judge Paul A. Chernoff Findings of Fact, Rulings of Law, and Order on Defendant's Amended Motion for a New Trial, October 31, 2007


NEWSPAPERS

"Mystery Shrouds Final Moments of Flight 990." *Boston Herald*, November 7, 1999.

"Woman Slain in Walpole park: Husband Says Body Found After Walk." *Boston Globe*, December 2, 1998.

"Murder Suspect's 25 Cats Stay in Legal Limbo for Now." *Boston Herald*, December 16, 1998.

"Walpole Murder Suspect Will Seek Dismissal of Case Today." *Boston Herald*, December 21, 1998.

"Plaintiff Can Sue in Wrongful Arrest." *Boston Herald*, September 6, 2004.

"Popular Wellesley Woman Found Slain." *Boston Herald*, November 1, 1999.

"Mourners Celebrate the Life of Murdered Wellesley Mother." *Boston Herald*, November 4, 1999.

"Hundreds Gather to Mourn Slain Woman." *Boston Globe*, November 4, 1999.

"Arundel Retrial Highlights New Types of DNA Testing." *Washington Post*, April 22, 1998.

"Proved Guilty by a Hair: Prosecutors Are Using Animal DNA to Win Murder and Assault Convictions." *Los Angeles Times*, December 21, 2001.

"Cases Using Animal DNA Include Two in Nebraska." *Omaha World-Herald*, January 30, 2000.

"Driver Allegedly Forced His Girlfriend into Crash." *Boston Herald*, December 31, 1999.

"Man Denies Forcing Car Crash That Killed Girlfriend in Quincy." *Boston Herald*, March 23, 2000.

"Defendant in Fatality Rejects Plea Bargain." *Quincy Patriot Ledger*, October 2, 2002.

"Doctor Held in Killing of Wife: Secret Life Alleged." *Boston Globe*, March 1, 2000.

"Wellesley Doc Held in Wife's Murder." *Boston Herald*, March 1, 2000.

"Sacco-Vanzetti relic Revives Interest." *Quincy Patriot Ledger*, February 26, 1998.

"Dark Secrets: Prosecutors Detail Doctor's Alleged Hooker Escapades." *Boston Herald*, March 2, 2000.

"Investigators Say Allergist Led Sordid Secret Life." *Boston Herald*, March 2, 2000

"Doctor Arraigned in Wife's Slaying Pleads Innocent: Held without Bail." *Boston Globe*, March 2, 2000

"Wellesley Doc 'in Fight for Life': From Start, Authorities Targeted Him as the Top Suspect in Wife's Killing." *Boston Herald*, March 5, 2000.

"Records: Doctor Feared He'd Be Prime Suspect." *Boston Herald*, March 3, 2000.

"Children Proclaim Doctor's Innocence." *Boston Herald*, March 3, 2000.

"Children Stand By Accused Father." *MetroWest Daily News*, March 3, 2000.

"Greineder Children in Media Spotlight." *MetroWest Daily News*, March 5, 2000.

"Wellesley Doc Denied Bail; Prosecutor: Wife May Have Discovered His Porn Habit." *Boston Herald*, April 11, 2000.

"Judge Raps Norfolk DA's Comments on Case." *Boston Globe*, April 11, 2000.

"Greineder Wants Evidence Tossed." *MetroWest Daily News*, July 12, 2000.

"Evidence in Wellesley Slaying Challenged." *Boston Globe*, July 19, 2000.

"Doc's Alleged Online Sexploits Ruled Admissible." *Boston Herald*, February 7, 2001.

"Judge Denies Bid to Move Wellesley Doc's Trial." *Boston Herald*, March 29, 2001.

"Perfect Case: Court TV Shines Again with Greineder Murder Trial." *Boston Herald*, June 7, 2001.

"Indiscretions Admitted: Lawyer Says Greineder Unfaithful, but No Killer." *Boston Herald*, May 25, 2001.

"Footprint Testimony Backs Case vs. Doc." *Boston Herald*, June 1, 2001.

"Expert: Doctor's DNA Found on Bloody Gloves." *Boston Herald*, June 8, 2001.

"Dirty Secrets: Testimony Details Slay Suspect's Kinky Side." *Boston Herald*, June 14, 2001.

"Accused Doc's Testimony Chills Torrid Courtroom." *Boston Herald*, June 19, 2001.

"Cross Fire: Prosecutor Grills Wellesley Allergist." *Boston Herald*, June 20, 2001.

"Doc's Blood Expert Doesn't Dispute Prosecution Case." *Boston Herald*, June 23, 2001.

"Last Expert Witness for Doctor Testifies." *Boston Globe*, June 23, 2001.

"Mystery Witness: Woman Claims She Saw Stranger after Murder in Wellesley." *Boston Herald*, June 26, 2001.

"11th-Hour Claim Halts Greineder Slaying Trial." *Boston Globe*, June 26, 2001.

"Doctor's Future in Jurors' Hands." *Boston Herald*, June 27, 2001.

"Guilty: Wellesley Allergist Gets Life in Prison." *Boston Herald*, June 30, 2001.

"Mabel's Sister, Niece Find Some Solace in Verdict." *Boston Herald*, June 30, 2001.

"Jury Had No Doubts He Did It." *Boston Herald*, June 30, 2001.

"A DNA Match: Bite Mark Links Killer to 1998 Slaying." *Boston Herald*, June 28, 2003.

"Wife-Killer Doc Appeals, Says Sex Talk Wrecked Case." *Boston Herald*, July 1, 2003.

WEBSITES

QuestGen Forensics DNA Testing and Mitochondrial Typing in Dogs, questgen.biz (accessed July 20, 2003).

McConnell, John C., A History of Superior Court Architecture in Massachusetts, sociallaw.com (accessed December 23, 2003).

Sherrod, The Reverend Marc, Breaking the Silence, sermon before Bethel Presbyterian Church (USA), October 19, 2003, bethelpcusa.org (accessed February 4, 2004).